W9-AAK-086

Fodor's
Virginia &
Maryland

By Francis X. Rocca

*Updated by Bob Willis
and John Bowen*

Fodor's Travel Publications, Inc.
New York • Toronto • London • Sydney • Auckland

**Copyright © 1995
by Fodor's Travel Publications, Inc.**

Fodor's is a registered trademark of Fodor's Travel Publications, Inc.

All rights reserved under International and Pan-American Copyright Conventions. Published in the United States by Fodor's Travel Publications, Inc., a subsidiary of Random House, Inc., New York, and simultaneously in Canada by Random House of Canada Limited, Toronto. Distributed by Random House, Inc., New York.

No maps, illustrations, or other portions of this book may be reproduced in any form without written permission from the publisher.

Third Edition

ISBN 0-679-02771-8

"The Road to Appomattox," by Geoffrey C. Ward with Ric Burns and Ken Burns, is excerpted from *The Civil War.* Copyright © 1990 by American Documentaries, Inc.

"A Serendipity Menu for Southern Maryland," © 1991 by Fred Powledge, is used by arrangement with the author.

"Pleasures of the Islands" excerpted from *Bay Country,* by Tom Horton. Copyright © 1987 Johns Hopkins University Press, Baltimore and London.

Fodor's Virginia & Maryland

Editors: Steven K. Amsterdam, Christopher Billy
Contributors: John Bowen, Mark Carnegie, Elinor Coleman, Michael Dolan, Alexander Parsons, Fred Powledge, Linda K. Schmidt, Bob Willis
Creative Director: Fabrizio La Rocca
Cartographer: David Lindroth
Illustrator: Karl Tanner
Cover Photograph: Catherine Karnow/ Woodfin Camp

Design: Vignelli Associates

Special Sales

Fodor's Travel Publications are available at special discounts for bulk purchases for sales promotions or premiums. Special editions, including personalized covers, excerpts of existing guides, and corporate imprints, can be created in large quantities for special needs. For more information contact your local bookseller or write to Special Marketing, Fodor's Travel Publications, 201 East 50th Street, New York, NY 10022. Inquiries from Canada should be directed to your local Canadian bookseller or sent to Random House of Canada, Ltd., Marketing Department, 1265 Aerowood Drive, Mississauga, Ontario L4W 1B9. Inquiries from the United Kingdom should be sent to Fodor's Travel Publications, 20 Vauxhall Bridge Road, London SW1V 2SA, England.

MANUFACTURED IN THE UNITED STATES OF AMERICA
10 9 8 7 6 5 4 3 2 1

Contents

Maps

Foreword

While every care has been taken to ensure the accuracy of the information in this guide, the passage of time will always bring change, and consequently the publisher cannot accept responsibility for errors that may occur.

All prices and opening times quoted here are based on information supplied to us at press time. Hours and admission fees may change, however, and the prudent traveler will avoid inconvenience by calling ahead.

Fodor's wants to hear about your travel experiences, both pleasant and unpleasant. When a hotel or restaurant fails to live up to its billing, let us know and we will investigate the complaint and revise our entries where the facts warrant it. Send your letters to the editors of Fodor's Travel Publications, 201 East 50th Street, New York, NY 10022.

Special thanks to Gil Stotler of the Baltimore Area Convention and Visitors Association and to Martha Steger and Susan Brinkerhoff Bland of the Virginia Division of Tourism.

Highlights and Fodor's Choice

Highlights

Virginia Few places in America have as rich a history as the Old Dominion, but that shouldn't stop you from discovering some of the newer attractions in the 10th state. While historical sites and settings such as the re-created town of **Colonial Williamsburg** and **Monticello**—Jefferson's home, recently refurnished with period pieces—remain surely worth visiting, more modern sights and local happenings make Virginia an ideal destination.

Newly opened **Nauticus,** the National Maritime Center in Norfolk, combines elements of science and industry museums with the entertainment value of theme parks. The "Virtual Adventures" submarine ride, a 70mm movie house, and dozens of interactive and CD-ROM–based exhibits use high-tech showmanship to explore nautical themes, such as shipbuilding, world commerce, and the marine environment. **Paramount's Kings Dominion,** off I–95 between Richmond and Fredericksburg, has added an enormous park-within-the-park with its new Wayne's World area, a tribute to the parent company's hit film.

If you have a hankering for less glitzy attractions, be sure to catch some of the local traditions. Make your way to Chincoteague Island in late July for the 70th annual **Pony Swim and Auction.** After the wild ponies of nearby Assateague Island are rounded up, they swim across the channel to Chincoteague, where the foals are auctioned off to benefit the volunteer fire department. The unsold ponies have to swim back home, but you can stay around for the carnival and the wonderful fish market. The 60th annual **Old Fiddler's Convention** will be sparking up the southeastern town of Galax in early August. Bluegrass musicians from around the world will gather for the oldest and largest convention of its kind in the United States.

Norfolk's **International Azalea Festival** is scheduled to be a kind of mini–World's Fair; each of the NATO countries will exhibit its traditional food, music, dance, and commerce at the Botanical Gardens. And 1995's most honored nation is the United Kingdom, whose ambassador will reign throughout the weeklong April festivities. For more wintry local flavor, the town of Monterey in the Shenandoah Valley holds the **Highland County Maple Festival** in mid-March, luring folks with simple pleasures, such as a buckwheat pancakes, tree tapping, and the crowning of the year's Maple Queen.

Whatever time of year you plan to visit, be sure to see at least some of the spectacular 105-mile **Skyline Drive** in **Shenandoah National Park.** One of the most lovingly preserved scenic routes in America, Skyline Drive offers panoramic views of the Blue Ridge Mountains; you'll get a sense of what the first Europeans settlers to the Blue Ridge saw when they arrived in 1716—and maybe a glance at the occasional bobcat or bear, still living in the wild.

Maryland After nearly a decade of planning and more than two years of construction, the **Baltimore Museum of Art** has opened its new wing, providing the largest space in Maryland devoted to modern art. The 35,000-square-foot addition houses 16 galleries that will be reserved for the BMA's diverse collection of 20th-century art. Included in the new galleries are important recent acquisitions, including 15 paintings by Andy Warhol (the world's second largest permanent display of his work). The new wing is directly adjacent to the Cone Wing, where a notable collection of early modern works includes pieces by Matisse and Picasso.

The venerable **USF *Constellation,*** built in Baltimore in 1797 and commissioned as the first ship of the U.S. Navy, was moved this year from its dock at the Inner Harbor. A recent underwater inspection by navy divers revealed that the ship was deteriorating badly and in dire need of repair. A funding campaign was organized to raise $5 million for the face-lift, and the ship was moved to a dry dock near Fort McHenry. Unfortunately, visitors won't be allowed back on board for at least another two years.

The **National Aquarium's Atlantic Coral Reef and Open Ocean exhibits** will reopen in early 1995 after a $14-million renovation (to repair the damage caused by a decade of salt-water corrosion). Through the glass-walled tanks of these exibits (which together hold 560,000 gallons of water), visitors can view the most realistic fabricated coral ever produced. The Aquarium's **Shark Tank** has recently reopened, as well.

Just a ten-minute drive from the Chesapeake Bay Bridge, in Grasonville on the Eastern shore (near U.S. 50), lies the **Horsehead Wetlands Center** (tel. 410/827–6694), a 310-acre preserve of pristine marshland. Administered by the Wildfowl Trust of North America, the Center is home to huge flocks of migrating waterfowl from October to March each year. Over 250 species of waterfowl are protected here under the auspices of the Trust's conservation/education programs. Included in the diverse flocks that make their home here year-round are canvasbacks, red heads, wood ducks, trumpeter swans, and dusky Canada geese. Miles of trails and boardwalks branch out from the Visitor's Center through the marshes to various blinds and observation towers; more adventurous tourists may want to explore these marshes by canoe (available for rent at the Visitor's Center).

Fodor's Choice

No two people will agree on what makes a perfect vacation, but it's fun and helpful to know what others think. We hope you'll have a chance to experience some of Fodor's Choices yourself while visiting Virginia and Maryland. For detailed information about each entry, refer to the appropriate chapters in this guidebook.

Sights

Skyline Drive on a bright fall day, Shenandoah National Park, VA

The Natural Bridge carved out of limestone by the Cedar Creek, Natural Bridge, VA

Manassas National Battlefield (Bull Run), a vast historic panorama, at Manassas, VA

U. S. Naval Base, one of the largest naval bases in the world, Norfolk, VA

Chesapeake Bay Bridge-Tunnel, VA, for an overwater and underwater experience

Assateague Island to see wild ponies, VA *and* MD

Calvert Cliffs to scavenge for fossils, Calvert County, MD

Historic Buildings and Monuments

Antietam Civil War Battlefield, Sharpsburg, MD

Virginia State Capitol, Richmond, VA

Monticello, Charlottesville, VA

Mount Vernon, Fairfax County, VA

Tomb of the Unknown Soldier, Arlington National Cemetery, Arlington, VA

Maryland State House, Annapolis, MD

Fort McHenry, Baltimore, MD

Historic Restorations

Appomattox Court House, Appomattox County, VA

Colonial Williamsburg, Williamsburg, VA

Museum of American Frontier Culture, Staunton, VA

Historic District, Frederick, MD

Historic St. Mary's City, St. Mary's County, MD

Museums

The Baltimore Museum of Art, Cone Collection, Baltimore, MD

Chesapeake Bay Maritime Museum, St. Michaels, MD

Chrysler Museum, Norfolk, VA

Mariners Museum, Newport News, VA

Virginia Air and Space Center and Hampton Roads History Center, Hampton, VA

Virginia Museum of Fine Arts, Richmond, VA

Walters Art Gallery, Baltimore, MD

B&O Railroad Museum, Baltimore, MD

The Ward Museum of Wildfowl Art, Salisbury, MD

Taste Treats

Wine tastings at Barboursville Vineyards, Barboursville, VA

Asparagus pizza at Crozet Pizza near Charlottesville, VA

Chincoteague Oysters at the Landmark Crab House, Chincoteague, VA

An ice-cream cone at the place where it was invented, Doumar's, Norfolk, VA

Soft-shell-crab sandwich at the Town Dock, St. Michaels, MD

Authentic Bavarian cuisine at Schmankerl Stube, Hagerstown, MD

Sampling wines at Boordy Vineyards, Hydes, MD

Lunch from the stalls at Lexington Market, Baltimore, MD

Arts and Entertainment

Barter Theatre, Abingdon, VA

Garth Newel Chamber Music Center, Hot Springs, VA

Wolf Trap Farm Park, Vienna, VA

U.S. Navy band summer open-air concerts, Annapolis, MD

Baltimore Symphony, Baltimore, MD

Center Stage, Baltimore, MD

Summer concerts at the Pier 6 Concert Pavilion, Inner Harbor, Baltimore, MD

After Hours

Ballroom dancing at the Homestead, Hot Springs, VA

The C&O, Charlottesville, VA

Whitey's, Arlington, VA

King of France Tavern, Annapolis, MD

The Explorer's Club, Baltimore, MD

Hotels

The Homestead, Hot Springs, VA, *$$$$*

Williamsburg Inn, Williamsburg, VA, *$$$$*

Harbor Court Hotel, Baltimore, MD, *$$$*

Inn at Perry Cabin, St. Michaels, MD, *$$$*

Victoriana Inn, St. Michaels, MD, *$$$*

Potomac View Farm, St. Mary's County, MD, *$$*

Prince George Inn, Annapolis, MD, *$$*

YMCA of Tidewater, Norfolk, VA, *$*

Restaurants

Hampton's, Harbor Court Hotel, Baltimore, MD, *$$$$*

Citronelle, Baltimore, MD, *$$$*

Eastern Standard, Charlottesville, VA, *$$$*

La Galleria, Norfolk, VA, *$$$*

The Polo Grill, Baltimore, MD, *$$$*

Tio Pepe's, Baltimore, MD, *$$$*

The Trellis, Williamsburg, VA, *$$$*

The Waterwheel, Warm Springs, VA, *$$$*

Haussner's Restaurant, Baltimore, MD, *$$*

Spinnakers Restaurant at Point Lookout Marina, St. Mary's County, MD, *$$*

Joe's Inn, Richmond, VA, *$*

Queen Bee, Arlington, VA, *$*

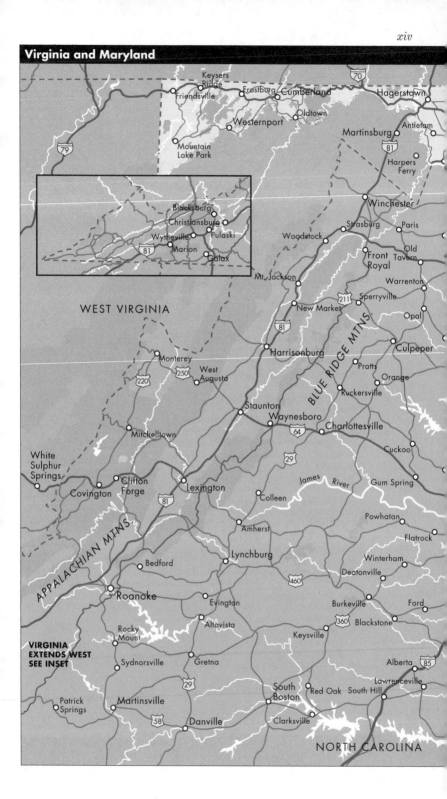

The United States

World Time Zones

Numbers below vertical bands relate each zone to Greenwich Mean Time (0 hrs.).
Local times frequently differ from these general indications,
as indicated by light-face numbers on map.

Algiers, **29**

Anchorage, **3**

Athens, **41**

Auckland, **1**

Baghdad, **46**

Bangkok, **50**

Beijing, **54**

Berlin, **34**

Bogotá, **19**

Budapest, **37**

Buenos Aires, **24**

Caracas, **22**

Chicago, **9**

Copenhagen, **33**

Dallas, **10**

Delhi, **48**

Denver, **8**

Djakarta, **53**

Dublin, **26**

Edmonton, **7**

Hong Kong, **56**

Honolulu, **2**

Istanbul, **40**

Jerusalem, **42**

Johannesburg, **44**

Lima, **20**

Lisbon, **28**

London (Greenwich), **27**

Los Angeles, **6**

Madrid, **38**

Manila, **57**

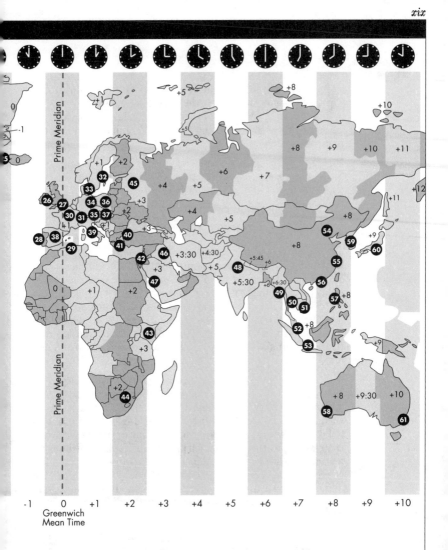

Mecca, **47**
Mexico City, **12**
Miami, **18**
Montréal, **15**
Moscow, **45**
Nairobi, **43**
New Orleans, **11**
New York City, **16**

Ottawa, **14**
Paris, **30**
Perth, **58**
Reykjavík, **25**
Rio de Janeiro, **23**
Rome, **39**
Saigon (Ho Chi Minh City), **51**

San Francisco, **5**
Santiago, **21**
Seoul, **59**
Shanghai, **55**
Singapore, **52**
Stockholm, **32**
Sydney, **61**
Tokyo, **60**

Toronto, **13**
Vancouver, **4**
Vienna, **35**
Warsaw, **36**
Washington, D.C., **17**
Yangon, **49**
Zürich, **31**

Introduction

The planter and the waterman are two curious human species—one long extinct, the other now endangered. Standing side by side, they evoke the histories and express the personalities of the bordering states of Virginia and Maryland, respectively.

Virginians have an extraordinary sense of place; a Virginian, if he lives in a house more than 50 years old, can tell you not only who built it but also about all the generations that have dwelt there up to his own. If the house is more than 150 years old, he will probably tell you Mr. Jefferson designed it (it's the spirit of history, not the letter, that Virginians cherish most).

The Virginia planter was very much connected to the land, at least to his own plantation. Many plantations in various stages of restoration, some of them still going concerns, can be toured today throughout the northern, eastern, and central parts of the state—Washington's august Mount Vernon, Jefferson's ingenious Monticello, and others less well known but also memorable. The heirloom silver in their grand dining rooms and the dirt floors of their slave quarters are eloquent evocations of antebellum Virginia.

Two centuries of life on the plantation go far to explain the curious combination of hauteur and hospitality that marks the Virginian personality to this day. Eighteenth-century aristocrats such as William Byrd of Westover, or his friends the Carters (whose descendants still live at nearby Shirley) used to show off their wealth by throwing lavish parties and taking solicitous interest in the affairs of their dependents and other inferiors. The condescension of one class and the deference of another melded into a common courtesy that visitors can still hear echoes of, in the tone of gracious reserve used by museum docents and waitresses alike.

Of all the crops raised on Virginia plantations, the most abundant was tobacco; the least likely, liberty. Yet this paternalistic, slave-holding system cultivated the interests and ideas that promoted the American Revolution. The rising landed gentry of Virginia composed the House of Burgesses (its chamber is now on view inside the reconstructed capitol in Williamsburg), which gave the colonists a long preparatory exercise in self-government. Though ultimately the Revolution meant far more than the self-interest of a certain class, it was crucial that plantation owners, alienated from a Crown that coveted their landed wealth, formed the preeminent Virginia contingent of revolutionaries.

The hard-won liberty was inequitably distributed, of course. Although the "peculiar institution" of slavery was more peculiar to the Deep South states, such as South Carolina and Georgia, than to Virginia—James Madison and George Mason, both Virginians, included abolition in an early draft of the Constitution—when rancor over the issue erupted into the Civil War, the Old Dominion took the lead in the rebellion. The capital of the Confederacy was in Richmond; the top commander of the Confederate army was a Virginian, Robert E. Lee; and two-thirds of the battles in the Civil War were fought in this state. Petersburg and Richmond were especially ravaged, but few places lay untouched. Today every town has at least one amateur historian who can point out the scenes of skirmishes or tell which buildings survived and which burned down. As he talks, the listener hears the mournful tone of Virginia's rich historical consciousness; much of the lore takes the form of lamentation.

But though they revere the past, Virginians have decided they prefer building to brooding. Jamestown's scrappy Captain John Smith told the very first generation of Virginia gentlemen, "Who does not work does not eat," and in a gentler tone the defeated but resilient Lee, after Appomattox, wrote to his relations at Shirley, "There is nothing left for us but work." Such industry has brought about change, often of a nature that would have startled Lee.

Consequently, the physical landscape has been markedly altered, in many respects shamefully. On the rolling plains in Albemarle and Orange counties ("Mr. Jefferson's Country") and in the still-remote southwestern highlands (a region through which the Wilderness Road once coursed), the roadsides are littered with fast-food outlets and discount malls in dumbfounding profusion. Manassas, where nearly 29,000 men died in two Civil War battles, has only temporarily fended off the encroachment of luxury town homes. Yet many Virginians regard the landscape itself as their preeminent luxury, and violations of it offend their sense of place. Great tracts of Virginia are legally protected from such disfigurement: More than a million acres are dedicated to national and state parks, an official wilderness that includes mountains, marshes, forests, and seashore.

In the beginning, all of America was Virginia—even Plymouth Rock in Massachusetts Bay, where the Pilgrims landed in 1620, was officially in northern Virginia, for all of English North America had been so named, after Elizabeth I the Virgin Queen, in the 16th century. Maryland, which was subtracted from Virginia and set up as its own colony in the 18th century, was named not for a reigning monarch but for a mere consort, Charles I's wife Queen Henrietta Maria. In the 3½ centuries since, it has lost border disputes with all its neighbors—Pennsylvania, West Virginia, and Virginia—to end up in its ungainly current shape, a quarter of the size of Virginia.

The map, however, shows only one aspect of history. Maryland's largest city, Baltimore, is almost three times as populous as any in Virginia, and Maryland has three-quarters the inhabitants of its grand southern neighbor. Though there is much less of it, Maryland has a terrain just as varied as Virginia's, from the mountains in the west through the central plateau to the jagged coast around the Chesapeake Bay. Virginia is also bounded by the bay, but the Chesapeake is by far the predominant feature in Maryland's geography, cleaving the Eastern from the Western shores. Divided by water, the inhabitants of the two shores have preserved quite different accents and customs. On the Western Shore itself, the Patuxent River separates Calvert and St. Mary's counties, which maintain subtly distinct identities and manners. On the Eastern Shore, the winding shoreline prolongs distance; in many cases it takes several times as long to drive to the next town as to sail to it across an inlet. If one were to straighten the shoreline of the Chesapeake Bay, it would stretch from Maryland to Hawaii with a few hundred miles to spare.

Most Marylanders lead terrestrial lives—they ride to work on subways and super-highways—but in spirit they are a waterborne people, bearing the legacy of a prominent maritime past. "Virginia is for lovers" was a hit promotional slogan in the 1970s; a Maryland T-shirt manufacturer matched it with a takeoff, "Maryland is for crabs." The second motto has the advantage, besides mild wit, of concrete truth, for crabs, along with oysters and other seafood from the Chesapeake Bay, remain a major Maryland industry.

Baltimore, on the Patapsco River, was an 18th- and 19th-century shipbuilding center, famous for the speedy Baltimore Clippers that were heavily employed in privateering, drawing the especial ire of the British in the early 1800s. When, in the War of 1812, British ships bombarded Fort McHenry in the harbor, Baltimoreans stood firm, and their flag-waving defiance inspired the "Star-Spangled Banner." Now Baltimore is the fifth-busiest port on the East Coast, and, since renovations and enhancements in the late '70s and early '80s, its Inner Harbor has been an attractive waterside recreation area, with shops, restaurants, and museums that draw millions of locals and out-of-towners alike each year.

Annapolis, on the banks of the Severn River, is one of the most important sailing cities in the world and home of the U.S. Naval Academy. All along both shores of the bay, towns such as St. Michaels, Tilghman's Island, and Solomons thrive on the weekend pleasures of yachtsmen.

Maryland's mythic hero—its cowboy, if you will—is the waterman, who prowls the Chesapeake in his skipjack, "drudging arshters" (dredging oysters) from the decks of America's last fleet of working sailboats. In the 1880s there were more than 1,500 of these native flat-bottomed sloops harvesting oysters with rakes and nets that were dragged over the oyster beds under sail power. Today, there are fewer than three dozen still plying the Chesapeake waters.

On one hand, in the great separateness of his life—spending days and nights on the water with his colleagues, and returning home to an isolated bayside or island village—the waterman is an anomaly in a state where half the population is concentrated in the Baltimore metropolitan area. But in another respect, the waterman provides a rich symbol of contemporary Maryland society: not in the manner in which he sets off to work, but in the variety of the catch he hauls back to the dock. Maryland has always been a land of diversity.

It is said that Maryland was founded as a Catholic colony. In one sense this is true, in that Cecil Calvert, the second Lord Baltimore, who organized the first expedition of colonists in 1633, was a member of the Church of Rome; half the members of that expedition were also Catholic. But Puritans and Anglicans were made welcome, too, a courtesy that was not reciprocated in most of the other English colonies. Maryland was, in fact, the first colony to enact legislation guaranteeing freedom of religion.

Diversity has been cause for turmoil. During the Civil War the state was dangerously ambivalent. Sitting below the Mason-Dixon line, with an economy based equally on agriculture and industry, Maryland found its popular sentiment divided between the agrarian South and the industrial North. The consensus was, in the tradition of tolerance, for compromise: to preserve the Union somehow without coercing the South. There was rioting (and the first bloodshed of that war) when Union troops appeared in Baltimore, and President Lincoln saw fit to incarcerate some city officials, including the mayor of the city and Francis Scott Key's grandson, an action that was strategically effective but probably unconstitutional. The state faced itself on the field of battle when the First Maryland Regiment of the Union army fought the First Maryland Regiment of the Confederate army at Front Royal, Virginia.

The planter and the waterman: One is patrician, landed, and gregarious; the other plebeian, afloat, and solitary. Both are enterprising and jealous of their independence, but they have proved to be congenial neighbors.

Between Virginia and Maryland, nature carved out the Chesapeake Bay, and politics carved out the District of Columbia. Maryland teeters between the cultures of North and South; it has been called the northernmost southern state and the southernmost northern state, with the efficiency of the North and the graciousness of the South. Virginia, by contrast, is quintessentially southern. It is tempting to draw further distinctions: Virginians are gracious, Marylanders fractious; Virginians are tragic, Marylanders sassy; Virginians are stalwart, Marylanders mercurial. There is plenty of evidence to disprove all such generalizations. Nevertheless, such comparisons help us to understand both states. Virginia and Maryland are best visited in tandem.

1 Essential Information

Before You Go

Visitor Information

Maryland Office of Tourism Development (217 E. Redwood St., 9th floor, Baltimore, MD 21202, tel. 410/333–6611, 800/543–1036, or 800/445–4558; TTY 410/333–6926, fax 410/331–6643).

Virginia Division of Tourism (1021 E. Cary St., Richmond, VA 23219, tel. 804/786–4484, 804/786–2051, or 800/847–4882 for brochures; fax 804/786–1919).

Virginia State Chamber of Commerce (9 S. 5th St., Richmond, VA 23219, tel. 804/644–1607 or 800/847–4882; fax 804/783–0903).

Washington Visitor Information Center (1455 Pennsylvania Ave. NW, Washington, DC 20004, tel. 202/789–7038, fax 202/289–8079) or the **Washington, D.C., Convention & Visitors Association** (1212 New York Ave. NW, Washington, DC 20005, tel. 202/789–7000, fax 202/789–8079).

Williamsburg Area Tourism and Conference Bureau (201 Penniman Rd., Drawer GB, Williamsburg, VA 23187, tel. 804/253–0192 or 800/368–6511, fax 804/229–2047).

Tours and Packages

If you want to see as much of Virginia and Maryland as possible in a realistic amount of time, then you might want to consider an escorted motor-coach tour. Group tours generally pack a lot of sightseeing into a relatively short time span, traversing a sizable portion of the area in as few as three days. This way, you're sure to hit all the traditional tourist spots and perhaps a few out-of-the-way places you might not be able to get to on your own. Keep in mind, though, that you can only spend as much time in one place as the tour itinerary allows. If freedom and flexibility are more important to you, pick up a map, decide where you want to go, plot a route, and experience the area on your own at a leisurely pace. Most major rental-car companies offer weekly rates with unlimited mileage.

When considering a tour, be sure to find out: (1) exactly what expenses are included, particularly tips, taxes, side trips, meals, and entertainment; (2) the ratings of all hotels on the itinerary and the facilities they offer; (3) the additional cost of single, rather than double, accommodations if you are traveling alone; and (4) the number of travelers in your group. Note whether the tour operator reserves the right to change hotels, routes, or even prices after you've booked, and check out the operator's policy regarding cancellations, complaints, and trip-interruption insurance. Many tour operators request that packages be booked through a travel agent; there is generally no additional charge for doing so.

Listed below is a sampling of operators and packages to give you an idea of what is available. For additional resources, contact your travel agent, the Maryland Office of Tourism Development, or the Virginia Division of Tourism.

General-interest **Maupintour** (Box 807, Lawrence, KS 66044, tel. 913/843–1211 or 800/255–4266) offers a seven-day jaunt through Baltimore and the Eastern Shore, including the Brandywine River valley, from May to October.

Domenico Tours (751 Broadway, Bayonne, NJ 07002, tel. 201/823–8687 or 800/554–8687) offers a three-day trip that takes in Chesapeake Bay and Tangier Island, plus a four-day tour of Virginia Beach. Other itineraries feature Williamsburg; Busch Gardens; Washington, D.C.; and Pennsylvania Dutch country, in various combinations.

Talmage Tours (1223 Walnut St., Philadelphia, PA 19107, tel. 215/923–7100 or 800/825–6243) offers a four-day trip to Williamsburg and Busch Gardens, as well as a four-day drive through the Shenandoah Valley, including Monticello.

Bill Rohrbaugh's Charter Service (3395 Main St., Box 690, Manchester, MD 21102, tel. 410/239–8000 or 800/543–9090) arranges charters, and offers regional itineraries, multilingual services, airport pick-up, and general group services.

Tauck Tours (11 Wilton Rd., Westport, CT 06881, tel. 203/226–6911 or 800/468–2825) has an eight-day tour that takes in Williamsburg, Richmond, Monticello, and Gettysburg, along with Philadelphia, Pennsylvania Dutch Country, Valley Forge, and Washington, D.C.

Brendan Tours (1537 Califa St., Van Nuys, CA 91411, tel. 818/785–9696 or 800/421–8446); **Collette Tours** (162 Middle St., Pawtucket, RI 02860, tel. 401/728–3805 or 800/832–4656); **Globus** and its more budget-minded sister, **Cosmos Tourama** (5301 S. Federal Circle, Littleton, CO 80123, tel. 303/797–2800 or 800/221–0090); **Mayflower Tours** (1225 Warren Ave., Downers Grove, IL 60515, tel. 708/960–3430 or 800/323–7604 outside the state); and **Parker Tours** (218–14 Northern Blvd., Bayside, NY 11361, tel. 718/428–7800 or 800/833–9600) also offer packages covering the attractions of the region.

Tips for British Travelers

Visitor Information Write or fax the **U.S. Travel and Tourism Administration** (Box 1EN, London W1A 1EN, tel. 071/495–4466, fax 071/409–0566) for a free "USA pack".

Passports and Visas British Visitor's Passports are **not** accepted. You need a valid 10-year passport to enter the United States (cost £15 for a standard 32-page passport, £30 for a 94-page passport). Application forms are available from most travel agents and major post offices and from the Passport Office (Clive House, 70 Petty France, London SW1H 9HD, tel. 071/279–3434 for recorded information or 071/279–4000). You do not need a visa if you are visiting either on business or pleasure, are staying 90 days or less, have a return ticket, are traveling with a major airline (in effect, any airline that flies from the United Kingdom to the United States), and complete visa-waiver form I–94W, which is supplied by the airline. For more information, or to apply for a visa, call the U.S. Embassy visa information line (tel. 089/200–2901; calls cost 48p per minute or 36p per minute cheap rate).

Customs Entering the United States, a visitor 21 or over can bring in 200 cigarettes or 50 cigars or 2 kilograms of tobacco; one liter of alcohol; and duty-free gifts to a value of $100. Restricted items include meat, meat products, fruits, vegetables, plants, and seeds. Never carry illegal drugs.

Returning to the United Kingdom, you may import duty-free 200 cigarettes, 100 cigarillos, 50 cigars, or 250 grams of tobacco; 1 liter of spirits or 2 liters of fortified or sparkling wine; 2 liters of still table wine; 60 milliliters of perfume; 250 milliliters of toilet water, plus £36 worth of other goods, including gifts and souvenirs.

Insurance Medical care in the United States is excellent, but it can be very expensive. Therefore, we recommend that you take out insurance to guard against health problems, motoring mishaps, theft, flight cancellation, and loss of luggage, with the emphasis on extra medical coverage. Most major tour operators offer holiday insurance, and details are given in brochures. Most companies provide a 24-hour contact telephone number in the event of an emergency. For free general advice on all aspects of holiday insurance, contact the **Association of British Insurers** (51 Gresham St., London EC2V 7HQ, tel. 071/600–3333). A proven leader in the holiday insurance field is **Europ Assistance** (252 High St., Croydon, Surrey CR0 1NF, tel. 081/680–1234).

Money Regardless of where you travel, it is always advisable to carry the major portion of your money in traveler's checks. U.S.-dollar checks can be used like cash in most restaurants and shops, so it's worth buying some in small denominations. Sterling checks can be very difficult to exchange, even in banks, and are not recommended. U.S. coins are 1 cent (penny), 5 cents (nickel), 10 cents (dime), 25 cents (quarter), and occasionally 50 cents (half dollar). Dollar bills that you are most likely to encounter are $1, $5, $10, $20, $50, $100. Be aware that all denominations are the same size and color, and look similar.

Credit Cards Most major credit cards are accepted throughout the region, including: American Express, Discover, MasterCard, VISA, and Diner's Club. A credit card is often requested as additional proof of identity. If your room payment or car rental is not being paid for by voucher or credit card, you will be asked to pay in cash.

Tipping Throughout the United States, it is customary to tip when service merits. A sufficient tip is 15% for meals in restaurants (not in cafeterias or fast-food establishments). At hotels, a tip of about 75¢ per bag is expected by bellboys. Airport porters, hotel doormen, and taxi drivers are also tipped.

Smoking As Americans are becoming more and more health conscious, smoking has become prohibited in many public places, and on domestic flights. Smoking is generally not permitted aboard public transport, in theaters, and only in special areas of many restaurants. Most hotels can provide nonsmoking rooms, which you should request when you make your reservations.

Electricity Electrical current in the United States is 110–115 volts, 60 cycles, AC. Standard plugs are two parallel flat pins. If you are traveling from abroad with electrical appliances, you will need an adaptor. Your hotel may have them available for guests, but if they don't, they'll probably be able to loan you a hair dryer or clothes iron.

Tour Operators The following is a selection of tour operators that service the Maryland and Virginia area. For more information of the region and a list of additional tour operators that offer both go-as-you-please and set itineraries, write or phone the **Virginia Division of Tourism** (182–184 Addington Rd., Seldon, Surrey CR2 8LB, tel. 081/651–4743).

American Eye (173 Wardour St., London W1V 3TA, tel. 071/437–9272) produces a series of packaged fly/drive tours to Maryland and Virginia, featuring Baltimore, Annapolis, Colonial Williamsburg, Amish country, the Brandywine Valley, and Washington, D.C. Their programs include a variety of itineraries with flights, hotels, and car hire included.

The Getaway Group (UK) Inc. (34 The Mall, Bromley, Kent BR1 1TS, tel. 081/313–0550) offers escorted motor-coach tours to the region, motor-home rental plans, and self-driving plans. The most comprehensive coverage of the region is "George Washington Country," a 16-day program with car rental included.

Key to America (15 Feltham Rd., Ashford, Middlesex TW15 1DQ, tel. 0784/248777) offers a 15-day Virginia fly/drive tour that combines scenic areas, beaches, and historical sights.

Kuoni Travel (Kuoni House, Dorking, Surrey RH5 4AZ, tel. 0306/742222) also has a 15-day fly/drive tour and an eight-day coach tour that includes Jamestown, Williamsburg, Richmond, Shenandoah National Park, and Washington, D.C.

Page & Moy Ltd. (136–140 London Rd., Leicester LE2 1EN, tel. 0533/552521) features Virginia on its tour of the Confederate States.

Premier Holidays (Westbrook, Milton Rd., Cambridge CB4 1YQ, tel. 0223/355977) features "The Virginian," a 13-day coach tour that covers the Chesapeake region, and a self-drive tour of Virginia.

Airlines and Airfares Washington's Dulles International Airport is the major gateway to the Chesapeake region for British travelers. **United** (tel. 0800/888555) and **British Airways** (tel. 081/897–4000) fly between London (Heathrow) and Washington. British Airways flies daily at 12:55 PM, with an additional Concorde flight three times a week. United has one non-stop flight daily, two in summer. Flying time is about 7½ hours (4½ hours on Concorde).

Peak-season round-trip fares to Washington start at around £350, but considerable reductions are available when you travel off-season or midweek. **Travel Cuts** (tel. 071/637–3161) and **Flightfile** (tel. 071/323–4203) are specialist ticket agencies that offer additional discounts (and absolutely no frills), with off-season fares starting at £250 round-trip.

When to Go

Spring brings horse racing to Baltimore, northern Virginia, and the Virginia Piedmont; the Preakness Stakes in Baltimore is a highly festive occasion, but many point-to-points and steeplechases are more interesting to watch and visit. Many public gardens are in full bloom and offer free visitations; garden clubs conduct tours of gracious private properties throughout both states. In Shenandoah National Park, Skyline Drive overlooks a blooming panorama that is just about as stirring as the autumn colors. At Jarrettsville, north of Baltimore, visitors are welcomed at the Harvey Smith Ladew Topiary Gardens, nearly 20 acres of the finest sculpted gardens in the country. If you happen to travel to Baltimore in early May, don't miss Sherwood Gardens, well known for hundreds of thousands of tulips (planted freshly each year) azaleas, pansies, and blossoming trees.

Summer draws the largest numbers of visitors, particularly at Virginia Beach, Ocean City, and other popular resorts on the bay and the ocean. Historical buildings and museums in both states tend to schedule longer opening hours to serve the crowds. Baltimore's Inner Harbor has become an East Coast mecca for tourists and yachtsmen. On warm days, the promenade is filled with visitors from around the world.

Autumn brings spectacular colors in the foliage of the rolling Piedmont region of Virginia and the Catoctin Mountains west of Baltimore; the temperatures become more comfortable for hiking and biking. Equestrian events resume, and in Maryland the sailboat and powerboat shows in Annapolis and the Waterfowl Festival in Easton attract thousands of visitors in October and November.

Winter temperatures may make it too cold to swim, yet the major resorts continue to draw vacationers with seasonal peace and quiet at much lower off-season rates. Other travelers come for romantic seclusion at a bed-and-breakfast in a little town. Virginia was the first southern state to develop skiing commercially, and now both downhill and cross-country skiing are popular activities at resorts in the Shenandoah Valley and western Maryland. Elsewhere in the region heavy snow is rarely seen, and because local residents are unaccustomed to driving under such conditions, a snowfall is a serious traffic hazard in this area.

Climate   Maryland enjoys a moderate climate with summer temperatures reaching into the 90s and winter days that usually stay in the 30s. Average temperature for the state is 64.4F°. Average rainfall is 41.6 inches, while snowfall is a modest 26.7 inches, except in the western Maryland mountains where it averages 82 inches. What follows are average daily maximum and minimum temperatures for major cities in Virginia and Maryland.

Baltimore	**Jan.**	43F	6C	**May**	74F	23C	**Sept.**	79F	26C
		29	− 2		56	13		61	16
	Feb.	43F	6C	**June**	83F	28C	**Oct.**	67F	19C
		29	− 2		65	18		50	10
	Mar.	52F	11C	**July**	86F	30C	**Nov.**	54F	12C
		36	2		70	21		40	4
	Apr.	63F	17C	**Aug.**	85F	29C	**Dec.**	45F	7C
		45	7		67	19		31	− 1

Norfolk	**Jan.**	49F	9C	**May**	76F	24C	**Sept.**	81F	27C
		34	1		58	14		65	18
	Feb.	50F	10C	**June**	83F	28C	**Oct.**	70F	21C
		34	1		67	19		56	13
	Mar.	58F	14C	**July**	88F	31C	**Nov.**	61F	16C
		40	4		72	22		45	7
	Apr.	67F	19C	**Aug.**	85F	29C	**Dec.**	52F	11C
		49	9		70	21		36	2

Information   For current weather conditions and forecasts for cities in the United
Sources   States and abroad, plus the local time and helpful travel tips, call the **Weather Channel Connection** (tel. 900/932–8437; 95¢ per minute) from a touch-tone phone.

Festivals and Seasonal Events

Late January: Lee-Jackson Day, the third Monday of the month, commemorates the birthdays of the Confederate generals Robert E. Lee (Jan. 19) and Stonewall Jackson (Jan. 21) with celebrations all over Virginia but especially in Lexington, where both men lived and taught. *Tel. 703/463–3777.*

Late January: Annapolis Heritage Antiques Show, in Annapolis, Maryland, one of the major mid-Atlantic events of its kind, lasts three days. *Tel. 410/383–9380.*

Mid-February: ACC Crafts Fair in Baltimore draws more than 800 exhibitors for three days of trading. *Tel. 410/659–7144.*

Late February: George Washington's Birthday is celebrated in Alexandria, Virginia, with a parade—175 floats and marching units—and a reenactment of a Revolutionary War skirmish at Fort Ward nearby. *Tel. 703/838–5005.*

Late March: Military Through the Ages, in Williamsburg, Virginia, uses authentic weapons in a series of reenactments of battles from the Middle Ages to the 20th century. *Tel. 804/229–1607.*

Late March: Maryland Days Weekend of St. Mary's City, Maryland, commemorates the founding of the colony at its original birthplace. *Tel. 410/862–0990.* (A celebration on a smaller scale takes place at the courthouse in Baltimore. *Tel. 410/889–6060.*)

Mid-April: Azalea Festival in Norfolk, Virginia, salutes NATO with battleship tours, a parade, an air show, outdoor concerts, a ball, and the crowning of a queen from the year's honored NATO member nation. *Tel. 804/622–2312.*

Late April: Historic Garden Week throughout Virginia is a time when grand private homes, otherwise closed to the public, open their doors to visitors. *Tel. 804/644–7776.*

Late April: Southern Maryland Celtic Festival and Highland Gathering, which takes place in Calvert County, features piping and fiddling competitions, dancing, games, and the foods and crafts of Scotland, Wales, Ireland, and England. *Tel. 410/535–3274.*

Early May: Virginia Gold Cup steeplechase horse races, held near Middleburg, have been among the most prominent social and sporting events of Virginia since the 1920s. *Tel. 703/253–5001.*

Mid-May: Flower Mart in Baltimore has been a rite of spring for most of this century; this outdoor vending of plants, flowers, and arts and crafts—accompanied by musical entertainment—benefits the Women's Civic League. *Tel. 410/837–5424.*

Mid-May: Maryland Preakness Celebration in Baltimore is a week-long festival including, among the more than 100 events: parades, street parties, fundraisers, and hot-air-balloon races. The culmination of all this fun is the annual running of the Preakness Stakes at Pimlico Racetrack in Baltimore, on the third Saturday in May. *Tel. 410/ 837–3030.*

Mid-May: Civil War Living History Weekend, a reenactment in New Market, Virginia, of a battle of 1864, is the oldest and possibly the largest event of its kind in the country. *Tel. 703/740–3101.*

Late May: Commissioning Week at the United States Naval Academy in Annapolis, Maryland, is a time of dress parades, traditional stunts such as the Herndon Monument Climb, and a spectacular aerobatics demonstration by the Navy's famous **Blue Angels** precision flying team. *Tel. 410/267–2291.*

Early June: Folklore Week at Smith Mountain Lake State Park near Roanoke, Virginia, brings demonstrations of Appalachian crafts and skills. *Tel. 703/297–5998.*

Early June: Eastern Shore Chamber Music Festival in Easton, Maryland, is two weekends of classical music performances at historical sites around town. *Tel. 410/745–2750.*

Mid-June: Deer Creek Fiddler's Convention is a twice-annual gathering at the Carroll County Farm Museum, in Westminster, and attracts some of the nation's finest bluegrass entertainers and fiddlers. *Tel. 410/876–2667.*

Late June: Hampton Jazz Festival in Hampton, Virginia—an event of national importance—brings together top performers in the different styles of jazz. *Tel. 804/838–4203.*

Late June: Virginia Horse Show, with a full program of competitions among Arabians, Half-Arabians, Morgans, saddlebreds, and others, takes place in Richmond, Virginia. *Tel. 804/228–3200.*

July 4: Independence Day celebrations in Baltimore culminate in a major show of fireworks over Inner Harbor. *Tel. 410/837–4636.*

Late July: Pony Swim and Auction in Chincoteague, Virginia, is the annual roundup of wild ponies from Assateague Island; the foals are auctioned off to support the volunteer fire department. *Tel. 804/ 336-9765 or 804/336-6161.*

Late July: Virginia Highlands Festival in Abingdon celebrates Appalachia with displays and demonstrations of arts and crafts, exhibitions of animals, sales of antiques, and performances of country music. *Tel. 703/628-8141.*

Early August: The Governor's Cup overnight yacht race boasts more than 300 sailboats that participate between Annapolis and St. Mary's City, Maryland, and culminates in a day-long party at St. Mary's College. *Tel. 410/862-0380.*

Early August: Seafood Feast-i-val in Cambridge, Maryland, is an all-you-can-eat extravaganza on the shore of the Choptank River. *Tel. 410/228-3575.*

Late August: Wine Festival in Middleburg, Virginia, features tastings of vintages from 20 Virginia wineries, plus grape stomping and musical entertainment. *Tel. 703/687-5219.*

Late August: Maryland State Fair, in Timonium, is 10 days of horse racing, midway fun, livestock judging, live entertainment, agricultural displays, farm implements, and plenty of food. *Tel. 410/252-0200.*

Late August: Civil War Reenactment at Manassas, Virginia, recreates the first and second battles of Bull Run. *Tel. 703/491-4045.*

Early September: Defender's Day celebrations at Fort McHenry in Baltimore commemorate—with music, drilling, mock bombardment, and fireworks—the battle that led to the writing of the national anthem. *Tel. 301/256-4152.*

Mid-September: Apple Harvest Festival in Winchester, Virginia, is a weekend of arts and crafts to celebrate the traditions of an important regional crop. *Tel. 703/665-8060.*

Late September: Virginia State Fair in Richmond is a classic conglomeration of carnival rides, livestock shows, displays of farm equipment, and lots of food for sale. *Tel. 804/228-3200.*

Late September: Maryland Wine Festival at the Carroll County Farm Museum, Westminster, features representatives from nearly a dozen of Maryland's wineries, who display their products, offer tastings, and give seminars on winemaking. *Tel. 410/876-2667.*

Early-mid-October: Autumn Glory Festival, at various western Maryland locations (Garrett County), is a celebration of the peak fall foliage, and features the State banjo and fiddle championships, Tournament of Bands, firemen's parades, Oktoberfest, arts, crafts, and antiques. *Tel. 301/334-1948.*

Early-mid-October: United States Sailboat and Powerboat Shows, the world's largest events of their kind, take place in Annapolis, Maryland. *Tel. 410/268-8828.*

Late October: Yorktown Day observances in Yorktown, Virginia, celebrate the Colonial victory in the American War of Independence (October 19, 1781) with 18th-century tactical demonstrations, patriotic exercises, and a stirring wreath-laying ceremony. *Tel. 804/898-3400.*

Late October: Virginia Festival of American Film is becoming a major event in the motion picture industry, with screenings in Charlottesville, Virginia, of important new movies and appearances by their stars. *Tel. 804/924-3378.*

Early November: Waterfowl Festival in Easton, Maryland, involves decoy exhibitions, carving demonstrations, duck-calling contests, and retriever exercises during a three-day weekend. *Tel. 410/822-4567.*

Late November: Waterfowl Week in Chincoteague, Virginia, is when the National Wildlife Refuge opens nature trails to motor vehicles, allowing visitors to watch the Canada and snow geese on their southward migration. *Tel. 804/336–6122.*

Late November–early January: Winter Festival of Lights, at Prince George's County (near Washington, D.C.), features a spectacular display of more than 150,000 multicolored lights in a drive-through setting. Highlights include a glittering giant tree, lighted train station and carousel, and Santa and his reindeer in lights. *Tel. 301/699–2545.*

Early December: Virginia Thanksgiving Festival at Berkeley Plantation in Charles City reenacts the original Thanksgiving of December 4, 1619, with performances of period music and the participation of costumed colonists and Native Americans. *Tel. 804/272–3226.*

Early December: Old Town Christmas Candlelight Tour of Alexandria, Virginia, visits historic houses for light refreshment and performances of period music of the season. *Tel. 703/463–3777.*

December 31: New Year's Eve festivities in Baltimore include a concert at the Harborplace amphitheater and a midnight fireworks display over Inner Harbor. *Tel. 410/332–4191.*

December 31: First Night Annapolis is a family-oriented, non-alcoholic, affordable celebration of the lively arts. The state capital is transformed into a stage with more than 150 performances by more than 40 local acts in historic homes, public buildings, schools, churches, and even shop windows. *Tel. 410/268–8553.*

What to Pack

Clothing   Visitors to the mountains and the caverns of Virginia will want to prepare for colder than average temperatures. Hiking along the Appalachian Trail, even during spring and fall, frequently requires a coat. A sweater is in order for a visit to Luray Caverns or Shenandoah Caverns at all seasons of the year.

Where dress is concerned, Baltimore and Richmond are relatively conservative. In the more expensive restaurants, men are expected to wear jacket and tie; in such public areas as art museums and theaters, patrons who are not neatly dressed and groomed are liable to feel conspicuous.

At the bay and ocean resorts, "formal" means long trousers and a collared shirt for men and shoes for everybody. A tie might never get tied during a stay in these areas.

Miscellaneous   Bring an extra pair of eyeglasses or contact lenses in your carry-on luggage. If you have a health problem that requires a prescription drug, pack enough to last the duration of the trip. In case your bags go astray, don't pack prescription drugs in luggage that you plan to check. Pack a list of the offices that supply refunds for lost or stolen traveler's checks. Bring along a good sunscreen, especially if you are planning to spend your time on, or near, the water.

Pack light, because porters and luggage trolleys can be hard to find at Washington airports. They are, however, readily available for inbound international passengers at Baltimore-Washington International Airport.

Luggage   Free airline baggage allowances depend on the airline, the route,
Regulations   and the class of your ticket; ask in advance. In general, on domestic flights, you are entitled to check two bags—neither exceeding 62 inches, or 158 centimeters (length + width + height), or weighing more than 70 pounds (32 kilograms). A third piece may be brought aboard; its total dimensions are generally limited to less than 45

inches (114 centimeters), so it will fit easily under the seat in front of you or in the overhead compartment. In the United States the Federal Aviation Administration gives airlines broad latitude to limit carry-on allowances and tailor them to different aircraft and operational conditions. Charges for excess, oversize, or overweight pieces vary.

Safeguarding Your Luggage Before leaving home, itemize your bags' contents and their worth in case they go astray. To minimize that risk, tag them inside and out with your name, address, and phone number. (If you use your home address, cover it so that potential thieves can't see it.) Put a copy of your itinerary inside each bag, so that you can easily be tracked. At check-in, make sure that the tag attached by baggage handlers bears the correct three-letter code for your destination. If your bags do not arrive with you, or if you detect damage, immediately file a written report with the airline before you leave the airport.

Insurance In the event of loss, damage, or theft on domestic flights, airlines' liability is $2,000 per passenger, excluding the valuable items such as jewelry, cameras, and more that are listed in the fine print on your ticket. Excess-valuation insurance can be bought directly from the airline at check-in. Your homeowner's policy may fill the gap; or firms such as **The Travelers Companies** (1 Tower Sq., Hartford, CT 06183, tel. 203/277–0111 or 800/243–3174) and **Wallach & Company, Inc.** (107 W. Federal St., Box 480, Middleburg, VA 22117, tel. 703/687–3166 or 800/237–6615) sell baggage insurance.

Traveler's Checks Traveler's checks are preferable in metropolitan centers, although you'll need cash in rural areas and small towns. The most widely recognized are **American Express**, **Citicorp**, **Thomas Cook**, and **Visa**, which are sold by major commercial banks, usually for a fee of 1% to 3% of the checks' face value. Both American Express and Thomas Cook issue checks that can be countersigned and used by you or your traveling companion, and they both provide checks, at no extra charge, denominated in six non-U.S. currencies. (Some foreign banks charge as much as 20% for cashing traveler's checks denominated in dollars.) Buy a few checks in small denominations to cash toward the end of your trip, so you won't be left with excess foreign currency. Record the numbers of the checks, cross them off as you spend them, and keep this list separate from the checks.

Getting Money from Home

Cash Machines Many automated-teller machines (ATMs) are tied to international networks such as **Cirrus** and **Plus**. You can use your bank card at ATMs to withdraw money from an account and get cash advances on a credit-card account if your card has been programmed with a personal identification number, or PIN. Check in advance on limits on withdrawals and cash advances within specified periods. On cash advances you are charged interest from the day you receive the money from ATMs as well as from tellers. Transaction fees for ATM withdrawals outside your home turf may be higher than fees for withdrawals at home.

For specific Cirrus locations in the United States and Canada, call 800/424–7787. For U.S. Plus locations, call 800/843–7587 and press the area code and first three digits of the number you're calling from (or of the calling area where you want an ATM).

Wiring Money You don't have to be a cardholder to send or receive funds through **MoneyGram® from American Express.** Just go to a MoneyGram agent, located in retail and convenience stores and in American Express travel offices. Pay up to $1,000 with cash or a credit card, anything over that in cash. The money can be picked up within 10 minutes in cash or with a check at the nearest MoneyGram agent. Call 800/926–9400 for locations and more information. There's no limit, and the recipient need only present photo identification. The cost, which includes a free long-distance phone call, runs from 3% to 10%, depending on the amount sent, the destination, and the method of payment.

You can also use **Western Union.** To wire money, take either cash or a cashier's check to the nearest agent or call 800/325–6000 and use MasterCard or Visa. Money sent from the United States or Canada will be available for pickup at agent locations in 100 countries within minutes. Once the money is in the system, it can be picked up at any one of 25,000 locations (call 800/325–6000 for the one nearest you; 800/321–2923 in Canada). Fees range from 4% to 10%, depending on the amount you send.

Traveling with Cameras, Camcorders, and Laptops

Film and Cameras If your camera is new or if you haven't used it for a while, shoot and develop a few test rolls of film before you leave. Store film in a cool, dry place—never in the car's glove compartment or on the shelf under the rear window.

Airport security X-rays generally aren't harmful to film with ISO below 400. To protect your film, carry it with you in a clear plastic bag and ask for a hand inspection. Such requests are honored at U.S. airports. Don't depend on a lead-lined bag to protect film in checked luggage—the airline may increase the radiation to see what's inside. Call the Kodak Information Center (tel. 800/242–2424) for details.

Camcorders and Videotape Before your trip, put camcorders through their paces, invest in a skylight filter to protect the lens, and check all the batteries.

Videotape is not damaged by X-rays, but it may be harmed by the magnetic field of a walk-through metal detector, so ask for a hand-check. Airport security personnel may ask you to turn on the camcorder to prove that it's what it appears to be, so make sure the battery is charged.

Laptops Security X-rays do not harm hard-disk or floppy-disk storage, but you may request a hand-check, at which point you may be asked to turn on the computer to prove that it is what it appears to be. (Check your battery before departure.) Most airlines allow you to use your laptop aloft except during takeoff and landing (so as not to interfere with navigation equipment).

Traveling with Children

Endowed with plenty of national parks, seashores, battlefields, and historic homes and restored towns—as well as theme parks and beach-town amusement piers—Virginia and Maryland make excellent destinations for family vacations. Driving distances are not wearisome and, outside of Virginia Beach and the northern Virginia suburbs of Washington, D.C., there are plenty of simple, low-cost accommodations and restaurants where children are more than welcome.

Publications Newsletter *Family Travel Times,* published 10 times a year by **Travel with Your Children** (TWYCH, 45 W. 18th St., New York, NY 10011, tel. 212/

206–0688; annual subscription $55), covers destinations, types of vacations, and modes of travel.

Books   *Great Vacations with Your Kids*, by Dorothy Jordon and Marjorie Cohen ($13; Penguin USA, 120 Woodbine St., Bergenfield, NJ 07621, tel. 800/253–6476), and *Traveling with Children—And Enjoying It*, by Arlene K. Butler ($11.95 plus $3 shipping per book; Globe Pequot Press, Box 833, 6 Business Park Rd., Old Saybrook, CT 06475, tel. 800/243–0495, or 800/962–0973 in CT), help plan your trip with children, from toddlers to teens. For basics with little ones, check *Take Your Baby and Go! A Guide for Traveling with Babies, Toddlers and Young Children*, by Sheri Andrews, Judy Bordeaux, and Vivian Vasquez ($5.95; Bear Creek Publications, tel. 800/326–6566). Also from Globe Pequot are *Recommended Family Resorts in the United States, Canada, and the Caribbean*, by Jane Wilford with Janet Tice ($12.95), and *Recommended Family Inns of America* ($12.95). TWYCH (*see above*) also publishes *Cruising with Children* ($22) and *Skiing with Children* ($29). Family Travel Guides catalog ($1; tel. 510/527–5849) lists about 200 books and articles on family travel.

Getting There
Air Fares   On domestic flights, children under 2 not occupying a seat travel free, and older children currently travel on the "lowest applicable" adult fare.

Baggage   The adult baggage allowance applies for children paying half or more of the adult fare.

Safety Seats   The FAA recommends the use of safety seats aloft and details approved models in the free leaflet **"Child/Infant Safety Seats Recommended for Use in Aircraft"** (available from the Federal Aviation Administration, APA–200, 800 Independence Ave. SW, Washington, DC 20591, tel. 202/267–3479; Information Hotline, tel. 800/322–7873). Airline policy varies. U.S. carriers allow FAA-approved models bearing a sticker declaring their FAA approval. Because these seats are strapped into regular passenger seats, airlines may require that a ticket be bought for an infant who would otherwise ride free.

Facilities Aloft   Some airlines provide other services for children, such as children's meals and freestanding bassinets (only to those with seats at the bulkhead, where there's enough legroom). Make your request when reserving. Biannually the February issue of *Family Travel Times* details children's services on three dozen airlines ($12, *see above*). "Kids and Teens in Flight" (free from the U.S. Department of Transportation's Office of Consumer Affairs, R–25, Washington, DC 20590, tel. 202/366–2220) offers tips for children flying alone.

Car Travel   To get a copy of the American Academy of Pediatrics' "Family Shopping Guide to Car Seats" send a self-addressed, stamped envelope to Safe Ride Program, American Academy of Pediatrics, 141 Northwest Point Blvd., Box 927, Elk Grove Village, IL 60009. Car crashes remain the leading cause of death for people ages 5–34, according to U.S. government statistics. And car seats are one of the top items recalled by the Consumer Product Safety Commission. If you are renting a car, ask if a free car seat is available and request it when you reserve.

Baby-sitting Services   Several local baby-sitting services in the two states are: **Babysitters of Tidewater** (tel. 804/489–1622) in Norfolk, Virginia; **Harbor City Sitter Service** (tel. 410/462–2977) in Baltimore, Maryland; **Summer Sitter** (tel. 301/289–3637) in Ocean City, Maryland; **Durham Sitters**

Agency (tel. 804/296–8732) in Charlottesville, Virginia; and **Nanny Connection** (tel. 804/379–9314) in Richmond, Virginia.

A hotel concierge or housekeeper can usually make baby-sitting arrangements.

Hints for Travelers with Disabilities

Organizations Several organizations provide travel information for people with disabilities, usually for a membership fee, and some publish newsletters and bulletins. Among them are the **Information Center for Individuals with Disabilities** (Fort Point Pl., 27–43 Wormwood St., Boston, MA 02210, tel. 617/727–5540 or 800/462–5015 in MA between 11 AM and 4 PM, or leave message; TTY 617/345–9743); **Mobility International USA** (Box 10767, Eugene, OR 97440, tel. and TTY 503/343–1284, fax 503/343–6812), the U.S. branch of an international organization based in Britain *(see below)* that has affiliates in 30 countries; **MossRehab Hospital Travel Information Service** (tel. 215/456–9603, TTY 215/456–9602); the **Travel Industry and Disabled Exchange** (TIDE, 5435 Donna Ave., Tarzana, CA 91356, tel. 818/344–3640, fax 818/344–0078); and **Travelin' Talk** (Box 3534, Clarksville, TN 37043, tel. 615/552–6670, fax 615/552–1182).

In the United Kingdom Important information sources include the **Royal Association for Disability and Rehabilitation** (RADAR, 12 City Forum, 250 City Rd., London EC1V 8AF, tel. 071/250–3222), which publishes travel information for people with disabilities in Britain, and **Mobility International** (228 Borough High St., London SE1 1JX, tel. 071/403–5688), an international clearinghouse of travel information for people with disabilities.

Travel Agencies and Tour Operators **Flying Wheels Travel** (143 W. Bridge St., Box 382, Owatonna, MN 55060, tel. 507/451–5005 or 800/535–6790) is a travel agency specializing in domestic and worldwide cruises, tours, and independent travel itineraries for people with mobility problems. Adventurers should contact **Wilderness Inquiry** (1313 5th St. SE, Minneapolis, MN 55414, tel. and TTY 612/379–3858 or 800/728–0719), which orchestrates action-packed trips such as white-water rafting, sea kayaking, and dog sledding to bring together people who have disabilities with those who don't.

Publications Several free publications are available from the U.S. Consumer Information Center (Pueblo, CO 81009): "New Horizons for the Air Traveler with a Disability" (include Dept. 608Y in the address), a U.S. Department of Transportation booklet describing changes resulting from the 1986 Air Carrier Access Act and from the 1990 Americans with Disabilities Act, and the Airport Operators Council's *Access Travel: Airports* (Dept. 5804), which describes facilities and services for people with disabilities at more than 500 airports worldwide.

Fodor's publishes *Great American Vacations for Travelers with Disabilities* ($18), detailing services and accessible attractions, restaurants, and hotels in Virginia and other U.S. destinations (available in bookstores, or call 800/533–6478). The 500-page *Travelin' Talk Directory* (*see* Organizations, *above;* $35 check or money order with a money-back guarantee) lists names and addresses of people and organizations who offer help for travelers with disabilities. Twin Peaks Press (Box 129, Vancouver, WA 98666, tel. 206/694–2462 or 800/637–2256) publishes the *Directory of Travel Agencies for the Disabled* ($19.95, plus $2 for shipping), listing more than 370 agencies worldwide. The Sierra Club publishes *Easy Access to National*

Parks ($16 plus $3 shipping; 730 Polk St., San Francisco, CA 94109, tel. 415/776–2211).

Hints for Older Travelers

Organizations   The **American Association of Retired Persons** (AARP, 601 E St. NW, Washington, DC 20049, tel. 202/434–2277) provides independent travelers who are members of the AARP (open to those age 50 or older; $8 per person or couple annually) with the Purchase Privilege Program, which offers discounts on lodging, car rentals, and sightseeing, and the AARP Motoring Plan, which furnishes domestic trip-routing information and emergency road-service aid for an annual fee of $39.95 per person or couple ($59.95 for a premium version). AARP also arranges group tours and cruises through AARP Travel Experience from American Express (400 Pinnacle Way, Suite 450, Norcross, GA 30071, tel. 800/927–0111 or 800/745–4567).

Two other organizations offer discounts on lodgings, car rentals, and other travel products, along with such nontravel perks as magazines and newsletters: the **National Council of Senior Citizens** (1331 F St. NW, Washington, DC 20004, tel. 202/347–8800; membership $12 annually) and **Mature Outlook** (6001 N. Clark St., Chicago, IL 60660, tel. 800/336–6330; $9.95 annually).

Note: For reduced rates, mention your senior-citizen identification card when booking hotel reservations, not when checking out. At restaurants, show your card before you're seated; discounts may be limited to certain menus, days, or hours. If you are renting a car, ask about promotional rates that might improve on your senior-citizen discount.

Educational   The nonprofit **Elderhostel** (75 Federal St., 3rd floor, Boston, MA
Travel   02110, tel. 617/426–7788) has offered inexpensive study programs for people 60 and older since 1975. Held at more than 1,800 educational and cultural institutions, courses cover everything from marine science to Greek myths and cowboy poetry. Participants usually attend lectures in the morning and spend the afternoon sightseeing or on field trips; they live in dormitory-type lodgings. Fees for programs in the United States and Canada, which usually last one week, run about $300, not including transportation.

Tour   **SeniorTours** (508 Irvington Rd., Drexel Hill, PA 19026, tel. 215/626–
Operators   1977 or 800/227–1100) arranges motorcoach tours throughout the United States and Nova Scotia, as well as Caribbean cruises.

Publications   *The 50+ Traveler's Guidebook: Where to Go, Where to Stay, What to Do*, by Anita Williams and Merrimac Dillon ($12.95; St. Martin's Press, 175 5th Ave., New York, NY 10010), is available in bookstores and offers many useful tips. "The Mature Traveler" ($29.95; Box 50820, Reno, NV 89513, tel. 702/786–7419), a monthly newsletter, contains many travel deals.

Hints for Gay and Lesbian Travelers

Organizations   The **International Gay Travel Association** (Box 4974, Key West, FL 33041, tel. 800/448–8550), which has a membership of 800 travel-related businesses, will provide you with names of travel agents and tour operators who specialize in gay travel.

Tour   Tour operator **Olympus Vacations** (8424 Santa Monica Blvd., No.
Operators and   721, West Hollywood, CA 90069; tel. 310/657–2220 or 800/965–9678)
Travel   offers all-gay and lesbian resort holidays. **Skylink Women's Travel**
Agencies   (746 Ashland Ave., Santa Monica, CA 90405, tel. 310/452–0506 or

800/225–5759) handles individual travel for lesbians all over the world and conducts international and domestic group trips annually. Toto Tours (1326 West Albion 3W, Chicago, IL 60626, tel. 312/274–8686) specializes in gay and lesbian travel and offers guided trips to such destinations as Costa Rica, the British Virgin Islands, the Florida Keys, Tanzania, Yellowstone National Park, the Grand Canyon, France, Alaska, the Canadian Rockies, and Munich, Germany.

Publications The premiere international travel magazine for gays and lesbians is *Our World* (1104 N. Nova Rd., Suite 251, Daytona Beach, FL 32117, tel. 904/441–5367; $35 for 10 issues). "Out & About" (tel. 203/789–8518 or 800/929–2268; $49 for 10 issues, full refund if you aren't satisfied) is a 16-page monthly newsletter with extensive information on resorts, hotels, and airlines that are gay-friendly.

Further Reading

Adventuring in Chesapeake Bay Country (Sierra Club Books), by John Bowen, is a comprehensive 450-page guide to the entire Chesapeake region and includes material on boating and fishing, conservation, sports, history, maps, and photos. Two illustrated maritime histories by Robert H. Burgess are *Chesapeake Circle* and *This Was Chesapeake Bay*. Another is Marion V. Brewington's *Chesapeake Bay: A Pictorial Maritime History*. James Michener's *Chesapeake*, a novel, covers nearly 400 years of history and is filled with facts about the area of Maryland's Eastern Shore around the Choptank River. *Chesapeake Bay* magazine, published in Annapolis, appears monthly with features on natural and human history and is available at newsstands in Maryland, Virginia, and Pennsylvania.

The Civil War Battlefield Guide, edited by Frances H. Kennedy, provides detailed information on more than 60 battlegrounds of the war, almost half of them in Virginia.

On Maryland, Carl Bode's *Maryland: A Bicentennial History* is useful. Jacques Kelly's *Maryland: A Pictorial History* makes for good reading, as does *Maryland: A Guide to the Old Line State*, written by the Federal Writer's Project during the Depression and updated in 1976 is an excellent guide. *Great Houses of Maryland*, by Susan Stiles Dowell, describes in detail 21 of the state's loveliest houses. *Day Trips From Baltimore* (Globe Pequot Press), by Gwyn and Bob Willis, offers dozens of one-day driving itineraries in every direction, utilizing Baltimore as the starting point. Francis F. Bierne's *The Amiable Baltimoreans* tells the city's history from the point of view of its elite.

On Virginia, *Virginia: A Guide to the Old Dominion*, published in 1940, remains valuable as history. For a detailed look at the state's political background, read Virginius Dabney's *Virginia: The New Dominion*. Mary Johnston's *To Have and To Hold* describes life in 17th-century Virginia, while William Styron's *The Confessions of Nat Turner* movingly tells the story of a 19th-century slave on a Virginia plantation. Douglas F. Freeman's two biographies, *George Washington* and *R.E. Lee: A Biography*, make wonderful introductions to the lives of two of Virginia's most famous sons. Fawn M. Brodie's *Thomas Jefferson: An Intimate History* is an excellent biography of the sage of Monticello; read also Jefferson's *Notes on the State of Virginia*. The novels of Ellen Glasgow, such as *Barren Ground*, *The Romantic Comedians*, and *They Stooped to Folly*, portray the first families of Richmond adjusting to the changes of the early 20th century. Before visiting Chincoteague and Assateague islands, children may enjoy reading Marguerite Henry's classic horse story, *Misty of Chincoteague.*

Arriving and Departing

By Plane

Flights are either nonstop, direct, or connecting. A **nonstop** flight requires no change of plane and makes no stops. A **direct** flight stops at least once and can involve a change of plane, although the flight number remains the same; if the first leg is late, the second waits. This is not the case with a **connecting** flight, which involves a different plane and a different flight number.

Airports and Airlines
Maryland

Baltimore Washington International Airport (tel. 301/261–1000, 410/859–7100, or 800/435–9294) is the principal airport in Maryland, served by Air Aruba (tel. 800/882–7822), Air Jamaica (tel. 800/523–5585), Air Ontario (tel. 800/776–3000), America West (tel. 800/247–5692), American Airlines (tel. 800/654–8880), British Airways (tel. 800/247–9297), Business Express (tel. 800/345–3400), Cayman Airways (tel. 800/422–9626), Colgan (tel. 800/272–5488), Continental Airlines (tel. 800/525–0280), Delta Airlines (tel. 800/221–1212), El Al (tel. 800/223–6700), Icelandair (tel. 800/223–5500), KLM–Royal Dutch Airlines (tel. 800/777–5553), Ladeco–Chilean Airlines (tel. 800/825–2332), Northwest Airlines (tel. 800/225–2525), TWA (tel. 800/221–2000), United Airlines (tel. 800/241–6522), and USAir (tel. 800/428–4322).

Virginia

Charlottesville-Albemarle Airport (tel. 804/973–8341) is served principally by USAir.

Richmond International Airport (tel. 804/226–3000) has scheduled flights by 12 airlines, including USAir, the major regional carrier.

Roanoke Regional Airport (tel. 703/362–1999) is served by eight carriers, principally USAir. The airport serves Virginia's Shenandoah Valley.

Patrick Henry International Airport (tel. 804/877–0221) in Newport News, and **Norfolk International Airport** (tel. 804/857–3200) are both served by USAir. The airports together serve the Hampton Roads, Williamsburg, and Eastern Shore regions of Virginia.

Tri-City Regional Airport (tel. 615/323–6271) in Blountville, Tennessee, is served by USAir; it's across the state line from southwestern Virginia.

Washington National Airport (tel. 703/419–8003) in Arlington, and **Washington Dulles International Airport** (tel. 703/661–2700), in Loudoun County, are both in northern Virginia; both are served by America West, American, Continental, Delta, Eastern, Northwest, TWA, United, and USAir; Dulles is served by many international airlines as well, including Air France (tel. 800/237–2747), British Airways (tel. 800/247–9297), and Lufthansa (tel. 800/645–3880).

Cutting Costs

The Sunday travel section of most newspapers is a good source of deals. When booking, particularly through an unfamiliar company, call the Better Business Bureau and your local or state Consumer Protection Bureau to find out whether any complaints have been registered against the company, pay with a credit card if you can, and consider trip-cancellation and default insurance.

Promotional Less expensive fares, called promotional or discount fares, are
Airfares round-trip and involve restrictions, which vary according to the
route and season. You must usually buy the ticket—commonly
called an APEX (advance purchase excursion) when it's for international travel—in advance (7, 14, or 21 days is usual), although some
of the major airlines have added no-frills, cheap flights to compete
with new bargain airlines on certain routes. These new low-cost carriers include **Markair** (tel. 800/627–5247), based in Anchorage, Alaska, and serving the West Coast, Kansas City, Minneapolis,
Cincinnati, Dallas, Atlanta, Colorado, Phoenix, Washington (D.C.),
Newark (NJ), and Chicago; and **ValuJet** (tel. 404/994–8258 or 800/
825–8538), based in Atlanta and flying to Jacksonville, Orlando,
Memphis, Louisville, Tampa, New Orleans, Ft. Meyers, Savannah,
West Palm Beach, Nashville, Ft. Lauderdale, and Washington
(D.C.).

With the major airlines the cheaper fares generally require minimum and maximum stays (for instance, over a Saturday night or at
least seven and no more than 30 days). Airlines generally allow some
return-date changes for a $25–$50 fee, but most low-fare tickets are
nonrefundable. Only a death in the family would prompt the airline
to return any of your money if you were to cancel a nonrefundable
ticket. However, you can apply an unused nonrefundable ticket toward a new ticket, again with a small fee. The lowest fare is subject
to availability, and only a small percentage of the plane's total seats
will be sold at that price. Contact the U.S. Department of Transportation's Office of Consumer Affairs (I–25, Washington, DC 20590,
tel. 202/366–2220) for a copy of "Fly-Rights: A Guide to Air Travel in
the U.S."

Consolidators Consolidators or bulk-fare operators—"bucket shops"—buy blocks
of seats on scheduled flights that airlines anticipate they won't be
able to sell. They pay wholesale prices, add a markup, and resell the
seats to travel agents or directly to the public at prices that still un-
dercut the airline's promotional or discount fares (higher than a
charter ticket but lower than an APEX ticket and usually without
the advance-purchase restriction). Moreover, some consolidators
sometimes give you your money back. Carefully read the fine print
detailing penalties for changes and cancellations. If you doubt the
reliability of a company, call the airline once you've made your booking and confirm that you do, indeed, have a reservation on the flight.

Discount Travel clubs offer members unsold space on airplanes, cruise ships,
Travel Clubs and package tours at as much as 50% below regular prices. Membership may include a regular bulletin or access to a toll-free hot line
giving details of available trips departing from three or four days to
several months in the future. Most also offer 50% discounts off hotel
rack rates, but double-check with the hotel to make sure it isn't offering a better promotional rate independent of the club. Clubs include **Discount Travel International** (114 Forrest Ave., Suite 203,
Narberth, PA 19072, tel. 215/668–7184; $45 annually, single or fami-
ly), **Entertainment Travel Editions** (Box 1014, Trumbull, CT 06611,
tel. 800/445–4137; price, depending on destination, $25–$48), **Great
American Traveler** (Box 27965, Salt Lake City, UT 84127, tel. 800/
548–2812; $49.95 annually), **Moment's Notice Discount Travel Club**
(425 Madison Ave., New York, NY 10017, tel. 212/486–0503; $45 an-
nually, single or family), **Privilege Card** (3391 Peachtree Rd. NE,
Suite 110, Atlanta GA 30326, tel. 404/262–0222 or 800/236–9732; domestic annual membership $49.95, international $74.95), **Travelers
Advantage** (CUC Travel Service, 49 Music Sq. W, Nashville, TN
37203, tel. 800/548–1116; $49 annually, single or family), and **World-**

wide Discount Travel Club (1674 Meridian Ave., Miami Beach, FL 33139, tel. 305/534–2082; $50 annually for family, $40 single).

Publications Both "Consumer Reports Travel Letter" (Consumers Union, 101 Truman Ave., Yonkers, NY 10703, tel. 914/378–2562 or 800/234–1970; $39 annually) and the newsletter "Travel Smart" (40 Beechdale Rd., Dobbs Ferry, NY 10522, tel. 800/327–3633; $37 annually) have a wealth of travel deals and tips in each monthly issue. *The Official Frequent Flyer Guidebook*, by Randy Petersen (4715–C Town Center Dr., Colorado Springs, CO 80916, tel. 719/597–8899 or 800/487–8893; $14.99, plus $3 shipping and handling), yields valuable hints on getting the most for your air travel dollars, as does *Airfare Secrets Exposed*, by Sharon Tyler and Matthew Wonder (Universal Information Publishing, $16.95 in bookstores). Also new and helpful is *202 Tips Even the Best Business Travelers May Not Know*, by Christopher McGinnis (Box 52927, Atlanta, GA 30355, tel. 404/659–2855; $10 in bookstores).

Enjoying the Fly at night if you're able to sleep on a plane. Because the air aloft is
Flight dry, drink plenty of fluids while on board. Drinking alcohol contributes to jet lag, as do heavy meals. Bulkhead seats, in the front row of each cabin—usually reserved for people who have disabilities, are elderly, or are traveling with babies—offer more legroom, but trays attach awkwardly to seat armrests, and all possessions must be stowed overhead.

Smoking Since February 1990, smoking has been banned on all domestic flights of less than six hours' duration; the ban also applies to domestic segments of international flights aboard U.S. and foreign carriers. On U.S. carriers flying to Virginia and Maryland, a seat in a no-smoking section must be provided for every passenger who requests one, and the section must be enlarged to accommodate such passengers if necessary as long as they have complied with the airline's deadline for check-in and seat assignment. If smoking bothers you, request a seat far from the smoking section.

By Car

Interstate 95 runs north–south through Maryland and Virginia, carrying traffic to and from New England and Florida and intermediate points. U.S. 50 links I–95 with Annapolis and Maryland's Eastern Shore. U.S. 97 links Baltimore with Annapolis. I–64 intersects I–95 at Richmond and runs east–west, headed east toward Williamsburg, Hampton Roads, and the bridge-tunnel to Virginia's Eastern Shore, and west toward Charlottesville and the Shenandoah Valley. At Staunton, I–64 intersects I–81, which runs north-south. Interstate 70 runs west from Baltimore's Beltway I–695, to Hancock in Western Maryland. Also, U.S. 40—The National Pike—travels east and west, the entire length of Maryland. Interstate 83 journeys south from Pennsylvania to the top of I–695, the Baltimore Beltway.

Car Rentals

All major car-rental companies are represented in Virginia and Maryland, including **Alamo** (tel. 800/327–9633); **Avis** (tel. 800/331–1212, 800/879–2847 in Canada); **Budget** (tel. 800/527–0700); **Hertz** (tel. 800/654–3131, 800/263–0600 in Canada); and **National** (tel. 800/227–7368). In cities, unlimited-mileage rates range from $20 per day for an economy car to $45 for a large car; weekly unlimited-mileage rates range from $179 to $206. This does not include tax, which in Virginia is 8% on car rentals, in Maryland 11.5%.

Extra Charges Picking up the car in one city and leaving it in another may entail substantial drop-off charges or one-way service fees. The cost of a collision or loss-damage waiver (*see below*) can be high, also. Some rental agencies will charge you extra if you return the car *before* the time specified on your contract. Ask before making unscheduled drop-offs. Be sure the rental agent agrees *in writing* to any changes in drop-off location or other items of your rental contract. Fill the tank just before you turn in the vehicle to avoid being charged for refueling at what you'll swear is the most expensive pump in town.

Cutting Costs Major international companies have programs that discount their standard rates by 15%–30% if you make the reservation before departure (anywhere from 24 hours to 14 days), rent for a minimum number of days (typically three or four), and prepay the rental. More economical rentals may come as part of fly/drive or other packages, even bare-bones deals that combine only the rental and an airline ticket (*see* Tours and Packages, *above*).

Insurance and Collision-Damage Waiver Until recently, standard rental contracts included liability coverage (for damage to public property, injury to pedestrians, and so on) and coverage for the car against fire, theft, and collision damage with a deductible. Due to law changes in some states and rising liability costs, several car-rental agencies have reduced the type of coverage they offer. Before you rent a car, find out exactly what coverage, if any, is provided by your personal auto insurer. Don't assume that you are covered. If you do want insurance from the rental company, secondary coverage may be the only type offered. You may already have secondary coverage if you charge the rental to a credit card. Only Diner's Club (tel. 800/234–6377) provides primary coverage in the United States and worldwide.

In general if you have an accident, you are responsible for the automobile. Car-rental companies may offer a collision-damage waiver (CDW), which ranges in cost from $4 to $14 a day. You should decline the CDW only if you are certain you are covered through your personal insurer or credit card company. In many states, laws mandate that renters be told what the CDW costs, that it's optional, and that their own auto insurance may provide the same protection.

By Train

Amtrak (tel. 800/872–7245) trains run out of Baltimore, Maryland, north toward Boston and south toward Washington, D.C., along the busy "northeast corridor." There is a rail station that serves both Baltimore (about 15 miles to the north) and Washington, D.C. (about 30 miles to the south), and is located at BWI Airport. Some trains running between New York and Chicago stop at Charlottesville, Virginia, and at two locations in western Virginia. Trains run between Newport News, Virginia, and New York City, stopping in northern Virginia, Richmond, and Williamsburg in between. Stops in Richmond and northern Virginia are also made on runs between New York City and Florida.

In addition, **The Maryland State Railroad Administration** (tel. 800/325–7245), or MARC, operates 14 daily commuter trains between Baltimore's Penn Station and Washington, D.C.'s Union Station. It also operates 10 trains from Baltimore's downtown Camden Station and from Union Station in Washington, D.C. There is free bus transportation between the BWI Airport Rail Station and the airport passenger terminal.

By Bus

Greyhound Lines (tel. 800/231–2222) serves the following locations in Maryland: Baltimore, Cambridge, Easton, Salisbury, and Ocean City. In Virginia it serves: Abingdon, Charlottesville, Fairfax, Fredericksburg, Hampton, Lexington, Newport News, Norfolk, Richmond, Roanoke, Springfield, Staunton, Virginia Beach, and Williamsburg.

Staying in Virginia and Maryland

Getting Around

By Plane USAir links the major airports in the region. For those who establish a vacation home on Maryland's Eastern Shore, commuter flights to and from Baltimore Washington International Airport can be a viable option.

Commuter Services **Cumberland Municipal Airport** (tel. 304/738–0002) serves Western Maryland; **Easton Municipal Airport** (tel. 410/822–0400), with Maryland Airlines, services Maryland's middle Eastern Shore; **Ocean City Municipal Airport** (tel. 410/289–0927) offers commuter, charter, and private facilities to Maryland's Atlantic seashore; **Salisbury/Wicomico County Airport** (tel. 410/548–4827) provides service to Maryland's lower Eastern Shore; **Washington County/Hagerstown Airport** (tel. 301/791–3333) has flights throughout midwestern Maryland.

By Car Except for a visit to central Baltimore, a car is by far the most convenient means of travel throughout Maryland and Virginia, and in many areas it is the only practical way to get around. (Where it exists, public transportation is clean and comfortable, but too often it bypasses or falls short of travel high points.) The state tourist offices of Maryland (tel. 800/543–1036) and Virginia (tel. 800/548–9797) publish official state road maps, free for the asking, that contain directories and other useful information. The maximum speed limit is 55 mph on major highways in Maryland, 65 mph in Virginia. A right turn on red is permitted in Maryland (unless signed otherwise), once you've brought the vehicle to a complete stop.

By Bus A bus excursion may be a practical way to visit Ocean City or Virginia Beach, but for most of the area bus travel would be an inconvenient alternative to the greater freedom of movement that driving allows.

Shopping

Western and southwestern Virginia are hunting grounds for bargains in English and American antique furniture, while the Williamsburg area is a virtual factory of reproduction Colonial furniture and crafts. Baltimore's "Antique Row," along the 800 block of North Howard Street, attracts smart antiques buyers. If you're traveling west on I–70 from Baltimore, visit New Market, "The Antiques Capital of Maryland," for a rewarding stop, especially on weekends.

Nationally known name-brand merchandise at reduced prices can be found at the large numbers of outlet stores near Annapolis and on Maryland's Eastern Shore. In the same areas, crafts shops offer quality sailing and hunting paraphernalia from brass deck fixtures to decoys. Williamsburg is another area with a major agglomeration of outlets.

Fresh produce can be found throughout the year at outdoor stands and at Baltimore's famous public markets. Many communities now offer farmer's markets, where the growers are invited to set up stands in public areas and offer their crops directly to the buyers. In northern Virginia, the arrival of the apple crop in the fall brings opportunities to find and sample fine varieties that do not reach stores or markets, either because they're produced in small numbers or because they have a short life. Both Maryland and Virginia have developed their wine industries, and many vineyards invite visitors to participate in the picking and tasting processes. Almost all are available for touring.

The sales tax in Virginia is 4.5%; in Maryland it is 5%.

Sports and Outdoor Activities

Biking The three regions of Virginia—coastal plain, piedmont, and mountains—give cyclists of all grades an opportunity to pedal through natural scenery and past historic sights. Also, national and regional trails cross Virginia. These include a 500-mile section of the **Trans-America Bicycle Trail** that extends from Breaks Interstate Park at the western fringe of the state to Yorktown on the coast and a 280-mile segment of the Maine–Richmond and Richmond–Florida coastal tracks. Multiday treks are organized by several companies.

For information, contact the **State Bicycle Coordinator** (VA Dept. of Transportation, 1401 E. Broad St., Richmond, VA 23219, tel. 804/786–2964).

Maryland offers excellent opportunities for serious cyclists by providing trails, canal towpaths, and even an old railroad route. *Best Bike Routes in Maryland,* a series of 10 maps covering scores of Maryland's touring and off-road routes, is printed on sturdy waterproof and tearproof paper (Box 16388, Baltimore, MD 21210, tel. 410/685–3626). The cost is $9.95 for one and $29.95 for the series. Also helpful is the **Maryland Department of Transportation** (Bicycle Affairs Coordinator, Room 218, State Hwy. Adm., 707 N. Calvert St., Box 717, Baltimore, MD 21203, tel. 800/252–8776), which can provide details concerning statewide bike routes.

Canoeing and Kayaking Virginia's main rivers—the James, York, Rappahannock, and Potomac—flow generally west to east and have numerous tributaries that wind through flatlands and extend deep into the mountains. Canoers and kayakers share the deepwater rivers with pleasure boaters, who sometimes make it difficult for nonmotorboats to operate. However, the **James below Richmond** is amenable. Paddlers also follow a tributary, the **Chickahominy River,** but it becomes shallow fairly quickly. A scenic upriver stretch of the **James near Balcony Falls** is navigable for some distance.

Isolated **Dragon Run** in coastal Middlesex County is one of the most pristine waterways in the state.

Shenandoah River trips start at **Front Royal** and **Bentonville.** The beautiful **Cowpasture River** follows the valleys deep into mountain fastness, creating such magnificent natural sights as Goshen Pass.

The **New River near Radford** is a favorite white-water site, and a choice canoeing destination. White-water rafting is recommended on weekends in October, when the dam at **Breaks Interstate Park** is opened. At least a half-dozen companies guide canoe, rafting, and tubing trips. For information, contact the **Virginia Tourism Development Group** (1021 E. Cary St., Richmond 23219, tel. 804/786–2051).

On Maryland's Eastern Shore, the Choptank River and Marshyhope and Tuckahoe creeks are the principal canoeing arteries. Western Maryland's rivers—sites of the Olympic Whitewater trials—have recently become famous, and there are numerous schools, tour planners, and outfitters throughout Western Maryland. The Savage and Youghiogheny rivers are especially popular with kayakers. The **Maryland Office of Tourism Development** (217 E. Redwood St., Baltimore 21202, tel. 800/543–1036) offer brochures.

Fishing   Virginia does not require a license for saltwater fishing in the ocean, in the bay, or in rivers up to the freshwater line. A license is required for freshwater fishing in rivers, lakes, and impoundments; a license valid for one year costs $30 for nonresidents, $12 for residents. The Chesapeake Bay area of Virginia harbors 18 catchable species, among them black drum, channel bass, copia, tarpon, striped bass, speckled trout, croaker, spot, weakfish, flounder, spadefish, and porgy. The **Virginia Commission of Game and Inland Fisheries** (Box 1104, Richmond 23230, tel. 804/367–1000) can provide further information.

Maryland fishing licenses valid for one year are $5 from the **Department of Natural Resources** (Box 1869, Annapolis 21404, tel. 301/974–3211). Fishing licenses can also be obtained at many sporting-goods stores; these licenses are valid for one week and cost $7 or more. The principal catches in Maryland are black drum (Tangier Sound, mid-May to mid-June, and off Tilghman Island, mid-June to late August); red drum or channel bass (Tangier Sound, same season); flounder (Tangier Sound, all summer); bluefish, white perch, weakfish, croaker, and trout (entire bay, April to December); and large-mouth bass (Choptank, Nanticoke, Pocomoke, and Wicomico rivers on the Eastern Shore).

Sailing   For a first-class cruise of the Chesapeake or the Atlantic, one can charter a yacht with a skipper and a crew. For those who have sailing experience, it's possible to hire a craft alone ("bareboat"), which requires that you demonstrate an ability with a vessel of that length. Some charter operations will offer several days of lessons to those who need to brush up or catch up before shoving off. Comprehensive insurance coverage should always be arranged in advance.

On a bareboat hire, be sure to inventory carefully the boat's equipment, from the sailing rig and deck equipment to the galley utensils, before signing the receipt; you will have to pay for anything that is missing when you return. Such a charge would be deducted from your security deposit, which is made in cash or with a certified check or credit-card charge. For a 30-foot craft, the deposit could be more than $600.

For a party of two to six sailors, a craft of 25 to 45 feet should be comfortable; fees for boats of this size range from $600 to $2,000 a week. Because demand is heavy from mid-May through October, it's a good idea to reserve as soon as you know your plans. The **Chesapeake Bay Yacht Charter Association** (Box 4022, Annapolis 21403, tel. 410/269–1194) prepares a list of charter companies on the bay. **Chesapeake Bay Magazine** (1819 Bay Ridge Ave., Suite 200, Annapolis 21403, tel. 410/263–2662) publishes the thorough *Guide to Cruising*

Chesapeake Bay for $24.95 plus $3 postage. The Maryland Department of Natural Resources publishes the *Cruising Guide to Maryland Waters,* which costs $18.

Skiing In the Shenandoah Valley, the Homestead Resort in Hot Springs started the southern ski industry in the 1950s and has since been joined by Wintergreen near Waynesboro, Massanutten near Harrisonburg, and other Virginia resorts. The **Division of Parks and Recreation** (203 Governor St., Richmond 23219, tel. 804/786–1712) provides further information on skiing facilities and seasons.

Wisp Mountain (Deep Creek Lake, Marsh Hill Rd., Box 629, McHenry, MD 21541, tel. 301/387–4911), in far Western Maryland, rises nearly 3,100 feet above sea level and overlooks Deep Creek Lake. It offers 23 slopes and 14 miles of trails, from novice to expert. It is easily accessible for weekenders from Baltimore and Washington. There are additional cross-country ski trails in the region.

Beaches

The busy, commercial, family-oriented Atlantic beaches at Ocean City (10 miles long) and Virginia Beach (6 miles long) have extensive boardwalks with man-made entertainments to compete with sea and sand. Assateague, the long Atlantic barrier island that lies in both Virginia and Maryland, is an utterly undeveloped national park with more than 30 miles of natural beach.

On the bay—on Virginia's Eastern Shore and in Calvert County on Maryland's Western Shore—there are beaches for fishing and swimming. The principal hazard for swimmers in the hot summer months are the sea nettles (jellyfish), whose stings are painful, long-lasting, and dangerous to some people.

National and State Parks

Assateague Island National Seashore in Maryland, a coastal barrier island with nearly 40,000 untamed acres, offers opportunities for camping, picnicking, hiking, boating, fishing, swimming, and biking. Many of the same activities are possible at a majority of the 18 Maryland state parks, including Point Lookout, which has a dramatic prospect of the bay from the southernmost tip of Maryland's Western Shore. Patapsco State Park near Baltimore offers horseback riding. The **Office of Tourism Development** (217 E. Redwood St., Baltimore 21202, tel. 800/543–1036) and the **State Forest and Park Service** (MD Dept. of Natural Resources, Tawes State Office Bldg., 580 Taylor Ave., Annapolis, MD 21401, tel. 410/974–3771; TDD 410/974–3683) can provide additional information about each of the state parks.

Virginia has four national parks. Shenandoah National Park's 195,000 acres vary over 3,500 feet in elevation; hiking, horseback riding, and fishing are popular in this mountainous area. George Washington National Forest (1.5 million acres) and Jefferson National Forest (700,000 acres), in western and southwestern Virginia respectively, offer camping, boating, hiking, fishing, swimming, hunting, and horseback riding. Mount Rogers National Recreation Area's 116,000 acres in southwestern Virginia contain the state's highest point—5,729 feet above sea level.

The 35 state parks of Virginia range in size from 500 acres to 4,500 acres. The **Division of Parks and Recreation** (203 Governor St., Richmond 23219, tel. 804/786–1712) has information on all of them.

Dining

The Chesapeake Bay blue crab, a specialty of Maryland, can be found at country crab houses and formal dining rooms in both states. It is prepared in several ways: steamed in the shell; broiled in a crab cake, with a "binder" of breading; or baked, as crab imperial, with a white cream and chardonnay sauce. The bay also yields an abundance of oysters in a good year, and clams are always popular. The state is also justly famous for its Maryland fried chicken (the eastern shore of Maryland is noted for hatching millions and millions of chickens and turkeys each year) and St. Mary's County stuffed ham.

Virginia ham, sugar cured and then baked, is no misnomer; it's a true local favorite and is available throughout the state. Other southern culinary traditions—most notably, fried chicken—are carried on with distinction in the eating places of the Old Dominion.

In the restaurants of the major cities and metropolitan areas, the traditional coexists with the innovative and the outlandish. Baltimore sustains at least a dozen ethnic cuisines, including both Neapolitan and northern Italian. The Virginia suburbs of Washington, D.C.—which cater to one of the country's most sophisticated dining markets—harbor a large population from Southeast Asia and thriving restaurants that prepare Vietnamese, Laotian, Cambodian, and Thai cuisine. Richmond and Norfolk serve their professional communities principally from New American, French, and other Continental menus.

Highly recommended restaurants are indicated by a star ★.

The following price categories are based on the average cost of a three-course dinner for one person, not including beverages, tax, and tip.

Category	Cost*
$$$$	over $30
$$$	$20–$30
$$	$10–$20
$	under $10

per person, excluding state tax (4.5% in Virginia, 5% in Maryland)

Lodging

The many 18th- and 19th-century houses in this region make it a natural area for bed-and-breakfast accommodations. The majority of B&Bs in Virginia and Maryland are Victorian structures with fewer than 10 rental units; a full or a Continental breakfast is typically included in the lodging rate, and rooms rarely have TV or telephone.

The large hotels of Baltimore, Richmond, Norfolk, and the Virginia suburbs of Washington, D.C., are in competitive markets where standards and prices remain high. The beach and mountain resorts in the region are among the oldest, largest, and most expensive in the country.

Highly recommended properties are indicated by a star ★.

The following rate categories (for all locations except Baltimore) apply to regular weekday rates during peak season for a double room (for two persons), do not reflect special weekend or package rates or seasonal promotions, and do not include taxes or service charges.

Category	Cost*
$$$$	over $120
$$$	$90–$120
$$	$50–$90
$	under $50

All prices are for a double room, excluding state tax (9.045% in Virginia, 10% in Maryland).

Home Exchange You can find a house, apartment, or other vacation property to exchange for your own by becoming a member of a home-exchange organization, which then sends you its annual directories listing available exchanges and includes your own listing in at least one of them. Arrangements for the actual exchange are made by the two parties to it, not by the organization. For more information about the process, contact the **International Home Exchange Association** (IHEA, 41 Sutter St., Suite 1090, San Francisco, CA 94104, tel. 415/673–0347 or 800/788–2489). Among the principal clearinghouses are **Intervac International** (Box 590504, San Francisco, CA 94159, tel. 415/435–3497), with three annual directories ($62 membership, or $72 to receive directories but remain unlisted); and **Loan-a-Home** (2 Park La., Apt. 6E, Mount Vernon, NY 10552, tel. 914/664–7640), which specializes in long-term exchanges (no charge to list your home, but directories cost $35 or $45 depending on the number you receive).

Apartment and Villa Rentals If you want a home base that's roomy enough for a family and comes with cooking facilities, a furnished rental may be the solution. It's generally cost-efficient, too, although not always—some rentals are luxury properties (economical only when your party is large). Home-exchange directories do list rentals—often second homes owned by prospective house swappers—and some services search for a house or apartment for you (even a castle if that's your fancy) and handle the paperwork. Some send an illustrated catalogue and others send photographs of specific properties, sometimes at a charge; up-front registration fees may apply.

Among the companies are **Rent-a-Home International** (7200 34th Ave. NW, Seattle, WA 98117, tel. 206/789–9377 or 800/488–7368) and **The Invented City** (*see* IHEA, *above*). **Hideaways International** (767 Islington St., Box 4433, Portsmouth, NH 03802, tel. 603/430–4433 or 800/843–4433) functions as a travel club. Membership ($99 annually per person or family at the same address) includes two annual guides plus quarterly newsletters; rentals are arranged directly between members, not by the club staff.

Credit Cards

The following credit card abbreviations are used: AE, American Express; D, Discover; DC, Diner's Club; MC, MasterCard; V, Visa. It's always a good idea to call ahead to confirm current credit card policies.

Great Itineraries

The following recommended itineraries, arranged by theme or area, are offered as a guide to planning individual travel.

Mother of Presidents Tour

Eight Virginians served as chief executive of the United States, and their homes can be found from the Shenandoah Valley east to the James River and north toward Washington, D.C.

Duration Six or seven days

The Main Route **One day:** In Staunton (just west of the junction of I–81 and I–64), visit the birthplace of Woodrow Wilson (28th president), then see the Museum of American Frontier Culture and take a walking tour of 19th-century and early 20th-century houses.

Two days: Take I–64 east. In Charlottesville see Monticello, the home of Thomas Jefferson (third president), and the college he founded, the University of Virginia. Next door is Ash Lawn, the more modest estate of James Monroe (fifth president). Head north on Route 20, stopping at the vineyards in Barboursville, which was the hometown of Zachary Taylor (12th president), on the way to Montpelier, the estate of James Madison (fourth president) outside Orange, a little town with a museum dedicated to Madison.

Two or three days: Return to I–64 and proceed east. In Richmond, among the many diversions of the State's capital and second-largest city, visit the White House of the Confederacy, home of the first and only Confederate president, Jefferson Davis. Less than an hour out of town are the plantation houses of William Henry Harrison (ninth president) and John Tyler (10th president).

One day: Take I–95 north to Fredericksburg, home town of George Washington (first president), where houses belonging to his mother and sister are among the 18th-century structures in the preserved Old Town neighborhood. A museum devoted to James Monroe is housed in his old law office.

One day: Take I–95 to Route 1 and go east to George Washington's Mount Vernon.

Information *See* Chapters 3, 4, and 5.

Civil War Tour

When Virginia voted, on April 17, 1861, to secede from the Union, it doomed itself to become a major battleground. Thus, much of this tour is in Virginia, with a brief foray across the Mason-Dixon line into Maryland. Richmond is the tour's hub.

Duration Eight or 10 days

The Main Route **One day:** Start at Hampton, on the peninsula, where Union general George McClellan in 1861 launched his drive toward Richmond. In Hampton visit the Syms-Eaton Museum to see the destruction that took place in the area during the Civil War. Across the channel is Fort Monroe—a Union stronghold in confederate territory, where Confederate president Jefferson Davis was imprisoned.

Two days: Drive northwest on I–64 up the peninsula to Richmond to visit the Museum and White House of the Confederacy and Richmond National Battlefield Park. Proceed 20 miles south on I–95 to

Petersburg, the city that was under siege for many months by Grant's army. While in Petersburg, visit Petersburg National Battlefield and the Siege Museum.

Two or three days: From Richmond proceed north on I–95 to Fredericksburg, site of the Old Stone Warehouse, which served as an arsenal and morgue during the Battle of Fredericksburg in December 1862. See four Civil War battlefields at Fredericksburg and Spotsylvania National Military Park. Return to I–95, and drive northwest to Manassas National Battlefield (Bull Run), where the Confederates won two important victories. Return to Richmond.

Two days: Take I–66 north from Richmond into Arlington and see Arlington National Cemetery and Arlington House (General Lee's house for 30 years, before the Union army confiscated it and turned the grounds into a national cemetery). Then head north on I–270 into Maryland. North of Frederick catch Route 34 out of Boonsboro, and follow it to the Antietam National Battlefield Site. (This part of Maryland is not covered in our guide, but background information is available at the site.) The battle of Antietam was the most fiercely fought, and bloodiest, single-day battle of the war. Not far to the south, at Harper's Ferry, you can walk the historic streets and see the Federal Arsenal where John Brown and his band of followers attempted their uprising. Return to Richmond.

Two or three days: Drive southwest on Route 360 from Richmond to Route 460. Proceed west into Appomattox and see Appomattox Court House, where General Lee surrendered to General Grant. From Appomattox you can continue west on Route 460 into Lynchburg to see Lynchburg's Monument Terrace, a Civil War memorial. Then take Route 29 north to Route 60 northwest into Lexington, where you can visit the Lee Memorial Chapel and Museum and the Virginia Military Institute Museum, with its displays on Stonewall Jackson.

Information *See* Chapters 3, 4, 5, and 7.

Military Tour

Duration Seven or eight days

The Main Route **One or two days:** Begin in Baltimore and see the USF *Constellation*, the first commissioned ship of the U.S. Navy and the oldest warship afloat. Drive, or take a tour boat, to Fort McHenry, birthplace of the "Star-Spangled Banner," our national anthem. Head north on I–95 35 miles to Havre de Grace to visit the U.S. Army Ordnance Museum.

Two days: Drive south on Route 3, I–97, to Annapolis and take a walking tour of the United States Naval Academy and the Colonial District of Annapolis. If you have time, take Route 4 south to visit the Naval Air Test and Evaluation Museum, at the Patuxent Naval Air Station in Lexington Park—the only facility in the country for testing naval aircraft. Then, returning to Annapolis, cross the bay on Route 50 into eastern Maryland to Route 13. Drive south on Route 13 to Wallops Island, site of the NASA Wallop's Flight Facility, and examine the spacecraft and the latest in 20th-century aerospace technology.

One day: Continue south on Route 13 and cross the mouth of the bay into Norfolk, Virginia, where you can visit the spectacular Norfolk Naval Base. Southwest of Norfolk, across the Elizabeth River, is the Portsmouth Naval Shipyard Museum.

One day: Proceed west on I–64 to Richmond, then on Route 60 into Lexington to visit the Virginia Military Institute, located in the basement of Jackson Memorial Hall. Along with a lot of Stonewall Jackson memorabilia, this museum houses many Virginian military artifacts.

One day: Take I–81 north to I–66 and go east to Arlington, Virginia, to visit Arlington National Cemetery, as well as the Tomb of the Unknown Soldier and graves of those who lost their lives in the two world wars and Korean War. Don't miss a stirring visit to the Vietnam Memorial Wall.

Information   *See* Chapters 3, 5, 7, 8, and 9.

Colonial Capitals Tour

Starting at Annapolis, this tour covers the Colonial capital, Historic St. Mary's City, swings over to Colonial Williamsburg, and ends up in Richmond.

Duration   Three or four days

The Main   **One or two days:** Begin in Annapolis and visit the 17th-century
Route   Maryland statehouse—the oldest state capitol in continuous legislative use. Congress convened here in 1783–84 and accepted the resignation of George Washington as commander in chief of the Continental Army. Head south on Route 4 to Route 5, and follow Route 5 into Historic St. Mary's City, birthplace of the original colony and the capital of Maryland from 1634 until 1694.

One day: Take Route 5 to Route 301 to reach Richmond, Virginia, where you can visit the Virginia State Capitol. Designed by Thomas Jefferson, it served as the capitol of the Confederacy during the Civil War.

One day: Route 64 takes you to Colonial Williamsburg, capital of Virginia in the years 1699–1780.

Information   *See* Chapters 4, 6, and 9.

Chesapeake Bay Tour

The natural beauty of the Chesapeake Bay and its tributaries has drawn people from all over the world for centuries. This tour begins near Baltimore and ends in Norfolk.

Duration   Five or six days

The Main   **Two days:** Start in Annapolis, Maryland, at City Dock, on the waterfront, and visit Market Square, an open dockside area the size of four city blocks. Less than an hour's drive south of Annapolis via Route 2, in St. Leonard, is Flag Ponds Nature Park—one of the few Chesapeake Bay beaches of Calvert County open to the public. A few miles south of Flags Ponds is the 1,600-acre Calvert Cliffs State Park. On the tip of the peninsula, in Solomons, is the Calvert Marine Museum, which recounts the history of the bay. Return to Annapolis.

Two days: On Maryland's Eastern Shore, about 10 miles northeast of Annapolis on Route 301, is Kent Island, the largest island in the bay and a thriving trading post since 1631. Take Route 50 to Route 33 and go 9 miles west to St. Michaels, historically a shipbuilding center, but now a harborside village. While in St. Michaels—the heartland of Maryland's Eastern Shore—visit the Chesapeake Bay Maritime Museum. Save time, though, for Easton, a highly polished gem of a town, with excellent facilities for dining and lodging. Oxford is well worth a visit, too, for its beautiful quaint waterfront. From here, you can take the nation's oldest free-running (non-cable) ferry across the Tred Avon River to Bellevue.

One day: If you find you have time, head to the quaint village on Tilghman on Tilghman Island. To get there continue on Route 33 to Knapp's Narrows Bridge and onto the island. In summer you'll see skipjacks (oyster boats), unique to the Chesapeake Bay. In winter a drive through Blackwater Wildlife Refuge, south of Cambridge on Route 50 at Route 331 is a pleasant activity. This is the southern feeding ground for hundreds of thousands of Canada geese and Snow geese.

One day: Take Route 50 to Route 13 south to Assateague and Chincoteague islands, with their wildlife and recreation areas. Here, you can visit the famous "wild ponies" (they are still wild and have been known to bite) who've inhabited the sandy islets for centuries. Continue down Route 13 to the Chesapeake Bay Bridge-Tunnel, which brings you to Virginia Beach, a popular summertime gathering place.

One or two days: East of Norfolk, Virginia, on the Cape where the mouth of the bay meets the ocean, historic Old Cape Henry Lighthouse marks the landing of the English on their way to Jamestown in 1607. Take Route 64 north from Norfolk to the Virginia peninsula and Newport News, where you will find the Mariner's Museum—a world history of seagoing vessels.

Information *See* Chapters 7, 9, and 10.

Western Virginia Tour

Duration Six to eight days

The Main Route **Two Days:** Take I–66 west from Washington, D.C., to scenic Skyline Drive and follow it south along the crest of the Blue Ridge Mountains. Nine miles west of Skyline Drive on Route 211 is Luray Caverns, the largest caverns in the state. After Waynesboro the drive becomes the Blue Ridge Parkway. Stop in Lexington to see the town's 19th-century architecture.

Two days: Head west from Lexington via Route 39, toward the West Virginia state line, to Bath County—and take a vacation from touring by immersing yourself in one of the warm springs and perhaps stopping at a resort for an elaborate meal. Take advantage of the facilities for golf, tennis, swimming, riding, or skiing, depending on the season.

One day: Return to Lexington and follow Route 81 south to Roanoke, at the bottom of the Shenandoah Valley. The railroad museum here commemorates an honored industry, and the birthplace of Booker T. Washington is nearby.

One to three days: I–81 marks the southern limit of most of Jefferson National Forest, where there are many opportunities for outdoor recreation. Take one of the many scenic roads south from Roanoke and enjoy the vistas.

Information *See* Chapter 4.

2 Portraits of the Chesapeake Region

The Road to Appomattox

By Geoffrey
C. Ward with
Ric Burns
and Ken
Burns

The thinning Confederate lines around Petersburg finally extended fifty-three miles. Grant's force had grown to 125,000. Lee's had dwindled to 35,000. "My own corps was stretched," John B. Gordon remembered, "until the men stood like a row of vedettes, fifteen feet apart. . . . It was not a line; it was the mere *skeleton* of a line." Soon the gaps between the men stretched to twenty feet.

Lee's only hope lay in moving his army safely out of the trenches and to the southwest, to link up with Johnston in the hills of North Carolina.

Grant wanted to ensure that he did not get away.

Lee moved first. On March 25, Confederates under Gordon mounted a sudden night assault that briefly won possession of an earthwork called Fort Stedman before superior Union firepower drove them off. It was merely "a little rumpus," Lincoln reported to his Secretary of War.

Grant counterattacked, sending Phil Sheridan, two infantry corps, and 12,000 cavalry racing around Lee's flank to block Lee's exit at a crossroads called Five Forks. There, on April 1, they routed a Confederate division under George Pickett, taking 4,500 prisoners. "They had no commanders," a northern newspaperman noted, "at least no orders, and looked for a guiding hand. A few more volleys, a new and irresistible charge . . . and with a sullen and tearful impulse, five thousand muskets are flung upon the ground."

When Grant got the news he simply said, "All right," and ordered an all-out Union attack all along the Petersburg line for 4:30 the next morning. Slowly, relentlessly, his men drove the Confederates out of their trenches. Among the southern dead left behind were old men and shoeless boys as young as fourteen.

A. P. Hill, who had served Lee faithfully in a dozen battles and had staved off disaster at Sharpsburg, could do nothing for him now. Two Union infantrymen shot him through the heart as he rode between the lines. "He is at rest . . ." Lee said, "and we who are left are the ones to suffer."

As the Union columns started into Petersburg, Lee's army slipped across the Appomattox. "This is a sad business," Lee told an aide. "It has happened as I told them in Richmond it would happen. The line has been stretched until it is broken."

Jefferson Davis was attending ten-o'clock services that Sunday morning at St. Paul's Episcopal Church in Richmond. His wife

This account is drawn from The Civil War, *based on the documentary filmscript by Geoffrey C. Ward, Ric Burns, and Ken Burns.*

and children had already left the city for safety farther south. The sexton handed him a message from his commander. A woman seated near Davis watched him read it: "I plainly saw the sort of gray pallor that came upon his face as he read [the] scrap of paper thrust into his hand."

"My lines are broken in three places," the note said. "Richmond must be evacuated this evening."

Davis hurried from the church, and ordered that his government move to Danville, 140 miles to the south. He took only a few belongings with him, but entrusted a heroic marble bust of himself to a slave, instructing him to hide it from the Yankees so that he would not be ridiculed.

The President of the Confederacy and his cabinet boarded the last train—a series of freight cars, each bravely labeled "Treasury Department," "Quarter Masters Department," "War Department." It was "Government on Wheels," said one man who watched it pass.

A slave dealer named Lumpkin failed to get his coffle of fifty chained slaves aboard the crowded train. A soldier with a bayonet barred him, until he unlocked his $50,000 worth of property in the street and let them go.

Chaos was all around them. Much of Richmond had been set afire by retreating Confederates. Mobs plundered shops, broke into abandoned houses. "Fierce crowds of skulking men and coarse . . . women gathered before the stores . . ." an eyewitness remembered. "Whiskey ran in the gutters ankle deep; and half-drunken women, and children even, fought to dip up the coveted fluid in tin pans, [and] buckets."

Rear Admiral Raphael Semmes blew up all that was left of the Confederate fleet anchored in the James, the shock shattering windows throughout the city. Then the fire on land spread to the Confederate arsenal, filled with gunpowder and artillery shells. A Confederate captain, on his way out of the city, described the bedlam left behind:

Every now and then, as a magazine exploded, a column of white smoke rose . . . instantaneously followed by a deafening sound. The ground seemed to rock and tremble. . . . Hundreds of shells would explode in the air and send [down] their iron spray. . . . As the immense magazines of cartridges ignited, the rattle as of thousands of musketry would follow, and then all was still, for the moment, except the dull roar and crackle of the fast-spreading fires.

Union troops occupied the city the next day, cheered by ecstatic crowds of blacks, and did their best to restore order. "Our . . . servants were completely crazed," a Richmond matron noted. "They danced and shouted, men hugged each other, and women kissed. . . . *Imagine* the streets crowded with these people!"

Two Union officers spurred their horses to the deserted Confederate Capitol. "I sprang from my horse," remembered Lieutenant Livingston de Peyster of New York, "first unbuckling the Stars and Stripes [from my saddle], [and] with Captain Loomis L. Langdon, Chief of Artillery, I rushed up to the roof. Together, we hoisted the first large flag over Richmond and on the peak of the roof drank to its success."

"Exactly at eight o'clock," a Richmond woman noted, "the Confederate flag that fluttered above the Capitol came down and the Stars and Stripes were run up. . . . We covered our faces and cried aloud. All through the house was the sound of sobbing. It was as the house of mourning." Nearby, another woman remembered, "We tried to comfort ourselves by saying in low tones (for we feared spies even in our servants) that the capital was only moved temporarily . . . that General Lee would make a stand and repulse the daring enemy, and that we would yet win the battle and the day. Alas, Alas, for our hopes."

Mrs. Robert E. Lee, too disabled by arthritis to travel, remained in Richmond. The Union commander posted a guard before her house to ensure no harm came to her—a black cavalryman. Mrs. Lee complained that the presence of a black soldier on her doorstep was "perhaps an insult," and was assigned a new guard, a white Vermonter—to whom she sent out meals on a little tray.

A Serendipity Menu for Southern Maryland

by Fred Powledge

Free At Last? The Civil Rights Movement and the People Who Made It, *published in 1991, is Fred Powledge's 14th book; he has also written on water resources, circus life, the food industry, and adoption.*

When my wife and I moved from New York City to southern Maryland a few years ago, we thought we were prepared for the shock. We eagerly traded the big city's arrogance for rural friendliness, a sky full of soot for one full of stars, a waterfront that was difficult to get to for one we could live on. But we weren't prepared for the gastronomical trauma.

From a place where you could chew your way through a dozen cultures in the space of a five-block stroll, we had entered an environment where restaurants seemed mere endproduct purveyors of fabricated food from distant manufacturers. Much of the seafood, even in this place bordered on three sides by the nation's richest estuary, was obviously not of local origin. The "catch of the day" was more likely to be the gullible customer than the microwaved red snapper that was placed before him. We loved our new home, but we mourned the loss of good eating.

Then serendipity set in. The delight of stumbling into unexpected pleasures had always been a vital part of eating out in New York, as well as when we were traveling, and we soon discovered that it worked in southern Maryland, too. Before long I was counting among my blessings the Jolly Gents' barbecue, reasonably authentic Colonial herb-garden sallet, Job's Daughters' funnel cake, and ham stuffed with kale.

My own grazing range for the past three years has been St. Mary's County, the peninsula bordered by the Patuxent and Potomac rivers and the western shore of Chesapeake Bay. My experience is somewhat local, but the county seems representative of much of nonurban Maryland and Virginia. Strangers still may wave when they pass on the road; you can phone or visit a government office and be treated politely; occasionally rowdy weather means the kerosene lamps on your mantel are not just for show. Best of all, a lot of people, including those who cook, still take pride in their work. It's the sort of place that encourages serendipity.

For instance, Farthing's Ordinary: This is one of the buildings in historic St. Mary's City, the partly restored first capital of Maryland and the fourth permanent English settlement in North America. As unlike Williamsburg as can be imagined, the small, low-key St. Mary's City contains this terrific but unadvertised and inadequately appreciated place to eat lunch. You can sit indoors, within the replica of an English ordinary, or tavern, or outside beneath a handsome grape arbor and have a delightful meal that pays some homage to Colonial appetites.

One recent menu at Farthing's Ordinary featured thin flour cakes with sausage, cabbage, and cheese; stuffed ham (more about that later) in not very Colonial pita; crab pie with fresh fruit; and the herb-garden sallet, a delicious salad that relegated iceberg lettuce to its rightful place at the back of the line. The little rolls came with butter that was whipped and flavored with strawberries, and the freshly brewed iced tea was accompanied by real lemon and real mint. The herb garden could be seen outside, next to the grape arbor.

I n rural and small-town America, which is to say much of the area around the Chesapeake, voluntarism is not just a concept hustled by politicians at election time. It means, among other things, fund-raising breakfasts, lunches, dinners, and in-between meals. This is a region of volunteer fire departments and rescue squads, and these groups raise some of their funds by selling food. Bake sales, all-you-can-eat breakfasts, turkey dinners—it seems as though there's always one you can go to.

Civic and religious organizations regularly hold what they term bull roasts, and they're always happy for the stranger to pay the modest price of admission and grab a plate. The bull is more likely to be steer or cow, and although it's large chunks of meat rather than halves or quarters that are cooked over open, slow fires, the result is delicious. If it weren't, the committee would find itself with a new chairperson, for a lot of local pride goes into these events.

Serendipity gets a big boost from fairs and festivals. When my wife and I were hunting for a house in the region a few years back, we wandered quite by chance into the Maryland Oyster Festival, an annual October celebration in St. Mary's County that features the U.S. finals for the world oyster-shucking championship and the selection of a local waterman to reign as King Oyster for the coming year. We gorged ourselves on scalded oysters (dipped into boiling water until they open) and decided that any county that held an Oyster Festival might make a great home.

And the county fair in St. Mary's is of manageable size, with a vest-pocket midway and just enough champion flop-ear rabbits, noisy roosters, and blue-ribbon heifers to round out a pleasant September Saturday. It's small enough that the big commercial purveyors of junk food don't show up. This leaves the field open to local organizations that, like the volunteer firehouses and church auxiliaries, want to raise money for a good cause. Job's Daughters is one example: The members of this group, who are daughters and granddaughters of Masons, make delicious funnel cake from scratch. And not far away are my favorites, the Jolly Gents, with their barbecue pit.

The Gents began around 1960 as an organization of hunters who held an annual dinner-dance that featured wild game. Robert L. Hill, one of the Gents, said that a typical menu included groundhog, muskrat (which many residents of the Chesapeake area insist they consider a heavenly treat), goose, rabbit, and domestic meats such as chicken and fish—and barbecue. The Gents sell their barbecue from a cinder-block booth each fall at the county fair.

Hill, a native of New Bern, North Carolina, and a staff member of the St. Mary's County Board of Education, noticed on arriving in Maryland that when people talked of barbecue, they meant beef, and they meant beef that was flavored with a tomato-base sauce.

Like all eastern North Carolinians (I am one, too, and I know), Hill believed there was more to barbecue than that. Why not offer two kinds of meat at the fair, he asked his brethren, beef with the usual red sauce, and also the North Carolina variety—roasted and minced pork, suffused with the traditional North Carolina flavoring made of vinegar, crushed red pepper, celery seed, and not a scintilla of tomato? "I didn't say North Carolina barbecue," Hill explained. "The people in Maryland are very turf conscious. The last thing in the world they would want to be eating would be North Carolina barbecue. If you called it pork barbecue, it would be all right."

The Gents tried cooking both kinds, and the eastern North Carolina variety did better than all right: It sold out. Since then the Gents have offered it at the Oyster Festival, a trade fair, political fund-raisers, family reunions, and the annual Blessing of the Fleet on the Potomac.

The county fair is also the place where you may get a chance to munch on championship St. Mary's stuffed ham. Some say the delicacy was born when plantation owners in southern Maryland gave their slaves the less upscale portions of ham, and the slaves promptly turned hog jowls into silk purses by stuffing them with greens and spices—and doing such a good job of it that the masters asked for the recipe. (A somewhat more somber explanation is offered by Alfred Dillow, president of the county historical society, who has pretty well tracked the dish back to England and thinks it arrived in 1634 with the original white settlers.)

The modern-day version of the delicacy is a corned ham into which Xs have been cut and a mixture of vegetables and spices stuffed into the openings. The whole thing is wrapped in cheesecloth (one recipe suggests an "old pillowcase") and simmered about 20 minutes to the pound, then served cold. The stuffing generally consists of kale or a mixture of kale and cabbage, with onions, scallions, mustard seed, celery seed, red and black peppers, and salt. For those who want further information on the subject, Alfred Dillow teaches a course, How to Stuff a Ham, each year at the St. Mary's County Technical Center. A written recipe by Charles Fenwick is published by the St. Mary's Nursing Center (Box 518, Leonardtown 20650, tel. 301/475–5681).

The spicy, peppery St. Mary's stuffed ham is a favorite in southern Maryland, especially around such holidays as Thanksgiving, Christmas, Easter, and Mothers' Day, and at county fair time, when restaurants, caterers, supermarkets, and grocery stores enter the annual stuffed-ham competition sponsored by the St. Mary's Nursing Center. Margie Hicks, the center's admissions coordinator, who supervises the contest, explained that the entries are judged by a panel of experts, then sliced into sandwiches that sell at the fairgrounds for $3 apiece—at a rate blindingly faster than hotcakes ("our biggest fund-raiser for the whole year"). In 1990 Hicks counted 17 restaurants and five grocery stores in the region that sell the ham. Most of them enter their product in the annual contest.

Southern Maryland includes a thriving and energetic community of Amish and Mennonite farmers, some of whom sell produce from roadside stands and their front porches. Most of them live along the roads around the tiny post office of Loveville, where on Valentine's Day the postmaster cancels "Love" stamps with a red-ink cancellation depicting a cupid and a heart. Travelers to the region might not be equipped to take advantage of the Silver Queen corn fresh from the field or the iridescent purple eggplant or tiny red potatoes, but they can stop to buy a shoofly pie or a bag of homemade ginger snaps. Stanley Zimmerman's stand on Highway 5, south of Loveville, and individual farms on Friendship School Road, which runs across the center of the county, are good places to look. At Charlotte Hall, in northern St. Mary's County, Amish and other communities hold a large farmers' market every Wednesday, Friday, and Saturday.

And then there's the seafood. The communities that embrace the Chesapeake have always shown an appreciation for the estuary's abundant life, especially those portions that are edible. As population growth and environmental degradation have taken their toll, some species of seafood have declined tragically. In recent years the oyster has been seriously damaged by a mysterious disease known as MSX. The situation is so severe that at the last Oyster Festival we attended almost as many people were eating clams—once considered almost a "trash" food in this area—as oysters.

The Maryland blue crab remains plentiful, despite warnings that pollution and overfishing may endanger it, too. At the present time, Marylanders who live by the seashore can still put out a crab pot (a debate rages over the relative merits of baiting it with chopped fish, chicken necks, or bull lips—yes, bull lips) and soon accumulate a bushel-basket full of the feisty creatures. What invariably follows is called a crab-feast, in which the crabs are steamed with a mixture of vinegar and spices (the virtual generic is Old Bay Seasoning, widely sold by a Baltimore company whose motto is "Entice with Spice") and then piled on a picnic table.

Access to the crabmeat is by force majeure; delicate diners will starve at a crab-feast. You tear the shell open by hand and apply your mouth to the meat, then pound on the claws with a small wooden mallet.

Those without access to the water can buy live crabs during the warm season from roadside entrepreneurs, or they can visit that

Chesapeake institution known as the crab house. Almost always this restaurant is as unpretentious as the act of eating crabs itself. The menu may be limited to steamed crabs, fried soft-shell crabs (as they mature, crabs periodically shed their hard coverings; a soft-shell is a crab caught in the midst of its molt), and crab cakes, which are fried patties of crab meat, spices, and a binder such as egg and mayonnaise. For the rare nonfeaster, the menu may also include hamburgers and hot dogs. Iced tea and very cold beer offset the effects of the spices. Napkins often consist of a roll of paper towels, with perhaps newspaper or butcher paper spread on the table. Cleanup then becomes a simple matter of balling up the paper and hauling the entire mess off to the dumpster.

A number of crab houses can be found within reasonable distance of our home in St. Mary's County, but my favorite is just a 10-minute boat ride down the creek. It took us two years to discover it, largely because it has no neon sign (or any other kind), it doesn't advertise, and it's open only on weekends during crab season, from mid-April to the end of October. It's known as B&M Seafood Restaurant (tel. 301/373–9819 or 301/373–2004), and it occupies space in a rambling old tavern, Clark's Landing Bar, close to the Patuxent River in Hollywood, Maryland. Bernie and Mary Weeks, the "B" and the "M," run the place.

Every morning between 3:30 and 5:00, depending on sunrise time, Bernie and often Mary cast off their 34-foot work boat from a dock across the creek from our home. They head out into the Chesapeake and check, empty, and rebait their crab pots—close to 500 of them at the beginning of the season, maybe 300 as the summer wears down.

Six to nine hours later, the Weekses return home with, they hope, enough crabs to make it all worthwhile. On a weekday, they work until dark repairing equipment and segregating the soft-shell crabs into special tanks. On a weekend, they tie on aprons and begin cooking. Bernie steams the hard-shells, and Mary fries soft-shells, makes crab cakes, and turns out her specialty—a crab cake with added ingredients that is run under the broiler on half an English muffin. She also prepares the macaroni salad that you can substitute for the french fries, which are just about the only store-bought item on the menu. The tomatoes for the salad come from the vines of friends and relatives. When the crabs run out, or when they decide not to let themselves get caught that week, Mary tells her customers the bad news. They almost always understand and come back the next weekend.

The Weekses started their restaurant as a part-time venture; now they find it "full-time and then some." They are aware that they're breaking several of the maxims of modern-day food service by their limited hours, lack of advertising, and insistence on supplying all their own ingredients rather than relying on distributors for fabricated and frozen products. To do it any other way, they say, would mean lower quality, and that would take all the fun out of their work. Besides, Mary told me, "It wouldn't be the same if we were open all year. That first crab in the spring is something to look forward to."

I t would be difficult for the casual traveler to discover the Weekses' somewhat hard-to-find crab house. Yet there are ways in which serendipity can be given a nudge. It has long been the saying among coastal-living people that the prudent mariner needs all the latest nautical charts and tables, but that "local knowledge" is also vital. It's the same with finding good food. Asking the culinary advice of perfect strangers about what and where to eat can, I'll admit, lead to disaster, since people's tastes differ so widely: One person's caviar is another's muskrat. But folks around the Chesapeake still exhibit a fierce loyalty to the institution of crab houses; they can be counted on to provide helpful information on how to find one, and they would probably be ashamed to steer you to a bad one.

Small-town newspapers almost invariably carry lists of fund-raising meals. A typical issue of our local semiweekly contained numerous announcements: The Animal Welfare League was holding its weekly bake sale down by the K Mart (their chocolate brownies are particularly good). The Knights of Columbus were planning a Sunday dinner (fried chicken, coleslaw, peas, mashed potatoes, gravy) for $6. The volunteer fire department in Valley Lee was putting on an all-you-can-eat breakfast that included scrambled eggs, ham, sausage, home fries, creamed chipped beef, hot spiced applesauce, biscuits, juices, and coffee for $4 (children pay half). The Leonardtown Volunteer Rescue Squad was holding a bake sale in front of the Ben Franklin variety store. Events of this sort often are advertised as well on signs along the highway.

I've found that the sort of tourism literature that's available at the welcome centers along interstate highways rarely mentions such local festivals as county fairs and seafood celebrations. But most state departments of agriculture maintain and distribute lists of just such events, and usually a telephone call to the department's public information office will start a copy on its way to you. In Maryland, the Agricultural Fair Board (50 Harry S Truman Pkwy., Annapolis 21401, tel. 301/841–5861) publishes an annual "Maryland Fair and Show Schedule"; the 1990 edition listed dates, places, and phone numbers for 80 events, ranging from all the county fairs to the Maryland Make It Yourself with Wool Contest to the Maryland State Beekeepers' 54th Annual Honey Show. That's a whole lot of barbecue, funnel cake, crab-feasting, homemade ginger snaps, and ham stuffed with kale.

Pleasures of the Islands

by Tom
Horton

A native of
Maryland's
Eastern
Shore,
Horton is a
writer and
analyst for
the nonprofit
environmental
group the
Chesapeake
Bay
Foundation.
This essay
appears in
his book Bay
Country,
winner of the
John
Burroughs
Medal for
nature
writing in
1988.

The water wakes long before the land. A raucous hen mallard, sassing the dawn, sails from behind a point of marsh, trailing gouts of liquid fire wherever first light catches her ripples on the cove's black, silken surface. A flight of quick-winged teal circles to land, pinions flailing a sound of far-off jingle bells from the chill air. Now the cove mirrors seamlessly the frosty gold thawing into day on the eastern horizon. The teal coming down could as well be flying up through the water's depths, like the ducks imbedded in expensive crystal paperweights. A burst of wind ruffles the illusion, and the breeze chuckles softly as the stiff marsh grass scratches its belly; then it is gone and the stillness of the island is pierced by one of the wildest songs on earth.

The geese are aloft, piping their haunting obligato to the grander, slower cadence of winter's coming. It is music that sets dogs to frenzied yelping along the great migration routes from Labrador to North Carolina, and makes people on the streets of large cities pause, cock an ear, and look skyward, stirred by a longing so old and deep we cannot articulate it much better than the dogs. Just as an old, popular tune on the radio can activate a hundred associations from one's youth, so does goose music evoke places and times out of some ancestral consciousness, when the flights heralded changing seasons to prehistoric hunters on these same shores—signified the glad prospect of roast goose in a season when the land would be otherwise lean. The tune no longer has survival value, but we still find it thrilling.

The same elemental shifts of season and weather which tug geese southward, and goad fish across whole oceans toward their natal streams, also whisper to something in our genes that it is time to be moving. We needn't heed such atavism, of course, but an impending snowstorm still sends us flocking to the supermarket with an almost delicious anticipation, to lay in stores well beyond any strictly rational need; and who could deny, watching the flow of Florida-bound Mercedes and Cadillacs on Interstate 95 each winter, that as soon as we are able to afford our druthers, we resume migrating?

The pleasure of migration is part of why I try faithfully to return each spring and fall to camp on islands like South Marsh in the Chesapeake Bay. The other reason has to do with the special nature of islands. South Marsh Island is five miles from the Somerset County mainland and consists of about three thousand low acres, owned by the state of Maryland, which with rare wisdom leaves it pretty much alone. Norfolk lies to the south, Wilmington to the north, and Baltimore and Washington to the west. Ocean City's teeming beaches on the east complete the circle. Six million people, conservatively, are busy carrying on the business of modern civilization within a hundred-mile radius of us. It is obscenely satisfying, in the midst of the conurbation, to be foraging for supper with our bare hands on this utterly lonesome, permanently unpeopled sweep of marsh. Not more than ten feet from shore, in the olive water off the camp, lies a trove of plump, salty oysters. To collect a bushel is the work of minutes, and the toughest chore is deciding how to eat them. We bicker, and then settle on steamed, raw, fried, and stewed. A short canoe trip to a nearby point of land yields an equal harvest of striated mussels. Gouged fresh from the peaty shore and steamed, they retain a delicate earthy taste that is the very essence of the tide marsh, a sort of estuarine equivalent of a mushroom. Fresh drinking water bubbles up sweet and pure from a rusting pipe sunk eight hundred feet deep here decades ago by a wealthy duck-hunting club. It taps a mammoth aquifer that runs beneath the bay, sloping west to east. Tonight we will wash down our fresh seafood with swigs of rain that fell on Appalachian slopes thousands of years ago, filtered a few inches a century through the geologic strata of half a state. In truth, we have also ferried over a case of beer to ease our transition to the natural life. Still, there is something heady and fulfilling about even so dilletantist a reversion to hunter-gatherer status.

Perhaps because they physically bound one's experiences and insulate the senses from the mainland's distractions, islands concentrate and render more vivid everything that happens on them. South Marsh and its neighbors, for example, might strike you as plain with their monolithic vegetational stands of needlerush and spartina grasses; but the rich light of a late afternoon sun can charge such places with a purity and strength of color to shame Van Gogh's palette, floating golden as Eldorado between blue blazes of autumn sky and water. On hot summer afternoons I have seen them, backlit before an approaching thunderstorm, glowing like neon emeralds. Without its islands, the bay would lose a vital texture.

Island communities are the original alternative societies, says the author John Fowles, and "that is why so many mainlanders envy them. Some vision of Utopian belonging, of social blessedness, of an independence based on cooperation, haunts them all." Even a cursory review of literature would show that, from the *Odyssey* to *Robinson Crusoe*, through *Misty of Chincoteague*, islands have commanded attention all out of proportion to their tiny share of the earth's land mass. In a complicated world, they seem alluringly defined and comprehensible. Special things, we feel, are bound to happen there. It seems no oddity that two of television's biggest recent hits, insipid though they may have been, were "Fantasy Island" and "The Love Boat" (boats, after all, are the ultimate islands). Mythically, islands are places of origins, which does not surprise me in light of my growing kinship with islands in the bay. Sometimes on still, clear evenings, it is possible to lie supine on South Marsh, cerebral cortex pressed into the damp peat and eyes locked on the starry galaxies, and complete a sort of primal circuit. Lulled by the amnion bay's gentle suck and glut in every indentation of the marshy edge, you may come close to reexperiencing the pleasures of the womb.

The Chesapeake Bay is favored with about fifty of the world's estimated one-half million islands. They range from Garrett in the mouth of the Susquehanna at bay's head, to Watts, a deepwater rendezvous for seventeenth-century pirates in Virginia. Uses of the islands include preserves for ducks, like South Marsh; preserves for the wealthy, like Gibson Island on the Magothy; isolation chambers, like heavily diked Hart-Miller, for the shiploads of polluted spoil that must be dredged constantly from Baltimore harbor's channels; and military bombing ranges, like cratered Bloodsworth Island in Dorchester County. It is from other islands—Smith, Deal, Tilghman, Kent, Hoopers, Tangier—that the watermen who harvest most of our seafood still choose to operate.

On the islands, elements of our human and natural heritage have been able to flourish well past the time they could still exist, unsullied, on the mainland. Water, even in the jet age, remains a surprisingly efficient barrier. If you doubt that, compare the cultures of Crisfield, where they say *aryster*, and St. Mary's County, where they say *oistuh;* or the Eastern Shore fishing community of Rock Hall with Baltimore City. Neither pair is separated by much more than a dozen miles, but they are water miles, and the insulation they provide is blessedly effective. This essential characteristic of islands enforces an interdependence, trust, and cooperation among their residents that we envy. It sometimes confounds me how the word *insular* ever got its slightly pejorative connotation.

I am convinced we are now living in the best of times—and probably the last of times—for appreciating the bay's islands. It is only in the last generation or two that the growth of road and bridge access, and of leisure time for boating and day-tripping, has begun allowing frequent and easy travel there for most of us. Modern bug repellents have also helped a lot, for these are often low and marshy places. At the same time, forces are at work that probably will extinguish, or greatly diminish, the islands' special qualities in many of our lifetimes. A number of bay islands already have vanished or dramatically receded from wind and wave erosion in the last century. That retreat will only accelerate as our profligate incineration of fossil fuels warms the global atmosphere and melts more of the polar icecaps, causing the sea level to rise at a rate unprecedented in many thousands of years. Right now it appears to be coming up at a foot a century, fast enough to doom thousands of precious island acres in a span of a few decades. It will not take until the islands are actually inundated. Long before that happens, storms riding in atop an elevated sea level will cause more erosion and property damage than they ever did in the past.

And perhaps even before physical forces decide the issue, the bay's declining natural-resources base, on which many waterfront communities depend for a living, could depopulate the islands. Already the difficulty of making a living on the water is reinforcing a trend toward gentrification of some islands, as growing numbers of city folks find the low price and availability of second homes there too good to pass up. On Tilghman Island in Talbot County, the man who owns both the biggest oyster company and a burgeoning tourist complex calculates that between 1978 and 1984 the former enterprise declined 40 percent, while the latter grew by 300 percent. So much of what is happening to the bay islands smacks to me of the irreversible. My advice is to revel in our favored-generation status, and celebrate them while we still can.

3 Shenandoah Valley and the Highlands

The Shenandoah Valley is best known as an outdoor destination—Shenandoah National Park is the most-often-visited park in the U.S. system—and the region's towns and cities, rich pockets of history and culture, are all too often bypassed by travelers skimming along the scenic Skyline Drive and Blue Ridge Parkway. In Staunton, you can visit the birthplace of Woodrow Wilson, the 28th president of the United States (and the eighth president from Virginia). Bath County, where the mineral waters flow, has been a fashionable resort for two centuries. Lexington, dense with historic sites, looks largely unchanged since the 19th century. Roanoke, nicknamed Star City of the South for an 88½-foot-high illuminated star atop a mountain within city limits, is the proud cultural and commercial center of western Virginia.

The Shenandoah Valley, about 150 miles long, lies between the Allegheny and Blue Ridge mountain ranges in northwestern Virginia, parallel to the western edge of the state and extending to Harpers Ferry in West Virginia. On the heights east of the valley, Shenandoah National Park's nearly 200,000 acres stretch more than 80 miles along the Blue Ridge, providing stunning vistas, hundreds of miles of hiking trails (including a section of the Appalachian Trail), and trout fishing in rushing streams. The park is a sanctuary for deer, bear, and red fox and a botanical treasury whose most spectacular specimens are blooming wild azaleas in spring and hardwood trees that turn glorious colors in autumn.

The Highlands, or the Appalachian Plateau, in the state's southwest corner, lie at an average elevation of 2,000 feet. This is a region heavily wooded and incised with gorges, one of them the legendary Cumberland Gap that leads into Kentucky and Tennessee. Here, near the southern end of the Blue Ridge, is Virginia's highest peak, Mt. Rogers (5,729 feet). Often neglected by travelers, the Highlands have a peculiar, rugged beauty and plenty of indoor and outdoor recreation: Seven state parks, three national parks, and six national forests can be counted in the area. The town of Abingdon boasts well-preserved 18th- and 19th-century buildings, two major regional festivals, and the state theater of Virginia, the Barter Theatre.

Essential Information

Important Addresses and Numbers

Visitor Information **Abingdon Convention & Visitors Bureau** (208 W. Main St., Abingdon 24210, tel. 703/676–2282).

Bath County Chamber of Commerce (Rte. 220, Box 57, Warm Springs 24484, tel. 703/839–5409).

Front Royal/Warren County Chamber of Commerce and Visitors Center (414 E. Main St., Front Royal 22630, tel. 703/635–3185 or 800/338–2576).

Harrisonburg-Rockingham County Convention and Visitors Bureau (800 Country Club Rd., Harrisonburg 22801, tel. 703/434–2319 or 703/434–3862).

Lexington Visitor Center (102 E. Washington St., Lexington 24450, tel. 703/463–3777).

Roanoke Regional Chamber of Commerce (310 1st St. SW, Roanoke 24011, tel. 703/983–0700).

Roanoke Valley Convention and Visitors Bureau (114 Market St., Roanoke 24011–1402, tel. 703/342–6025 or 800/635–5535).

Shenandoah Valley Travel Association (Box 1040, New Market

22844–1040, tel. 703/740–3132; I–81, Exit 264, Rte. 211 W, tel. 703/332–3972).

Staunton/Augusta Travel Information Center (1303 Richmond Ave., Staunton 24401, tel. 703/885–8504).

Emergencies Throughout the region, dial **911** for emergency assistance.

Hospitals **Roanoke: Roanoke Memorial Hospital** (Belleview Ave. and Jefferson St., tel. 703/981–7000).
Staunton: Kings' Daughters' Hospital (1410 N. Augusta St., tel. 703/887–2000).

Arriving and Departing

By Plane **Roanoke Regional Airport** (tel. 703/362–1999) has flights by eight carriers, principally USAir (tel. 800/428–4322).

Tri-City Regional Airport (tel. 615/323–6271), located just across the state line in Blountville, Tennessee, is served by USAir and Delta.

By Car I–81 and U.S. 11 run north–south the length of the Shenandoah Valley and continue south into Tennessee. I–66 west from Washington, D.C., which is 90 miles to the east, passes through Front Royal to meet I–81 and U.S. 11 at the northern end of the valley. I–64 connects the same highways with Charlottesville, 30 miles to the east. Route 39 into Bath County connects with I–81 just north of Lexington. I–77 cuts off the southwest tip of the state, running north–south.

By Train **Amtrak** (tel. 800/872–7245) has service three days a week to Staunton, en route between New York and Chicago. The same train stops at Clifton Forge for The Homestead resort in Bath County. A complimentary shuttle bus on Sunday, Wednesday, and Friday connects Roanoke (Campbell Court and Roanoke Airport Sheraton) and Clifton Forge Rail Station.

By Bus **Greyhound Lines** (tel. 800/231–2222) schedules several trips daily to and from Abingdon (465 W. Main St., tel. 703/628–6622) and Roanoke (26 Salem Ave., tel. 703/343–5436) on its transcontinental routes between major U.S. cities. Lexington (U.S. 11 north of bridge, tel. 800/231–2222) and Staunton (1211 Richmond Rd., tel. 703/886–2424) have daily service to and from New York and points south.

Guided Tours

The **Historic Staunton Foundation** (tel. 703/885–7676) offers free one-hour walking tours of Staunton Saturday morning at 11, Memorial Day through October, departing from the Woodrow Wilson Birthplace at 24 North Coalter Street. A brochure is available for a self-guided tour.

For $8, the **Lexington Carriage Company** (tel. 703/463–5647) will take visitors around town in a horse-drawn carriage for 45–50 minutes, from April through October. A walking-tour brochure is available at the Lexington Visitor Center (102 E. Washington St., tel. 703/463–3777).

Exploring

The Shenandoah Valley

Numbers in the margin correspond to points of interest on the Shenandoah Valley and the Highlands map.

❶ Belle Grove, on Route 11 in **Middletown,** just west of I–81 (Exit 302) in the northern valley, is a fitting first stop on a tour of the Shenandoah. The elegant farmhouse is a monument to the rural and the refined, two qualities that exist in harmony in the architecture here and throughout this region. Completed in 1794 after consultation with Thomas Jefferson, the building bears such signature Jeffersonian touches as fan windows; the four chimneys that tower over the structure are made of Virginia limestone. This was the headquarters of the Union general Philip Sheridan during the Battle of Cedar Creek (1864), a crucial defeat for the Confederacy. Part of the battle was fought on the farm, and an annual reenactment is held in October with as many as 2,000 participants. Today it is a 165-acre working farm. *Rte. 11, Middletown, tel. 703/869–2028. Admission to the house: $4 adults, $3.50 senior citizens, $2.50 children 6–12; admission to reenactment varies. Open mid-Mar.–mid-Nov., Mon.–Sat. 10–4, Sun. 1–5. Open for Christmas candlelight tours; call for schedule.*

❷ Ten miles southeast of Belle Grove, the town of **Front Royal** marks the northern limit of **Shenandoah National Park,** which is easily reached from I–66 and I–81 (and I–64 farther south). The park extends more than 80 miles south along the Blue Ridge, with several gaps in the range forming passes between the Shenandoah Valley on the west and the Piedmont on the east. The name Shenandoah means "Daughter of the Stars" in a Native American language, and the metaphor is apt indeed, for some 60 peaks of the Blue Ridge Mountains stretch skyward within the park's vast boundaries. Hardwood and pine forests shroud the slopes, with mountain meadows rampant with wildflowers opening up to gorgeous panoramas that can be viewed at leisure from numerous turnoffs. Hikers and campers find deep natural environments just yards from the highway (*see* Hiking in Sports and Outdoor Activities, *below*), trout fishers may wade into more then 25 streams in seven counties, horses can be rented for wilderness trail rides, and naturalists conduct daily guided hikes throughout the summer. The seasonal activities of the park, supervised by rangers, are outlined in the *Shenandoah Overlook,* a free newspaper you can pick up on entering the park. *Park Superintendent, Box 348, Rte. 4, Luray 22835, tel. 703/999–2229. Park (and Skyline Drive) admission: $5 car; $2 motorcycle, bicycle, or pedestrian.*

The most popular way to see Shenandoah National Park is by car on **Skyline Drive,** a spectacular route that winds 105 miles south from Front Royal to Waynesboro over the mountains of the park. The drive offers panoramas of the valley to the west and the rolling country of the Piedmont to the east; white-tailed deer are often seen along the route. But the fame of Skyline Drive has its drawbacks: The holiday and weekend crowds in high season—spring and fall—can slow traffic to much less than the maximum speed of 35 mph and strain the facilities of the few lodges, campsites, and eating places along the way. Winter brings further problems, for many facilities are closed from November through April, and treacherous road conditions can cause the closing of parts of the drive itself. Neverthe-

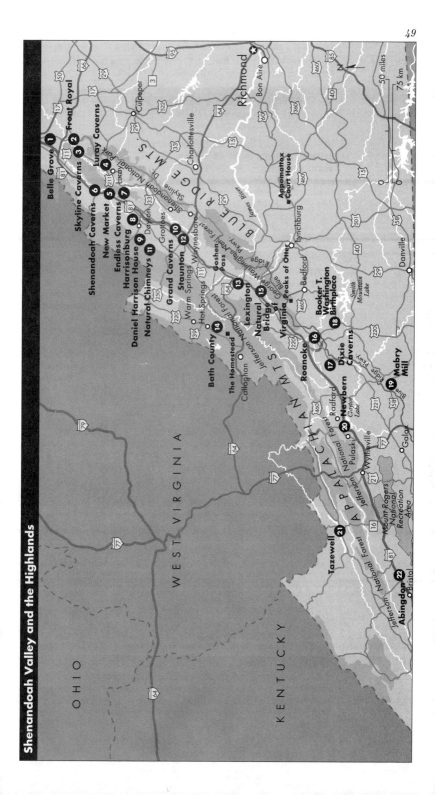

Shenandoah Valley and the Highlands

49

less, for easily accessible wilderness and exciting views, few routes can compete with this one; just come during the fine weather—and bring a sweater, for temperatures can be brisk.

You'll also want that sweater when you visit the caverns that honey-comb the hills, a number of which are open to the public. The best known is **Luray Caverns** (*see below*), but others are stretched out along the main routes down the valley and over the hills.

3 **Skyline Caverns** is known for its anthodites, or spiked nodes that grow from ceilings at an estimated rate of one inch every 7,000 years, and for its chambers with appropriately descriptive names such as the Capitol Dome, Rainbow Trail, Fairytale Lake, and Cathedral Hall. *1 mi from northern entrance to Skyline Dr., Box 193, Front Royal 22630, tel. 703/635–4545 or 800/296–4545. Admission: $9 adults, $8 senior citizens, $4 children 6–12. Open Mar. 15–June 14, weekdays 9–5, weekends 9–6; June 15–Labor Day, daily 9–6; Nov. 15–Mar. 14, daily 9–4.*

4 **Luray Caverns,** 9 miles west of Skyline Drive on Route 211, are the largest caverns in the state. For millions of years water has seeped through the limestone and clay to create a variety of suggestive rock and mineral formations. The world's only "stalacpipe organ" is composed of stalactites (calcite formations hanging from the ceilings of the caverns) that have been tuned to concert pitch and are tapped by electronically controlled rubber-tipped plungers. The organ is played electronically for every tour and may be played manually on special occasions. A one-hour tour begins every 20 minutes. *Rte. 211, Luray, tel. 703/743–6551. Admission: $11 adults, $9 senior citizens and active-duty military, $5 children 7–13. Open mid-June–Labor Day, daily 9–7; mid-Mar.–mid-June and Labor Day–mid-Nov., daily 9–6; mid-Nov.–mid-Mar., weekdays 9–4, weekends 9–5.*

5 **New Market,** 12 miles west of Luray on Route 211 and just off I–81, marks the site of a costly Confederate victory late in the Civil War. Here 247 cadets from the Virginia Military Institute, some as young as 15 years old, were mobilized to improve the odds against superior Union numbers. Fighting under their cadet flag, 10 of the boys died on the field of honor. At the Hall of Valor, focal point of the 260-acre **New Market Battlefield Historical Park,** the sacrifice is commemorated in a stained-glass window mosaic, unconventional and dignified. This circular building contains a chronology of the war, and a short film deals with Stonewall Jackson's legendary campaign in the Shenandoah Valley. A farmhouse that figured in the fighting still stands on the premises; its outbuildings have been reconstructed and equipped to show a prosperous farm of the period. On the ridge over a precipitous 200-foot drop to the Shenandoah River are two overlooks with views of the nearby countryside and the Alleghenies. The battle is reenacted at the park each May. *I–81 (Exit 264), New Market, tel. 703/740–3102. Hall of Valor admission: $5 adults, $2 children. Open daily 9–5; closed Thanksgiving, Christmas, and New Year's Day. Farmhouse admission free with Hall of Valor admission. Open mid-June–Labor Day, daily 9–5.*

A separate **New Market Battlefield Military Museum** stands in the area where the battle began. The front of the building is a replica of Arlington, Robert E. Lee's house near Washington, D.C. The museum has more than 1,500 artifacts from all American wars beginning with the Revolution and including Desert Storm; 60% deal with the Civil War. A movie on the Battle of New Market is shown. *Box 1131,*

New Market 22844, tel. 703/740–8065. Admission: $5 adults, $4 senior citizens, $2.50 children 7–15. Open Mar. 15–Dec. 1, daily 9–5.

⑥ Shenandoah Caverns offer spectacular calcite formations, among them a series resembling strips of bacon, formed by water dripping through long, narrow cracks in the limestone. The lighting effects are most noticeable where the sparkling calcite crystals are differentiated by colored lights. As at Luray, most of the formations are wet and shiny and continue to grow at an imperceptible rate. *I–81 (Exit 269), Box 1, Shenandoah Caverns 22847, tel. 703/477–3115. Admission: $8 adults, $7 senior citizens, $4 children 8–14. Accessible for visitors with disabilities. Open mid-June–Aug., daily 9–6:15; mid-Apr.–mid-June and Sept.–mid-Oct., daily 9–5:15; mid-Oct.–mid-Apr., daily 9–4:15.*

Three miles south of New Market on Route 11 (or Exits 264 or 257 off
⑦ I–81) are **Endless Caverns,** discovered in 1879 by two boys and a dog chasing a rabbit, and opened to the public in 1920, whose seemingly endless configurations have baffled numerous explorers. The tour is enhanced by lighting effects, especially at "Snow Drift," where a sudden illumination emphasizes the white powdery appearance of the "drift" in a brown and yellow tinted room. *Box 859, New Market 22844, tel. 703/740–3993 or 800/544–2283. Admission: $9 adults, $8.10 senior citizens, $4.50 children 3–12. Open mid-Mar.–mid-June and Sept.–early Nov., daily 9–5; mid-June–Labor Day, daily 9–7; Sept.–Nov., daily 9–5; mid-Nov.–mid-Mar., daily 9–4.*

⑧ Harrisonburg (Exit 251 from I–81 leads to Main Street), settled in 1739, is often bypassed as a workaday market town for the rich farmlands that surround it and the newly established agricultural industries that have settled here. But a visit here can be enlightening: It's not unusual to see plainly dressed Mennonites driving horse-drawn buggies past modern aluminum-and-glass buildings—an image that has been created by the merging of two otherwise separate ways of life. The city is also a center of higher education, with James Madison University and Eastern Mennonite College in town and Bridgewater College nearby.

An informative stop while you're here is the Harrisonburg–Rockingham County Historical Society's **Warren-Sipe Museum,** which features an electric map that traces Stonewall Jackson's famous 1862 Valley Campaign, as well as other displays. *301 S. Main St., tel. 703/434–4762. Admission free. Open early May–Oct., Wed.–Sat. 10–4.*

In nearby Dayton—on Route 42, a few miles south of Harrison-
⑨ burg—a not-for-profit foundation is restoring the **Daniel Harrison House** (circa 1749), which was a fortified frontier home and is decorated in prosperous frontier style. Costumed interpreters discuss how the furnishings—beds with ropes as slats and hand-quilted comforters—were made. *Box 366, tel. 703/879–2280 or 703/433–0373. Admission free. Open mid-May–Oct., weekends 1–4.*

⑩ ⑪ Off I–81, the **Grand Caverns** and **Natural Chimneys** stand in adjacent Augusta County, at Exits 235 and 240, respectively. Among the caverns' features is an underground room that's classified as one of the largest of its kind in the East. Since their discovery in 1806, the caverns have inspired artists such as Porte Crayon, whose drawings appeared in many 19th-century magazines. The Natural Chimneys, near the town of Grottoes, stand tall and slender like the pillars of an Egyptian temple ruin. The seven free-standing limestone pylons date back 500 million years, but their origins are unknown. They were created by some form of natural action. Facilities include connecting nature trails and a swimming pool. Every June and August a jousting tournament is held at the site. *Grand Caverns: I–81 (Exit 235). Admission: $9 adults, $7 senior citizens and military, $6 children. Open Apr.–Oct., daily 9–5; Mar., weekends 9–5. Natural Chimneys: I–81 (Exit 240), west to Bridgewater and follow signs to Grottoes, tel. 703/249–5729. Admission: $5 per car. Open daily 9–dark.*

⑫ Staunton (pronounced Stan-ton), off I–64, 11 miles west of the southern end of Skyline Drive at Waynesboro, is a town with a distinguished past. This was once the seat of government of the vast Augusta County, formed in 1738 and encompassing present-day West Virginia, Kentucky, Ohio, Illinois, Indiana, and the Pittsburgh area. Staunton was briefly the capital of Virginia, when the General Assembly fled here from the British in 1781. And here Woodrow Wilson was born in 1856.

The restored **Woodrow Wilson Birthplace and Museum** has period antiques, items from Wilson's political career, and some original pieces from when this museum was the residence of Wilson's father, a Presbyterian minister. Among the memorabilia exhibited is Wilson's presidential limousine, a 1919 Pierce-Arrow sedan, on display in the garage. *24 N. Coalter St., tel. 703/885–0897. Admission: $6 adults, $5.50 senior citizens, $4 students 13–18, $2 children 6–12. Open Mar.–Nov., daily 9–5; Dec., daily 10–4; Jan.–Feb., Mon.–Sat. 10–4. Closed major holidays.*

The **Museum of American Frontier Culture,** an outdoor living museum, re-creates the beginnings of agrarian life in America in four genuine 18th-century farmsteads: American, Scots-Irish, German, and English. The attention to authenticity here is painstaking. Master craftsmen were brought from Ulster, Northern Ireland, to thatch the roofs on farm buildings transported from County Tyrone. Livestock have been backbred and ancient seeds germinated in order to create an environment accurate in all details. The museum is off I–81, at Exit 222 to Route 250 West. *230 Frontier Dr., tel. 703/332–7850. Admission: $7 adults, $6.50 senior citizens, $3 children 6–12. Open Dec.–mid Mar., daily 10–4; mid-Mar.–Nov., daily 10–5. Closed Thanksgiving, Christmas, and New Year's Day.*

The **Statler Brothers Museum,** on the edge of downtown Staunton, about 2 miles from I–81, features memorabilia of more than 25 years, including awards, collected by the Staunton-born country-music singing group. The building that houses the museum is a former school the brothers attended. *501 Thornrose Ave., tel. 703/885–7297. Admission free; tours run weekdays at 2 PM.*

The 470-mile **Blue Ridge Parkway,** a continuation of Skyline Drive, extends south through the George Washington National Forest to Great Smoky Mountains National Park in North Carolina and Tennessee. Although the parkway is less pristine, the higher mountains offer even better views than those of Skyline Drive: **Peaks of Otter Recreation Area,** (tel. 703/586–4357), about 25 miles northeast of Roanoke, rewards drivers and hikers with a 360° panorama of old, soft-sloping mountains—the rougher Alleghenies are visible in the distance. Trails of varying difficulty lead the way up the two main peaks: Sharp Top and Flat Top—the highest of the two at 4,004 feet. The hills rise above the shores of Abbott Lake, a bucolic picnic spot. A pleasant lakeside lodge (tel. 703/586–1081) and campground below are an ideal base for local trekking. Like the drive, the parkway has a variety of lodges, waysides, and self-guided nature walks on a section of the Appalachian Trail; unlike the drive, admission to the parkway and its attractions is free.

🔞 In **Lexington,** 30 miles south of Staunton on I–81 (which parallels the Blue Ridge Parkway), two deeply traditional Virginia colleges sit side by side, each with a memorial to a soldier who was also a man of peace.

Washington and Lee University, the sixth-oldest college in the United States, was founded in 1749 as Augusta Academy and later renamed Washington College in gratitude for a donation from George Washington. After Robert E. Lee served as its president following the Civil War, it received its present name. Today, with 1,850 students, the university occupies a campus of white-column, redbrick buildings around a central colonnade. The Lee Chapel and Museum on campus contains many relics of the Lee family. Edward Valentine's statue of the recumbent general, behind the altar, is especially moving: The pose is natural and the expression gentle, a striking contrast to most monumental art. Here one can sense the affection and reverence that Lee inspired. *Tel. 703/463-8768. Admission free. Open Apr.–Oct., Mon.–Sat. 9–5, Sun. 2–5; Nov.– Mar., Mon.–Sat. 9–4, Sun. 2–5.*

Cyrus McCormick is honored at the **McCormick Museum and Wayside,** which sits about a mile off I–81. Follow the signs to Walnut Grove farm; now a livestock research center, this mill farmstead is where McCormick developed the first mechanical wheat reaper. *S.R. 606, a few miles north of Lexington, tel. 703/377-2255. Admission free. Open daily 8:30–5.*

Adjacent to Washington and Lee University are the imposing Gothic buildings of the **Virginia Military Institute,** founded in 1839, with about 1,300 cadets. Here the **George C. Marshall Museum** preserves the memory of the World War II army chief of staff. Exhibits trace his brilliant career, which began when he was aide-de-camp to John "Black Jack" Pershing in World War I and culminated when, as secretary of state, he devised the Marshall Plan, a strategy for reviving postwar Western Europe. Marshall's Nobel Peace Prize is on display; so is the Oscar won by his aide Frank McCarthy, who produced the Academy Award–winning Best Picture of 1970, *Patton.* An electronically narrated map tells the story of World War II. *Tel. 703/ 463-7103. Admission: $3 adults, $2 senior citizens, $1 children 7– 18, free to students with valid ID and active-duty military. Open Mar.–Oct., daily 9–5; Nov.–Feb., daily 9–4. Closed Thanksgiving, Christmas, and New Year's Day.*

The **Virginia Military Institute Museum,** located in the lower level of Jackson Memorial Hall, displays Stonewall Jackson's stuffed and mounted horse, Little Sorrel, and the general's coat, pierced by the bullet that killed him at Chancellorsville. *Tel. 703/464-7232. Admission free. Open Mon.–Sat. 9–5, Sun. 2–5.*

Jackson's private life is on display a few blocks away at the **Stonewall Jackson House,** where he is revealed as a man devoted to physical fitness and the Presbyterian faith, careful with money, musically inclined, and fond of gardening. There is nothing remote about the modest professor one meets here, in the only house he ever owned, furnished now with period pieces and some of the general's belongings. He lived here only two years, while teaching physics and military tactics to the cadets, until the Civil War put his tactical genius to bloody use. *8 E. Washington St., tel. 703/463-2552. Admission: $4 adults, $2 children 6–12. Open Sept.–May, Mon.–Sat. 9–5, Sun. 1–5; June–Aug., Mon.–Sat. 9–6, Sun. 1–6.*

Time Out **Sweet Things** (106 W. Washington St., tel. 703/463–6055) is one of those rare places that still make old-fashioned milkshakes, sundaes, and homemade ice cream and frozen yogurt in special flavors, served in homemade cones.

---

14 The drive to **Bath County** in the west, on the 35-mile stretch of Route 39 north and west from Lexington, provides a scenic side trip whose most prominent feature is the 3-mile Goshen Pass, which follows the Maury River through the mountains. Before the coming of railroads, it was the principal stagecoach route into Lexington. The sunlight shining through the thick, variegated foliage creates a brilliant kaleidoscope at any time of year. Starting in May, the scene becomes lush with rhododendrons and other flowering plants. A day-use park enables picnickers to bask in this still underused sylvan refuge, where visitors can fish, swim, and inner-tube in the river.

As residents are proud to point out, there are no traffic lights in all of Bath County, just four billboards and only 10 year-round inhabitants per square mile. For more than 200 years this peaceful area has been a popular resort. Visitors came originally for the healing thermal springs, whose treatments are less fashionable today—though the sulfur waters still flow at **Warm Springs, Hot Springs,** and **Bolar Springs,** their temperatures ranging from 77°F to 104°F. On Route 645, in Warm Springs, you may want to stop by **Gristmill Square,** where five restored historic buildings have been converted into a gift shop, inn, and the Waterwheel Restaurant (*see* Dining and Lodging, *below*).

Of the numerous resorts in Bath County, **The Homestead** (Hot Springs, tel. 703/839–5500 or 800/336–5771, fax 703/839–7670), 5 miles south of Warm Springs on Route 39, has long been an attraction in its own right (*see* Dining and Lodging, *below*). It was built in 1891 and is still owned by the founding M.E. Ingalls family. Every imaginable luxury and diversion is available to its guests, whose number at any one time may reach 1,000. You can still drink from the springs around which the spa was built in the 19th century, when wealthy vacationers from the North traveled here on private rail cars. The oldest of the resort's three golf courses was laid out in 1892; its first tee is the oldest in continuous use in the United States and it is the oldest golf course in Virginia. A pretty good golfer named Sam Snead got his start on this course. The first skiing in the South took place here in 1959–60. Tennis, horseback riding, carriage riding, fishing, lawn bowling, skeet, trap, and archery are available. The sprawling redbrick main building looks almost like a movie-set version of a Colonial mansion grown to fantastic size.

15 About 20 miles south of Lexington on I–81 is the **Natural Bridge of Virginia.** The Monocan Indians called it the Bridge of God, but today it is destined for less heavenly uses; in addition to being the popular tourist attraction of a private corporation, the impressive limestone arch supports part of U.S. 11. The bridge has been gradually carved out of the rock by Cedar Creek, which rushes on 215 feet below. Surveying the structure for Lord Halifax, George Washington carved his own initials in the stone; Thomas Jefferson bought it (and more than 150 surrounding acres) from George III. The after-dark sound-and-light show may be overkill, but viewing and walking under the bridge itself and along the wooded pathway beyond are worth the price of admission. The bridge complex also includes dizzying caverns that descend 34 stories into the earth and a wax museum that gives a factory tour of the state-of-the-art process by which the figures are made. *Just off I–81, tel. 703/291–2121 or 800/533–1410. Ad-*

mission to single attraction: $8 adults, $7 senior citizens, $4 children; any two attractions: $10.50 adults, $8.50 senior citizens, $5.50 children; for all three: $13 adults, $11 senior citizens, $7.50 children. Sound-and-light show, $7. Open May–Aug., daily 9–9; Sept., Nov., Mar.–Apr., daily 10–6; Dec.–Feb., Wed.–Sun. 10–4.

16 The quiet and cheerful city of **Roanoke,** situated 54 miles south of Lexington, is a hub for the railroad and the arts. In Market Square, at the heart of the city, a restored warehouse called **Center in the Square** contains the Mill Mountain Theatre (musicals, Shakespeare, contemporary drama) and three museums: the Science Museum of Western Virginia and Hopkins Planetarium, the Roanoke Valley History Museum, and the Roanoke Museum of Fine Arts. *Center in the Square, tel. 703/342–5700. Museums open Mon.–Sat. 10–5, Sun. 1–5; opening days vary with museums.*

The **Science Museum of Western Virginia** has displays on Virginia's natural history. Many exhibits are interactive and especially appealing to youngsters. Shows are given in the planetarium. *Tel. 703/342–5710. Combined admission, museum and planetarium: $5.75 adults, $4.25 senior citizens and children. Museum admission: $4 adults, $2.50 senior citizens and children. Open Mon.–Sat. 10–5, Sun. 1–5.*

The **Roanoke Valley History Museum** displays a curious collection of regionalia, including relics of the local Native Americans, whose word for "shell wampum" forms the root of "Roanoke." A permanent exhibit explores the history of volunteer rescue units in America. *Tel. 703/342–5770. Admission: $2 adults, $1 senior citizens and children. Open Tues.–Sun.*

The collection of the **Roanoke Museum of Fine Arts** is strongest in regional works, particularly Appalachian folk art. The exhibition space extends into the Center on Church annex across the alley, which is linked by a second-floor gallery bridge; the gallery of 19th-century American art was tripled in size in 1990. *Tel. 703/342–5760. Admission free.*

Just a pleasant stroll away from Market Square, the **Virginia Museum of Transportation** is devoted almost exclusively to trains, for Roanoke got its start as a railroad town and is today the headquarters of the Norfolk and Western Railway (formerly the Norfolk Southern). The dozens of original train cars and engines, many built here in town, include a massive Nickel Plate locomotive. The collections are unique, an unabashed display of civic pride peculiar to Roanoke; the museum captures the spirit of the town. *303 Norfolk Ave., tel. 703/342–5670. Admission: $4 adults, $3 senior citizens, $2 children 13–18, $1.75 children 3–12. Open Mon.–Sat. 10–5, Sun. noon–5. Closed Mon. Jan.–Feb.*

After you've gotten back on I–81, take Exit 132, which links up with **17** Route 11/460, to **Dixie Caverns.** Here visitors can wander inside a mountain and ascend into an enormous chamber called the Cathedral Room, and into smaller cavities with names such as Turkey Wing and Wedding Bell, all hung with beautiful stalactites and flows that look like taffy. There's also a mineral shop—good for souvenirs—attached to the caverns. *5753 W. Main St., Salem, tel. 703/380–2085. Admission: $5.50 adults, $3.50 children 5–12. Open daily 9:30–6.*

Time Out Residents of Roanoke may steer you to more respectable and more expensive establishments, not because they are ashamed of the **Texas Tavern** (114 Church Ave.) but because they want to keep it to themselves. A sign proclaims, WE SERVE A THOUSAND, TEN AT A TIME—and there are just 10 stools. The tavern is often packed, especially late at night; chili is the specialty. This spot is not recommended for families.

⑱ A restored plantation 20 miles southeast of Roanoke, **Booker T. Washington's birthplace** is now a national monument and a museum of life under slavery. Washington, born in slavery, was a remarkable educator who went on to advise presidents McKinley, Roosevelt, and Taft and to take tea with Queen Victoria. More important, he started Tuskegee Institute in Alabama and inspired generations of African-Americans. Covering 224 acres, the farm presents restored buildings, tools, crops, animals, and, in summer, interpreters in period costume. The plantation is on Route 122, 6 miles east of Burnt Chimney (the junction of Routes 116 and 122). *Rte. 122, tel. 703/721-2094. Admission: $1 adults, $3 families, free for senior citizens. Open daily 8:30–5. Closed Thanksgiving, Dec. 25, Jan. 1.*

The Highlands

The Highlands is the only region of the state where the atmosphere retains a residue of the frontier wilderness that enthralled adventurers such as Daniel Boone and provided a setting for their heroic exploits. The shortest route southwest through this rugged region is I–81; the scenic option is to continue south on the Blue Ridge Parkway to I–77, then take I–77 west to I–81.

⑲ **Mabry Mill,** just north of Meadows of Dan and the parkway's junction with U.S. 58 at mile marker 176, is the Blue Ridge Parkway's point of greatest interest. Here are a sawmill and a restored waterpowered gristmill, producing cornmeal and buckwheat flour (for sale). Regular demonstrations showcase blacksmithing and other trades. *Tel. 703/952–2947. Admission free. Open May and Sept.–Oct., daily 8–6; June–Aug., daily 8–7.*

Chateau Morrisette Winery Inc. is a superb vantage point for spectacular views of nearby hills. Tours of the winery are given, and tastings allow visitors to sample the dozen different wines produced on the premises. *On Winery Rd. off Rte. 716 west of Blue Ridge Pkwy., tel. 703/593–2865. Admission: $1. Open Mon.–Sat. 10–5. Closed Thanksgiving, Christmas, and New Year's.*

⑳ The **Wilderness Road Regional Museum** in **Newbern** is 40 miles southwest of Roanoke, off I–81. Settlers used to lodge here on their way west along the Wilderness Road, a route from Pennsylvania through the Cumberland Gap that had been used originally by Native Americans. The man who founded Newbern in 1810 built this house in the same year, and the structure has since served as private home, tavern, post office, and store. Today the house contains an eclectic collection: antique dolls, swords and rifles, an old loom, and other artifacts of everyday life. Museum guides will point out the several other 19thcentury structures in town. *I–81 (Exit 98), tel. 703/674-4835. Admission free. Open Tues.–Sat. 10:30–4:30, Sun. 1:30–4:30.*

Largely to the north of I–81, the 700,000 acres of campgrounds, picnic areas, and lakes of the **Jefferson National Forest,** distributed in scattered patches across southwestern Virginia, provide a habitat for bobcat, black bear, and bald eagle. Here are more than 1,000 miles of hiking trails and hundreds of streams for fishing, with trout in abundance. *U.S.D.A. Forest Supervisor, 210 Franklin Rd. SW, Roanoke 24001, tel. 703/265–6054.*

The portion of Jefferson National Forest south of I–81 (and west of I–77) is the **Mount Rogers National Recreation Area,** where Mt. Rogers (at 5,729 feet, it is the highest mountain in Virginia) is traversed by an extensive network of riding and hiking trails. The Appalachian Trail crosses the border into Tennessee here. Hunting and fishing are permitted in season. *Rte. 1, Box 303, Marion 24354, tel. 703/783–5196.*

㉑ North of Mt. Rogers, Route 16 links I–81 with **Tazewell** in Tazewell County, where the **Crab Orchard Museum and Pioneer Park,** on the site of an archaeological dig just west of the town, has geological and industrial exhibits. These 110 acres were part of a hunting ground for the Shawnee and Cherokee nations, and many of the traditional tools and pieces of furniture have been recovered. European settlement and the ensuing history are illustrated by displays of artifacts, and further exhibits show the social impact of farming and regional mining. Farm buildings and crafts shops nearby are fully accessible to the disabled. *Rtes. 19/460, Tazewell, tel. 703/988–6755. Admission: $4 adults, $3.50 senior citizens, $2 children 13–18, $1.25 children 4–12. Open Apr.–Oct., Mon.–Sat. 9–5, Sun. 1–5; Nov.–Mar., Mon.–Sat. 10–5.*

㉒ West of Mt. Rogers, off I–81, is **Abingdon,** a cultural crossroads in the wilderness: The town of nearly 10,000 residents draws tens of thousands of visitors annually with a fine theater company (*see below*) and exuberant local celebrations. By far the most popular attraction here is the **Virginia Highlands Festival** during the first two weeks of August, when 150,000 people come to hear live performances of music ranging from bluegrass to opera, to visit the exhibitions of mountain crafts, and to browse among the wares of more than 100 antiques dealers. This is followed by the **Burley Tobacco Festival,** held in September, where country-music stars perform and prize farm animals are proudly displayed. *Washington County Chamber of Commerce, 179 E. Main St., 24210, tel. 703/628–8141.*

From April through the Christmas season, audiences flock to the prestigious **Barter Theatre,** America's longest-running professional repertory theater. Founded during the Depression by local actor Robert Porterfield, the theater got its name in the obvious way: Early patrons who could not afford the 40¢ tickets were offered admission for the equivalent in produce. Hume Cronyn, Ned Beatty, and Gregory Peck are among the many stars who began their careers at the Barter, which today presents the classics of Shakespeare as well as works by contemporary playwrights such as David Mamet. Although times have changed since Noël Coward was given a Virginia ham for his contributions, the official policy still permits you to barter for your seat. But don't just show up at the box office with a bag of arugula—all trades must be approved by advance notice. *133 W. Main St., tel. 703/628–3991 or 800/368–3240.*

Off the Beaten Track

Big Stone Gap, about 60 miles west of Abingdon along Alternate U.S. Route 58, stands among the mountains that inspired the early 20th-century novel and later movie, *The Trail of the Lonesome Pine,* by John Fox, Jr. The tragic story of June Tolliver, mountain feuding, and vigilante law is retold every year during the summer months in an outdoor theater, where local performers have acted in this production for more than 30 years. The organization that sponsors the play also manages the 1880s **June Tolliver House,** where rooms are furnished from the period and local arts and crafts, including coal carvings and quilts, are sold. *Climpon Ave., tel. 703/523–4707. Admission free; donations accepted. Performance admission: $7 adults, $5 senior citizens, $4 children 4–12. Performances mid-June–Labor Day, Thurs.–Sat. 8:15. House open June–mid-Dec., Tues.–Sun. and during theater intermission.*

Also in the area is the **Southwest Virginia Historical Museum**, housed in a Victorian mansion built during the coal boom of 1888–1893. Exhibits include the mine-manager's home furnishings. *Tel. 703/523–1322. Admission: $2 adults, $1 children. Open Memorial Day–Labor Day, daily 9–5; Labor Day–Dec. 30 and Mar.–Memorial Day, Tues.–Sun. 9–5; closed Jan.–Feb. and major holidays.*

What to See and Do with Children

Barter Theatre (*see above*), Abingdon, has performances for children June–early August.

Mill Mountain Zoo, Roanoke, has 43 species of exotic and native animals, including a Siberian tiger and red pandas. *Box 13484, Roanoke 24034, tel. 703/343–3241. Admission: $3.50 adults, $2 children 2–12. Open (weather permitting) mid-Apr.–Sept., daily 10–6; Oct.–Feb., daily 10–5; Mar.–mid-Apr., daily 10–4:30.*

Science Museum of Western Virginia (*see above*), Roanoke.

Endless, Grand, Luray, New Market, Shenandoah, and **Skyline Caverns** (*see above*).

Shopping

Antiques **Virginia Made Shop** (I–81 Exit 222, Staunton, tel. 703/886–7180) specializes in English and Irish antique pine furniture.

The area around **Harrisonburg** once was a good place to find bargains on antiques and collectibles at estate sales and the like, but dealers have made this as impossible here as elsewhere in the country. Still, there are more than 25 antiques shops in the area—on or near Rte. 11. Contact the Harrisonburg-Rockingham County Convention and Visitors Bureau (*see* Essential Information, *above*) for a list or drive through communities such as Bridgewater, Dayton, Elkton, Mt. Crawford, Mt. Sydney, Verona, and Weyer's Cave.

Crafts **Rooftop of Virginia CAP Crafts** (206 N. Main St., Rte. 58, 6 mi west of I–70 Galax, tel. 703/236–7131) is an unusual enterprise: a clearinghouse run as a nonprofit corporation by the community, selling the wares of local artisans.

Markets The **Dayton Farmers Market** (Rte. 42 south of Dayton, Box 2-H, Dayton 22821, tel. 703/879–9885), an 18,000-square-foot area, has everything from homemade baked goods and fresh fruits and vegetables to crafts such as butter churns and speckleware made by the Mennonites. It's one place to mingle with the industrious and pleasant Mennonites who live in the vicinity, as well as with students from James Madison University in nearby Harrisonburg. *Open Thurs. 9–6, Fri. 9–8, Sat. 9–5.*

Sports and Outdoor Activities

Participant Sports

Camping The **Big Meadows Campground** (Mistix, tel. 800/365–2267), located approximately at the midpoint of **Shenandoah National Park**, accepts reservations; other campsites are available on a first-come, first-served basis. *Shenandoah National Park, Box 348, Luray 22835, tel. 703/999–2266. Park admission: $5 car.*

Canoeing Rentals are available through **Front Royal Canoe** (Rte. 340 S, near Front Royal, tel. 703/635–5440), **Downriver Canoe** (Rte. 613, near Front Royal, tel. 703/635–5526), and **Shenandoah River Outfitters** (Rte. 684, RFD 3, Luray 22835, tel. 703/743–4159).

Fishing To take advantage of the trout that abound in some 50 streams of Shenandoah National Park, you will need a Virginia fishing license; it's available in season (early April to mid-October) at concession stands along Skyline Drive.

Golf The 18-hole course at **Massanutten Village** (on Rte. 644 near Harrisonburg, tel. 703/289–9441) meanders under inspiring mountain peaks. **Caverns Country Club Resort** (Rte. 211, Luray, tel. 703/743–6551) has an 18-hole course along the Shenandoah. **The Homestead** (Rte. 39, Hot Springs, tel. 703/839–5500 or 800/336–5771, fax 703/839–7670) has three courses. **Wintergreen** (Rte. 664, Wintergreen, tel. 804/325–2200 or 800/325–2200) offers 36 holes, half in the mountains, half in the valley.

Hiking The 2,000-mile wilderness footpath from Maine to Georgia known as the **Appalachian Trail** is no relic of pioneer days but a creation of the 1920s and 1930s that provides challenging hiking opportunities. The stretch of the trail that runs the length of Shenandoah National Park takes hikers along the skyline of the Blue Ridge Mountains to views of some of the most stunning prospects of the Piedmont to the east and the valley to the west. Wildlife that auto traffic would scare away—such as the white-tail deer, for whom the park is a refuge—often step quietly into view. Because the trail's main pathway is never more than a few hundred yards from Skyline Drive (the two arteries intersect repeatedly), and there are parking lots every few miles, one can embark on any kind of hike. Maintained by the National Park Service, with the help of volunteers, the trail has a smooth surface and—given the steep terrain—a gentle grade. Three-sided emergency shelters offer protection from unexpected storms. Hiking neophytes and experienced backpackers will all set their own pace here, and deep-wilderness lovers will head farther into the backcountry by means of the 500 miles of marked side trails within the park. A number of walking trails at intervals along the parkway lead to historical relics such as pioneer farmsteads and natural phenomena such as geologic formations and forests. Park service information sheets show distances, degrees of difficulty, and other information.

Skiing **The Homestead** (Rte. 39, Hot Springs, tel. 703/839–5500 or 800/336–5771) has cross-country, downhill, and night skiing. **Massanutten Village Ski Resort** (off Rte. 33, 10 mi east of Harrisonburg on Rte. 33; tel. 703/289–9441) offers equipment rental, night skiing, and snow making. **Wintergreen** (Rte. 664, Wintergreen, tel. 804/325–

2200 or 800/325–2200) maintains 17 downhill slopes and five chair lifts.

Tennis   **The Homestead** (Rte. 39, Hot Springs, tel. 703/839–5500 or 800/336–5771) has 19 tennis courts. **Caverns Country Club Resort** (Rte. 211, Luray, tel. 703/743–6551) has four courts. **Wintergreen** (Rte. 664, Wintergreen, tel. 804/325–2200 or 800/325–2200) maintains 25 outdoor tennis courts. Many hotels throughout the region provide courts or arrange for guests to use nearby facilities.

Spectator Sports

Equestrian   The **Virginia Horse Center** stages competitions—show jumping,
Events   hunter trials, multibreed shows—several days a week. A new $7 million indoor arena opened in 1992, permitting year-round operation. *Lexington, tel. 703/463–2194. Admission policy varies with event.*

The **Roanoke Valley Horse Show** (tel. 703/389–7847), in June, is one of the top all-breed shows, attracting more than 1,000 entries each year. *Salem Civic Center, 1001 Blvd., Box 886, Salem.*

Horse Racing   **Charles Town Race Track,** in West Virginia, 30 minutes northwest of Front Royal, has thoroughbred racing Friday and Saturday evenings at 7 and Monday, Wednesday, and Sunday afternoons at 1. *Charles Town, WV, tel. 304/725–7001. Admission: $4 clubhouse, $2 grandstand.*

Jousting   **Natural Chimneys Recreation Area,** in Mount Solon, south of Harrisonburg, hosts jousting tournaments in June and August. The day's entertainment typically includes a parade and crafts exhibitions. Campsites are available. *Tel. 703/350–2510. Prices vary according to event.*

Dining and Lodging

Accommodations in private homes and reconverted inns are available through **Blue Ridge Bed & Breakfast Reservation Service** (Rte. 2, Box 3895, Berryville 22611, tel. 703/955–1246 or 800/296–1246).

Highly recommended establishments are indicated by a star ★.

Abingdon   **The Tavern.** This cozy restaurant—built in 1779 and standing as the
Dining   oldest building in town—was a field hospital during the Civil War. Today, it has two small dining rooms and a cocktail lounge, all with fireplaces, stone walls, and brick floors. In warm weather you can dine outdoors on a balcony overlooking historic Court House Hill, or on a brick patio surrounded by trees and flowers. The menu features fresh seasonal seafood, Indonesian Cornish hen, and rack of lamb. There is live music nightly. *222 E. Main St., tel. 703/628–1118. Reservations advised. Dress: casual. AE, MC, V. $$*

Dining and   **Martha Washington Inn.** Constructed as a private house in 1832,
Lodging   turned into a college dormitory in 1860, and used as a field hospital during the Civil War, the Martha Washington has been an inn since 1935. The rooms are furnished with antiques, some have fireplaces, and the inn is located opposite the Barter Theatre. The restaurant menu includes roast quail, mountain trout stuffed with crabmeat, scampi, and—for dessert—Martha's hot fudge cake. Friday buffet and Sunday brunch are featured at the First Ladies Table, and complimentary afternoon tea is offered daily on the porch of the inn. *150 W. Main St., 24210, tel. 703/628–3161 or 800/533–1014, fax 703/628–8885. 50 rooms with bath, 11 suites. Facilities: restaurant, bar, whirlpool in some suites. AE, D, DC, MC, V. $$$–$$$$*

Lodging **Alpine Motel.** The spacious rooms of this clean motel have the basic amenities, a modern decor with soft, creamy colors, and tile bath; each room has a striking view of Virginia's highest mountain peaks: Mt. Rogers and Whitetop. The nearby Barter Theatre is the major attraction in the area. The motel is located away from the road; it's popular with families and traveling salespeople. *882 E. Main St., 24210, tel. 703/628–3178. 19 rooms. AE, D, MC, V. $*

Bath County **Waterwheel Restaurant.** Part of a complex of five restored buildings, *Dining* this restaurant is in a gristmill that dates from 1700. A walk-in wine ★ cellar, set among the gears of the original waterwheel, has 100 varieties of wine; diners may step down and make their own selections. The dining area is decorated with Currier and Ives and Audubon prints. Entrées change; recent choices included salmon steak, broiled and stuffed with smoked salmon, and chicken Fantasio (breast of chicken stuffed with wild rice, sausage, apple, and pecans). Desserts include such Old Virginny recipes as apple brown Betty, a deep-dish apple pie baked with bourbon. On Sunday, a moderately priced but hearty brunch is served. *Grist Mill Sq., Warm Springs, tel. 703/839–2231. Reservations advised. Dress: casual. D, MC, V. Open nightly May–Oct. Closed Mon. night Nov.–Apr. $$$*

Lodging **The Homestead.** The Homestead in Hot Springs is to the luxury re- ★ sort what the Rolls-Royce is to the family wagon. Host to a prestigious clientele since 1761—Thomas Jefferson was the first of eight American presidents to visit—the Homestead has evolved from a country spa famed for its mineral waters to a state-of-the-art resort and conference facility that spans 15,000 acres. From the glorious columns of the entry hall to the stunning views of the Appalachian Mountains, magnificence surrounds guests from first moment to last. Rooms in the older section of the hotel (which includes the tower and the south wing) have elegant Victorian decor and Chippendale-reproduction furnishings. The newer section features well-appointed duplexes with fireplaces and private bars. Four miles of streams stocked with rainbow trout, 100 miles of riding trails, skeet and trap shooting, and three 18-hole golf courses are just a few of the sport and leisure facilities available. The natural mineral springs and spa offer up-to-the-minute treatment and weight-training equipment. An orchestra plays nightly in the gorgeous formal dining room, which features such regional specialties as Virginia lamb in its six-course extravaganzas. *Rte. 220, Hot Springs 24445, tel. 703/839–5500 or 800/336–5771, fax 703/839–7670. 592 rooms. Facilities: 7 restaurants (one has orchestra and dancing), indoor pool, 2 outdoor pools, 19 tennis courts, 3 golf courses, bowling alley, horseback riding, movie theater, extensive spa services and facilities. AE, MC, V. Rates are MAP or European plan. $$$$*

★ **Inn at Gristmill Square.** Occupying two of five restored buildings at the same site as the Waterwheel Restaurant, the rooms of the inn have a Colonial Virginia decor. Four units are in the original miller's house; the main building, formerly a country store, has a modern addition in period style. Near the inn and the restaurant, a blacksmith shop and a hardware store have been combined and converted into a gift shop. The inn is a state historical landmark. *Rte. 645, Box 359, Warm Springs 24484, tel. 703/839–2231, fax 703/839–5770. 9 rooms, 5 suites, 2 apartments. Facilities: restaurant, bar, 3 tennis courts, outdoor pool, sauna. D, MC, V. $$$*

Roseloe Motel. Some rooms in this modest, clean hostelry have a kitchenette; each has a refrigerator. The conventional decor differs from room to room—the larger rooms are in the addition—but the homelike atmosphere prevails throughout. The motel is located halfway between Warm Springs and Hot Springs, and the fresh mountain air is bracing. Also convenient to this accommodation is the Garth Newel Music Center, ¼ mile away. *Rte. 2 (Box 590), Hot Springs 24445, tel. 703/839–5373. 14 rooms. MC, V. $*

Blue Ridge Parkway Lodging ★

Doe Run Lodge. This resort at Groundhog Mountain, a rustic lodge on the crest of the Blue Ridge, offers grand vistas of the Piedmont and proximity to golf, skiing, and hunting. Each unit has a fireplace, and floor-to-ceiling windows allow full appreciation of the view. Reserve well in advance to stay in the more than 100-year-old log cabin. *Mile Post 189, Rte. 2, Box 338, Hillsville 24343, tel. 703/398–2212 or 800/325–6189, fax 703/398–2833. 39 chalets, 3 villas. Facilities: restaurant, 3 tennis courts, outdoor pool, hiking trails, conference center, sauna, stocked fishing pond. AE, MC, V. $$$*

Wintergreen. December through March, guests at this 11,000-acre resort may ski and golf on the same day for the price of a lift ticket; all year long there's an extensive choice of sports options. This makes Wintergreen a popular weekend getaway attraction for active Washingtonians, especially in summer, when temperatures in the mountains are significantly lower than elsewhere. Accommodations range from studio apartments to houses with seven bedrooms, and all buildings are wood structures built to blend in with the natural surroundings. The resort is proud of its award-winning environmental awareness; 6,700 acres are protected as natural forest area, and a staff biologist plans nature walks. Ask about discounted packages. *Rte. 664, Wintergreen 22958, tel. 804/325–2200 or 800/325–2200, fax 804/325–6760. 350 units. Facilities: 6 restaurants, bar, indoor pool, 5 outdoor pools, 25 tennis courts, lake swimming, canoeing, 2 18-hole golf courses, 17 downhill ski slopes, 25 miles of hiking trails, equestrian center, exercise room, sauna, Jacuzzi. AE, MC, V. $$$*

Peaks of Otter Lodge. This unpretentious lodge is so popular that reservations are accepted beginning October 1 for the following year. Every room looks out on Abbott Lake from a private terrace or balcony, and the folksy decor adds to the peaceful ambience—unlike the suites, rooms have neither TVs nor phones. The restaurant serves the area's ubiquitous fried trout and offers a prix fixe menu. *Rte. 664, Box 489, Bedford 24523, tel. 703/586–1081, fax 703/586–4420. 59 rooms, 3 suites. Facilities: restaurant, fishing, hiking trails. MC, V. $$*

Callaghan Lodging

Milton Hall. This restored 1874 house, built as a getaway place by English nobility, is located on 44 acres adjacent to the George Washington National Forest. The location is good for hunting, fishing, hiking, and other outdoor activities, and the staff provides dinner and box lunches for guests who make arrangements in advance. *Off I–64 (Exit 10) at Callaghan. R.R. 3, Covington 24426, tel. 703/965–0196. 5 rooms, 1 suite. MC, V. Full breakfast and afternoon tea included in rates. $$$*

Harrisonburg Lodging

Joshua Wilton House. A row of trees guards the privacy of this late-19th-century house decorated in the Victorian style and set on a large yard at the edge of downtown. Guests relax in the sun room and on the back patio; high tea is served on Wednesday afternoon. Ask for room 4; it has a canopy bed and a view of the Blue Ridge Mountains looming over Main Street. Room 2 has a fireplace. *412 S. Main St., Harrisonburg 22801, tel. 703/434–4464. 5 rooms. Facilities: restaurant. AE, MC, V. Rates include breakfast. $$*

Lexington Dining

Wilson-Walker House. The elegant cuisine and stately atmosphere of this excellent restaurant are an affordable treat, particularly during the $5 chef's-special luncheon and the $10 sunset-special dinner.

Period furnishings lend grace to the early 19th-century Greek Revival house, which is an ideal setting in which to enjoy the kitchen's creative concoctions. Regional fare is interpreted with style and splash—seafood dishes are a specialty, particularly the hazelnut crabcakes. Burgers, pasta, and other, more mundane offerings are also available. *30 N. Main St., tel. 703/463–3020. Reservations required for dinner. Dress: casual but neat. AE, MC, V. Closed Sun. and Mon. $$–$$$*

The Palms. Once a Victorian ice-cream parlor, this property is now a full-service restaurant with indoor and outdoor dining. Wood booths line the walls of the plant-filled room whose pressed-metal ceiling is one of the original details of this 1890 building. Food is prepared and presented with care; specialties of the house include broccoli-cheese soup, charbroiled meats, and teriyaki chicken. There is a Sunday brunch. *101 W. Nelson St., tel. 703/463–7911. No reservations. Dress: casual. MC, V. $*

Dining and **Maple Hall.** This country inn of 1850, located 6 miles north of the
Lodging Lexington historic district, is a former plantation house set on 56 acres. Rooms are furnished with period antiques and modern amenities. Dinner is served in three ground-floor rooms and on a glassed-in patio of this elegant farmhouse. Watercolors by local artists adorn the cream-color walls; the main dining room has a large decorative fireplace, and in one of the other rooms the fireplace is used in cold weather. The menu changes monthly. Among notable entrées that the chef is likely to offer are beef fillet with a green peppercorn sauce; veal sautéed with mushrooms in hollandaise sauce; and chicken Chesapeake, a chicken breast stuffed with spinach and crabmeat. When weather permits, there is dining on an outdoor patio. *Rte. 11, 24450, tel. 703/463–6693, fax 703/463–7262. 21 rooms. Facilities: restaurant (reservations advised; no lunch), hiking trails, trout pond, outdoor pool, tennis court. MC, V. $$$*

Luray **Parkhurst Inn.** This redbrick building, built as a restaurant in the
Dining 1930s, gutted by fire in the 1940s, and turned into a motel in the 1950s, was restored to its original function in 1978. In addition to a glass-enclosed porch where meals are served within sight of greenery all year long, the main dining room has white walls decorated with baskets and mirrors. Another dining room is finished in knotty pine, and still another is distinguished by a crystal chandelier. The menu, international in character, has featured roast duck with orange sauce; curried chicken accompanied by fresh-fruit condiments; beef strips sautéed with mushrooms, topped with a blue-cheese sauce, and baked; and veal Oscar (with Alaskan king crab, asparagus, and béarnaise). The commendable wine list is more heavily Virginian every year, and local vintages are available by the glass. *Rte. 211 W, tel. 703/743–6009. Dress: casual but neat. AE, DC, MC, V. No lunch. $$–$$$*

Lodging **Jordan Hollow Farm.** The oldest of the four buildings is the dining hall, but it was originally created as a farmhouse in 1790; the youngest structure, built of hand-hewn logs almost 200 years later, contains the inn's most luxurious rooms, which include a fireplace, whirlpool, and TV. The inn's setting, on a 45-acre horse farm near the tiny town of Stanley, 6 miles from Luray, lets you gaze out over pastures full of horses toward a backdrop of the Blue Ridge Mountains. Guided tours on horseback are varied in length and terrain to match the rider's experience. *Rte. 2, Box 375, Stanley 22851, tel. 703/778–2285. 21 rooms. Facilities: restaurant, bar, stables. D, DC, MC, V. $$–$$$*

Natural Bridge Lodging **Natural Bridge Hotel.** Within walking distance of the spectacular rock arch (there is also shuttle-bus service), the hotel boasts a beautiful setting and family recreational facilities. Long porches with rocking chairs allow leisurely appreciation of the prospect of the Blue Ridge Mountains. Rooms have ersatz Colonial Virginia decor. *U.S. 11, Box 57, 24578, tel. 703/291-2121 or 800/533-1410. 180 rooms. Facilities: cafeteria, snack bar, outdoor pool, 2 tennis courts, walking trails. AE, D, DC, MC, V. $$*

Newbern Dining ★ **Valley Pike Inn.** This family-owned restaurant in Newbern, off I-81, features fried chicken, country-baked ham, roast beef, homemade buttermilk biscuits, and old-fashioned fruit cobblers (no liquor is served). Wood walls and floors add to the farmhouse atmosphere found in this inn that was built in 1830 at what was then a stagecoach stop. *Off I-81 (Exit 98), tel. 703/674-1810 or 703/980-6757. Reservations advised for 5 or more. Dress: casual. MC, V. No lunch. Closed Jan.-Apr., Mon.-Thurs.; May-Dec., Mon.-Wed. $*

Radford Lodging **Best Western Radford Inn.** Rooms are decorated in Colonial Virginia style, and the views of the Blue Ridge Mountains are not utterly spoiled by the surrounding parking lot. Service and amenities (such as a bathroom phone) distinguish this facility from other highway motels of similar ambience and location. *1501 Tyler Ave. (Rte. 177), Box 1008, 24141, tel. and fax 703/639-3000; 800/528-1234. 104 rooms. Facilities: restaurant, bar, indoor pool, whirlpool, sauna, gym. AE, D, DC, MC, V. $$*

Roanoke Dining **The Library.** This quiet, elegant restaurant in the Piccadilly Square shopping center, decorated with shelves of books, specializes in seafood dishes. *3117 Franklin Rd. SW, tel. 703/985-0811. Reservations required. Jacket required. AE, DC, MC, V. Closed Sun. $$$$*

★ **La Maison du Gourmet.** One by one, starting in 1978, the 12 rooms of this brick Georgian Colonial house built in 1927 have been converted into dining rooms; one accommodates 50 people, another (a former bedroom) only 15. A second-floor terrace, used in warmer weather, overlooks the elaborate formal gardens that cover much of the 2-acre property. Dining rooms are variously distinguished by crystal chandeliers, fireplaces, slate floors, and bare wood floors. The tableside preparation of steak Diane is a sight: Filet mignon in a Bordelaise sauce is flambéed, then served with fresh mushrooms and scallions. The menu also offers a range of veal, chicken, and lamb entrées. *5732 Airport Rd., tel. 703/366-2444. Reservations advised. Dress: casual but neat. AE, D, DC, MC, V. Lunch served weekdays at 11. Dinner Mon.-Sat. Closed Sun. $$$*

Billy's Ritz. Music in the background on weekends and a friendly clientele, evenly divided between under-30s and over-30s, create a relaxing and convivial atmosphere at this downtown restaurant. Chicken teriyaki and cobb salad are among the selections on a diversified menu that includes steaks, chops, and seafood. *102 Salem Ave., tel. 703/342-3937. Reservations not required. Dress: casual. Open nightly at 5, lunch weekdays 11:30-2:30. AE, DC, MC, V. $$*

The Homeplace. Here's a prime restaurant for old-fashioned cooking served family-style, including fried chicken, mashed potatoes and gravy, green beans, pinto beans, baked apples, and hot biscuits. No alcohol is served. *I-81, Exit 141, Rte. 311 N, near Salem, tel. 703/384-7252. No reservations. Dress: casual. Dinner Thurs.-Sat. 4:30-8, Sun. 11:30-6. D, MC, V. $$*

Lodging **Patrick Henry Hotel.** Strategically located at I-581 and Elm Avenue, this hotel is easy to reach and central to downtown attractions. The interior is attractively decorated, particularly the elegant lobby, and antiques in the restored rooms make each guest quarter unique. *617 S. Jefferson St., 24011, tel. 703/345-8811 or 800/833-4567, fax 703/342-9908. 124 rooms, many with kitchenette. Facilities: restaurant, lounge, access to health facilities. AE, MC, V. $$-$$$*

Holiday Inn Civic Center. The convenient downtown location—at I-581 and Williamson Road—of this 30-year-old facility helps to make it a popular accommodation with business travelers. The conventional two-story building is ringed by parking space; a pool surrounded by a courtyard with a pebble surface adds some privacy. The contemporary rooms have soundproofing and wood furniture, and the lobby is a model of modern Holiday Inn style, with sturdy but ordinary furnishings. *501 Orange Ave., 24016, tel. and fax 703/342-8961; 800/465-4329. 153 rooms, 2 parlors. Facilities: restaurant, lounge, outdoor pool. AE, D, DC, MC, V. $$*

Smith Mountain Lake Lodging **Bernard's Landing.** A lakeside resort 45 minutes southeast of Roanoke, Bernard's offers one- to three-bedroom condominiums with water views, for periods of up to two weeks. All units have full kitchen facilities; the decor of each condo is by design of the respective owner. Businesspeople schedule conferences here year-round, and summer vacationers are attracted by the variety of sports facilities. *Rte. 940, Box 462, Moneta 24121, tel. 703/721-8870 or 800/572-2048, fax 703/721-8383. 63 units. Facilities: restaurant, 2 outdoor pools, 6 tennis courts, 2 racquetball courts, sauna, Jacuzzi, weight room, playground, boating and fishing available. AE, D, MC, V. $$$*

Staunton Dining **Rowe's Family Restaurant.** A homey restaurant with a bright, comfortable dining room filled with booths, Rowe's has been operated by the same family since 1947. House specialties include Virginia ham, steak, chicken, and homemade pies—try mincemeat. *I-81 (Exit 222), tel. 703/886-1833. Reservations not required. Dress: casual. D, MC, V. $*

Dining and Lodging **Belle Grae Inn.** The sitting room and music room of a restored Victorian house have been converted into formal dining rooms appointed with brass wall sconces, Oriental rugs, and candles at the tables. The kitchen prepares breast of chicken with artichoke hearts, Bermuda onions, red peppers, and balsamic vinegar sauce. Classic entrées on the prix fixe menu include grilled lamb chops with mint sauce and grilled medallions of beef with béarnaise sauce. An adjacent bistro, more casual and less expensive, offers entrées such as chicken Parmesan and London broil at lunch and dinner. Eighteen rooms available for overnight guests are furnished with rocking chairs and canopied or brass beds; the lodging rates are moderate and include breakfast. *515 W. Frederick, 24401, tel. 703/886-5151, fax 703/886-6641. Reservations advised. Dress: casual but neat. AE, D, MC, V. $$$*

Lodging **Frederick House.** Three restored town houses dating to 1810 make up this inn in the center of the historic district. All rooms are decorated with antiques, and smoking is not allowed on the premises. A pub and a restaurant are adjacent. *28 N. New St., 24401, tel. 703/885-4220 or 800/334-5575. 14 rooms. AE, D, DC, MC, V. Rates include breakfast. $$*

Wytheville Lodging **Boxwood Inn.** This 1835 home located between Roanoke and Abingdon is surrounded by mountains and has been restored in recent years to reflect its early 19th-century appearance. A yard featuring English boxwoods adds to the atmosphere, and the inn is within walking distance of crafts and antiques shops. Breakfast is included in the room rate. *460 E. Main St., 24382, tel. 703/228-8911. 8 rooms. MC, V. $$*

The Arts

Dance   **Roanoke Ballet Theatre** (tel. 703/345–6099) attracts guest artists from around the world for performances in spring and fall at theaters around town and the Shenandoah Valley.

Music   **Garth Newel Music Center** (Hot Springs, tel. 703/839–5018) has weekend chamber-music performances in summer; you can make reservations and plan to picnic on the grounds.

Washington and Lee University's **Lenfest Center for the Performing Arts** (Lexington, tel. 703/463–8000) sponsors a variety of concerts, recitals, and dramatic events during the school year and hosts community-sponsored programs.

The Roanoke Symphony (tel. 703/343–9127) performs monthly in January, February, May, September, and October and gives a summer picnic-with-the-pops performance in July and August.

Roanoke Valley Chamber Music Society (tel. 703/375–2333) hosts distinguished visiting performers from October to May at the Olin Theater on the campus of Roanoke College.

Theater   **Barter Theatre** (133 W. Main St., Box 867, Abingdon, tel. 703/628–3991 or 800/368–3240) has performances Tuesday–Sunday nights from April through December. Plays change every four weeks.

Lime Kiln Arts Theater (Lexington, tel. 703/463–3074) performs in the ruins of a lime kiln—outdoor rock walls, with lush hillsides. Here, dramatic works (previous visiting artists have ranged from Russian clowns to Vietnamese puppets) and original musicals are staged Monday–Saturday and contemporary concerts are given on Sunday throughout the summer.

Mill Mountain Theatre (Center in the Square, downtown Roanoke, tel. 703/342–5740) offers year-round professional theater, plus a festival of new works.

Roanoke Comedy Club (213 Williamson Rd., tel. 703/982–5693) combines dinner and laughs Wednesday–Friday nights, with headliners, feature acts, and amateur night.

4 Richmond and the Piedmont

Richmond is the heart of Virginia. Centered on the fall line of the James River, about 75 miles upriver from the Chesapeake Bay, Richmond completes the transition from Tidewater Virginia into the Piedmont, the central section of rolling plains that reaches toward the mountain barrier in the west. Not only is Richmond the capital of the commonwealth, it was also the capital of the Confederacy. As a result, the city is studded with historic sites.

Richmond has a long tradition as an industrial center, as well. It was, at the start of the Civil War, the most industrialized city in the South, and it remains home base to national industries such as Reynolds Metals and tobacco manufacturers. In recent years, Richmond has added high technology to traditional economic bases that include shipping and banking.

After years of urban decay, it has transformed itself into a lively and sophisticated modern town. It's one of the South's preeminent art cities, flourishing with avant-garde painting and sculpture, in addition to the magnificent traditional works and artifacts such as Fabergé eggs exhibited in the Virginia Museum of Fine Arts. Drive beyond the historic downtown area and you'll find a fascinating array of charming and distinctive residential neighborhoods.

After Richmond, the most prominent city in this region is Charlottesville, 71 miles northwest of Richmond, at the core of what Virginians call Mr. Jefferson's country. While the influence of the third president of the United States is inescapable throughout the commonwealth (and far beyond its borders), in Albemarle and Orange counties Jefferson's presence is especially visible. Here are buildings and sites associated with him and the giants among his contemporaries. Here, too, are the locales of many crucial events in early American history.

Since 1819, when Jefferson founded the University of Virginia in Charlottesville, the area has been a cultural center. In recent years the countryside has been discovered by celebrities in search of privacy, among them the actresses Jessica Lange and Sissy Spacek. A growing community of writers and artists is making this affluent area a colony of the intelligentsia, the fashion-conscious, and others who appreciate a historic, out-of-the-way setting.

Essential Information

Important Addresses and Numbers

Visitor Information **Virginia Division of Tourism** (1021 E. Cary St., Richmond 23219, tel. 800/932–5827) offers a state guide and map. For information concerning specific attractions contact the **Old Bell Tower** (Capitol Sq., Richmond, tel. 804/786–4484) on the capitol grounds.
Charlottesville/Albemarle Convention and Visitors Bureau (Rte. 20 S, Box 161, Charlottesville 22902, tel. 804/977–1783).
Metro Richmond Convention and Visitors Bureau (6th St. Marketplace, 5500 E. Marshall St., Box C–250, 23219, tel. 804/782–2777 or 800/365–7272). Other visitor centers are located at 1710 Robin Hood Road (Exit 78 off I–95 and I–64) and at Richmond International Airport (Exit 197 off I–64).
Lynchburg Visitors Information Center (216–12th St., Lynchburg 24504, tel. 804/847–1811).
Department of Tourism/Petersburg Visitors Center (15 Bank St., Petersburg 23803, tel. 804/733–2400 or 800/368–3595). Also visit the center at 425 Cockade Alley.

Emergencies Throughout the region, dial **911** for emergency assistance.

Hospitals **Martha Jefferson Hospital** (459 Locust Ave., Charlottesville, tel. 804/293–0193), **Lynchburg General Hospital** (1901 Tate Springs Rd., tel. 804/947–3000), and **Virginia Commonwealth University Hospital** (401 N. 12th St., Richmond, tel. 804/786–9151) are open 24 hours.

Pharmacy **CVS Pharmacy** (2730 W. Broad St., Richmond, tel. 804/359–2497).

Arriving and Departing

By Plane **Richmond International Airport** (tel. 804/226–3000), 10 miles east of the city, off I–64, has scheduled flights by 12 airlines, including American (tel. 800/433–7300), Delta (tel. 800/221–1212), United (tel. 800/241–6522), and USAir (tel. 804/293–6111 or 800/428–4322). A taxi ride downtown from the airport costs $18–$20.

Charlottesville-Albemarle Airport (tel. 804/973–8341), 8 miles north of Charlottesville on Route 29, is served principally by USAir Express, United Express, American Eagle, and Comair via Delta Connection.

Lynchburg Regional Airport (tel. 804/582–1150) on Route 29 South is served principally by USAir Express and United Express.

By Car Richmond is at the intersection of Interstates 95 and 64, which run north–south and east–west, respectively. U.S. 1 also runs north–south by the city. Charlottesville is where U.S. 29 (north–south) meets I–64. U.S. 460 between Richmond and Roanoke and Route 29 south from Charlottesville meet in Lynchburg.

By Train **Amtrak** (tel. 800/872–7245) service between New York City and Newport News or Florida passes daily through Richmond Station (7519 Staples Mill Rd., Richmond, tel. 804/264–9194).

Union Station (810 W. Main St., Charlottesville, tel. 804/296–4559) is a stop on Amtrak's runs between New York and Chicago (three times a week) and between New York and New Orleans (daily).

Amtrak's *Silver Crescent* runs between New York and New Orleans and stops daily at Lynchburg's Kemper Street Station.

By Bus **Greyhound Lines** (tel. 800/231–2222) serves Charlottesville (310 W. Main St., tel. 804/295–5131) and Richmond (2910 N. Blvd., tel. 804/254–5910).

Getting Around Richmond and the Piedmont

By Car Having a car is advisable—though not necessary—in Richmond and indispensable for visiting Charlottesville and Lynchburg. I–64 is the main highway linking Richmond and Charlottesville.

By Bus and Trolley **Greater Richmond Transit** (tel. 804/358–4782) operates bus and trolley service in Richmond. Buses run daily, 5 AM–12:30 AM; fares are 75¢–$1.20 (exact change). Trolley service in downtown Richmond is free: The Riverside run operates every 7 minutes weekdays 11–5 and every 30 minutes 5–midnight; the Broad Street–Shockoe Slip run operates weekdays 11–3.

By Taxi Cabs are metered in Richmond; they charge $1.50 per mile, $1.50 drop charge.

Guided Tours

Orientation On weekends the **Richmond Cultural Link Trolley,** leaving from the Science Museum on West Broad Street, makes a 90-minute loop with stops at 34 cultural and historic landmarks. You can proceed at your own pace, getting on and off as you choose. *Tel. 804/358–4782. Cost: $5 adults, $2.50 children 5–12. Runs Sat. 10–5, Sun. 12:30–5:30.*

Special-interest The **Historic Richmond Foundation** (tel. 804/780–0107) organizes tours on subjects such as women of Richmond, architecture, the canal system, the Civil War, the Revolution, homes and gardens, battlefields, and walking tours ($5). It also runs daily two- to four-hour driving tours of the city in air-conditioned vans, for $15–$20. Reservations are required.

Richmond Discoveries (tel. 804/795–5781, fax 804/795–1164) is a private company that offers an array of excursions in the Richmond area, including trips that highlight Civil War history, horseback tours, and customized rambles for large groups or small families.

Boat Tours **Historic Richmond Foundation** (tel. 804/780–0107) schedules scenic-tour and dining cruises.

Annabel Lee **Riverboat Cruises** (tel. 804/222–5700) ply the waters from April to December and feature lunch, brunch, dinner, dancing, live riverboat show, and James River plantation cruises.

Exploring

Richmond

Numbers in the margin correspond to points of interest on the Piedmont and Richmond maps.

 Richmond's historic attractions lie north of the James River, which bisects the city with a sweeping curve. The heart of old Richmond is the Court End district, downtown. Running west from here is Main Street, which is lined with banks; stores are concentrated along Grace Street. Another east–west thoroughfare, Cary Street, becomes, between 12th and 15th streets, the cobblestoned center of Shockoe Slip, a fashionable shopping-and-entertainment zone converted from several blocks of warehouses. The downtown area gives way to gracious residential neighborhoods as one moves farther west; Monument Avenue, 140 feet wide and divided by a verdant median, is lined with statues of Civil War heroes and the stately homes of some of the first families of Virginia. A block south, a series of streets fanning out southwesterly from Park Avenue creates the gaslighted Fan District, a treasury of restored turn-of-the-century town houses that has been the "hip" neighborhood for at least a decade.

Our tour begins in the **Court End** district, which contains seven National Historic Landmarks, three museums, and 11 more buildings on the National Register of Historic Places—all within eight blocks. At any one of the museums you will receive a self-guided walking tour with the purchase of a discount block ticket ($11 adults, $10 senior citizens, $5 children 7–12; groups of 10 or more, $8 per person), good for all admission fees.

 One of those museums, the **John Marshall House,** was built in 1790 by the future chief justice of the United States, who also served as secretary of state and ambassador to France. The house, now fully

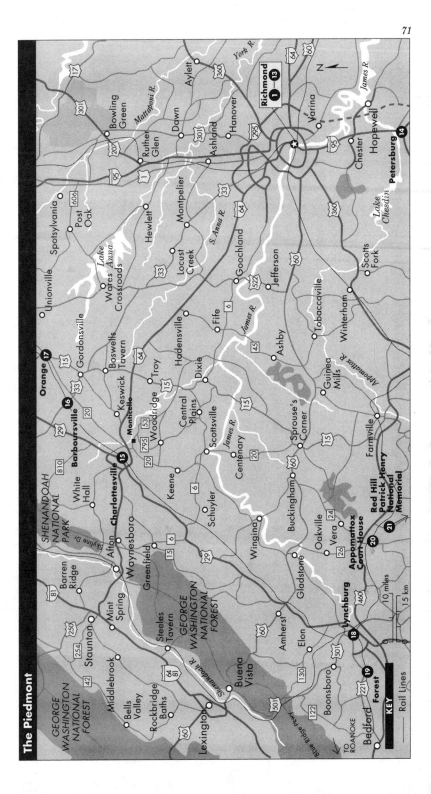

The Piedmont

York R.

Richmond **1** **13**

James R.

Hopewell **14**

Petersburg

Chester

Lake Chesdin

Varina

Scotts Fork

Winterham

Tobaccaville

Guinea Mills

Farmville

Sprouse's Corner

Appomattox R.

Jefferson

Goochland

Ashby

Dixie

Fife

Hadensville

Troy

Boswells Tavern

Central Plains

Scottsville

Buckingham

Oakville

Vera

Gladstone

Appomattox Court House **20**

Red Hill Patrick Henry National Memorial **21**

Lynchburg **18**

Forest **19**

Bedford

Boonsboro

Amherst

Elon

Buena Vista

Lexington

Rockbridge Baths

Bells Valley

Middlebrook

Staunton

Mint Spring

Steeles Tavern

Greenfield

Waynesboro

Afton

White Hall

Charlottesville **15**

Barboursville **16**

Orange **17**

Gordonsville

Keswick

Monticello

Woodridge

Keene

Schuyler

Wingina

Centenary

Centenary

GEORGE WASHINGTON NATIONAL FOREST

SHENANDOAH NATIONAL PARK

Skyline Dr.

Shenandoah R.

Barren Ridge

TO ROANOKE

Blue Ridge Pkwy.

Aylett

Hanover

Dawn

Bowling Green

Ruther Glen

Ashland

Montpelier

Hewlett

Spotsylvania

Post Oak

Wares Crossroads

Lake Anna

Unionville

Locust Creek

S. Anna R.

James R.

KEY
——— Rail Lines

10 miles

15 km

N

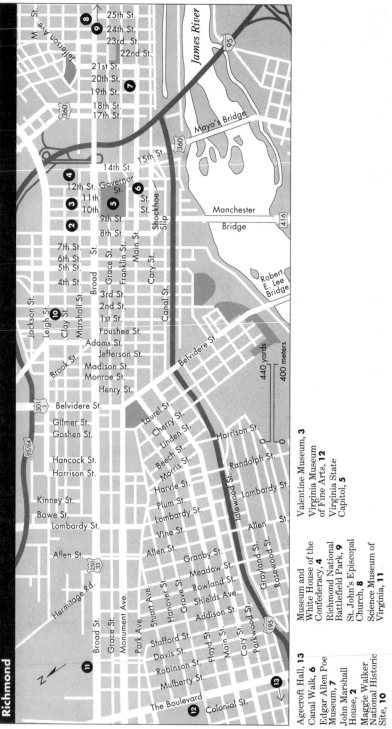

Richmond

James River

I-95

Mayo's Bridge

360

Manchester
Bridge

416

Robert
E. Lee
Bridge

301

95/64

250
33

195

N

Jefferson Ave.
W. St.

25th St.
24th St.
23rd. St.
22nd St.

21st St.
20th St.
19th St.
18th St.
17th St.

15th St.

14th St.
Governor St.
12th St.
11th
10th
9th St.
8th St.

7th St.
6th St.
5th St.
4th St.

Shockhoe Slip
St. St.

Broad St.
Grace St.
Franklin St.
Main St.
Cary St.
Canal St.

3rd St.
2nd St.
1st St.
Foushee St.
Adams St.
Jefferson St.
Madison St.
Monroe St.
Henry St.

Jackson St.
Leigh St.
Clay St.
Marshall St.
Brook St.

Belvidere St.

Gilmer St.
Goshen St.

Hancock St.
Harrison St.

Kinney St.
Bowe St.
Lombardy St.

Allen St.

Hermitage Rd.

Broad St.
Grace St.
Monument Ave.
Park Ave.
Stuart Ave.
Hanover St.
Grove St.
Stafford St.
Davis St.
Robinson St.
Mulberry St.

The Boulevard

Laurel St.
Cherry St.
Linden St.
Beech St.
Morris St.
Harvie St.
Plum St.
Lombardy St.
Vine St.
Allen St.
Granby St.
Meadow St.
Rowland St.
Shields Ave.
Addison St.

Belvidere St.
Harrison St.
Randolph St.
Lombardy St.
Idlewood St.
Allen St.
Grayland St.
Rosewood St.

Floyd St.
Main St.
Cary St.
Parkwood St.

Colonial St.

440 yards
400 meters

0   0

Agecroft Hall, **13**
Canal Walk, **6**
Edgar Allen Poe
Museum, **7**
John Marshall
House, **2**
Maggie Walker
National Historic
Site, **10**

Museum and
White House of the
Confederacy, **4**
Richmond National
Battlefield Park, **9**
St. John's Episcopal
Church, **8**
Science Museum of
Virginia, **11**

Valentine Museum, **3**
Virginia Museum
of Fine Arts, **12**
Virginia State
Capitol, **5**

restored and furnished, combines neoclassical motifs and the Federal style; it has wood paneling and wainscoting, arched narrow passageways, and a mix of period pieces and heirlooms. *9th and Marshall Sts., tel. 804/648–7998. Admission: $3 adults, $2.50 senior citizens, $1.25 children 7–12. Open Apr.–Sept., Tues.–Sat. 10–5, Sun. 1–5; Oct.–Mar., Tues.–Sat. 10–4:30, Sun. 1–4:30.*

❸ The **Valentine Museum** impressively documents the life and history of Richmond. **Wickham House** (1812), a part of the Valentine, is more rightly called a mansion; it was designed by architect Alexander Parris, the creator of Boston's Faneuil Hall. John Wickham was Richmond's wealthiest citizen of the time, and Daniel Webster and Zachary Taylor were frequent guests at the house, which is stunning inside. Not all at the museum is opulence, however—the slave quarters, also meticulously restored, provide a chilling contrast to the mansion's splendor. The Valentine Riverside, on the site of the former Tredegar Iron Foundry (*see* Canal Walk, *below*) in the heart of downtown, is an extensive renovation-in-progress; call ahead to find out what's open and what's showing. *1015 E. Clay St., tel. 804/ 649–0711. Admission: $3.50 adults, $3 senior citizens, $2.75 students, $1.50 children 7–12. Open Mon.–Sat. 10–5, Sun. noon–5.*

❹ The **Museum and White House of the Confederacy** are best seen in that order. The former offers elaborate permanent exhibitions on the Civil War era. The "world's largest collection of Confederate memorabilia" features such relics as the sword Robert E. Lee wore for his surrender at Appomattox. At the White House next door, preservationists have painstakingly re-created the interior as it was during the Civil War, when Jefferson Davis lived here. A brick house built in 1818, the building has been stuccoed to give the appearance of large stone blocks. Despite its name, it has always been painted gray. Group dinners with a Civil War theme are held here. *1201 E. Clay St., tel. 804/649–1861. Admission to one site: $4 adults, $3.50 senior citizens, $2.25 children 7–12; both sites: $7 adults, $5 senior citizens, $3.50 children. Open Mon.–Sat. 10–5, Sun. 1–5.*

❺ The **Virginia State Capitol** was designed by Thomas Jefferson in 1785, modeled on a Roman temple in the south of France. It contains a wealth of sculpture: busts of each of the eight presidents that Virginia has given the nation, and a famous life-size—and lifelike—statue of George Washington by Houdon. In the old Hall of the House of Delegates, Robert E. Lee accepted the command of the Confederate forces in Virginia (a bronze statue marks the spot where he stood). Elsewhere on the grounds, at the Old Bell Tower, you can get travel information for the entire state. *Capitol Sq., tel. 804/786–4344. Admission free. Open Apr.–Nov., daily 9–5; Dec.–Mar., Mon.–Sat. 9–5, Sun. 1–5.*

❻ **Canal Walk,** beginning south of the capitol at 12th and Main streets, follows the locks of the James River–Kanawha Canal proposed by George Washington to bring ships around the falls of the James River. Along the course of the walk, plaques note historic points of interest. At 12th and Byrd streets, a restored lock has been incorporated into Kanawha Park, where, under the archway, a free slide show (daily 9–5) recounts the history of the canal. The walk continues over a footbridge to Brown's Island, across from the ruins of the Tredegar Iron Foundry, a vital supplier of cannons throughout the Civil War. The island, terminus of the scenic walk, boasts a heliport and sculptures and hosts concerts in the warmer months.

On leaving downtown Richmond, follow Main Street east to the Church Hill Historic District to reach the **Edgar Allan Poe Museum** in the Old Stone House. Poe grew up in Richmond, and, although he never lived in this structure of 1737, his disciples have made it a shrine, displaying some of the writer's possessions. The Raven Room is hung with illustrations inspired by his most famous poem. *1914 E. Main St., tel. 804/648–5523. Admission: $5 adults, $4 senior citizens, $3 students. Open Tues.–Sat. 10–4, Sun.–Mon. 1:30–4.*

Three blocks north is Broad Street, which leads east to **St. John's Episcopal Church.** For security reasons, the rebellious Second Virginia Convention met here instead of at Williamsburg, and it was in this church on March 23, 1775, that Patrick Henry delivered the speech in which he demanded, "Give me liberty or give me death!" The speech is reenacted every Sunday in summer at 2 PM. Those planning a Saturday visit should call ahead, especially in May and June; weddings often close the church to the public. *2401 E. Broad St. at 24th St., tel. 804/648–5015. Admission: $2 adults, $1.50 senior citizens, $1 children 7–18. Open Mon.–Sat. 10–4, Sun. 1–4.*

At the eastern end of Broad Street, the visitor center for **Richmond National Battlefield Park** is the launching point for tours of the Richmond battlefield and others nearby. Three campaigns were fought here: the Seven Days Battle (1862) and the Battle of Cold Harbor (1864), both Confederate victories, and the Battle of Fort Harrison (1864), a Union victory. Here you can see a movie about the city during the war and a slide show about the battlefields, then pick up a map for a self-guided tour. *3215 E. Broad St., tel. 804/226–1981. Admission free. Open daily 9–5. Closed Christmas Day.*

Maggie Walker National Historical Site, the home of a pioneering African-American businesswoman and educator, is now part of the battlefield-system tour administered by Battlefield Park personnel. Visitors may take a 30-minute tour of the furnished 22-room brick house where she lived from 1904 to 1934 and see a movie detailing her accomplishments. *110½ E. Leigh St., tel. 804/780–1380. Admission free. Open Wed.–Sun. 9–5.*

Continuing west on Broad Street, one finds the **Science Museum of Virginia** housed in the old train station, a massive domed building on the north side of the street. Aerospace and Crystal World are among the instructive exhibits here, many of which strongly appeal to children. The biggest spectacle is in the Universe Theater, also a planetarium, where an Omnimax screen draws the audience into the movie or the star show. *2500 W. Broad St., tel. 804/367–1080. Admission to museum: $4.50 adults, $4 senior citizens and children 4–17; Omnimax and planetarium: $3 adults, $2 senior citizens and children, with general admission. Open Mon.–Sat. 9:30–5, Sun. noon–5 (Fri. until 9 in summer).*

Go two blocks farther west on Broad Street and turn south on the Boulevard to find the **Fan District**—a fashionable neighborhood of restored turn-of-the-century town houses—and the **Virginia Museum of Fine Arts.** The museum's most startling pieces are Duane Hanson's true-to-life wax figures; their unglamorous everyday attire and provocative poses frequently lead visitors to think the figures are living persons. Among the more important works are paintings by Goya, Renoir, Monet, and Van Gogh; African masks, Roman statuary, Oriental icons; and five Fabergé eggs. *Boulevard and Grove Ave., tel. 804/367–0844. Admission: $4 suggested. Open Tues.–Sun. 11–5 (Thurs. until 8).*

Just west of the Fan District, in the Windsor Farms neighborhood, ⑬ stands **Agecroft Hall,** built in Lancashire, England, in the 15th century and transported here in 1925. Set amid gardens, the country manor-house contains an extensive assortment of Tudor and early Stuart art and furniture (1485–1660) and a few priceless collector's items, such as a Ming vase. *4305 Sulgrave Rd., tel. 804/353–4241. Admission: $4 adults, $3.50 senior citizens, $2 students. Open Tues.–Sat. 10–4, Sun. 12:30–5.*

The Piedmont

⑭ **Petersburg,** 20 miles south of Richmond on I–95, was the so-called last ditch of the Confederacy. A major railroad hub, the city was a crucial link in the supply chain for Lee's army. Grant laid siege to it for 10 months, and its capitulation in 1865 precipitated the evacuation of Richmond and the subsequent surrender at Appomattox.

At the **Petersburg National Battlefield,** visitors can tread ground that absorbed the blood of more than 60,000 Union and Confederate soldiers. A pronounced depression in the ground is the eroded remnant of the Crater, the result of a 4-ton gunpowder explosion set off by Northern forces in one failed attack. The 1,500-acre park is laced with several miles of earthworks and includes two forts. In the visitor center, maps and models convey background information vital to the self-guided driving tour. Visitors park at specified spots on the tour road and proceed on foot to nearby points of interest. *Rte. 36, Petersburg, tel. 804/732–3531. Admission: $4 car, $2 cyclist or pedestrian. Open mid-June–Aug., daily 8–7; Sept.–mid-June, daily 8–5.*

All Petersburg attractions listed below are located in Old Towne and can be found easily by walking around or asking someone to direct you. Petersburg's visitor centers sell a variety of passes that offer reduced admission to Old Towne museums and attractions, including the Appomattox Iron Works.

In Old Towne Petersburg the Civil War is examined from a purely local perspective. Exhibits at the **Siege Museum** concentrate on details of ordinary civilian life in embattled Petersburg during the last year of the war. A short film narrated by the actor Joseph Cotten dramatizes the upheaval. *15 W. Bank St., tel. 804/733–2402. Admission: $2 adults, $1.50 children. Open Mon.–Sat. 9–5, Sun. 12:30–5.*

The **Trapezium House of 1817** is named for its geometric shape: four sides, none of them parallel. The construction is said to have followed a Caribbean superstition learned by the builder from one of his servants—that parallel lines and right angles harbor evil spirits. No parallels or right angles occur in the house. *N. Market St., tel. 804/733–2400. Admission: $1 adults, 75¢ children. Open Feb.–Nov., Mon.–Sat. 10:30–3:30, Sun. 12:30–3:30.*

The **Centre Hill Mansion** (1823) has been furnished with Victorian antiques, including a grand piano 3 yards long, in accord with the period of its last remodeling—in 1901. The house had previously been remodeled in the 1840s. *Centre Hill Ct., tel. 804/733–2400. Admission: $2 adults, $1.50 children. Open Mon.–Sat. 9–5, Sun. 12:30–5.*

Farmers Bank (1817) is one of the oldest bank buildings in the nation. This Federal-style brick building was restored by the Association for the Preservation of Virginia Antiquities. *19 Bollingbrook St., tel. 804/733–2400. Admission: $1 adults, 75¢ children. Open Feb.–Nov., Mon.–Sat. 9:30–3:30.*

Appomattox Iron Works, a still active relic of the early industrial age, features craftsmen and interpreters who work in the more than 20 blacksmith and machine shops the way their ancestors did in the 19th century. Also on the grounds are a restaurant, a tavern, and a company store. *20–28 Old St., tel. 804/733–7300 or 800/232–4766. Admission: $6.95 adults; $5.95 senior citizens, students 12 and older, and active-duty military; $4.50 children 6–11. Open daily 10–5; closed Christmas Day.*

⓯ Charlottesville, 20 miles east of Waynesboro and the southern end of the Skyline Drive, is the epitome of Virginia's Piedmont area, and the major attraction in the Piedmont is nearby Monticello, the distinguished home that Thomas Jefferson designed and built for himself. In Charlottesville, the **visitor bureau** (*see* Important Addresses and Numbers, *above*) on Route 20 distributes a walking-tour map of the downtown historic district, though there is little to see here. The downtown pedestrian shopping mall stretches along six blocks of Main Street, with fountains, outdoor restaurants, and restored buildings lining a brick-paved street.

A good place to start is the **Thomas Jefferson Visitors Center,** where the exhibit "Thomas Jefferson at Monticello" provides extensive background information on both house and owner, and artifacts recovered during recent archaeological excavations are on display. A stop here is a must, either before or after visiting Monticello, because there is so much that is not explained on the house tour. *Rte. 20 S from Charlottesville (I–64 Monticello, Exit 121), tel. 804/977–1783. Open Mar.–Oct., daily 9–5:30; Nov.–Feb., daily 9–5.*

Monticello, the most famous of Jefferson's homes and his monument to himself, is a masterwork that was constructed over a period of 40 years, 1769–1809. Typical of no single architectural style, it is characteristic of Jefferson, who made a statement with every detail. The staircases are narrow and hidden because he considered them unsightly and a waste of space; and contrary to plantation tradition, his outbuildings are in the back, not on the east side, where his guests would arrive. In these respects and in its overall conception, Monticello was a revolutionary structure, a neoclassical repudiation of the prevalent English Georgian style and of the colonial mentality behind it. As if to reflect this subversive aspect, a concave mirror in the entrance hall presents you with your own image, upside down. Throughout the house are Jefferson's inventions, including a seven-day clock and a "polygraph," a two-pen contraption that allowed him to make a copy of his correspondence as he wrote it. The Thomas Jefferson Center for Historic Plants features interpretive gardens, exhibits, and a sales area. Tour guides are happy to answer questions, but they must move visitors through the house quickly because another group is always waiting. It is impossible to see everything in one visit. *Rte. 53, tel. 804/984–9800. Admission: $8 adults, $7 senior citizens, $4 children 6–11. Open Mar.–Oct., daily 8–5; Nov.–Feb., daily 9–4:30. Closed Christmas Day.*

Modest **Ash Lawn–Highland,** on Route 795, 3 miles southwest of Monticello, is—like its grand neighbor—marked by the personality of the president who lived in it and who held more major national offices than any other man of his era. It is no longer the simple farmhouse built in 1799 for James Monroe, who lived in the L-shaped single story at the rear; a later owner added the more prominent two-story section, though the furniture is mostly original, and it is not hard to imagine Monroe here at his retreat. Small rooms are crowded with gifts from notable persons and with souvenirs from his time as envoy to France. Such coziness befits the fifth U.S. president, the first to come from the middle class. Ash Lawn–Highland today is a working plantation, where spectacular peacocks roam the grounds. *Rte. 795 (southwest of Rte. 53), tel. 804/293–9539. Admission: $6 adults, $5.50 senior citizens, $3 children 6–11; group rates available. Open Mar.–Oct., daily 9–6; Nov.–Feb., daily 10–5.*

Its proximity to Monticello and Ash Lawn–Highland has made **Historic Michie Tavern** on Route 53 a popular attraction. Most of the complex was built 17 miles from here at Earlysville, in 1784, and moved here piece by piece in 1927. Costumed hostesses lead visitors into a series of rooms, where they play recorded interpretations of the interiors. A visit here is not as entertaining or educational as the tour of the Rising Sun Tavern in Fredericksburg, for the narration is less informative and the conditions too tidy. The restaurant's "Colonial" lunch is fried chicken. The old gristmill has been converted into a gift shop. *Rte. 53, tel. 804/977–1234. Admission: $5 adults; $4.50 senior citizens, students, military; $1 children under 12. Open daily 9–5, except Dec. 25 and Jan. 1.*

At the west end of town, the **University of Virginia,** one of the nation's most distinguished institutions of higher education, was founded and designed by Thomas Jefferson, who called himself its "father" in his own epitaph. A poll of experts at the time of the U.S. bicentennial designated this complex "the proudest achievement of American architecture in the past 200 years." Students vie for the rooms in the original pavilions that flank the lawn, a graduated expanse that flows down from the Rotunda, a half-scale replica of the Pantheon in Rome. Behind the pavilions, gardens and landscaping are laced with serpentine walls. Tours begin indoors in the rotunda, entrance on the lawn side, lower level. *Tel. 804/982–3200. Free 30-min.–1-hr. historic tours daily at 10, 11, 2, 3, 4. Rotunda open daily 9–4:45; closed during winter break.*

Time Out **Martha's Café** (11 Elliewood Ave., tel. 804/971–7530) is a pleasant place to have lunch with University of Virginia students; try the enchiladas or a vegetarian entrée. In warm weather, ask for a table on the patio, which is lush with potted plants.

Between Monticello and Ash Lawn–Highland, at the intersection of Routes 53 and 735, is **Jefferson Vineyards** (Rte. 9, Box 293, Charlottesville 22902, tel. 804/977–3042). Home to Gabriele Rausse, the "guardian angel of Virginia vineyards," the establishment is open March–November, daily 11–5.

Afton Mountain Vineyards (Rte. 3, Box 574, Afton 22920, tel. 703/456–8667), which in recent years has won international awards for its Chenin Blanc and Gewürtztraminer, also thrives on its stunning panoramic views of Piedmont landscape and ridgelines. Tours and tastings are free Wednesday–Monday 10–6 (until 5 in winter). Contact the **Jeffersonian Wine Grape Growers Society** (Rte. 5, Box 429, Charlottesville 22901, tel. 804/296–4188) to get brochures about other vineyards in the foothills around Charlottesville.

The pastoral background of Route 20 as it winds its way to Orange, 25 miles northeast of Charlottesville, makes the drive a pleasure in itself. Near **Barboursville** on Route 33, the **Barboursville Vineyards** are the oldest vineyards in a state whose young wine industry is already the third-largest in the United States, after those of California and New York. They were planted in 1976 by the sixth generation of an Italian viticulturalist dynasty on the former plantation of James Barbour, governor of the commonwealth from 1812 to 1814. The extensive ruins of his house, gutted by fire in 1884, afford a structural look at Jeffersonian architecture—the third president designed the building to resemble his own Monticello. During the first three weekends of August, "Shakespeare at the Ruins" presents outdoor performances of the Bard's classics amid this awesome setting; theatergoers have the option to purchase a modest dinner provided by a local caterer. *Rte. 777, RFD 1, Box 136, tel. 703/832–3824. Admission free. Tastings: Mon.–Sat. 10–5; Sun. 11–5; tours: Sat. 10–4:30; closed Sun.*

⑰ On Route 20, just west of **Orange,** is the residence of the fourth president of the United States, James Madison. Yet **Montpelier** in its present state has more to do with its 20th-century owners, the Du Pont family, who enlarged and redecorated it. This dual legacy poses a dilemma in the restoration, for today the house only vaguely resembles itself as it was in Madison's time. Markings on walls, floors, and ceilings, which show the locations of underlying door and window frames and other features, are guides to the restoration in progress. The process is slow, to the credit of the diligent preservationists of the National Trust. With a little imagination and attention to the guide's eloquent and evocative narration, one can appreciate the history of this mostly empty house. The building can be seen only on a guided tour of 1½ to two hours, which begins with a slide show on the history of the house, followed by a bus tour of the farm and paddock area, a tour of the mansion, and free time to wander the grounds, gardens, and the cemetery where James and his wife, Dolley, and other Madisons are buried. The annual Montpelier Hunt Races (steeplechase), which have been held since 1934, are run on the first Saturday in November, at which time the house tour does not run. Admission to the races is $5. *Rte. 20, 4 mi south of Orange, tel. 703/672–2728. Admission: $6 adults, $5 senior citizens, $1 children 6–12. Open daily 10–4.*

In the town of Orange, **St. Thomas's Episcopal Church** (1833) is the one surviving example of Jeffersonian church architecture, a replica of Charlottesville's demolished Christ Church, which Jefferson designed. St. Thomas's, where Robert E. Lee worshipped during the winter of 1863–64, boasts a Tiffany window. *119 Caroline St., tel. 703/672–3761. Admission by contribution. Tours by appointment with the James Madison Museum.*

Next door to the church, the **James Madison Museum** presents a comprehensive exhibition on the Founding Father most responsible for the Constitution. The collection includes some of the china and glassware recovered from the White House before the British torched it during the War of 1812. The fourth president's tiny Campeachy chair, an 18th-century recliner, betrays his small stature. *129 Caroline St., tel. 703/672–1776. Admission: $3 adults, $2.50 senior citizens, 50¢ children 6–16. Open Mar.–Nov., weekdays 9–4, weekends 1–4; Dec.–Feb., weekdays 9–4.*

⑱ Well to the south in the Piedmont, 60 miles southwest of Charlottesville on Route 29, is the city of **Lynchburg.** Although its founder, John Lynch, was a Quaker pacifist, the city's most prominent landmark is **Monument Terrace,** a war memorial: At the foot and head of the 139 limestone and granite steps that lead to the Old City Courthouse are statues honoring a World War I doughboy and a Confederate soldier. Visitors who hesitate to make the climb should at least catch the dramatic view from the bottom of Court House Hill, at Main and Ninth streets. Self-guided walking tours designed by, and available from, the Lynchburg Visitors Information Center cover the historic Riverfront and Diamond Hill sections.

The **Confederate Cemetery** and garden of 60 roses (representing the history of the plant from 1565 to 1900) are next to the **Pest House Medical Museum,** which provides a brief but informative look into medical practices and instruments at the time of the Civil War and later. The 1840s frame building was the office of Dr. John Jay Terrell. *4th and Taylor Sts., tel. 804/384–8337. Admission: $1. Open daily sunrise to sunset; tours by appointment.*

Another hilltop landmark, northwest of Monument Terrace, is **Point of Honor,** a mansion on Daniel's Hill that was built in 1815 on the site of a duel. Once part of a 900-acre estate, this red-brick house surrounded by lawns retains a commanding view of the James River. The facade is elegantly symmetrical, with two octagonal bays joined by a balustrade on each of the building's two stories. The interiors have been restored and furnished with pieces authentic to the early 19th-century Federal period, including wallpaper whose pattern is in the permanent collection of the Metropolitan Museum of Art in New York. *112 Cabell St., tel. 804/847–1459. Admission: $3 adults, $1 children 13–18. Open daily 1–4.*

⓳ In **Forest,** less than 5 miles southwest of Lynchburg, you can visit **Jefferson's Poplar Forest,** an even more impressive piece of octagonal architecture. This Palladian hermitage (the president conceived and built it as his "occasional retreate," where he sometimes stayed between 1806 and 1813) exemplifies the architect's sublime sense of order that is so evident at Monticello. Erected on a slope, the front of the house is one story high, its rear elevation two stories. The octagon's center is a square, skylit dining room flanked by two smaller octagons. The attraction here is the economy of space throughout, never mind the unfinished state of the restoration. Every July 4th, on Independence Day, a free celebration is held here. *Rte. 661, Forest, tel. 804/525–1806. Admission: $5 adults, $4 senior citizens, $1 children. Open Apr.–Nov., Wed.–Sun. and major holidays 10–4.*

⓴ Twenty miles east of Lynchburg, an American shrine, the village of **Appomattox Court House,** has been restored to its appearance of April 9, 1865, when General Lee surrendered the Army of Northern Virginia to General Grant. Among the 27 structures in the national historical park, most of which can be entered, is the reconstructed McLean House, in whose parlor the articles of surrender were signed. The self-guided tour is well planned and introduced by exhibits and slide shows in the reconstructed courthouse. First-person interpreters cast as soldiers and villagers answer questions in the summer. *Rte. 24, tel. 804/352–8987. Admission: $2 adults. Open June–Aug., daily 9–5:30; Sept.–May, daily 8:30–5.*

㉑ Thirty-five miles southeast of Lynchburg or 26 miles south of Appomattox Court House is **Red Hill Patrick Henry National Memorial.** The final home of Revolutionary War patriot Patrick Henry, whose "Give me liberty or give me death" speech inspired a generation, has been restored near an original law office and contains numerous Henry-family furnishings. Other buildings, including a coachman's cabin and stable, stand near a garden and a boxwood maze. Henry's grave is located on the property. *S.R. 501, Brookneal 24528, tel. 804/376–2044. Admission: $3 adults, $2 senior citizens, $1 students. Open Apr.–Oct., daily 9–5; Nov.–Mar., daily 9–4.*

What to See and Do with Children

At Charlottesville's **Virginia Discovery Museum** children can step inside a giant kaleidoscope or into basketball star Ralph Sampson's uniform. Plays and musical performances are given, and the hands-on exhibits are intended to develop both the imagination and such basic skills as shoelace tying. *400 Ackley La., tel. 804/977–1025. Admission: $3 adults, $2 senior citizens and children 1–13. Open Tues.–Sat. 10–5, Sun. 1–5; free first Sun. of each month.*

Petersburg's **Softball Hall of Fame Museum** features videos of great games and memorabilia of players inducted into the United States Slo-Pitch Softball Association Hall of Fame. *3935 S. Crater Rd., tel. 804/733–1005. Admission: $1.50 adults, $1 senior citizens and students. Open weekdays 9–4, Sat. 11–4, Sun. 1–4; closed holidays.*

The **Paramount King's Dominion** entertainment complex in Doswell is great for children, but parents will need to bring lots of money and patience; lines often begin forming an hour before the park opens. A monorail takes visitors through a game preserve, and there are more than 100 rides, including a stand-up roller coaster and, since 1994, "The Hurler"—another scary coaster located in a section of the park whose theme is the parent company's popular *Wayne's World* movies. *I–95 (Doswell Exit), tel. 804/876–5000. Admission: $26.95 adults and children over 6, $21.95 senior citizens, $18.95 children 3–6. Parking: $4. Open June, daily 10–8; July–Aug., daily 10–10; Apr.–May and Sept.–Oct., weekends 9:30–8.*

Shopping

Shopping Districts   **6th Street Marketplace,** Richmond, has specialty shops, chain stores, and eating places.

Shockoe Slip, on East Cary Street between 12th and 15th streets in Richmond—a neighborhood of tobacco warehouses in the 18th and 19th centuries—is now full of boutiques and branches of upscale specialty stores.

Downtown Mall on Main Street, Charlottesville, is a six-block brick pedestrian mall with specialty stores, restaurants, and bars in restored 19th- and early 20th-century buildings.

Food Markets   The **Farmers Market** at 17th and Main streets, Richmond, makes fresh farm produce available directly to the consumer. Art galleries, boutiques, and antiques shops, many in converted warehouses and factories, are nearby.

Lynchburg's **Community Market** (12th and Main Sts., tel. 804/847–1499), one of Virginia's oldest (1783), still sets up weekdays 7–2, Saturdays 6–2. Vegetables, homemade foods, fruits, and handmade crafts are for sale.

Sports and Outdoor Activities

Participant Sports

Golf   **The Crossings** (Jct. I–95 and I–295, Glen Allen, tel. 804/266–2254), north of Richmond, has an 18-hole course open to the public.

Jogging   Joggers in Richmond use the running track in the park around the **Randolph Pool** (Idlewood Ave.) and the fitness track in **Byrd Park,** off the Boulevard.

Rafting   **Richmond Raft** (tel. 804/222–7238) offers guided white-water rafting through the heart of the city on the James River (class 3 and 4 rapids), float trips upriver, and overnight camping and rafting trips from March through November.

Spectator Sports

The **Richmond Coliseum** (tel. 804/780–4956) hosts ice shows, basketball, wrestling, and tennis tournaments; the coliseum seats 12,000.

Auto Racing In September and March, races (NASCAR Miller Genuine Draft, Autolite Platinum; Winston Cup, respectively) are held at the **Richmond Fairgrounds Raceway** (I–64 Laburnum Ave. Exit, tel. 804/329–6796 or 804/329–7223 for ticket information).

Baseball The Richmond Braves, a Triple-A farm team for Atlanta, play at **The Diamond** (tel. 804/359–4444), a 12,500-seat stadium.

Basketball In the Richmond area, games at Randolph-Macon College, the University of Richmond, Virginia Commonwealth University, and Virginia Union University are listed in the *Times-Dispatch* and the *News Leader*.

The **University of Virginia** in Charlottesville is nationally or regionally ranked in several varsity sports. In season, you can watch the Cavaliers play first-rate ACC basketball in University Hall. There are also football at Scott Stadium, baseball, soccer, and lacrosse. The *Cavalier Daily* has sports listings.

Dining and Lodging

The established upmarket dining rooms of Richmond are dependable and respected, and the adventurous will keep an eye out as well for the intriguing new bistros, particularly in the Fan District, that often lead brief but exciting lives. Charlottesville, with a population of writers and artists, offers esoteric Asian and French cuisines.

Richmond's hotel rates are fair for a city of its size, but standards of service lag behind those of many smaller communities; it has a smaller range of choices for the money than, for example, Williamsburg, but it does boast some luxurious accommodations. Lodging in Charlottesville will be almost impossible during University of Virginia commencement week (in May) and hard to find when a home basketball game is scheduled. A B&B service for the area is **Guesthouse Bed & Breakfast** (Box 5737, Charlottesville 22905, tel. 804/979–7264). For $1 you can get a brochure about local B&Bs.

Highly recommended establishments are indicated by a star ★.

Charlottesville **C&O Restaurant.** A boarded-up storefront hung with an illuminated
Dining Pepsi sign conceals one of the best restaurants in town. The stark
★ white formal dining room upstairs (seatings at 6:30 and 9:30) features fine regional French cuisine. Among the appetizers is a *terrine de campagne* (pâté of veal, venison, and pork); the entrées include coquilles St. Jacques. The wine list offers 300 varieties. A lively and less formal bistro (open daily) downstairs serves pâtés, cheese, and light meals. *515 E. Water St., tel. 804/971–7044. Reservations advised. Jacket and tie strongly recommended (casual dress downstairs). MC, V. Closed Sun. $$$$*

★ **Eastern Standard.** Specialties in the formal dining room upstairs include rainbow trout stuffed with shiitake mushrooms, wild rice, and fontina cheese; oysters cooked in a champagne and caviar sauce; and loin of lamb with mint pesto. Curries and stir-fry Asian dishes are also offered. The crowded and lively bistro downstairs serves pastas and light fare to taped music, primarily jazz and rock. *Downtown Mall, tel. 804/295–8668. Reservations advised. Dress: casual. AE, MC, V. No lunch. Closed Sun. $$$*

Old Mill Room. A fireplace, wrought-iron chandeliers, and prints and posters depicting the gristmill built here in 1834 set the mood in this dining room of the Boar's Head Inn, 1½ miles west of Charlottesville on Route 250 West. Waiters and waitresses in Colonial dress serve such offerings as veal Oscar (veal topped with crabmeat, asparagus spears, and béarnaise sauce) and prime rib. Light fare is available in the tavern downstairs. *Boar's Head Inn, U.S. 250, tel. 804/296–2181. Reservations advised. Dress: casual. AE, DC, MC, V. $$$*

★ **Crozet Pizza.** With 18 toppings to choose from, including snow peas and asparagus spears, this popular parlor 12 miles west of Charlottesville has some of Virginia's best pizza. On the weekend, take-out must be ordered hours in advance. Diners in the restaurant find hardwood floors and booths, portraits of the owners' forebears, and one wall covered with business cards from around the world. *Rte. 240, Crozet, tel. 804/823–2132. Reservations not required. Dress: casual. No credit cards. Closed Sun., Mon. $$*

Hardware Store. Deli sandwiches, burgers, salads, seafood, and ice cream from the soda fountain are today's merchandise in this former Victorian hardware store. Some of the original wood paneling and brick walls remain from 1890. Outdoor dining is popular in the warm-weather months. *316 E. Main St., tel. 804/977–1518. Reservations not required. Dress: casual. MC, V. Closed Sun. No dinner Mon. $$*

Lodging **Boar's Head Inn.** A gristmill built in 1834 of brick and wood construction has the character today of a late Victorian English inn. At this luxurious resort on two small lakes, 1½ miles west of Charlottesville on Route 250, the simple but elegant rooms and suites are furnished chiefly with antiques. Some suites have fireplaces, some are efficiencies; some rooms have king- or queen-size beds. *U.S. 250, Box 5307, 22905, tel. 804/296–2181, fax 804/977–1306. 173 rooms, 11 suites. Facilities: 3 restaurants, 3 pools, 17 tennis courts, 3 squash courts, racquetball court, biking, fishing, dry-rock saunas, massage, hot-air ballooning. AE, D, DC, MC, V. $$$$*

★ **Mayhurst.** A Victorian home built in 1859 by a grandnephew of James Madison makes a cozy and comfortable B&B surrounded by 36 acres of woods and hiking trails near Orange, about 30 miles northeast of Monticello. All rooms are decorated with early Victorian antiques. *U.S. 15, Box 707, Orange 22960, tel. 703/672–5597. 6 rooms, 1 guest house. Facilities: pond fishing, swimming. MC, V. $$$$*

Omni Charlottesville. This relatively new, attractive addition to the luxury chain looms over the Downtown Mall. The triangular rooms at the point of the wedge-shaped building get light from windows on two sides. Blond wood and maroon fabrics, in a mixture of modern and Colonial styles, decorate the guest quarters, and potted plants soften the look of the bright atrium lobby. Ask about weekend discounts and "supersaver" and "B and B" discounts in summer. *235 W. Main St., 22902, tel. 804/971–5500 or 800/843–6664, fax 804/979–4456. 208 rooms, 3 suites. Facilities: restaurant, nightclub, bar, indoor pool, outdoor pool, hot tub and saunas, whirlpool, exercise room. AE, DC, MC, V. $$$$*

Prospect Hill. This former plantation house was rebuilt in Victorian times, when columns and decorative cornice borders were added. Four furnished rooms and one suite are in the main house, where dinner (one sitting) is a leisurely production by the family of innkeepers. But the prize quarters are the eight refurbished rooms and suites in dependencies (outbuildings)—one is a cottage, one a carriage house, and several have Jacuzzis. The B&B is 20 miles east of Monticello. *Rte. 3, Box 430, Trevilians 23093, tel. 703/967-0844 or 800/277-0844, fax 804/967-0102. 13 rooms. Facilities: restaurant, pool. MC, V. MAP rates. $$$$*

★ **200 South Street Inn.** Two historic houses, one of them a former brothel, have been combined and restored to create this old-fashioned inn in the historic district. Furnishings throughout are English and Belgian antiques. Several rooms come with a canopy bed, sitting room, fireplace, and whirlpool. *200 South St., 22901, tel. 804/979-0200, fax 804/979-4403. 17 rooms, 3 suites. AE, MC, V. $$$$*

High Meadows. Two styles of architecture are joined by a hall in this bed-and-breakfast listed on the National Register of Historic Places and located 15 miles south of Monticello. Five rooms in the Victorian section and three rooms in the Federal section feature curtains and bed hangings of fabrics with a handcrafted look. By arrangement, the kitchen will prepare hot gourmet baskets (cassoulet is one option) to take away for afternoon and evening meals. *Rte. 4, Box 6, Scottsville 24590, tel. 804/286-2218. 12 rooms, 4 suites, 1 cottage. AE, MC, V. Rates include breakfast. $$$*

Sheraton Charlottesville. This modern Sheraton hotel, situated on a hill 7 miles north of town, overlooks the Blue Ridge Mountains. Rooms have contemporary furnishings in muted tones, two restaurants feature Continental dining, and full conference facilities are available. *2350 Seminole Trail (U.S. 29), 22901, tel. 804/973-2121 or 800/325-3535, fax 804/978-7735. 240 rooms. Facilities: 2 restaurants, bar, indoor pool, outdoor pool, 2 tennis courts. AE, D, DC, MC, V. $$$*

★ **Silver Thatch Inn.** Four-poster beds and period antiques are just part of the charm at this 18th-century white-clapboard Colonial farmhouse. The inn is set off a tranquil road a few miles north of town, and the friendly hosts provide complimentary transportation to the airport and help guests arrange outdoor activities at nearby locations. The restaurant has an award-winning wine cellar and is quite popular. As visitors often discover to their chagrin that the dining room is booked solid, guests should reserve a table in advance to sample offerings such as roast quail, the fresh fish, and rabbits and chickens locally raised on organic farms. *3001 Hollymead Dr., 22901, tel. 804/978-4686, fax 804/973-6156. 7 rooms. Facilities: restaurant, outdoor pool, 2 tennis courts. DC, MC, V. $$$*

Best Western Cavalier Inn. Teal and plum are the dominant colors of the contemporary furnishings in the guest rooms, which were renovated in 1991. The nearby grounds of the University of Virginia are delightful for strolling, and full exercise facilities are free to guests at a fitness club 3 miles from the hotel. Monticello is within easy driving distance. *105 Emmet St., 22905, tel. 804/296-8111 or 800/528-1234, fax 804/296-3523. 118 rooms. Facilities: restaurant, bar, outdoor pool. AE, D, DC, MC, V. Rates include Continental breakfast. $$*

English Inn. This inn is a model treatment of the B&B theme on a large but comfortable scale that includes a three-story atrium lobby with cascading plants. A Continental breakfast is served in a 150-year-old Tudor-style dining room with fireplace. The suite accommodations have a sitting room, wet bar, king-size bed, and reproduction antiques; other rooms have modern furnishings. *2000 Morton Dr., 22901, tel. 804/971-9900 or 800/338-9900, fax 804/973-6156. 67 rooms, 21 suites. Facilities: restaurant, bar, indoor pool, sauna, exercise equipment. AE, DC, MC, V. Rates include Continental breakfast. $$*

Econo Lodge. Parents of University of Virginia students make up a large part of the clientele at this budget chain motel. It's handily located in the university neighborhood, across from the sports arena. Brown tones predominate the furnishings. *400 Emmet St., 22903, tel. 804/296-2104. 60 rooms. Facilities: outdoor pool. AE, D, DC, MC, V. $*

Richmond Dining

La Petite France. The emerald green walls and tuxedoed waiters signal a formal and traditional dining atmosphere. Reproductions of 18th-century English landscapes and portraits hang on the walls. The diners seated at the 40 tables covered with white linen cloths are largely middle-aged and quiet; one dish they frequently order is lobster whiskey (lobster meat baked in a puff pastry with whiskey sauce). Among other specialties are Chateaubriand and Dover sole amandine. *2108 Maywill St., tel. 804/353-8729. Reservations advised. Jacket and tie suggested. AE, DC, MC, V. Closed Sun., Mon. $$$*

★ **Mr. Patrick Henry's Inn.** Two houses circa 1858 were restored and joined to create this restaurant and inn (three suites upstairs have kitchenette and fireplace). Antiques and fireplaces in the dining room contribute to the Colonial ambience, an English pub is in the basement, and there's a garden café. Especially popular dishes are the crisp roast duck with crushed-plum sauce, and crab cakes (crabmeat and spices in a puff pastry). *2300 E. Broad St., tel. 804/ 644-1322. Reservations advised. Jacket and tie advised upstairs. AE, DC, MC, V. $$$*

Amici Ristorante. Authentic northern Italian cuisine, including game specialties such as stuffed quail, duck, and venison sautéed in juniper berry sauce, are regularly on the menu alongside calamari, fresh pasta, and veal dishes. A cozy atmosphere prevails on the first floor of the restaurant, where the walls around the booths are adorned with flowered tapestries and oil paintings of Italy. The second floor is more formally decorated, and the white walls are trimmed with stenciled grapes and vines. *3343 W. Cary St., tel. 804/ 353-4700. Reservations advised. Dress: casual. MC, V. $$*

Joe's Inn. Spaghetti is the specialty—especially the Greek version, with feta and provolone cheese baked on top—and the sandwiches are distinguished for their generous proportions. Regular customers predominate at this local hangout in the Fan District, yet they make newcomers feel right at home. *205 N. Shields Ave., tel. 804/ 355-2282. Reservations not required. Dress: casual. AE, MC, V. $*

Lodging

Omni Richmond. This luxury hotel in the James Center Complex is conveniently located next door to Shockoe Slip. While the rooms are furnished in contemporary style, the impressive marble lobby calls to mind a Venetian foyer with its green velvet chairs, equestrian statues, and Romanesque-style vases. *100 S. 12th St., 23219, tel. 804/344-7000 or 800/843-6664, fax 804/648-6704. 363 rooms, 12 suites. Facilities: 3 restaurants, bar, indoor pool, outdoor pool, sun deck, 2 racquetball courts, 2 squash courts, indoor track, Nautilus, whirlpool, saunas. AE, D, DC, MC, V. $$$$*

★ **Jefferson Grand Heritage Hotel.** A staircase of 26 steps, reputedly used as a model for a grand staircase in the movie *Gone with the Wind*, graces the lobby of this famous downtown hotel. Built in 1895, the Jefferson is a National Historic Landmark restored to its former glory. Mauves, grays, blues, and dark woods are dominant in the relatively small rooms, which have reproduction 19th-century furnishings. Guests receive passes to the YMCA spa across the street. *Franklin and Adams Sts., 23220, tel. 804/788-8000 or 800/424-8014, fax 804/225-0334. 274 rooms, 26 suites. Facilities: 3 restaurants, bar. AE, D, DC, MC, V. $$$*

Radisson Hotel. Guest rooms in this wedge-shaped hotel in the business district have views of the Richmond skyline or the James River; triangular rooms at the point of the wedge have both views. The wallpaper is uniformly gray, carpeting is brown or pewter, and bedspreads have a paisley pattern whose colors match the carpeting. Guests get free covered parking and free transportation on request to area attractions and the airport. The three-story atrium lobby features an operating waterfall. Two concierge floors have additional amenities. *555 E. Canal St., 23219, tel. 804/788-0900 or 800/333-3333, fax 804/788-7087. 296 rooms, 10 suites. Facilities: restaurant, bar, nightclub, indoor pool, health club with Jacuzzi, saunas. AE, D, DC, MC, V. $$$*

Richmond Marriott. The lobby of this luxury hotel near the 6th Street Marketplace has crystal chandeliers and marble flooring. Rooms are furnished in a contemporary style, and concierge service is available. *500 E. Broad St., 23219, tel. 804/643-3400 or 800/228-9290, fax 804/788-1230. 400 rooms. Facilities: 3 restaurants, nightclub, indoor pool, exercise room, tanning parlor. AE, D, DC, MC, V. $$$*

Days Inn North. This three-story redbrick motel is 2 miles northwest of downtown in a neighborhood of government and private offices. Guest rooms renovated in 1990 have clunky but dependable hotel furniture and predominantly mauve fabrics. Rooms are entered directly from the parking lot. *1600 Robin Hood Rd., 23220, tel. 804/353-1287 or 800/325-2525, fax 804/355-2659. 87 rooms. Facilities: restaurant, bar, outdoor pool. AE, D, DC, MC, V. $$*

Massad House Hotel. The four-story Massad House is not fancy, but it's clean and convenient and just five blocks from the capitol. On the north and south sides, rooms look out over alleyways and face other nearby buildings. A handful look out at undistinguished 4th Street, with a row of office buildings whose merit is silence after 6 PM. Guest rooms are small, with dressers doubling as writing desks by virtue of kneeholes. *11 N. 4th St., 23219, tel. 804/648-2893. 64 rooms. Facilities: restaurant. AE, MC, V. $*

The Arts and Nightlife

The Arts

Dance, music, and theater performances take place all year long at the **University of Virginia** in Charlottesville; the *Cavalier Daily* will have details.

McGuffey Art Center (201 2nd St. NW, Charlottesville, tel. 804/295-7973), housed in a converted school building, contains the studios of painters and sculptors and is the sight for many musical and theatrical performances.

Theater **Barksdale Theatre** (Hanover Tavern, Richmond, tel. 804/537-5333), founded in 1953, was the first dinner theater in the country. Performances are given Wednesday through Saturday evenings, and there are Sunday matinees.

Carpenter Center (Richmond, tel. 804/782-3900), a restored 1928 motion picture palace, is now a performing-arts center, offering year-round opera, road shows, symphony, and ballet.

The Mosque (Main and Laurel Sts., Richmond, tel. 804/780-4213), an ornate, Moorish-style auditorium, is worth a visit in itself even when no performances are scheduled.

Swift Creek Mill Playhouse (Colonial Heights, Richmond, tel. 804/ 748–5203), a dinner theater, is housed in a 17th-century gristmill.

Theatre Virginia (Richmond, tel. 804/367–0831), an Equity theater maintained by the Virginia Museum of Fine Arts, has a strong repertory.

Music   **The Richmond Symphony** (tel. 804/788–1212), more than 30 years old, often features internationally known soloists. Members of the orchestra perform chamber concerts as The Sinfonia, and the Richmond Pops hosts popular guest artists.

Dance   **Concert Ballet of Virginia** (Box 25501, Richmond 23260, tel. 804/ 780–1279) performs modern and experimental works; the **Richmond Ballet** (614 N. Lombardy St., 23220, tel. 804/359–0906) is the city's professional classical ballet company.

Nightlife

Comedy   **Ma's British Pub/Comedy Club** (109 S. 12th St., Richmond, tel. 804/ 643–JOKE) offers comedy on weekend nights. Reservations are required.

Folk   **Potter's Pub** (7007 Three Choppet Rd., Village Shopping Center, Richmond, tel. 804/282–9999) encourages audience participation.

Miller's (109 W. Main St., Downtown Mall, Charlottesville, tel. 804/ 971–8511), a large and comfortable bar, hosts folk and jazz musicians.

Jazz   **Bogart's** (203 N. Lombardy St., Richmond, tel. 804/353–9280) is a cozy club, with music on weekends.

Rock   **Flood Zone** (18th and Main Sts., Richmond, tel. 804/643–6006), a converted recording studio, has live music for dancing—or for listening while watching from the balcony.

5 Northern Virginia

Northern Virginia, which extends from the District of Columbia westward to the Blue Ridge, is unlike any other section of the state. Much of it has been subsumed into the official and residential life of the nation's capital—and has prospered as a result. The affluent and cosmopolitan northern Virginians may look more to Washington than to the rest of the commonwealth for direction, yet they take pride in being Virginians and in protecting the historic treasures they hold in trust for the rest of the nation.

Old Town Alexandria appears unsuburbanized; its more than 2,000 18th- and 19th-century buildings are listed collectively in the National Register of Historic Places. Fairfax and Arlington counties thrive as satellites of Washington (Tysons Corner in Fairfax County is said to have more commercial office space than Miami, Florida, and serves more than 400 corporations employing 70,000 people) and contain some of America's most precious acreage: Mount Vernon and Arlington Cemetery included. Fredericksburg, only an hour from the nation's capital, seems farther away: It's a quiet, well-preserved southern town, with a 40-block National Historic District. But Fredericksburg was once the scene of bloody conflict—as was Manassas (Bull Run), 26 miles from Washington, the site of some of the most significant battles of the Civil War. In 1994 this area almost became home to a Disney history theme park. It would have meant big business for this region (the state approved incentives to encourage the project), but opponents to the development prevailed, raising concerns about the Disney-scale traffic and the company's cultural sensitivity to history. Instead, the gracious lifestyle of the Old South survives, and the diversions here still include fox hunting and steeplechasing.

Essential Information

Important Addresses and Numbers

Visitor Information
Alexandria Convention and Visitor's Bureau (Ramsay House, 221 King St., Alexandria 22314, tel. 703/838–4200, TDD 703/838–6494).
Arlington County Visitor Center (735 S. 18th St., Arlington 22202, tel. 703/358–5720 or 800/677–6267).
Fairfax County Convention and Visitors Bureau (8300 Boone Blvd., Suite 450, Tysons Corner 22182, tel. 703/790–3329).
Fairfax County Visitor's Center (7764 Armistead Rd., Suite 160, Lorton 22079, tel. 703/550–2450 or 800/7-FAIRFA).
Fredericksburg Visitor Center (706 Caroline St., Fredericksburg 22401, tel. 703/373–1776 or 800/678–4748).
Loudoun County Conference and Visitor Bureau (108D South St. SE, tel. 703/777–0518 or 800/752–6118).

Emergencies
Throughout the region, dial **911** for emergency assistance.

Hospitals
Alexandria Hospital (4320 Seminary Rd., Alexandria, tel. 703/504–3000).
National Hospital for Orthopedics and Rehabilitation (2455 Army Navy Dr., Arlington, tel. 703/553–2417) has a 24-hour emergency room.
Medic 1 Clinic (3429 Jefferson Davis Hwy., Fredericksburg, tel. 703/371–1664) is open 9–9, but call ahead.

Arriving and Departing

By Plane Three major airports serve both northern Virginia and the Washington, D.C., area: The busy and often crowded **Washington National Airport** (tel. 703/685–8000) in Arlington has scheduled daily flights by all major U.S. carriers; **Washington Dulles International Airport** (tel. 703/661–2700), in Loudoun County, 26 miles northwest of Washington, is a modern facility served by the major U.S. airlines and many international carriers. **Baltimore-Washington International Airport** (tel. 410/859–7111 for information and paging), located 10 miles south of Baltimore off Route 295, also serves the metropolitan Washington area, including Northern Virginia. It is almost as close to some areas as Dulles.

By Car I–95 runs north–south along the eastern side of the region. I–66 runs east–west, perpendicular to I–95, cutting off the top third of the region.

By Train **Amtrak** (tel. 800/872–7245) has scheduled stops in Alexandria (110 Callahan Dr., tel. 703/836–4339) and Fredericksburg (Caroline St. and Lafayette Blvd., no tel.) as part of its East Coast service.

By Bus **Greyhound Lines** (tel. 800/231–2222) provides scheduled service to Fairfax (4103 Rust Rd., tel. 703/273–7770), Fredericksburg (1400 Jefferson Davis Hwy., tel. 703/373–2103), and Springfield (6583 Backlick Rd., tel. 703/451–5800).

Guided Tours

Orientation **Doorways to Old Virginia** (tel. 703/548–0100) and **Accent on Alexandria** (tel. 703/751–5756) are two private companies that offer tours of historic Old Town; many tours begin at the **Ramsay House Visitor Center** (221 King St., tel. 703/838–4200).

Exploring

Northern Virginia

Numbers in the margin correspond to points of interest on the Northern Virginia and Mount Vernon and Environs maps.

First in war, first in peace, and first stop on a tour of the Virginia suburbs of Washington, D.C., is George Washington—his house, that is, at **Mount Vernon,** 16 miles south of the nation's capital. It is the most visited historic house museum in the United States after the White House. Washington considered himself a farmer, and although his farmhouse was a formal one, none of the embellishments disguised its working nature; in the ornate dining room, for example, guests ate at a simple trestle table assembled from boards and sawhorses. The long portico with its eight columns faces east across the Potomac; as the riverbank opposite remains forested, the views match the period authenticity of Mount Vernon's interior. About 25% of the furnishings are original; the others are carefully selected and authenticated antiques. The outbuildings, including kitchen and stable, have been precisely restored. Beyond them, George and Martha Washington are laid to rest in a tomb on the estate. *Rte. 235, tel. 703/780–2000. Admission: $7 adults, $6 senior citizens, $3 children 6–11. Open Apr.–Aug., daily 8–5; Sept.–Oct., daily 9–5; Nov.–Feb., daily 9–4; Mar., daily 9–5.*

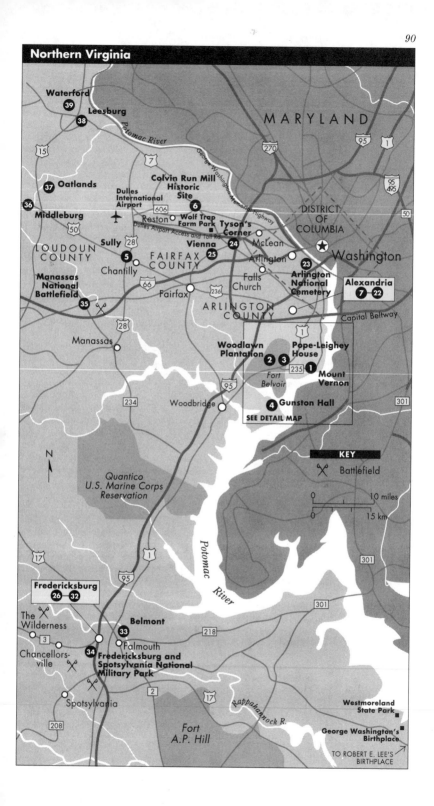

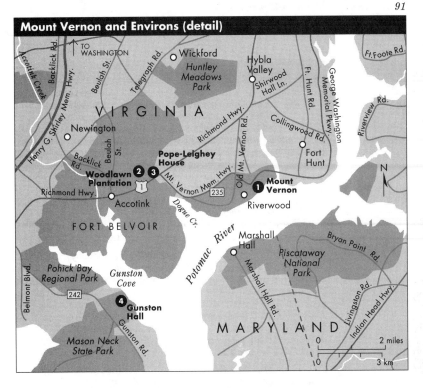

Mount Vernon and Environs (detail)

② Three miles west of Mount Vernon is the circa 1800 **Woodlawn Plantation,** home of Major Lawrence and Nellie Custis Lewis, the nephew and granddaughter of George and Martha Washington. The Federal-style mansion was designed by William Thornton (architect of the Capitol) to resemble Kenmore, Lewis's boyhood home in Fredericksburg, and offers a commanding view of the river and countryside. The mansion was built atop Grey's Hill on land Washington gave as a wedding present to his nephew. It was well furnished to accommodate a growing family and to entertain notable guests. Today, the house, which is owned by the National Trust for Historic Preservation, has many original and period furnishings. The well-maintained, formal gardens include the largest collection of Heritage Roses on the East Coast. *U.S. 1 and Rte. 235, tel. 703/ 780–4000. Admission: $5 adults, $3.50 senior citizens and students. Open mid-Feb.–Dec., daily 9:30–4:30; Jan. and early Feb., weekends 9:30–4:30. Closed Thanksgiving, Christmas Day.*

③ On the grounds of Woodlawn, but having no connection with the Washington family, is Frank Lloyd Wright's **Pope-Leighey House,** a 1930s Usonian home constructed of cypress, brick, and glass. In contrast to Woodlawn mansion, Pope-Leighey House was designed to satisfy the post–World War II housing needs of middle-class Americans. Scheduled to be torn down in 1964 for highway construction, it was dismantled by the National Trust for Historic Preservation and reassembled here and furnished with original Wright pieces. The longer you look at this house, and the more that it is explained, the better you come to appreciate its subdued beauty and utility. Together, Woodlawn and Pope-Leighey houses offer a unique opportunity to compare two celebrated architects at the same site. *U.S. 1* *and Rte. 235, tel. 703/780–4000. Admission: $4 adults, $3 senior citizens and students. Open Mar.–Dec., daily 9:30–4:30; Jan.–Feb., weekends 9:30–4:30. Woodlawn/Pope-Leighey combination admission: $8 adults, $6 senior citizens and students.*

❹ On the Potomac, 6 miles south of Mount Vernon as the crow flies (but 15 miles via Routes 1 and 242), is the rarely crowded **Gunston Hall.** This was the home of another George—George Mason—one of the framers of the Constitution, who in the end refused to sign it because it failed to prohibit slavery, to restrain adequately the powers of the federal government, and to include a bill of rights. The interior of the house, with its carved woodwork in styles ranging from Chinese to Gothic, has been meticulously restored, using paints made from the original formulas and with carefully carved replacements for the intricate mahogany medallions in the moldings. The grounds, whose formal gardens feature boxwood hedges, may look familiar; the last scene of the movie *Broadcast News* (1987) was filmed here, by the gazebo. *Rte. 242, tel. 703/550–9220. Admission: $5 adults, $4 senior citizens, $1.50 children. Open daily 9:30–5.*

❺ **Sully,** a Federal-style home, has changed hands many times since 1795, when it was built by Richard Bland Lee. Citizen action in the 20th century saved it from destruction during construction of nearby Dulles Airport. In the 1970s the house was restored to Federal style and today features an 18th-century-style garden. There's a special Civil War festival and re-enactment held here every April ($5 adults, $2 children.) *Rte. 28 near Chantilly, tel. 703/437–1794. Admission: $3 adults, $1 children. Open Mar.–Dec., Wed.–Mon. 11–4; Jan.–Feb., weekends 11–4.*

❻ **Colvin Run Mill Historic Site** dates from the first decade of the 19th century, although the country store, which is still open for business, was added in the early 20th century. In addition to the restored mill, there's a small museum inside the miller's home. The mill operates on an irregular schedule, so call ahead for opening times as well as information concerning interpretive programs offered. *Rte. 7 at Great Falls; for information: Fairfax County Park Authority, 3701 Pender Dr., tel. 703/759–2771. Admission: $3 adults, $1 children. Open Mar.–Dec., Wed.–Mon. 11–5; Jan.–Feb., weekends 11–5.*

❼ Nine miles north of Mount Vernon, where the Mount Vernon Memorial Highway becomes the George Washington Memorial Parkway, the suburban city of **Alexandria** maintains an identity distinct from that of Washington, D.C., across the Potomac. Established in 1749, the city dwarfed Georgetown—Washington's oldest neighborhood—in the days before the Revolution.

Numbers in the margin correspond to points of interest on the Old Town Alexandria map.

Old Town Alexandria is the historic area of the city; its main arteries are Washington Street (the parkway as it passes through town) and King Street, which divide the town east–west and north–south, respectively. The shopping (art, antiques, and specialty) is of high quality, as are the sights. Most points of historic interest are on the east (Potomac) side of Washington Street. Visit them on foot if you are prepared to walk for 20 blocks or so; parking is usually scarce, but parking garages within walking distance of the Visitor's Bureau (*see below*) provide some relief. On Saturday parking costs $2 all day; it's $3 after 6 PM.

❽ The **Alexandria Convention and Visitor's Bureau,** where you should begin your tour, will issue a 72-hour parking permit for the two-hour

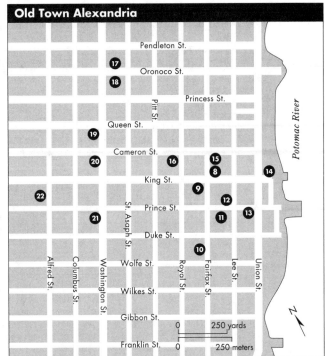

Old Town Alexandria

metered zones and will provide a walking-tour map. The bureau also has a translation service, and can issue tickets for museums and local events. The bureau is located in Ramsay House, the home of the town's first postmaster and Lord Mayor, William Ramsay. The white clapboard structure was built in 1724 in Dumfries (about 25 miles south along the Potomac) and moved here in 1749, and is believed to be the oldest house in Alexandria. Ramsay was a Scot, as a swatch of his tartan on the door proclaims. *221 King St., tel. 703/838-4200. Open daily 9-5 except Thanksgiving, Christmas, and New Year's.*

Across the way, at the corner of Fairfax and King streets, is the **Stabler-Leadbeater Apothecary Shop,** the second-oldest apothecary in the country, which was patronized by George Washington and the Lee family. Here, on October 17, 1859, Lieutenant Colonel Robert E. Lee received the orders to move to Harpers Ferry, West Virginia, to suppress John Brown's insurrection. The shop now houses a small museum of 18th-century apothecary paraphernalia, including a fine collection of about 800 apothecary bottles. *105-107 S. Fairfax St., tel. 703/836-3713. Admission free; suggested donations $1 per person. Open Mon.-Sat. 10-4.*

Two blocks south on Fairfax Street, just beyond Duke Street, sits the redbrick **Old Presbyterian Meeting House.** Except for during a six-decade hiatus, it has been an active house of worship since 1774, when Scottish pioneers established the church; a Presbyterian congregation still meets at 8:30 and 11 on Sunday mornings. The **Tomb of the Unknown Soldier of the American Revolution** lies in a corner of the churchyard, where many prominent Alexandrians—including Dr. James Craik, physician to both Washington and Lafayette—are interred. If the church door is locked during visiting hours, walk around back to the sanctuary to locate a staff member. *321 S. Fairfax St., tel. 703/549–6670. Open weekdays 9–5, weekends when staff available.*

To the north, the block of Prince Street between Fairfax and Lee is known as **Gentry Row,** after the 18th- and 19th-century inhabitants of its imposing three-story houses. On the corner at Lee is the **Athenaeum,** a reddish-brown Greek Revival edifice that stands in contrast to its many redbrick Federal neighbors. Built in 1852 as a bank, it now houses the gallery of the Northern Virginia Fine Arts Association, which shows the work of local artists. *201 Prince St., tel. 703/548–0035. Admission free. Open Wed.–Fri. 11–4, Sat. 11–1, Sun. 1–4.*

The block on Prince between Lee and Union has an array of humbler but very photogenic redbrick houses, many built by 19th-century sea captains, and accordingly this is **Captain's Row.** According to legend, the cobblestones that pave the street were laid by Hessian mercenaries in the employ of the British, who were then being held as prisoners of war.

Prince terminates at the bustling waterfront; two blocks north, at King and Union streets, is the **Torpedo Factory Art Center,** where 180 artists and craftspersons have their studios (and sell their wares) in a renovated waterfront building where torpedo parts were manufactured during the two world wars. The center also houses exhibits of the city's archaeology program (one of the nation's largest and oldest) and laboratories where you can observe work in progress. *105 N. Union St., tel. 703/838–4565. Admission free. Open daily 10–5. Archaeology section (tel. 703/838–4399) open Tues.–Fri. 10–3, Sat. 10–5, Sun. 1–5.*

Walking west on Cameron Street, visitors will find the grand **Carlyle House** (1753) two blocks away at Fairfax Street. The Georgian structure was the manor house of a riverside estate, the home of John Carlyle, a Scottish merchant who was one of Alexandria's founders. General Edward Braddock met here with five royal governors in 1755 to plan the strategy and funding of the early campaigns in the French and Indian War. The decor of the house remains 18th-century, with the original woodwork, Chippendale furniture throughout, and decorative items that include Chinese export porcelain. An architectural exhibit on the second floor explains how the house was built. *121 N. Fairfax St., tel. 703/549–2997. Admission: $3 adults, $1 children 11–17. Open Tues.–Sat. 10–4:30, Sun. noon–4:30.*

Gadsby's Tavern Museum, one block west at Royal Street, is two buildings: the tavern and the hotel. The tavern was built in 1770, the hotel 22 years later. General Washington reviewed his troops for the last time from the steps of this building. Lafayette was entertained here during his visit in 1824. The rooms in the tavern have been convincingly restored to look as they did in the 1790s. *134 N. Royal St., tel. 703/838–4242. Admission: $3 adults, $1 children. Open Apr.–Sept., Tues.–Sat. 10–5, Sun. 1–5; Oct.–Mar., Tues.–Sat. 10–4, Sun. 1–4.*

Among the town's attractions is the **Boyhood Home of Robert E. Lee,** where he lived on and off for 13 years. The Georgian town house (1795) is furnished with antiques that reflect life in the 1820s. *607 Oronoco St., tel. 703/548–8454. Admission: $3 adults, $1 children 11–17. Open Feb.–mid-Dec., Mon.–Sat. 10–4, Sun. 1–4.*

⑱ Across the street from the Lee home, the **Lee-Fendall House** was built in 1785 by an in-law and lived in by Lees until 1903. The interior reflects styles from a variety of periods and includes furniture that belonged to the family. The labor leader John L. Lewis lived here from 1937 to 1969. *614 Oronoco St., tel. 703/548–1789. Admission: $3 adults, $1 children 11–17. Open Tues.–Sat. 10–4, Sun. noon–4.*

⑲ Two blocks south, at the corner of Queen and Washington streets, **Lloyd House** (1794) stands as a fine example of Georgian architecture. Now part of the Alexandria Library System, it houses a collection of rare books and documents related to city and state history. *220 N. Washington St., tel. 703/838–4577. Admission free; tours on request if a docent is available. Open weekdays 9–6, Sat. 9–5.*

⑳ At Cameron Street, **Christ Church** looks much the same as it did when George Washington worshipped here. His pew and that of Robert E. Lee, who was confirmed in the church, are marked by silver commemorative plaques. The churchyard contains the graves of several Confederate dead. *Washington and Columbus Sts., tel. 703/549–1450. Admission free; donation requested. Open Mon.–Sat. 9–6, Sun. 9–5.*

Time Out Sightseers may welcome the opportunity to stop for a pint of Guinness or Harp and a ploughman's lunch of pickles and cheese at **Murphy's Restaurant and Pub** (713 King St.). This brick-wall pub and restaurant, on two floors of an 18th-century building, resounds with an Irish sing-along at night.

㉑ At the corner of Washington and Prince streets, the **Lyceum,** like the Athenaeum, is of Greek Revival design. Since it was built in 1839, the structure has served as library, hospital, residence, and office building; in the 1970s it was restored and now houses three art galleries, a gift shop, and a museum of local history. *201 S. Washington St., tel. 703/838–4994. Admission free. Open Mon.–Sat. 10–5, Sun. 1–5.*

㉒ Two blocks west, on Alfred Street, the **Friendship Fire House** (107 S. Alfred St.) occupies a building dating from 1855. According to local tradition, George Washington helped found the volunteer fire company in 1774 and served as its honorary captain. Among the early fire engines that will be displayed is one that Washington bought for the company for about $140—it was one of the finest of its time.

Numbers in the margin correspond to points of interest on the Northern Virginia map.

Don't miss the stirring panorama of the famous buildings and monuments of Washington, D.C., that can be seen by heading north from Alexandria on the George Washington Memorial Parkway. Then, at Memorial Bridge, cross the river into Washington and turn back **㉓** again to Virginia to make the most impressive approach to **Arlington National Cemetery** (tel. 703/695–3157): Behind you in Washington is the Lincoln Memorial; ahead of you, high atop a hill, is Robert E. Lee's Arlington House; a little below it Jacqueline Kennedy Onassis is interred, next to the eternal flame marking the grave of John F. Kennedy.

All these monuments are aligned with the bridge, and the effect of the arrangement is stunning. In the cemetery, thousands of veterans are interred beneath simple white headstones. Among the many famous Americans who lie here are William Howard Taft, Oliver Wendell Holmes, George C. Marshall, Joe Louis, and the brothers John and Robert Kennedy. In and around the **Tomb of the Unknown**

Soldier are the graves of men and women who lost their lives in two world wars, Korea, and Vietnam. Also, soldiers of the Gulf War are interred here. The tomb is guarded constantly by members of the Old Guard: First Battalion (reinforced), 3rd Infantry. The changing-of-the-guard ceremony takes place every half-hour from 8 AM to 5 PM, April to September, and hourly October to March. *Tel. 703/697–2131. Admission free. Open Oct.–Mar., daily 8–5; Apr.–Sept., daily 8–7.*

Within the cemetery is **Arlington House,** where Robert E. Lee lived for 30 years until his work obliged him to leave the proximity of the Union capital. During the Civil War, the Union confiscated the estate when Arlington began to function as a cemetery. The massive Greek Revival house, with its templelike appearance, is furnished with antiques and reproductions. The view of Washington from the portico is as magnificent as the sight of the house from the bridge. *Tel. 703/557–0613. Admission free. Open Oct.–Mar., daily 9:30–4:30; Apr.–Sept., daily 9:30–6.*

Perhaps the best way to see Arlington National Cemetery is by taking the **Tourmobile** narrated-tour buses, which set out from the visitor center and stop at Arlington House, the Tomb of the Unknown Soldier, and the Kennedy graves. If you want to spend time at any one place, you can catch the next tour bus when you're ready to move on. *Tel. 202/554–7020. Cost: $3 adults, $1.50 children. Buses operate 8:30–6 in summer, 9:30–4:30 in winter.*

㉔ Northwest of Arlington on Route 7, at the eastern edge of Vienna, the shopping mecca of **Tysons Corner** has some of the most upscale shops in the Washington, D.C., area, many of them located in and around two major malls.

㉕ In **Vienna,** a couple of miles northwest of Tysons Corner, is **Wolf Trap Farm Park for the Performing Arts** (tel. 703/255–1860), a national park devoted to the performing arts. Drama, dance, and music performances are given in a partially covered amphitheater and in two 18th-century barns transported from upstate New York. Picnicking is permitted at wood tables on the grounds.

㉖ **Fredericksburg,** 50 miles south of Washington, D.C., on I–95, rivals Alexandria and Mount Vernon in the number of its associations with the Washington family. The first president lived across the Rappahannock River at Ferry Farm from age six to 16; later he bought a house for his mother here, near his sister and brother.

Numbers in the margin correspond to points of interest on the Fredericksburg map.

㉗ Washington's only sister, Betty, married her cousin Fielding Lewis in 1750, and they built **Kenmore** a few years later. The plain exterior belies a lavish interior; these have been called some of the most beautiful rooms in America. The plaster moldings in the ceilings are even more ornate than those of Mount Vernon. Equally elegant are the furnishings, which include a large standing clock that belonged to Betty's mother. In the reconstructed kitchen next door, following the tour, you can enjoy tea and a fresh rendition of Mary Washington's gingerbread. *1201 Washington Ave., tel. 703/373–3381. Admission: $5 adults, $2.50 children. Open Mar.–Nov., daily 9–5; Dec.–Feb., daily 10–4.*

㉘ In 1760 George Washington's brother Charles built as his home what became the **Rising Sun Tavern,** a watering hole for such revolutionaries as the Lee brothers, Patrick Henry, Washington, and Jefferson. An actress dressed in period costume and portraying the

Chatham
Manor, **32**

Mary Washington
House, **29**

Hugh Mercer
Apothecary
Shop, **30**

James Monroe
Museum and
Memorial
Library, **31**

Kenmore, **27**

Rising Sun
Tavern, **28**

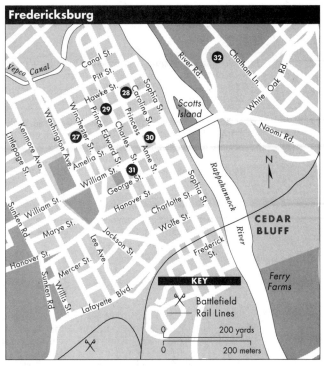

character of "wench" leads the tour, allowing you to observe the activity at this busy institution entirely from her perspective. Visitors are served spiced tea in the tap room. *1306 Caroline St., tel. 703/ 371–1494. Admission: $3 adults, 75¢ children. Open Mar.–Nov., daily 9–5; Dec.–Feb., daily 10–4.*

㉙ On Charles Street is the modest white **Mary Washington House,** which the future president purchased for his mother in 1772. Here she spent the last 17 years of her life, tending the charming garden where her boxwood still flourishes—and where many a bride and groom come today to exchange vows. *Charles and Lewis Sts., tel. 703/373–1569. Admission: $3 adults, $1 children 6–18. Open Mar.– Nov., daily 9–5; Dec.–Feb., daily 10–4. Closed Thanksgiving, Dec. 24–25, and Dec. 31–Jan. 1.*

Dr. Hugh Mercer, a Scotsman who served as a brigadier general of the Revolutionary army, may have been more careful than most other Colonial physicians, yet his methods make today's visitors cringe.
㉚ A costumed hostess at the **Hugh Mercer Apothecary Shop** describes explicitly the procedures for amputations and cataract operations; she also tells about therapeutic bleeding and shows off the gruesome devices used in Colonial dentistry. This look at life two centuries ago is informative (if mildly nauseating). *Caroline and Amelia Sts., tel. 703/373–3362. Admission: $3 adults, $1 children. Open Mar.–Nov., daily 9–5; Dec.–Feb., daily 10–4.*

㉛ The **James Monroe Museum and Memorial Library,** a tiny one-story building where the man who would later be the nation's fifth president practiced law from 1787 to 1789, is the repository of many of Monroe's possessions, which were collected and preserved by his family. Here is the desk at which Monroe signed the nation's single most enduring declaration of foreign policy, the Monroe Doctrine. *908 Charles St., tel. 703/899–4559. Admission: $3 adults, 75¢ children. Open daily 9–5.*

Time Out   The **Made in Virginia Store Deli** (101 William Tell St.) is a good place to stop for quiche or a gourmet sandwich (the "Thomas Jefferson" is turkey and bacon). Triple-chocolate cheesecake and almond pound cake are formidable entries on the menu of rich desserts.

㉜ **Chatham Manor** is a fine example of Georgian architecture, built between 1768 and 1771 by William Fitzhugh on a site overlooking the Rappahannock and the town of Fredericksburg. Fitzhugh, a plantation owner, frequently hosted such luminaries as Washington and Jefferson. At the time of the Civil War, Union forces commandeered the house and converted it into a headquarters and hospital. President Lincoln conferred here with his generals; Clara Barton, founder of the American Red Cross, and the poet Walt Whitman tended the wounded. Later its owners restored the house and gardens and gave the property to the National Park Service. Concerts are performed here in summer. *Chatham La., tel. 703/371–0807. Admission free. Open daily 9–5, except Christmas Day and New Year's Day.*

Numbers in the margin correspond to points of interest on the Northern Virginia map.

㉝ In Falmouth, on Route 1001, just off U.S. 17 north of Fredericksburg, is the 18th-century estate of **Belmont,** which was acquired in 1916 by Detroit-born artist Gari Melchers, who returned from Europe at the outbreak of World War I. The house is furnished with antiques; the stone studio Melchers built in 1924 houses the largest collection of his works anywhere. *224 Washington St., tel. 703/899–4860. Admission: $3 adults, $1 children 6–18. Open Mar.–Nov., Mon.–Sat. 10–5, Sun. 1–5; Dec.–Feb., Mon.–Sat. 10–4, Sun. 1–4; closed major holidays.*

㉞ Four Civil War battlefields in this area—Fredericksburg, Chancellorsville, the Wilderness, and the Spotsylvania Courthouse—together constitute the **Fredericksburg and Spotsylvania National Military Park.** All are within 17 miles of Fredericksburg. The in-town visitor center for the park has two floors of exhibits and a slide show on the fighting. On the fields, signs and exhibits recount details of the battles. *1013 Lafayette Blvd. (U.S. 1), tel. 703/371–0802. Admission free. Open mid-June–Labor Day, daily 8:30–6:30; Sept.–mid-June, weekdays 9–5, weekends 9–6.*

㉟ West of Washington is a monumentally important Civil War battleground: **Manassas National Battlefield,** or Bull Run. Here the Confederacy won two important victories—in July 1861 and August 1862—and Stonewall Jackson won his nickname. The self-guided tour begins at the visitor center, where exhibits and audiovisual presentations greatly enhance a visit. It's a 26-mile drive from Washington; take I–66 west to Route 234 (don't be fooled by the earlier Manassas exit for Route 28), and the visitor center is ½ mile north on the right. *Tel. 703/361–1339. Admission: $1 adults, free for senior citizens. Open daily 8:30–dusk. Visitor center open daily 8:30–5 (until 6 June–Aug.).*

On leaving Manassas, return to I–66 and take it west to U.S. 15, the road to horse country. The major towns here in Loudoun County are Leesburg, Middleburg, and Waterford, where old Virginia still carries on, with gracious homes, fox hunts, and steeplechases.

36 The area that is now **Middleburg** was surveyed by George Washington in 1763, when it was known as Chinn's Crossroads. It was considered strategic because of its location midway on the Winchester–Alexandria route (roughly what is now Route 50). The community, incorporated in 1787, has numerous horse events; polo matches are played Sundays June–August (tel. 703/777–0775).

37 **Oatlands,** 5 miles north of Middleburg on Route 15, is a former 5,000-acre plantation built by a great-grandson of Robert "King" Carter, one of the wealthiest planters in Virginia before the Revolution. The manor house was built in 1803 in Greek Revival style; a stately portico and half-octagonal stair wings were added in 1827. The house has been meticulously restored, and the manicured fields that remain host public and private equestrian events from spring to fall, among them the Loudoun Hunt Point-to-Point in April, a race that brings out the entire community for picnics on blankets and tailgates. The Draft Horse and Mule Day also attracts crowds in late summer, when competing teams flex their muscles in pulling contests and craftspersons spread their wares for an all-day fair. A restored English garden of 4½ acres is bordered by terraced walls. *Tel. 703/777–3174. Admission: $5 adults, $4 students and senior citizens. Additional admission for special events. Open Apr.–Dec., Tues.–Sat. 10–4:30, Sun. 1–4:30. Closed Jan.–Mar. and Thanksgiving.*

38 **Leesburg,** a staging area during the French and Indian War, is one of the oldest towns in northern Virginia, and it retains numerous fine Colonial and Revolutionary buildings that now house business offices, shops, restaurants, and residences. When the British burned Washington during the War of 1812, James and Dolley Madison fled to Leesburg with many government records, including official copies of the Declaration of Independence and the U.S. Constitution.

One mile north of Leesburg, the 1,200-acre estate of **Morven Park** is home to the Westmoreland Davis Equestrian Institute, a private riding school; the **Morven Park Carriage Museum,** which boasts more than 100 horse-drawn vehicles; and the **Museum of Hounds and Hunting.** The mansion, the work of three architects in 1781, is a Greek Revival building that bears a striking resemblance to the White House—and has been used as a stand-in for it in films. Two governors have lived here. The price of admission includes entrance to the two museums and to 16 rooms in the Morven Park mansion. *Rte. 7, Leesburg, tel. 703/777–2414. Admission: $5 adults, $4 senior citizens, $2 children 12 and under. Open Apr.–Oct., Tues.–Sun. noon–5; Nov., weekends noon–5; special Christmas tours during the 1st 3 weeks of Dec., Tues.–Sun. noon–5.*

39 **Waterford,** another historic community, was founded by a Quaker miller and for many decades has been synonymous with fine crafts; its annual early October Homes Tour and Crafts Exhibit attracts as many as 15,000 visitors. Festival activities include Revolutionary War military camps with marching fife and drum corps, Civil War skirmishing, and visits to 18th-century buildings. Waterford and more than 1,400 acres around it were declared a National Historic Landmark in 1970. For information on events, contact the **Tin Shop/ Waterford Foundation** (2nd St., Box 142, Waterford 22190, tel. 703/ 882–3018).

Touring the well-tended countryside is a pleasure. Scenic drives and sites capture the horsey atmosphere of this fine green country, which in recent decades has become an important wine-producing region. Among the wineries worth visiting are: **Meredyth, Piedmont, Loudoun Valley, Swedenburg, Tarara,** and **Willowcroft Farms** (*see* Off the Beaten Track, *below*). The **Loudoun County Conference and Visitor Bureau** (*see* Important Addresses and Numbers, *above*) provides information on tours.

The history of the area is detailed in exhibits at the **Loudoun Museum,** in Leesburg, which displays art and artifacts of daily life from the time of the Native American tribes to the 20th century. *16 W. Loudoun St. SW, tel. 703/777–7427. Admission free; donation requested. Open Mon.–Sat. 10–5, Sun. 1–5.*

What to See and Do with Children

Reston Animal Park, at the intersection of Routes 7 and 606 in Reston (Fairfax County), is inhabited by a gibbon, emus, giant tortoises, zebras, and other exotica as well as domestic farm animals. Children can take pony and elephant rides; the entire family can go on a hayride. *Hunter Mill Rd. at Lake Fairfax, tel. 703/759–3636 or 703/759–3637. Admission weekdays: $5.95 adults, $4.95 senior citizens and children; weekends: $6.95 adults, $5.95 senior citizens and children. Open late Mar.–mid-June and Labor Day–late Nov., weekdays 10–5, weekends 10–6; mid-June–Labor Day, daily 10–5. Special events every weekend are included in admission price.*

At **Claude Moore Colonial Farm,** a family in costume re-creates the activities of a tenant farm in the 1770s. They plant, cultivate, and harvest crops, and tend the livestock. Seasonal harvest celebrations and 18th-century market fairs are among special events. The farm is located at Turkey Run, at the intersection of Routes 123 and 193, in McLean. *Admission: $2 adults, $1 senior citizens and children 3–12. (Fees slightly higher for special events.) Open Apr.–mid-Dec., Wed.–Sun. 10–4:30.*

Wolf Trap Farm Park, in Vienna, schedules performances for children throughout the year, including mime, puppets, animal shows, music, drama, and storytelling. During the summer, free daily performances take place at the outdoor Theater in the Woods (tel. 703/255–1827), but reservations are required. On Labor Day weekend, a three-day International Children's Festival brings together performers from the United States and abroad. *Rte. 7, I–495, tel. 703/642–0862. Admission varies with event.*

Off the Beaten Track

On display at Alexandria's **George Washington Masonic National Memorial** are furniture and regalia that Washington used while he was charter master of the local Masonic lodge. Exhibits demystify the international organization, explaining many of its traditions, aims, and activities. Every 45 minutes until 4 PM, an elevator tour takes visitors to the top of the 333-foot structure for a grand view of the town and nearby Washington. The memorial is a 20-minute walk from the river; it can also be reached by DASH bus west on King Street (60¢ fare, exact change, includes transfer for return trip). *Shooter's Hill. Admission free. Open daily 9–5.*

Meredyth Vineyards (Rte. 628, south of Middleburg, tel. 703/687–6277), established in 1972, has been in the forefront of promoting the recent Virginian industry of winegrowing. Tours and tastings are offered daily 10–4. Nearby is **Piedmont Vineyards and Winery** (Rte. 626, tel. 703/687–5528), which offers tours daily 10–5. **Swedenburg**

Estate Vineyard (Rte. 50, east of Middleburg, tel. 703/687–5219) has tours daily 10–4.

Shopping

Shopping Malls

The enormous **Potomac Mills Mall** (2700 Potomac Mills Circle, tel. 703/491–4050), just south of Washington on I–95, houses more than 200 stores and manufacturers' outlets, including Swedish furniture giant IKEA.

Tysons Corner Center (1961 Chain Bridge Rd.), at the junction of Routes 7 and 123, contains 240 retailers, including Bloomingdale's (tel. 703/556–4600), Nordstrom (tel. 703/761–1121), and Woodward and Lothrop (tel. 703/893–6400) department stores. Next door, **The Galleria at Tysons II** (2001 International Dr.) has another 125 stores, including Saks Fifth Avenue (tel. 703/761–0700) and Neiman Marcus (tel. 703/761–1600). **Crystal City**'s street-level and underground stores, on the Metro line, include conventional shops as well as the more unusual, such as Geppi's (1675 Crystal Square Arcade, tel. 703/521–4618), which sells comic-book and baseball-card collectibles.

Specialty Stores

Antiques The **Old Towns** of Alexandria and Fredericksburg are dense with antiques shops—many of them quite expensive—that are particularly strong in the Federal and Victorian periods. The respective visitor centers have maps and lists of the dozens of stores in each town. Arlington's **Law's Antique World** (2900 Clarendon Blvd., tel. 703/525–8300) also rates highly.

Clothing **Brooks Brothers** (tel. 703/556–6566) and **Liz Claiborne** (tel. 703/893–7904) are among the many clothing stores at Tysons Corner.

Gifts **Brookstone** (tel. 703/356–0280), the **Nature Company** (tel. 703/760–8930), and **The Museum Company** (tel. 703/760–9784) are part of the Tysons Corner selections.

Jewelry The first area branch of the New York jeweler **Tiffany & Co.** (8045 Leesburg Pike, tel. 703/893–7700) is a few minutes from the mall in Fairfax Square.

Toys **The Disney Store** (tel. 703/448–8314) and **F. A. O. Schwarz** (tel. 703/893–6660) are both at Tysons Corner. **Ringling Bros. Barnum & Bailey Store** (8607 Westwood Center Dr., Vienna, tel. 703/790–2550) and **Warner Bros. Studio Store** (tel. 703/691–0422) at Fair Oaks Mall have unique gifts for children.

Sports and Outdoor Activities

Biking The Arlington Parks and Recreation Bureau (tel. 703/838–4343, TDD 703/838–6463) has a free map of the **Arlington County Bikeway System,** available on request. The Fredericksburg Visitor Center (tel. 703/373–1776) has mapped rides of 3, 9, and 20 miles, which highlight the historical and natural beauty of the town. The **Mount Vernon Bicycle Trail** (tel. 703/285–2598), 19 miles of asphalt, runs along the shore of the Potomac and through Alexandria (bike maps sold at Ramsay House). The **Burke Lake Park Bicycle Trail** (tel. 703/ 323–6600), in Fairfax County, is 4.7 miles long and circles the lake. The **Washington & Old Dominion Railroad Regional Trail** (tel. 703/ 729–0596), better known to hikers, follows the roadbed of the "Virginia Creeper" tracks from Shirlington (near I–95) to Purcellville, 44 miles away in the Allegheny foothills.

Golf **Algonkian Park** (600 Potomac View Rd., Sterling, tel. 703/450– 4655), **Burke Lake Golf Course** (Fairfax Station, tel. 703/323–1641), **Pohick Golf Course** (10301 Gunston Rd., tel. 703/339–8585), **Twin Lakes Golf Course** (6100 Clifton Rd., tel. 703/631–9099), and **Shannon Green Resort** (Rte. 3, Fredericksburg, tel. 703/786–8385) have 18-hole public courses.

Hiking **Great Falls National Park** (Box 66, Great Falls 22066, tel. 703/285– 2966), 15 miles north of Washington, is one of the most spectacular natural areas in and around the nation's capital. Five clifftop paths look down on Mather Gorge, the rocky narrows that make the Potomac River churn. Visit the one-time town of Matildaville, and look across to the Maryland side, where boats re-create canal rides. *Admission: $3 per vehicle, good for 7 days. Open year-round, daily 7–dark; visitor center open Apr.–Oct., daily 10–6; Nov.–Mar., daily 10–5.*

Tennis Dozens of public tennis courts are available all over the Virginia suburbs of Washington; many are lighted and are accessible to the disabled. **Fairfax County Park Authority** (tel. 703/246–5700) maintains a directory of tennis courts within its jurisdiction.

Dining and Lodging

Alexandria has more restaurants per square foot than any other city in the commonwealth, yet the establishments of King Street tend to be jammed Friday and Saturday nights, so reservations are necessary for diners who don't want to reconnoiter the side streets. In Arlington, many small restaurants of the Little Saigon neighborhood, on and around Wilson Boulevard, serve Southeast Asian cuisine at moderate prices. Fairfax County has more than 1,000 dining establishments, including good seafood and ethnic restaurants (a Chinese restaurant favored by George Bush among them) at Tysons Corner, Vienna, Great Falls, McLean, and elsewhere.

Proximity to the nation's capital makes this a relatively high-price hotel market, but standards of luxury and comfort are commensurately high. Bed-and-breakfasts tend to be more elegant here because many serve as romantic weekend hideaways for regular customers from Washington. **Bed & Breakfast Ltd.** (Box 12011, Washington, DC 20005, tel. 202/328–3510) and **Princely Bed & Breakfast Ltd.** (819 Prince St., Alexandria 22314, tel. 703/683–2159) are reservations services that arrange accommodations in historic homes in Alexandria

Highly recommended establishments are indicated by a star ★.

Alexandria **Gadsby's Tavern.** Here's a tavern in Old Town Alexandria whose de-
Dining cor, cuisine, and entertainment are all about 200 years old. As you dine, John Douglas Hall, dressed as a gentleman of the 18th century, performs on the lute and recounts the latest news and gossip of Colonial Virginia. Built in 1792, the tavern was a favorite of George Washington, who is commemorated on the menu by George Washington's Favorite Duck, a cornbread-stuffed roast duck with

fruit-and-madeira sauce. Other period offerings include Colonial Game Pye (lamb, pork, and rabbit), Sally Lunn bread, and a rich English trifle. *138 N. Royal St., tel. 703/548–1288. Reservations advised. Dress: casual; jacket and tie requested in evening. AE, DC, MC, V. $$*

King Street Blues. Not the place for power-lunching or princely wooing, this informal eatery just off King Street in the heart of Old Town is popular for its relaxed ambience and hearty but quirky southern menu. The whimsical decor is a mix of neon and papier-mâché constructions—it's an ideal setting for the friendly, twentysomething waiters hustling around in T-shirts and shorts. Diners of all ages, though, come to enjoy the baked pecan-crusted catfish, the Thai chicken and noodle salad, the glazed pork chops, and the fish special of the day; wash your choice down with the excellent house beer. *112 N. St. Asaph St., tel. 703/836–8800. Dress: casual. AE, D, DC, MC, V. $$*

★ **Le Gaulois.** Simple, dark-blue plastic-covered tables stand in this quiet country bistro, surrounded by scenes of southern France on white plaster walls. Among the specialties are pot-au-feu gaulois (a beef-and-chicken stew with whole vegetables) and cassoulet, a rich bean casserole with sausage and beef. More than half a dozen wines from France and California are available by the glass. *1106 King St., tel. 703/739–9494. Reservations advised. Dress: casual but neat. Closed Sun. AE, DC, MC, V. $$*

★ **Taverna Cretekou.** Whitewashed stucco walls and brightly colored macramé tapestries bring a Mediterranean ambience to the center of Old Town. On the menu are lamb *Exohikon* (baked in a pastry shell) and swordfish kabob. All the wines served are Greek, and in the warm months you can dine in the canopied garden. *818 King St., tel. 703/548–8688. Reservations advised. Dress: casual. AE, D, MC, V. Closed Mon. $$*

Hard Times Café. Recorded country-and-western music and framed photographs of Depression-era Oklahoma set the tone at this casual, crowded, two-floor hangout. Three kinds of chili—Texas (spicy), Cincinnati (sweeter), and vegetarian—are served: Texas chili is typically served over spaghetti—a "Chili-mac"; Cincinnati comes with cheese, onions, beans, or all three. A tuna-fish sandwich, chicken salad, and chicken wings are alternatives to the more combustive cuisine. About 30 domestic and Mexican beers are available. *1404 King St., tel. 703/683–5340. No reservations. Dress: casual. AE, MC, V. No lunch Sun. $*

Lodging **Holiday Inn Eisenhower Metro.** Built 20 years ago and recently renovated, this hotel is conveniently located in a suburban area 1½ miles from the Amtrak station and within walking distance of the Eisenhower Metro station. Decor is standard modern: light-color walls and curtains with shades of mauve and teal. The rooms facing east overlook Old Town Alexandria. *2460 Eisenhower Ave., 22314, tel. 703/960–3400 or 800/465–4329, fax 703/329–0953. 202 rooms, 1 suite. Facilities: restaurant, bar, indoor pool, exercise room; golf, tennis nearby. AE, D, DC, MC, V. $$$*

★ **Holiday Inn Old Town.** The distinctive mahogany-paneled lobby of this well-known chain hotel suggests a men's club in the city, and guest-room decor follows this motif, with hunting-and-horse prints on the walls. Bathrooms have marble floor and tub, and the phones have computer-modem capabilities. The hotel chain has decreed this member to be one of its 20 best, worldwide, in large part because of the extraordinary service: Staff will bring exercise bicycles to rooms on request and provide touring bicycles for use in the area without charge. Because this is the hotel closest to the center of Old Town, its guests in some rooms on the fifth and sixth floors can enjoy a picturesque roofscape of 18th- and 19th-century buildings and the river beyond—but only in autumn after the trees have shed their leaves. *480 King St., 22314, tel. 703/549–6080 or 800/465–4329, fax 703/684–6508. 227 rooms. Facilities: restaurant, lounge, complimentary English tea in afternoon, secured parking, beauty shop, barbershop, indoor pool, sauna. AE, D, DC, MC, V. $$$*

★ **Morrison House.** This small hotel in Old Town is decorated in Federal style throughout, the rooms are furnished with four-posters, and afternoon tea is served as it would have been 200 years ago, though the four-story redbrick building has been here only since 1985. English butlers will unpack guests' bags on request, and the marble bathrooms have telephones and hair dryers. *116 S. Alfred St., 22314, tel. 703/838–8000, fax 703/684–6283. 42 rooms, 3 suites. Facilities: 2 restaurants, lounge. AE, DC, MC, V. $$$*

Arlington
Dining

The View. Picture windows on three sides of this restaurant on the 14th floor of the Key Bridge Marriott Hotel more than fulfill the promise of its name: The Washington Monument and the spires of Georgetown University are among the most prominent landmarks to be seen across the Potomac. The interior is heavily burgundy—the carpeting, the leather banquettes, the wallpaper, even the ceiling. Prominent entrées have been broiled lobster, served out of its shell with an unusual cucumber flan; and New York strip steak, broiled in Jack Daniels sauce and served in medallions with hot peppers. This is a grazing restaurant; all the entrées are also available as appetizers, in one form or another. A salad of seasonal fruit is served warm with chicken and quail. At the popular Sunday brunch buffet, swordfish and oysters are among the more than 50 items offered. *Key Bridge Marriott, 1401 Lee Hwy., tel. 703/524–6400. Reservations advised. Dress: casual but neat. AE, D, DC, MC, V. No lunch. $$$$*

Queen Bee. Arlington's Little Saigon area has lots of terrific Vietnamese restaurants, but this is one of the best. The atmosphere is unassuming, the service is cordial, and the food is always excellent. Spring rolls are moist and delicately flavorful, and don't pass up the green-papaya salad with sausage and beef jerky. The Saigon pancake—accented with a mix of crab, pork, and shrimp—is another reason why diners often wait in line for a table at this popular establishment. *3181 Wilson Blvd., tel. 703/527–3444. Dress: casual but neat. MC, V. $$*

★ **Red Hot & Blue.** Photos of famous customers, such as John Grisham and B. B. King, adorn the walls of this joint where patrons inhale (among other dishes) pork ribs and shoulders prepared Memphis-style—smoked over a pit, then spiced or sauced—or pulled-pig sandwiches, all served with a choice of beans, cole slaw, potato salad, or french fries. *1600 Wilson Blvd., tel. 703/276–7427. Reservations not required. Dress: casual. MC, V. $*

Lodging

Holiday Inn National Airport. This is your basic, familiar high-rise Holiday Inn, set just off the highway, with modern, cheerful decor and a convenient location a mile from the airport. Rooms have the standard furnishings in pastels or earthtones. The casual **Fred's Place,** suitable for family dining, offers an American menu. *1489 Jefferson Davis Hwy., 22202, tel. 703/416–1600 or 800/465–4329, fax 703/416–1615. 295 rooms, 11 suites. Facilities: restaurant, bar, outdoor pool; racquetball club adjacent. AE, D, DC, MC, V. $$$$*

Marriott Crystal Gateway. This elegant, modern Marriott caters to the business traveler and those who want to be pampered. Its two towers rise 17 stories above the highway; inside you'll find black marble, blond wood, Oriental touches, and lots of greenery. Rooms have contemporary styling. *1700 Jefferson Davis Hwy., 22202, tel. 703/920–3230 or 800/228–9290, fax 703/979–6332. 563 rooms, 131 suites. Facilities: 3 restaurants, lounge, nightclub, indoor pool, outdoor pool, spa with whirlpool, sauna, exercise rooms. AE, DC, MC, V. $$$$*

Ritz Carlton Pentagon City. In the middle of a vast shopping mall, five minutes from National Airport, this hotel greets guests with Persian carpets and an 18th-century grandfather's clock. Upstairs, the rooms have either a rose or a blue color scheme, with silk drapes, silk floral-pattern wallpaper, and framed botanical prints. The furniture is reproduction Federal. The building's insulation from the noise of air traffic and its lavish appointments together make it a paragon among airport hotels. *1250 S. Hayes St., 22202, tel. 703/415–5000 or 800/241–3333, fax 703/415–5060. 345 rooms, 42 suites. Facilities: 2 restaurants, bar, indoor pool, whirlpool, exercise room, steam room, sauna. AE, D, DC, MC, V. $$$$*

Best Western Arlington. There are essentially two hotels situated here on 6 acres: the three units of a 30-year-old low-rise building that was renovated in 1986, and an executive tower built in 1987. The tower combines shades of rose and light green in a typically modern decor; the rooms of the low-rise tend to be a bit darker, with rust carpeting and touches of mauve. All rooms have ample seating space, and some have pullout sofa beds. The hotel is just 2 miles from the District of Columbia, and there's easy access to I–395. Shuttle service to the nearby National Airport is free. *2480 S. Glebe Rd., 22206, tel. 703/979–4400 or 800/426–6886, fax 703/685–0051. 325 rooms. Facilities: restaurant, outdoor pool, exercise room, Jacuzzi, gift shop, games room, laundry and valet service. AE, D, DC, MC, V. $$*

Fairfax
Dining and
Lodging

The Bailiwick Inn. Red brick and green shutters distinguish this bed-and-breakfast in an 18th-century building that stands opposite the historic Fairfax County Courthouse. The rooms, named for eminent Virginians, have reproduction furniture, period detail, and 1990s bathrooms. Four rooms have a fireplace; two have a Jacuzzi. The location at the meeting of Routes 123 and 236 is particularly convenient for business travelers. The quite good restaurant offers an expensive but tasty prix fixe menu. *4023 Chain Bridge Rd., 22030, tel. 703/691–2266, fax 703/934–2112. 13 rooms, 1 suite. AE, MC, V. Facilities: restaurant, gift shop. Rates include full breakfast. $$$*

Fredericksburg
Dining

Le Lafayette. When you dine here, expect well-prepared French cuisine made with fresh Virginia ingredients and served in the Colonial setting of a 1771 Georgian-style house. The menu includes both brook trout and Chesapeake Bay seafood, plus imaginative Continental dishes such as grilled breast of duck in red currant sauce over fresh, braised red cabbage; poached fillet of salmon in saffron broth with mussels, leeks, and tomatoes; and pecan-crusted rack of lamb. *623 Caroline St., tel. 703/373–6895. Dress: casual. AE, D, DC, MC, V. Closed Mon. $$$*

Ristorante Renato. This unlikely Italian restaurant in the center of the Colonial town justifies its presence with a strong if conventional menu. "Romeo and Juliet" is veal and chicken topped with mozzarella and swimming in white-wine sauce; shrimp scampi Napoli has a lemon-butter sauce. White tablecloths and candles decorate the tables in the three quiet dining rooms, and the main dining room, with a view of the street corner, has red carpeting, stone walls, and a fireplace. *422 Williams St., tel. 703/371–8228. Reservations advised on weekends. Dress: casual. AE, MC, V. $$*

Goolrick's Pharmacy. This 1940s pharmacy with a soda fountain and Formica tables serves soft drinks in paper cups set in metal stands, and offers breakfast and light meals. *901 Caroline St., tel. 703/373–3411. No reservations. Dress: casual. Closed Sun.* $

Lodging **Best Western Johnny Appleseed.** This family-oriented two-story motel, a five-minute drive from the battlefields, is situated on a commercial highway strip. Rooms are of the basic motel variety, and queen-size beds are available; efficiencies have stove and microwave oven. The most pleasant views are of the pool. A truckstop across the street can be a source of predawn racket. *543 Warrenton Rd. (U.S. 17 and I–95), 22406, tel. 703/373–0000 or 800/528–1234, fax 703/373–5676. 87 rooms. Facilities: restaurant, outdoor pool, playground, nature trail, volleyball. AE, D, DC, MC, V.* $$

Hampton Inn. This cheerful motel on the interstate, near the historic district, has a U-shaped layout, with rooms on two stories that face the parking spaces, and a pool at the center. The rooms have a pink-and-green color scheme and the basic furnishings. Seven restaurants are within walking distance. *2310 Plank Rd., 22401, tel. 703/371–0330 or 800/426–7866, fax 703/371–1753. 165 rooms, 2 equipped for guests with disabilities, 1 suite. Facilities: outdoor pool. AE, D, DC, MC, V. Rates include Continental breakfast.* $$

The Richard Johnston Inn. This is a three-story row house across the street from the visitor center, with parking in the rear under the magnolia trees. Empire-style and Chippendale antiques and polished wood floors with Oriental rugs show that care has gone into the restoration. Two suites, with wet bar and wall-to-wall carpeting, open onto a patio. *711 Caroline St., 22401, tel. 703/899–7606. 7 rooms. AE, MC, V. Rates include breakfast.* $$

Great Falls **L'Auberge Chez François.** Alsatian cuisine is served here, 12 miles *Dining* west of Tysons Corner, in a country-inn atmosphere. The building, ★ of white stucco and dark exposed beams, is set on 6 acres, with a garden that can be seen from the dining room. Three fireplaces, flowered tablecloths, and stained glass set the mood for such specialties as salmon soufflé—a fillet of salmon topped with a mousse of scallops and salmon and a white-wine or lobster sauce. *332 Springvale Rd. (Rte. 674), tel. 703/759–3800. Reservations required 2 weeks in advance. Jacket required. AE, DC, MC, V. No lunch. Closed Mon.* $$$$

Loudoun **Hyatt Dulles.** This 14-story hotel is linked to Dulles International **County** Airport 3 miles away by a free shuttle service every half-hour. *Lodging* Soundproof guest rooms are suite-size; the parlor area (seats four) is separated from the bed by a credenza. Rooms have blond-wood furniture, floral paintings, and a mauve color scheme with liberal touches of gray, violet, and teal. A pianist performs, morning and afternoon, near the fountain in the two-story atrium. This is warmer and more elegant than the standard airport hotel. *2300 Dulles Corner Blvd., Herndon 22070, tel. 703/713–1234 or 800/223–1234, fax 703/713–3410. 317 rooms. Facilities: restaurant, bar, indoor pool, whirlpool, exercise room, sauna. AE, D, DC, MC, V.* $$$$

Lansdowne Conference Resort. The windows of this modern retreat that's located 45 minutes from Washington overlook the fields and rolling hills of the northern corner of Virginia. Polished wood furniture, carpets, handsome wall decorations, and marble-accented bathrooms evoke the classy feel of this property. Tall windows in the dining room, where regional cuisine is served, look toward Sugarloaf Mountain. Among its many specialties, the menu features hot smoked salmon with a sage hollandaise sauce; Maine lobster tail with *arborio* (Italian rice) and spring vegetables; and cilantro and garlic roasted leg of lamb. The pastry chef's buffet is an award winner. *44050 Woodridge Pkwy., Leesburg 22075, tel. 703/729–8400 or*

800/541–4801, fax 703/729–4111. 305 rooms. Facilities: 3 restaurants, bar, fitness center, golf, tennis, squash, racquetball, volleyball, indoor pool, outdoor pool, billiards, conference rooms. Weekend packages available. $$$$

Middleburg
Lodging

Middleburg Country Inn. This historic three-story structure, built in 1820 and enlarged in 1858, was the rectory of St. John's Parish Episcopal Church until 1907. Its medium-size rooms are furnished in antiques and period reproductions and have working fireplaces. A full country breakfast is served, and, when weather permits, guests can enjoy their meals alfresco. There's also a complimentary afternoon tea. *209 E. Washington St., Box 2065, Middleburg 22117, tel. 703/687–6082 or 800/262–6082, fax 703/687–5603. 7 rooms. Facilities: parlor, VCRs and video library. AE, D, MC, V. $$–$$$*
Middleburg Inn and Guest Suites. This is not an historic building, but the atmosphere conveys 18th-century-style living. Large rooms are furnished with canopied beds, antiques, and period reproductions. *105 W. Washington St., Middleburg 22117, tel. 703/687–3115 or 800/432–6125. 4 suites, 1 cottage. MC, V. $$–$$$*

Tysons Corner
Dining

Clyde's of Tysons Corner. A branch of a popular Georgetown pub, Clyde's has four basically art deco dining rooms, which offer a choice of styles. The **Palm Terrace,** for example, has high ceilings and lots of greenery; another room is a formal dining room. The long, eclectic menu always includes fresh fish, often in such preparations as trout Parmesan. The wine list is equally long. Quality is high, service attentive. *8332 Leesburg Pike, tel. 703/734–1900. Reservations advised. Dress: casual. AE, D, DC, MC, V. $$$*

Lodging

Ramada Hotel. This high-rise property on the highway, 10 miles west of Arlington, has a convention center and rooms styled in contemporary furnishings in mauves, greens, and pastel shades. The restaurant, Café Fennel, serves popular American fare. *7801 Leesburg Pike (Rte. 7 and I–495), 22043, tel. 703/893–1340 or 800/228–2828, fax 703/847–9520. 391 rooms, 13 suites. Facilities: restaurant, nightclub, indoor pool, sauna, whirlpool, exercise room. AE, D, DC, MC, V. $$$*

The Arts and Nightlife

The Arts

Northern Virginia is only minutes from the substantial cultural offerings in Washington, D.C., including the Kennedy Center.

Fairfax County Council of the Arts (tel. 703/642–0862) acts as a clearinghouse for information about performances and exhibitions throughout northern Virginia.

Music and Dance

Wolf Trap Farm Park (Vienna, tel. 703/255–1860 or 703/938–2404) operates in a grand outdoor pavilion during the warmer months, in The Barns—18th-century farm buildings transported from upstate New York—at other seasons. Top performers appear here in programs from the entire range of musical entertainment. Dance is featured frequently, as are children's programs (tel. 703/255–1827). This is one of the major performing-arts venues in the greater Washington area.

George Mason University Center for the Arts (tel. 703/993–8888) frequently opens jazz, classical, opera, dance, and theater performances by premier artists to the public. The concert hall seats 2,000; other venues are more cozy.

Theater   **The Harris Theater** (tel. 703/993–2503) of George Mason University presents student drama performances.

Lazy Susan Dinner Theater (Rte. 1 and Furnace Rd., Woodbridge, tel. 703/550–7384) offers a varied year-round program.

Gunston Arts Center (2700 S. Lang St., Arlington, tel. 703/358–6960) is home to the Washington Shakespeare Company, Signature Theatre, and other groups.

Nightlife

Blues   **Whitey's** (2761 Washington Blvd., Arlington, tel. 703/525–9825) is crowded, noisy, and irresistible—a dive with a loyal following of diverse ages and backgrounds. **Where the Buffalo Roam Restaurant** (216 William St., Fredericksburg, tel. 703/373–2833) offers blues and rock-and-roll.

Irish and Folk   **Murphy's Restaurant and Pub** (713 King St., Alexandria, tel. 703/548–1717) has boisterous entertainment and, in winter, a blazing fire. **The Old Brogue** (760-C Walker Rd., Great Falls, tel. 703/759–3309) has lively music.

Jazz   **Two Nineteen** (219 King St., Alexandria, tel. 703/549–1141) has jazz upstairs, a bar in the basement. **Ice House Café** (706 Elden St., Herndon, tel. 703/437–4500) also swings.

Rock   **Roratonga Rodeo** (2711 Wilson Blvd., Arlington, tel. 703/525–8646) features live music Saturday–Thursday. You can figure out the type of cuisine served by the strands of jalapeño peppers hanging over the tables.

Singles   **Clyde's of Tysons Corner** (8332 Leesburg Pike, Vienna, tel. 703/734–1901) is famous in the D.C. area as a gathering place for unattached professionals. **Sitting Duck** (Evans Farm Inn, 1696 Chain Bridge Rd., McLean, tel. 703/356–8000), an English pub, has a piano bar Friday through Sunday.

Excursions

The C&O Canal and Great Falls

In the 18th and early 19th centuries, the Potomac River was the main transport route between vital Maryland ports and the seaports of the Chesapeake Bay. But though it served as an important link with the country's western territories, the Potomac had a major drawback for a commercial waterway: Rapids and waterfalls along its 190 miles made navigation of the entire distance by boat impossible.

To make the flow of goods from east to west more efficient, engineers proposed that a canal with elevator locks be built parallel to the river. George Washington founded a company to build the canal, and in 1802 his firm opened the Patowmack Canal on the Virginia side of the river.

In 1828 Washington's canal was replaced by the **Chesapeake & Ohio Canal,** known as the C&O. Stretching from downtown Washington to Cumberland, Maryland, the C&O moved barges through 75 locks, and by the mid 19th-century it carried a million tons of goods a year. But by the time it had opened, newer technology was already starting to make canal systems obsolete. The Baltimore & Ohio Railroad—which opened the same day as the C&O—finally put the canal out of business in 1924. After Palisades residents defeated a 1950s proposal to build a highway over it, the canal was turned into a national park.

The twin parks of **Great Falls**—on either side of the river 13 miles west of Georgetown—are also now part of the national park system. The 800–acre park on the Virginia side is a favorite spot for outings, not least because the steep, jagged falls roar into a narrow gorge, providing one of the most spectacular scenic attractions in the East.

Escorted Tours A tour of the visitor center and museum at **Great Falls Park** (tel. 703/ 285–2966) in Virginia takes 30 minutes. Staff members conduct special tours and walks year-round. On the Maryland side, the old **Great Falls Tavern** (tel. 301/299–2026) serves as a museum and headquarters for the rangers who manage the C&O Canal. During warm weather, replicas of the old mule-drawn boats carry visitors along this stretch of the canal; similar trips also begin in Georgetown.

Getting Around *By Car* To reach the Virginia side of Great Falls Park, take the scenic and winding Route 193 (Exit 13 off Route 495, the Capitol Beltway) to Route 738, and follow the signs. It takes about 25 minutes to drive to the park from the Beltway. You can get to the Maryland side of the park by following MacArthur Boulevard from Georgetown or by taking Exit 41 off the Beltway, following the signs to Carderock.

By Foot, Canoe, or Bicycle The C&O Canal Park and its towpath are favorite destinations for joggers, bikers, and canoeists. Most recreational bikers consider the 13 miles from Georgetown to Great Falls an easy ride; there's only one short stretch of rocky ground near Great Falls where bikers need to carry their cycle. Storm damage has left parts of the canal dry, but many segments remain intact and navigable by canoe. You can rent canoes or bicycles at **Fletcher's Boat House,** just upriver from Georgetown (*see* Exploring, *below*).

Exploring *Numbers in the margin correspond to points of interest on the C&O Canal and Great Falls map.*

This tour moves from Georgetown northwest along the Potomac to Great Falls Park. The canal itself is worth a day's stroll or ride.

❶ The towpath along the canal in **Georgetown** passes traces of that area's industrial past, such as the Godey Lime Kilns near the mouth of Rock Creek, as well as the fronts of numerous houses dating to 1810. From mid-April through early November mule-drawn barges leave for 90-minute trips from the Foundry Mall on Thomas Jefferson Street NW, half a block south of M Street. No reservations are required for the public trips. *For information, tel. 202/653–5190 or 301/299–2026. For group reservations and rates, tel. 301/299–3613. Cost: $6 adults, $3.50 senior citizens and children under 13.*

❷ **Fletcher's Boat House** (4940 Canal Rd. NW, tel. 202/244–0461) rents canoes and bicycles and sells fishing tackle and D.C. fishing licenses. Fishermen often congregate here to try their luck with shad, perch, catfish, striped bass, and other freshwater species. Be sure to call ahead; hours vary seasonally.

❸ **Chain Bridge**—named for the chains that held up the original structure—links the district with Virginia. The bridge was built to enable cattlemen to bring Virginia herds to the slaughterhouses on the Maryland side of the Potomac. The Virginia side of the river in the area around Chain Bridge is known for its good fishing and narrow, treacherous channel.

Glen Echo is a charming village of Victorian houses that was founded in 1891 when brothers Edwin and Edward Baltzley fell un-

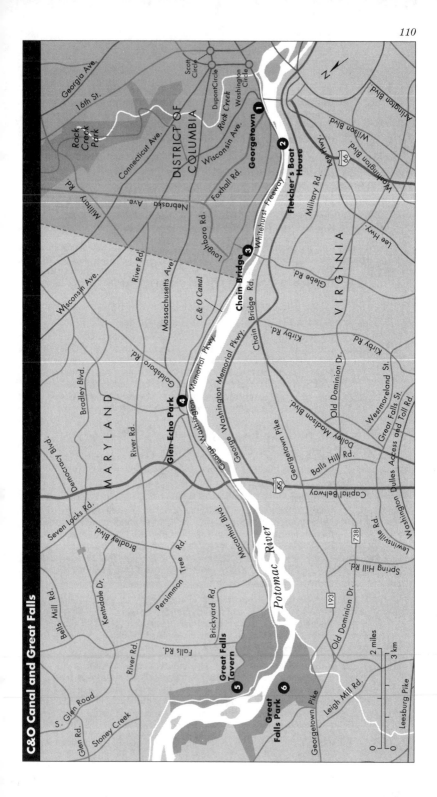

C&O Canal and Great Falls

der the spell of the short-lived Chautauqua movement, an organization that promoted liberal and practical education among the masses. Their compound served a stint as an amusement park and is now run by the National Park Service as an arts and cultural center.

❹ **Glen Echo Park** (7300 MacArthur Blvd., tel. 301/492-6282) is noted not only for its whimsical architecture, including a stone tower left from the Chautauqua period, but also for its splendid 1921 Dentzel carousel. The park is also the site of frequent folk festivals, and dances are held in the ornate Spanish Ballroom. For scheduling information, check the "Weekend" section in Friday's *Washington Post* or the free weekly *City Paper*.

The nearby **Clara Barton House,** one of the most striking Victorian structures in Glen Echo, has been preserved as a monument to the founder of the American Red Cross. Barton moved here toward the end of her life, using the place for a while to store Red Cross supplies and as the organization's headquarters. Today the building is furnished with original period artifacts. *5801 Oxford Rd., Glen Echo, MD, tel. 301/492-6245. Admission free. Open daily 10-5; guided tours hourly on the ½ hour.*

❺ **Great Falls Tavern,** on the Maryland side of Great Falls Park, features displays of canal history and a platform from which to look at the falls. Better yet, walk over the Olmsted Bridges out to a small island in the middle of the river for a spectacular view. On the canal walls are "rope burns" caused by decade upon decade of friction from barge lines. Half a mile west a flood marker shows how high the Potomac can go—after a hurricane in 1972 the river crested far above the ground where visitors stand. Canal barge trips start here between April and October. The tavern ceased being a hostelry long ago, so if you're hungry head for the snack bar a few paces north of the tavern. *Park, tel. 301/299-2026. Admission: $4 per vehicle, $2 per person without vehicle, good for 7 days for MD and VA sides of the park. Open daily sunrise-sunset. Tavern, snack bar, and museum, tel. 301/299-3613. Open daily 9-5.*

❻ The Virginia side of **Great Falls Park,** not accessible from the Maryland side, offers the best views of the Potomac, as well as trails leading past the old Patowmack Canal and among the boulders and forests lining the edge of the falls. Horseback riding is permitted— maps are available at the visitors center—but you can't rent horses in the park. Swimming and wading are prohibited, but there are fine opportunities for fishing (a Virginia, Maryland, or D.C. license is required for anglers 16 and older), rock climbing (climbers must register at the visitor center beforehand), and white-water kayaking (*below* the falls only, and only by experienced boaters). Despite frequent signs and warnings, each year some visitors dare the powerful currents and lose. It's best to keep away from even the most benign-looking ripple. *Tel. 703/285-2966. Admission: $4 per vehicle, $2 per person without vehicle, good for 7 days for MD and VA sides of the park. Open daily 8 AM until dark. Closed Dec. 25.*

6 Williamsburg, Jamestown, Yorktown

Virginia's single largest historical attraction is the re-creation of an 18th-century American city—its buildings, its trades, its daily life, and even some of its citizens, portrayed by costumed interpreters. Colonial Williamsburg, a careful restoration of the former Virginia capital, gives visitors the chance to walk into another century and see how earlier Americans worked and socialized. The streets may be unrealistically clean for that era, and you'll find hundreds of visitors exploring the buildings with you, but the rich detail of the re-creation and the sheer size of the city could hold your attention for days. A ticket or pass (price is based on duration of visit) admits the holder to sites in the restored area, but it costs nothing just to walk around, watch the comings and goings, and absorb the atmosphere.

The 23-mile Colonial Parkway joins Williamsburg with two other significant historical sites on or near the peninsula bounded by the James and York rivers. Jamestown Island was the location of the first permanent English settlement in North America; Yorktown was the site of the final major battle in the American War of Independence. The sites themselves are maintained today by the National Park Service, which provides visitors with background information. Close by are the more purely entertaining Jamestown Settlement and the Yorktown Victory Center—both run by the Jamestown-Yorktown Foundation—which, like Colonial Williamsburg, re-create the buildings and lives and activities of the 18th century, using interpreters in period dress who speak with visitors as though they were living 200 years ago.

Essential Information

Important Addresses and Numbers

Visitor Information **Williamsburg Area Convention and Visitors Bureau** (Drawer GB, 201 Penniman Rd., Williamsburg 23187, tel. 804/253–0192 or 800/368–6511).
Colonial Williamsburg (Box 1776, Williamsburg 23187–1776, tel. 800/447–8679).
Colonial National Historical Park (Box 210, Yorktown 23690, tel. 804/898–3400).

Emergencies Throughout the region, dial **911** for emergency assistance.

Hospitals In Williamsburg, **Williamsburg Community Hospital** (6005 1238 Mt. Vernon Ave., tel. 804/253–6000; emergency room, 804/253–6005). **Riverside Regional Medical Center** (500 J. Clyde Morris Blvd., tel 804/594–2000; emergency room, tel. 804/594–2050), in Newport News, is near many areas of York County.

Arriving and Departing

By Plane **Newport News/Williamsburg International Airport,** in Newport News but close to Williamsburg, is served primarily by USAir (tel. 800/428–4322). **Norfolk International Airport** hosts American (tel. 800/433–7300), Delta (tel. 800/221–1212), United (tel. 800/241–6522), TWA (tel. 800/221–2000), and USAir (tel. 800/428–4322).

By Car Williamsburg is west of I–64, 51 miles southeast of Richmond; the Colonial Parkway joins Williamsburg with Jamestown to the southwest and Yorktown to the southeast.

By Train **Amtrak** (tel. 800/872–7245) trains stop at Williamsburg (468 N. Boundary St., tel. 804/229–8750) on their way from New York, Washington, and Richmond to Newport News.

By Bus **Greyhound Lines** (468 N. Boundary St., Williamsburg, tel. 804/229–1460 or 800/231–2222) has seven departures daily, both westbound (to Richmond) and eastbound (to Norfolk).

Guided Tours

Interpreters well versed in Williamsburg and Colonial history are available to lead groups on tours of the Historic Area (tel. 800/228–8878).

Interpre-Tours, Ltd. (tel. 804/785–2010), Williamsburg's oldest tour company, provides guides for groups that want personalized tours of the area, as well as special programs and destination management.

Orientation Colonial Williamsburg's hour-long guided **walking tours** of the historic area depart from the Greenhow Lumber House daily from 9 to 5. Reservations should be made on the day of the tour at the Lumber House; tours are free to Patriot's Pass holders.

Special- Colonial Williamsburg's **Lanthorn Tours** takes visitors on an evening
interest walking tour of selected trade shops where jewelry and other products are made in 18th-century style. A separate ticket is required for this program and may be purchased at the visitor center or Lumber House. **Carriage and wagon rides** are available daily, weather permitting. General ticket holders may purchase tickets on the day of the ride at the Lumber House.

Exploring

Colonial Williamsburg

Numbers in the margin correspond to points of interest on the Williamsburg and Environs and Colonial Williamsburg maps.

❶ **Colonial Williamsburg,** 51 miles southeast of Richmond, is the foremost attraction in this area, and it's a marvel: Although improbably sanitary, it's an otherwise convincing re-creation of the late-18th-century city. This was the capital of Virginia from 1699 to 1780, succeeding Jamestown and then succeeded by Richmond. Williamsburg has long ceased to be politically important, but now that it resembles itself in its era of glory, it ranks as a jewel of the commonwealth. The restoration project, begun in 1926, was inspired by a local pastor, W.A.R. Goodwin, and financed by John D. Rockefeller, Jr. Rockefeller died in 1960, but the work of the archaeologists and historians of the Colonial Williamsburg Foundation continues to this day, and the restored area of the city is operated by the foundation as a living-history museum.

In Colonial Williamsburg, 88 original 18th-century and early 19th-century structures have been meticulously restored, and another 40 have been reconstructed on their original sites. There are two architectural anomalies here: a 19th-century Federal house, privately owned and closed to the public, and a Victorian Carpenter's Gothic building, operated as a museum by the Association for the Preservation of Virginia Antiquities. In all, 225 period rooms have been furnished from the foundation's collection of more than 100,000 pieces

Williamsburg and Environs

KEY

Rail Lines
Ferry
Battlefield

0 ___ 10 miles
0 ___ 15 km

of furniture, pottery, china, glass, silver, pewter, textiles, tools, and carpeting.

Period authenticity also governs the landscaping of the 90 acres of gardens and public greens. The restored area covers 173 acres—surrounded by another "greenbelt," controlled by the foundation, that guards against the encroachment of development that could destroy the illusion of the Colonial city.

Despite its huge scale, Williamsburg can seem almost cozy. One million visitors come here annually, and all year long hundreds of costumed interpreters, wearing bonnets or three-cornered hats, rove and ride through the streets. Dozens of skilled craftspersons, also in costume, demonstrate and explain their trades inside their workshops. They include the shoe maker, the cooper, the gunsmith, the blacksmith, the musical instrument maker, the silversmith, and the wig maker. Their wares are for sale nearby. Four taverns serve food and drink that approximate the fare of 200 years ago.

Because of the sheer size of Williamsburg and the large numbers of visitors (especially in the warmer months), the best plan may be to begin a tour early in the day; it's a good idea to spend the night before in the area. The foundation claims that visitors must allow three or four days to do Williamsburg justice, but that will depend on one's own interest in the period—and one's interest often increases on arrival. Everyone should allow at least one full day to tour the city. Families will soon realize that this is a place where they can spend a lot of pocket money.

 The **visitor center** is the logical first stop at Colonial Williamsburg. Here visitors can park free; buy their tickets; see a 35-minute intro-

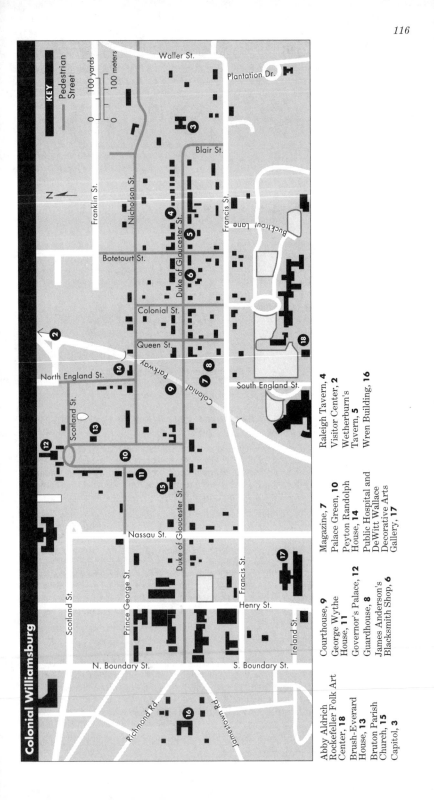

Colonial Williamsburg

KEY

Pedestrian Street

Waller St.

Plantation Dr.

Blair St.

Franklin St.

Nicholson St.

Duke of Gloucester St.

Botetourt St.

Francis St.

Bucktrout Lane

Colonial St.

Queen St.

Colonial Parkway

North England St.

South England St.

Scotland St.

Nassau St.

Duke of Gloucester St.

Prince George St.

Francis St.

Henry St.

Scotland St.

N. Boundary St.

S. Boundary St.

Ireland St.

Richmond Rd.

Jamestown Rd.

Abby Aldrich Rockefeller Folk Art Center, **18**
Brush-Everard House, **13**
Bruton Parish Church, **15**
Capitol, **3**

Courthouse, **9**
George Wythe House, **11**
Governor's Palace, **12**
Guardhouse, **8**
James Anderson's Blacksmith Shop, **6**

Magazine, **7**
Palace Green, **10**
Peyton Randolph House, **14**
Public Hospital and DeWitt Wallace Decorative Arts Gallery, **17**

Raleigh Tavern, **4**
Visitor Center, **2**
Wetherburn's Tavern, **5**
Wren Building, **16**

ductory movie, *Williamsburg—the Story of a Patriot*; and pick up a *Visitors Companion* guide, with a list of regular events and special programs and a map of the Historic Area. *I–64 (Exit 238), tel. 804/220–7645 or 800/447–8679. Admission: Patriot's Pass ($29 adults, $17 children 6–12, prices subject to change), good for one year, admits bearer to every Colonial Williamsburg–run site, including Carter's Grove Plantation, the Governor's Palace, DeWitt Wallace Decorative Arts Gallery, and the Abby Aldrich Rockefeller Folk Art Center. A range of less expensive tickets allows more restricted visits. Tickets are also sold at the Lumber House in the historic area. Open daily 9–5. Some sites close in winter on a rotating basis (Carter's Grove closed Jan.–mid-Mar.).*

Visitors must tour the restored area on foot because all vehicular traffic is prohibited to preserve the Colonial atmosphere. Shuttle buses run continuously to and from the visitor center, following a route along the perimeter of the area. Vans for people with disabilities are permitted by prior arrangement, and some structures have wheelchair ramps. Other services for visitors with disabilities are also available (tel. 804/220–7644).

The spine of the restored area is the broad **Duke of Gloucester Street,** which is almost precisely a mile long. On Saturday at noon, from March to October, the Junior Fife and Drum Corps marches the length of the street and performs a stirring drill. Along this artery alone, or just off it, are two dozen attractions.

❸ At the east end of the street is the **capitol,** the building that made this town so important. It was here that the pre-Revolutionary House of Burgesses (dominated by the ascendant gentry) challenged the royally appointed council (an almost medieval body made up of the bigger landowners). The House eventually arrived at the resolutions that amounted to rebellion. An informative tour explains the development, stage by stage, of American democracy from its English parliamentary roots. In the courtroom a guide recites the harsh Georgian sentences that were meted out: For instance, theft of more than 12 shillings was a capital crime. Occasional reenactments, such as witch trials, dramatize the evolution of our jurisprudence.

What stands on the site today is in fact a reproduction of a structure of 1705 that burned down in 1747. Dark-wood wainscoting, pewter chandeliers, and towering ceilings contribute to a handsome impression. That an official building would have so ornate an interior was characteristic of aristocratic 18th-century Virginia. This was in telling contrast to the plain town meeting halls of Puritan New England, where other Founding Fathers were governing themselves at the same time.

Walking west on Duke of Gloucester Street, visitors encounter a dozen 18th-century shops—including those of the apothecary, the wig maker, the silversmith, and the milliner.

Less than ⅕ mile from the capitol, on the north side of the street, is
❹ **Raleigh Tavern,** the scene of pre-Revolutionary revels and rallies that were often joined by Washington, Jefferson, and other major figures. The spare but elegant blue-and-white Apollo Room is said to have been the first meeting place of Phi Beta Kappa, the scholastic honorary society founded in 1776. The French general Marquis de Lafayette was feted here in 1824. In 1859 the original structure burned, and today's building is a reconstruction based on archaeological evidence and period descriptions and sketches of the building.

Across the street and a few steps farther west is the original
⑤ Wetherburn's Tavern, which offered refreshment, entertainment,
and lodging beginning in 1743. This is possibly the most accurately
furnished building in Colonial Williamsburg, for the contents con-
form to a room-by-room inventory taken in 1760. Excavations at this
site have yielded more than 200,000 artifacts. The outbuildings include the original dairy and a reconstructed kitchen. Vegetables are
still grown in the small garden.

Between Botetourt and Colonial streets, on the south side of Duke
⑥ of Gloucester Street, **James Anderson's Blacksmith Shop** is where
smiths forge the nails, tools, and other iron hardware that is used in
construction throughout the town. The shop itself was recently reconstructed by costumed carpenters using 18th-century tools and
techniques—a project that was featured on public television.

Two blocks farther west, on the south side of Duke of Gloucester
⑦ Street, the original **Magazine** (1715), an octagonal brick warehouse,
was used for storing arms and ammunition—at one time, 60,000
pounds of gunpowder and 3,000 muskets. It was used for this purpose by the British, then by the Continental army, and again by the
Confederates during the Civil War. Today, 18th-century firearms
are on display within the arsenal. Behind and to the left is the
⑧ Guardhouse, which once served in the defense of the magazine's le-
thal inventory; now it contains a replica fire engine (1750) that is
seen on the town streets in the warmer months; special interpretive
programs about the military also are scheduled here.

The magazine sits on the southern half of **Market Square,** an open
green between Queen and Palace streets along Duke of Gloucester
Street, and extending a block on either side. This was the outdoor
site for the vending of cattle, seafood, dairy products, fruit, and vegetables. It was also the venue for slave auctions.

Across the street from the magazine is the site of the original
⑨ Courthouse of 1770, which continued to be used by municipal and
county courts until 1932. Civil and minor criminal matters and cases
involving slaves were adjudicated here; other trials were conducted
at the capitol. Stocks, once used to punish misdemeanors, are located outside the building; modern-day visitors take perverse pleasure in photographing each other clapped in the stocks. The exterior
of the Courthouse recently has been restored to its original appearance. Visitors often participate in scheduled reenactments of court
sessions.

Around the corner from the courthouse, extending north from Duke
⑩ of Gloucester Street, the broad **Palace Green** runs up the center of
Palace Street, with the governor's palace at the far end and a notable
historic house on each side of it.

Walking along the west side of Palace Green toward the palace, you
⑪ first encounter the **George Wythe House,** residence of Thomas
Jefferson's law professor, also a signer of the Declaration of Independence. General Washington used the house as a headquarters
just before his victory at Yorktown. The large brick structure, built
in the mid-18th century, is conspicuously symmetrical: Each side
has a chimney, and each floor has two rooms on either side of a center
hallway. The garden in back is similarly divided. The outbuildings,
including a smokehouse, kitchen, laundry, privies, and a chicken
coop, have been reconstructed.

⑫ The **Governor's Palace** was built in 1720 by His Majesty's Governor
Alexander Spotswood. Seven British viceroys, the last of them Lord

Dunmore in 1775, lived in this mansion, whose design and decor heralded the power of the Crown. Helping to make this point are 800 guns and swords arrayed on the walls and ceilings of several rooms. Some of the furnishings are in fact original, and the rest are matched to an extraordinary inventory of 16,000 items. Lavishly appointed as it is, the palace is furnished to the time just before the Revolution. During the Revolution, it housed the Commonwealth's first two governors, Patrick Henry and Thomas Jefferson. The original residence burned down in 1781, and today's reconstruction stands on the original foundation.

A costumed guide greets visitors at the door of the Governor's Palace and conducts them through the building, offering commentary and answering questions. Notable among the furnishings are several pieces made in Williamsburg and actually owned by Lord Dunmore, the last royal governor. Social events are described on the walk through the great formal ballroom. The supper room leads to the formal garden and the planted terraces beyond.

🔞 From the palace, turn left on Scotland Street at the **Brush-Everard House,** which was built in 1717 by John Brush, a gunsmith, and later owned by Thomas Everard, who was twice mayor of Williamsburg. The yellow wood-frame house contains remarkable ornate carving work but is open only for special-focus tours.

From the house, continue to England Street, the site of **Robertson's Windmill,** where—on the outskirts of the Historic Area—rural trades such as basket making, pit sawing, and coopering (barrel making) are demonstrated. The windmill operates only when the weather is willing.

Follow England Street south to Nicholson Street and turn left at the **Peyton Randolph House,** the home of a prominent colonist and revolutionary who served as attorney general under the British, then as Speaker of the House of Burgesses, and later as president of the first and second Continental Congresses. The oak-paneled bedroom and Randolph family silver are highlights, but unfortunately, this is another building open only for special tours.

Continue east to the **military encampment.** During warm weather, "Join the Continental Army," an interactive theater performance, enables visitors to experience military life on the eve of the Revolution. Under the guidance of costumed militia-men, visitors drill and make camp in a 45-minute participatory program. If you want to join the ranks for a little while, you can volunteer at the site.

🔞 On Duke of Gloucester Street, west of Palace Street, the brick Episcopal **Bruton Parish Church,** built in 1715, has served continuously as a house of worship. One of its 20th-century pastors, W.A.R. Goodwin, provided the impetus for Williamsburg's restoration. The church tower, topped by a beige wooden steeple, was added in 1769; during the Revolution its bell served as the local liberty bell. The white pews, tall and boxed in, are characteristic of the starkly graceful Colonial ecclesiastical architecture of the region. The stone baptismal font is believed to have come from an older Jamestown church. Many local eminences, including one royal governor, are interred in the graveyard. The church is open to the public; contributions are accepted.

Time Out At the west end of Duke of Gloucester Street, for a block on both sides, **Merchant's Square** has more than 30 shops and restaurants, including ones serving fast food. Services include two banks.

16 Beyond Merchant's Square, at the west end of Duke of Gloucester Street, where it faces the capitol a mile away, the **Wren Building** is part of the College of William and Mary, founded in 1693 and the second-oldest college in the United States after Harvard University. The campus extends to the west; the Wren Building (1695) was based on the work of the celebrated London architect Sir Christopher Wren, who never visited Colonial America. Its redbrick outer walls are original, but the interiors were gutted by fire several times, and the present quarters are largely reconstructions of the 20th century. The faculty common room, with a table covered with green felt and an antique globe, suggests Oxford and Cambridge universities, the models for this New World institution. Jefferson studied and later taught law here to James Monroe and others. College undergraduates lead visitors on tours of the building, including the chapel where Peyton Randolph is buried.

Along with all the handsome public buildings, restored homes, reconstructed shops, and costumed interpreters of Colonial Williamsburg, museums bequeathed by three modern-day benefactors add another cultural dimension that goes well beyond Colonial history.

17 The **Public Hospital** on Francis Street is a reconstructed insane asylum of 1773 that provides a shocking glimpse of bedlamite squalor. It also serves as cover for an edifice of 1985 that houses very different exhibitions; visitors pass through the hospital lobby into the **DeWitt Wallace Decorative Arts Gallery.** Here English and American furniture, textiles, prints, metals, and ceramics of the 17th to the early 19th century are grouped by medium. Prizes among the 8,000 pieces in the collection are a full-length portrait of George Washington by Charles Willson Peale and a royally commissioned case clock surmounted by the detailed figure of a Native American.

18 On South England Street, ½ mile from the DeWitt Wallace Gallery, the **Abby Aldrich Rockefeller Folk Art Center** is best reached by the shuttle bus because there is no direct path. This is a showcase for American "decorative usefulware": toys, furniture, weather vanes, coffeepots, quilts. There are also folk paintings, rustic wood and metal sculpture, and needlepoint pictures. The exhibition spaces represent typical 19th-century domestic interiors. Since the 1920s, the 2,000-piece collection has grown from the original 400 pieces acquired by the wife of Colonial Williamsburg's first and principal benefactor.

19 **Carter's Grove,** 8 miles east of Williamsburg on U.S. 60 East, examines 400 years of history, starting in 1619 with Wolstenholme Towne. The settlement has been reconstructed after extensive archaeological investigation and equipped with recorded narrative. Exhibits of the Winthrop Rockefeller Archaeology Museum, opened in 1991, provide further insight. The 18th century is represented by slave dwellings reconstructed on their original foundations, where costumed interpreters explain the crucial role African-Americans played on plantations. Finally, visitors may tour the mansion, built in 1755 by Carter Burwell, whose grandfather, "King" Carter, made the family fortune as one of Virginia's wealthiest landowners and greatest explorers. It was extensively remodeled in 1919 to express its owner's fascination with the past, and additions were made in the 1930s. The interior is notable for the original wood paneling and elaborate carvings. A one-way scenic country road, used also for biking, leads from Carter's Grove through woods, meadows, marshes, and streams back to Williamsburg. Visitors also may return to the Historic Area on Route 60. *Tel. 804/220–7645. Admis-*

sion: $10 or Patriot's Pass. Open Tues.–Sun. 9–5. Closed early Jan.–mid-Mar.

㉑ Three miles east of Williamsburg, **Busch Gardens Williamsburg** is a 360-acre amusement and theme park with more than 30 rides and nine re-creations of European and French Canadian hamlets. Competitors drive bumper cars on the "Autobahn"; ride the new "Drachen Fire" and the established "Loch Ness Monster" roller coasters at speeds of up to 70 miles an hour; swing on a pendulum ride, "DaVinci's Battering Ram," said to be based on a design by Leonardo himself. Water adventures include a "Rhine River" cruise and "rafting" the "Roman Rapids." In a medieval English village, a jet flight simulator is piloted by a gnome searching for the magic crystal of Zed. Shows and rides are included in the admission price; food is additional. Costumed actors add character to the themed areas, and two covered trains circle the park while cable-car gondolas pass overhead. The park is thronged with families in warm months. *U.S. 60, tel. 804/253–3350. Admission: $27.95 one day adults, $21.50 children 3–6, free for children under 2. Open Apr., Sat. 10–10, Sun. 10–7; mid-May–mid-June, Sun.–Fri. 10–7, Sat. 10–10; mid-June–July, daily 10–10; Aug., Sun.–Fri. 10–10, Sat. 10–midnight; Sept.–Oct. 31, Fri.–Tues. 10–7; Nov., weekends 10–7. Parking $2–$6.*

Jamestown and Yorktown

Not far from Colonial Williamsburg are two important but smaller historical sites maintained by the National Park Service, each with a neighboring attraction that re-creates, on a much smaller scale than that of Colonial Williamsburg, the daily activities of an 18th-century town using costumed interpreters who converse with visitors about aspects of Colonial life.

㉒ **Jamestown Island,** the site of the first permanent English settlement in North America (1607) and the capital of Virginia until 1699, is 9 miles southwest of Williamsburg on the Colonial Parkway, separated from the mainland by a narrow isthmus. That Jamestown is no longer inhabited makes its historical significance all the more stirring to the imagination. Redbrick foundation walls approximately delineate the settlement, and artists' conceptions of the original buildings can be seen at several locations. Audio stations narrate the evolving story of Jamestown. The only standing structure is the ruin of a church tower from the 1640s, now part of the Memorial Church built in 1907; the markers within indicate the original church's foundations. Other monuments around the site also date from the tercentenary celebration in 1907. Statues portray the founder of Jamestown, Captain John Smith, and his advocate, the Native American princess Pocahontas, whose pleas saved Smith from being beheaded. Ranger-guided tours of the site take place daily. Living-history programs are presented daily in summer and on weekends in spring and autumn. The museum in the visitor center contains one of the most extensive collections of 17th-century artifacts in the United States. A 5-mile nature drive that rings the island is posted with historically informative signs and paintings. *Tel. 804/229–1733. Admission: $8 car, $2 cyclist or pedestrian. Visitor center open daily 9–5 (until 6 in summer, but gates close at 5:30).*

On leaving the island, visitors can stop at the reconstructed **Glasshouse** to observe a demonstration of glassblowing, an unsuccessful business venture of the early colonists. The products of today are for sale in a gift shop.

Adjacent to Jamestown Island, and not to be confused with it, is a living-history museum called **Jamestown Settlement.** A version of the early James Fort has been built here, and within it "colonists" cook, make armor, and describe their hard life living under thatched roofs and between walls of wattle and daub (stick framework covered with mud plaster). The largest structure in the complex is the church, where attendance was required twice a day. In the "Indian Village" you can enter a wigwam and see buckskin-costumed interpreters cultivate a garden and make baskets, tools, and pottery. This is one museum where everything may be handled—children especially enjoy this. Visitors may stroll to the pier and inspect large-scale reproductions of the ships in which the settlers arrived: *Godspeed, Discovery,* and *Susan Constant.* The *Godspeed* is a seaworthy vessel that retraced the original voyage in 1985. Visitors may climb aboard the *Susan Constant* and interrogate the sailor-interpreters. Jamestown Settlement's indoor museum, opened in 1990, has exhibits on the lives of the Powhatans and their English-born neighbors; permanent and changing exhibits explore their interaction and world conditions that encouraged colonization. There's also a 20-minute docudrama, "Jamestown: The Beginning," as told from a Native American perspective. *Rte. 31 off Colonial Pkwy., tel. 804/ 229–1607. Admission: $7.50 adults, $3.75 children 6–12. Combination ticket for Jamestown Settlement and Yorktown Victory Center: $9 adults, $4.40 children 6–12. Open daily 9–5, except Christmas Day and New Year's Day.*

㉒ **Yorktown,** on the Colonial Parkway 14 miles southeast of Williamsburg, is where the combined American and French forces surrounded British troops under Lord Cornwallis in 1781 and forced an end to the American War of Independence. In Yorktown today, as at Jamestown, two major attractions complement each other: Yorktown Battlefield, the historical site, is operated by the National Park Service; Yorktown Victory Center, an informative entertainment, is operated by the state's Jamestown-Yorktown Foundation. The town of Yorktown remains a living community, albeit a small one.

The museum in the visitor center at **Yorktown Battlefield** has on exhibit General George Washington's original field tent, pitched and furnished as it was during the fighting. Dioramas, illuminated maps, and a short movie about the battle make the sobering point that Washington's victory was hardly inevitable. A look around from the observation deck on the roof can help one to visualize better the events of the campaign. Guided by a taped audio tour rented ($2) from the gift shop, visitors may explore the battlefield by car, stopping at the site of Washington's headquarters, a couple of crucial redoubts (breastworks dug into the ground), and the field where surrender took place. *Tel. 804/898–3400. Admission free. Visitor center open daily 8:30–5 (until 6 in summer).*

On the western edge of the battlefield, at the **Yorktown Victory Center,** visitors follow the "Road to Revolution" walkway beginning at the orientation area: Textual and graphic displays cover the principal events and personalities of the period. The trail enters the main museum, where the story of Yorktown's critical role in the achievement of American independence is told, and where life-size tableaux feature six "witnesses," including an African-American patriot, a loyalist, a Quaker, two Continental Army soldiers, and the wife of a Virginia plantation owner. An action-packed, half-hour movie dramatization (more melodramatic than the one at the battlefield) is screened continuously. Outdoors, in a Continental Army encampment, interpreters costumed as soldiers and female auxiliaries reenact and discuss daily camp life, including the firing of muskets, drilling, the use of medical treatments, and cooking. In another outdoor area, costumed interpreters re-create 18th-century farm life and demonstrate the gardening of herbs, vegetables, flax, and tobacco. *Old Rte. 238 off Colonial Pkwy., tel. 804/887–1776. Admission: $3.75 adults, $1.75 children 6–12. See Jamestown Settlement, above, for ticket prices. Open daily 9–5. Closed Christmas Day and New Year's Day.*

Route 238 leads into **Yorktown,** whose Main Street is an array of preserved 18th-century buildings on a bluff overlooking the York River. First settled in 1691, Yorktown had become a thriving tobacco port and a prosperous community of several hundred houses by the time of the Revolution. Nine buildings from that time still stand, not all of them open to visitors. **Moore House,** where the terms of surrender were negotiated, and the elegant **Nelson House,** the residence of a Virginia governor and a signer of the Declaration of Independence, are open for tours in summer. The **Swan Tavern,** a reconstruction of a structure of 1722, now houses an antiques shop. On Church Street, Grace Church, built in 1697 and damaged in the War of 1812 and the Civil War, was rebuilt and remains an active Episcopal congregation; its walls are made of native marl (a mixture of clay, sand, and limestone containing fragments of seashells). On Main Street, the **Somerwell House,** built before 1707, and the Sessions House (before 1699)—the oldest houses in town—are privately owned and closed to the public. The latter was used as local headquarters by the Union forces during General George McClellan's Peninsula Campaign of the Civil War.

Within 35 miles to the west of Williamsburg on Route 5, along the north bank of the James River, are four historic plantations.

㉓ Sherwood Forest, built in 1720 and said to be the longest wood-frame house in the United States at 300 feet, was the retirement home of John Tyler, 10th president of the United States. Tyler, who came into office when William Henry Harrison died a month after his inauguration, was a Whig who dissented from the party line on abolition in favor of the proslavery position of the Democrats. He died in 1862, having served briefly in the congress of the Confederate States of America. His house remains in the Tyler family and is furnished with heirloom antiques; it can be toured by appointment, but the dozen acres of grounds and the five outbuildings, including a tobacco barn, are open daily. *Rte. 5 (Box 8), tel. 804/829–5377. Admission to grounds: $3. Grounds open daily 9–5. House tour: $7.50 adults, $6.50 senior citizens, $4 students group discounts offered. House open Apr.–Dec., daily 9–5; Jan.–Mar. by appointment.*

㉔ Westover was built in 1735 by the flamboyant Colonel William Byrd II (1674–1744), an American aristocrat who spent much of his time and money in London. He was in Virginia frequently enough to serve in both the upper and lower houses of the Colonial legislature at Williamsburg and to write one of the first travel books about the region (as well as a notorious "secret diary," a frank and thorough account of plantation life and Colonial politics). He lived here with his library of 4,000 volumes. Westover's interior, celebrated for its moldings and carvings, is open to visitors only during Garden Week in late April. The grounds are arrayed with tulip poplars at least 100 years old, and gardens of roses and other flowers are well tended. Three wrought-iron gates, imported from England by the colonel, are mounted on posts topped by figures of eagles with spread wings. Byrd's grave is here, inscribed with the eloquent, immodest, and apt epitaph he composed for himself. *Rte. 5, 7000 Westover Rd., tel. 804/829–2882. Admission: $2 adults, $1.50 children. Open daily 9–5:30.*

㉕ Evelynton Plantation originally was part of Westover estate and is believed to have been part of the dowry of William Byrd II's eldest daughter, Evelyn. However, her father refused to allow her to wed her favorite suitor, and she never married. The plantation was purchased in 1846 by the Ruffin family, which had settled on the south shore of the James River in the 1650s. Edmund Ruffin, a celebrated agronomist prior to the Civil War, was a strident secessionist who fired the first shot at Fort Sumter. Evelynton was the scene of fierce skirmishing during the 1862 Peninsula Campaign; the manor house and outbuildings were destroyed during the war. The present Colonial revival–style house on a hill at the end of a cedar-and-dogwood alley was built two generations later, using 250-year-old brick, under the direction of renowned architect Duncan Lee. The house is furnished in 18th-century English and American antiques and has handsomely landscaped lawn and gardens. Since it opened to the public in 1986, it has earned a reputation for artistic, abundant flower arrangements in every season. The house, gardens, and grounds are part of a 2,500-acre working plantation still operated by Ruffin descendants. *Rte. 5, 6701 John Tyler Hwy., tel. 804/829–5075 or 800/473–5075. Admission: $6 adults, $5 senior citizens, $3 children 7–12. Open daily 9–5, except Thanksgiving, Christmas Day, and New Year's Day. Afternoon tea is held on the terrace during Historic Garden Week and the Christmas season. Flower arranging seminars are held three times a year; call for details.*

Virginians say that the first Thanksgiving was celebrated at **㉖ Berkeley** on December 14, 1619, not in Massachusetts. This plantation was the birthplace of Benjamin Harrison, a signer of the Declaration of Independence, and of William Henry Harrison, who was briefly president in 1841. Throughout the Civil War, the Union general George McClellan used Berkeley as headquarters; during his tenure, his subordinate general Daniel Butterfield composed the melody "Taps" on the premises. The brick Georgian house, built in 1726, has been carefully restored following a period of disrepair after the Civil War. It is furnished not with original pieces but with period antiques. The gardens are in excellent condition, particularly the boxwood hedges. A restaurant has seating indoors and out. *Rte. 5, then follow signs, tel. 804/829–6018. Admission: $8.50 adults (10% reduction for senior citizens, AAA members), $4 children 6–12. Open daily 8–5, except Christmas Day.*

㉗ Shirley, a few minutes farther west and the oldest plantation in Virginia, has been occupied by a single family, the Carters, for 10 generations. Their claim to the land goes back to 1660, when it was settled by a relative, Edward Hill. Robert E. Lee's mother was born here, and the Carters seem to be related to every notable Virginia family from the Colonial and antebellum periods. The approach to the elegant 1723 Georgian manor is a dramatic one: The house stands at the end of a drive lined by towering Lombardy poplars. Inside, the hall staircase rises for three stories with no visible support. Family silver is on display, ancestral portraits are hung throughout, and rare books line the shelves. *501 Shirley Plantation Rd., tel. 804/829–5121. Admission: $7 adults, $6 senior citizens, $5 youth 13–21, $3.50 children 6–12. Open daily 9–4:30, except Christmas Day.*

What to See and Do with Children

Busch Gardens Williamsburg (*see* Exploring Williamsburg, *above*).

In the summer, **Colonial Williamsburg** (tel. 800/447–8679) offers special programs, tours, and experiences for children.

Water Country USA, 3 miles east of Williamsburg and Busch Gardens on Route 199, has a dozen aquatic rides: Among them, the "Amazon" is a trip through tunnels and waterfalls on an inner tube big enough for two, and the "Jet Stream" is a flume the rider can slide down on an inner tube. A wave pool five times Olympic size is quiet for 10 minutes, then produces waves for 13 minutes. *Rte. 199 off I–64 (Exit 242–B), tel. 804/229–9300 or 800/343–7946. Admission: $17.95 adults, $15.95 children 3–6. Open Memorial Day–Labor Day, daily 10–7; Labor Day–Memorial Day, weekends 10–7.*

Shopping

Crafts   In the restored area of Colonial Williamsburg, nine stores and shops have been reconstructed to create the milieu of the Colonial merchant. Among the available wares typical of the 18th century are silver tea services, jewelry, pottery, pewter and brass items, ironwork, tobacco and herbs, candles, hats, baskets, books, maps and prints, and even baked goods. Two crafts houses sell approved reproductions of the antiques on display in the houses and museums. *Craft House, Merchant Sq., tel. 804/220–7747; Craft House Inn, tel. 804/220–7749.*

Outlets   The **Williamsburg Pottery Factory** (Rte. 60, tel. 804/564–3326), less than 10 minutes west of Williamsburg, is an attraction in itself, and its parking area is usually crammed with tour buses. This enormous outlet store on 200 acres sells luggage, clothing, furniture and home furnishings, food and wine, china, crystal, and pottery. It's the foremost among more than 100 outlet stores on the outskirts of Williamsburg.

Sports and Outdoor Activities

Participant Sports

Biking   Colonial Williamsburg ticket holders can rent bicycles at the **Williamsburg Lodge** on South England Street; others can try **Bikesmith** (515 York St., tel. 804/229–9858). The pamphlet *Biking through America's Historic Triangle,* available at bike shops, maps a 20-mile route.

Golf   **Colonial Williamsburg** (tel. 804/220–7696 or 800/447–8679) operates three courses—the 18-hole Golden Horseshoe Course, rated one of the top 12 in the country; the 18-hole Golden Horseshoe Green; and the nine-hole Spotswood Course. **Kingsmill Resort** (tel. 804/253–1703 or 800/832–5665), near Busch Gardens, has three courses.

Tennis   **Colonial Williamsburg** (tel. 804/220–7794 or 800/447–8679) has 10 tennis courts (four clay, two rubber, and two asphalt at the Williamsburg Inn and two asphalt at Williamsburg Woodlands); **Kingsmill** (tel. 804/253–3945 or 800/832–5665) has 13 clay and two hard courts open to the public; additional public courts in

Williamsburg are at **Kiwanis Park** on Long Hill Road and at **Quarterpath Park** on Pocahontas Street.

Spectator Sports

The **College of William and Mary** fields varsity or club teams in football, basketball, baseball, track, wrestling, field hockey, soccer, swimming, tennis, and gymnastics. The listings in the weekly *Virginia Gazette* give specifics.

Beaches

Along Water Street (Route 238) in Yorktown is a public beach for swimming and fishing. The public beach just over the bridge across the York River, at Gloucester Point, has boat ramps. Beware of sea nettles (jellyfish) in July and August.

Dining and Lodging

Ethnic cuisines are rare in this area, but the heavy tourist traffic from throughout the United States and abroad has kept standards high at restaurants with French and other Continental menus. Dining rooms within walking distance of the Colonial Williamsburg's restored area are often crowded, and reservations (tel. 800/447–8679) are necessary. Restaurants range from the sophisticated fare at the luxurious Williamsburg Inn's Regency Room to the light period fare available at some of the restored taverns; most places accept credit cards.

Williamsburg's 8,000 hotel rooms are above average in quality and price for Virginia, with vacancies scarce in summer and some rate reductions available in winter. The **Williamsburg Motel/Hotel Association** (tel. 800/446–9244), representing 73 hostelries, provides free lodging reservation services year-round.

Highly recommended establishments are indicated by a star ★.

Charles City
Lodging

Edgewood Plantation. The Victorian wood house, built in 1849, stands out among its redbrick Colonial neighbors. Three stories high, it sits behind a porch on five largely wooded acres, ½ mile west of Berkeley Plantation and less than an hour from Williamsburg. Two large suites at the front of the house have private bath; elsewhere, two rooms share one bath. All rooms are decorated with Victorian antiques and country crafts, the likes of which are for sale in a shop on the ground floor—and there's an antiques shop out back as well. Breakfast is served in the formal dining room or in the cozier kitchen, as guests prefer. *Rte. 5 (for reservations, write 4800 John Tyler Memorial Hwy.), 23030, tel. 804/829–2962 or 800/296–3343. 7 rooms. Facilities: outdoor pool, hot tub. MC, V. Rates include breakfast. $$$$*

Williamsburg
Dining

Regency Room. This restaurant in the Williamsburg Inn is the place to dine for those who seek elegant decor, attentive service, and quality cuisine. Crystal chandeliers, Oriental silk-screen prints, and full silver service set the tone. Rack of lamb is carved at the table; other specialties are lobster bisque and rich ice-cream desserts. *S. Francis St., tel. 804/229–1000. Reservations advised. Jacket and tie required at dinner and Sun. brunch. AE, MC, V. $$$$*

Aberdeen Barn. Barn walls decorated with saws, pitchforks, oxen yokes, and the like surround lacquered wood tables set with linen napkins. The menu reflects more elaborate fare than typical country cooking. House specialties include slow-roasted prime ribs of beef; babyback Danish pork ribs barbecued with a sauce of peach preserves and Southern Comfort; and shrimp scampi sautéed in garlic, white wine, parsley, and butter. An ample but not esoteric wine list is dominated by Californian vintages. *1601 Richmond Rd., tel. 804/ 229–6661. Reservations advised. Dress: casual. AE, MC, V. No lunch. $$$*

Berret's Restaurant and Raw Bar. Situated just behind Merchants Square, Berret's boasts a choice location and lively nautically themed surroundings with a colorful tile wall and paintings by regional artists. The outdoor raw bar is popular on sunny days; the restaurant, which also has some outdoor seating, specializes in fish and shellfish dishes—try the softshell crabs with peanut-bourbon butter. *199 S. Boundry St., tel. 804/253–1847. Reservations advised. Dress: casual. AE, MC, V. $$$*

Le Yaca. A mall of small boutiques seems an unlikely setting for a convincingly country-French dining room with soft pastel colors, hardwood floors, candlelight, and a central open fireplace where a nightly spectacle is the specialty of the house: leg of lamb roasting on a spit. A rosemary-and-garlic sauce complements individual servings of the lamb. For dessert, the kitchen offers its square version of a chocolate truffle, *marquis au chocolat*: a concoction of chocolate, cream, eggs, and sugar that is frozen and served atop crème anglaise. *1915 Pocahontas Trail, tel. 804/220–3616. Reservations advised. Dress: casual but neat. AE, DC, MC, V. Closed Sun., early Jan. $$$*

★ **The Trellis.** Although the restaurant is in a Colonial building, its hardwood floors, ceramic tiles, and green plants evoke the atmosphere of a country inn in the Napa Valley. Executive chef Maurice Desaulniers has won national recognition for the imaginative menu, which changes with the seasons. Diners have a choice of five cozy dining rooms—in one, you can watch the mesquite fire—and 8,000 bottles of wine. The grilled seafood specialties are particularly good, but whatever you have, be sure to save room for dessert—Death by Chocolate is a must for any sweet tooth. *Merchants Sq., tel. 804/229–8610. Reservations advised. Dress: casual. AE, MC, V. $$$*

Yorkshire Inn Steak and Seafood House. A cream color dominates the decor, with red carpeting in one dining room and gold in the other; brass chandeliers and candles light the rooms. The views of a motel swimming pool and a parking lot will not distract diners from the menu, which offers predominantly seafood. Recent entrées have included blackened tuna; trout stuffed with crab imperial; and shish kebab in traditional (beef tenderloin, tomato, green pepper) and seafood (lobster-tail meat, shrimp, scallops) versions. The wine cellar is highly diversified, with representatives of Germany and Greece among the customary French and Californian vintages. *700 York St., tel. 804/229–9790. Reservations advised. Dress: casual. AE, MC, V. $$$*

Bray Dining Room. From the dining room of this modern restaurant guests can watch the goings-on at the Kingsmill golf course through the picture windows that overlook the 18th green. This grill is atypical of its genre in that it features gourmet cuisine including steaks, beef, and seafood; the house specials are the grilled tuna and the swordfish. A guitar player performs in the evening, and breakfast is served daily. *Kingsmill Resort, 100 Golfclub Rd., tel. 804/253–3900. Reservations advised. Dress: casual (no jeans or tank tops). AE, D, DC, MC, V. No dinner Mon. $$*

The Cascades. Its location on the grounds of the visitor center means that this restaurant is full of tourists for breakfast and dinner; local residents come for Sunday brunch, when most of the visitors are off touring the restored area. Large windows look on to landscaped lawns and a waterfall, and at night the scene is illuminated. The all-American fare is a credit to its genre and features a broiled seafood platter with a distinctive baked crab imperial, which tastes like a lightly seasoned crab cake. The ample country chicken dinner begins with cheddar-cheese soup, includes sugar-cured ham with the fried chicken, and concludes with pecan pie. The daily Hunt Breakfast buffet includes fried chicken, oysters in season, and fruit waffles. *Visitor-center area, tel. 804/229–1000. Dress: casual. $$*

The Lafayette Restaurant. The interior of this restaurant, located a short walk from the restored area, is well lighted by bay windows in the daytime and by chandeliers at night, and the French colonial decor just bears up under scrutiny. Better can be said about the Continental cuisine: The stuffed shrimp has more crabmeat than one might expect, and the spareribs come with an especially tangy barbecue sauce, from the kitchen's own recipe. *1203 Richmond Rd., Williamsburg, tel. 804/229–3811. Reservations accepted. Dress: casual. AE, DC, MC, V. No lunch. $$*

The Lobster House. A captain's wheel and other nautical paraphernalia adorn the wood-paneled walls of this restaurant, where diners select Maine lobsters from a tank and enjoy them boiled or stuffed with unadulterated crabmeat. Shrimp comes fried or steamed, along with the usual "turf" options of filet Mignon or New York strip steak. The most distinctive item on the menu is peanut butter pie. *1425 Richmond Rd., tel. 804/229–7771. Reservations advised. Dress: casual. AE, DC, MC, V. No lunch. $$*

Lodging **Williamsburg Inn.** This award-winning grand hotel—built in 1932—
★ is owned and operated by Colonial Williamsburg and is known for its individually furnished rooms in the English Regency style and gracious service. A number of nearby Colonial houses and taverns, which provide more exclusive surroundings for those who desire them, are furnished with period reproductions and serviced by the staff of the inn. So is Providence Hall, which is adjacent to the inn but which has a less formal atmosphere, with rooms in contemporary Oriental decor overlooking tennis courts, a private pond, and a wooded area. Together these structures have 235 rooms. *136 E. Francis St. (Box 1776), 23187–1776, tel. 804/229–1000 or 800/447–8679, fax 804/220–7096. Facilities: restaurant, lounge, gift shop, outdoor pool, tennis, golf, hiking trails. AE, D, MC, V. $$$$*

Fort Magruder Inn. Although this is primarily a convention facility, it's a comfortable and convenient option for individuals and families, too. The inn was built in 1976 on a Civil War battlefield, and some rooms overlook the surviving fortifications. A neo-Colonial motif is the decor for all rooms. *6945 Pocahontas Trail, 23187, tel. 804/220–2250 or 800/582–1010, fax 804/220–3215. 303 rooms. Facilities: restaurant, bar, indoor pool, outdoor pool, sauna, whirlpool, fitness room, 2 tennis courts, playground. AE, DC, MC, V. $$$*

★ **Liberty Rose.** On a hilltop-acre lot 1 mile from the restored area, this slate-roof, white-clapboard house is surrounded by century-old beech, oak, and poplar. The inn was constructed in the early 1920s and renovated in 1986; furnishings include Victorian antiques and a decor characterized by heavy use of lace and silk. Most remarkable is that every room has windows on three sides. The large suite on the first floor has a TV and VCR; its unique bathroom has a clawfoot tub, a red-marble shower, and large mirrors. Breakfast is served on a sun porch. *1022 Jamestown Rd., 23185, tel. 804/253–1260 or 800/545–1825. 2 rooms, 2 suites. MC, V. Rates include full breakfast. $$$*

Quality Suites. The five-story, all-suites hotel, built in 1987, sits on 11 wooded acres next to a shopping center, less than 1 mile from the restored area. There is no large meeting facility or restaurant to attract conventioners, but this well-appointed hostelry offers a convenient retreat from the bustle of Colonial Williamsburg. Guest rooms are furnished in a heavily mauve California-contemporary decor. *152 Kingsgate Pkwy., 23185, tel. 804/229–6800 or 800/333–0924, fax 804/220–3486. 169 suites. Facilities: indoor pool, sauna, whirlpool. AE, D, DC, MC, V. $$$*

Williamsburg Hospitality House. This four-story redbrick building, constructed in 1973, faces the College of William and Mary; ask for a room that looks onto the cobblestone courtyard with a fountain at the center. Guest quarters have Chippendale reproduction furnishings and matching decor. Its convenient location two blocks from Colonial Williamsburg makes it a popular choice. *415 Richmond Rd., 23185, tel. 804/229–4020 or 800/932–9192, fax 804/220–1560. 300 rooms, 9 suites. Facilities: restaurant, bar, outdoor pool. AE, D, DC, MC, V. $$$*

The Williamsburg Woodlands. Formerly the Motor House and another official Colonial Williamsburg hostelry, this recently renovated motel features rooms with contemporary furnishings in a variety of buildings. All are set in a pine grove adjacent to the visitor-center area. *102 Visitor Center Dr., 23185, tel. 804/229–1000 or 800/447–8679, fax 804/221–8942. 315 rooms. Facilities: restaurant, lounge, 3 outdoor pools, miniature golf, putting green, tennis, fitness trail, horseshoes, shuffleboard, ping-pong, playground. AE, MC, V. $$$*

Governor's Inn. Although this accommodation is only three blocks from the visitor center, shuttle-bus service is available. Rooms here are furnished with two double beds, and the lodging provides quality at a moderate rate. *506 N. Henry St., 23185, tel. 804/229–1000, fax 804/220–7019. 200 rooms. Facilities: games room with pool tables, pinball and video games, outdoor pool, gift shop. AE, MC, V. $$*

Heritage Inn. The three-story building houses a charming and comfortable 25-year-old inn that's decorated inside and out in Colonial style. Room furnishings include postered headboards, prints of Colonial Williamsburg, and an armoire concealing a TV. Some quarters open directly onto the parking lot, but this is an unusually quiet, leafy site, and the pool is set in a garden. *1324 Richmond Rd., 23185, tel. 804/229–6220 or 800/782–3800, fax 804/229–2774. 54 rooms. Facilities: restaurant, outdoor pool. AE, DC, MC, V. $$*

War Hill Inn. Erected in 1970, the inn was designed by a Colonial Williamsburg architect to resemble a period structure: A two-story redbrick building at the center has two wood-frame wings. Inside, guests find appropriate antiques and reproductions. The setting is a 32-acre operating cattle farm, 4 miles from the Colonial Williamsburg information center. Those in search of privacy will want the two-room cottage or the first-floor suite (other rooms open onto a common hallway). All rooms have cable TV. *4560 Long Hill Rd., 23188, tel. 804/565–0248. 5 rooms. AE, MC, V. $$*

Bassett Motel. Dogwood trees and many flower beds (azaleas and tulips in the spring, begonias in the fall) distinguish the site of this well-run, family-oriented, single-story brick property on the quieter east side of Williamsburg. Rooms are variously furnished, some with tables, some with desks, in a cream color scheme. *800 York St. (U.S. 60), 23185, tel. 804/229–5175. 18 rooms. MC, V. $*

Governor Spotswood Motel. This one-story redbrick motel has been extended gradually, section by section, for more than 50 years, most recently in 1990; all rooms have been renovated since 1980. The decor reflects the influence of Colonial Williamsburg, but in classic motel design each room faces its parking space. There's lots of surrounding lawn and a sunken garden setting for the swimming pool. Seven of the 19 kitchen units are in cottages. *1508 Richmond Rd., 23185, tel. 804/229–6444 or 800/368–1244, fax 804/253–2410. 78 rooms. Facilities: outdoor pool, shuffleboard court, playground. AE, D, DC, MC, V. $*

Taverns The following taverns serve Colonial-style foods in reconstructed Colonial settings. Smoking is not permitted in any of the taverns. Hours change according to season, so check by calling the reservations number (tel. 800/828–3767). Dress is casual and dinner reservations are recommended. All taverns are moderately priced and accept American Express, MasterCard, and Visa.

Chownings Tavern. This reconstructed 18th-century alehouse serves light meals, including Brunswick stew, Welsh rarebit, oysters, and sandwiches, all complemented by Chowning's especially good bread and drink. It's open every night; in summer, guests may eat outside under the arbor. *Duke of Gloucester St.*

Christiana Campbell's Tavern. Almost as popular today as it was in the Colonial era, this pub features seafood from the Chesapeake Bay, served in period (crab cakes) and nonperiod (spicy jambalaya) dishes. *Waller St.*

Kings Arms. This is one of Williamsburg's most "genteel" establishments. The fare and the atmosphere mimic those experienced by Founding Fathers such as George Washington and Thomas Jefferson when they sat down to eat Virginia ham, hearty chicken pot pie, and Sally Lunn bread over a political discussion. Weather permitting, guests may eat light meals in a garden behind the tavern. *Duke of Gloucester St.*

Shields Tavern. The newest member of the tavern foursome recalls tavern-keeping in the early 18th century by a man named James Shields. Some outdoor seating is available in proper weather. *Duke of Gloucester St.*

Yorktown Dining **Nick's Seafood Pavilion.** Fish and shellfish are prominent on a menu that includes seafood shish kebab (lobster, shrimp, scallops, tomatoes, peppers, mushrooms, and onion, served with rice pilaf and topped with brown butter), a buttery lobster pilaf, Chinese dishes, and baklava for dessert. *Water St., tel. 804/887–5269. Dress: casual. AE, DC, MC, V. $$$*

Lodging **Duke of York Motel.** All rooms in the two two-story buildings of the motel face the water and are only a few steps from a public beach. The motel also boasts an outdoor swimming pool and a restaurant where three meals are served daily from Memorial Day to Labor Day, breakfast and lunch at other times of year. *508 Water St., 23690, tel. 804/898–3232. 57 rooms. Facilities: restaurant, outdoor pool. DC, MC, V. $–$$*

The Arts and Nightlife

The Arts

Music **Busch Gardens Williamsburg** (U.S. 60, tel. 804/253–3350) hosts a variety of popular song and dance shows (country, gospel, opera, German folk) in several theaters; the largest is the 5,000-seat Royal Palace, which features pop stars.

W&M Hall (tel. 804/221–4000) at the College of William and Mary, with 10,000 seats, is another venue for concerts by well-known artists on tour.

Old Dominion Opry (3012 Richmond Rd., tel. 804/564–0200), in Williamsburg, offers family-oriented live country music and comedy. Shows run Monday through Saturday beginning at 8 PM.

Theater   **The Virginia Company** (tel. 804/220–7645 or 800/HISTORY) in Colonial Williamsburg presents rollicking 18th-century plays (mostly English) throughout the year, with performances during the warmer months in the open-air Playbooth Theater on the site of the first theater in the country. Colonial Williamsburg also offers a variety of plays, concerts, cultural events, and historical reenactments in the evening.

Student drama at the **College of William and Mary** (tel. 804/221–4000) takes place during the school year.

Nightlife

Rock   **J. B.'s Lounge** (Fort Magruder Inn, 6945 Pocahontas Trail, Williamsburg, tel. 804/220–2250) has a bar, live music (Tuesday–Saturday), and a transient crowd.

Rockin' Robin Restaurant & Lounge (Econo Lodge, 1402 Richmond Rd., tel. 804/253–8818) has a dance floor and features music from the 1950s and 1960s. Sandwiches as well as complete meals are on the menu.

Tavern   **Chowning's Tavern** (tel. 800/447–8679) has lively "gambols," or colonial games, along with music and entertainment on a regular basis.

7 Hampton Roads Area and the Eastern Shore

Tidewater Virginia is technically defined as the area east of the fall line of the rivers flowing into the Chesapeake Bay, although, in the popular imagination, the term "Tidewater" has also come to stand for a sort of aristocratic southern gentility. The eastern end of the Tidewater, however, around the mouth of the Chesapeake Bay along Virginia's brief stretch of Atlantic shoreline, cannot be so easily characterized. Norfolk is defined today by its role as a port, with a strong shipbuilding industry and military presence, while Virginia Beach thrives as the state's most populous city and chief beach town, complete with its own crowded boardwalk.

At the end of the Williamsburg peninsula, the enormous harbor of Hampton Roads—where the James, Elizabeth, and Nansemond rivers flow together and on into Chesapeake Bay—has played a crucial role in the discovery and settlement of the nation, the struggle for independence, and the conflict that nearly dissolved the Union. A history of violence and hardship provides a dramatic background for the prosperous present day in an area now dedicated to recreation and tourism.

On the north side of the port, the city of Hampton hosts a major weekend jazz festival in June and an even bigger Bay Days extravaganza, with fireworks and boat races, for three days in September. Newport News, builder of the navy's biggest nuclear ships and port of embarkation during both world wars, reminds visitors of its personality in several ways, but the Fall Festival in October is one of the most fun things to do. Yorktown Day, also in October, celebrates the winning of American independence when the British surrendered here. Poquoson, long recognized for its seafood and its construction of seafaring "log canoes," boasts its credentials at a September Seafood Festival.

On the south side of Hampton Roads, the city of Norfolk accommodates the U.S. headquarters of the North Atlantic Treaty Organization. NATO is saluted during the Azalea Festival in the third week of April, a time of parades, air shows, dances, and exhibitions. The celebrating resumes at Harborfest, on the first full weekend in June, when more than a million visitors gather to watch the tall ships arrive. Nearly 200 free events, including concerts and festivals, are held in Town Point Park, adjacent to Waterside.

Just across the Elizabeth River from Norfolk is the city of Portsmouth, with gracious English-basement homes from the 1700s, brick sidewalks, and an impressive seawall and waterfront. From April to October, the Riverside Festival Marketplace bustles with activity that features music, art, food, and festivals. The Old Town Ghost Walk in October and the Holiday Lights in December are especially interesting.

Virginia Beach, on the Atlantic east of Norfolk, is one of the most popular East Coast resorts. This is no sleepy seaside retreat but a bustling entertainment center with beach and boardwalk, a place whose greatest appeal may lie with the young (of all ages). Recent traditions include the free Valentine Dance at the Cavalier Hotel.

Virginia's "other" coastline, the Eastern Shore, is a long, narrow finger of land extending south from Maryland, separating the Chesapeake Bay from the Atlantic Ocean. Connected to the rest of the state only by the Chesapeake Bay Bridge-Tunnel, it has its own natural beauty, largely undisturbed, and uncolonized by weekenders from Washington.

Essential Information

Important Addresses and Numbers

Visitor Information
Chincoteague Chamber of Commerce (Box 258, Chincoteague 23336, tel. 804/336–6161).
Eastern Shore of Virginia Chamber of Commerce and Tourism Commission (Drawer R, Melfa 23410, tel. 804/787–2460).
Hampton Convention and Visitors Bureau (710 Settlers Landing Rd., Hampton 23669, tel. 804/727–1102 or 800/800–2202).
Norfolk Convention and Visitors Bureau (end of 4th View St., 23503, tel. 804/441–1852 or 800/368–3097).
Portsmouth Convention and Visitors Bureau (801 Crawford St., Portsmouth 23704, tel. 804/393–8481 or 800/767–8782).
Newport News Tourism and Conference Bureau (8 San Jose Dr., Suite 3B, Newport News 23606, tel. 804/873–0092 or 800/333–7787).
Virginia Beach Visitor Information Center (2100 Parks Ave., Virginia Beach 23451, tel. 804/437–4888 or 800/822–3224).

Emergencies Throughout the region, dial **911** for emergency assistance.

Hospitals Eastern Shore: **Northampton-Accomack Memorial Hospital** (9507 Hospital Ave., Nassawadox, tel. 804/442–8777). Newport News: **Newport News General Hospital** (5100 Marshall Ave., tel. 804/247–7357). Chesapeake: **Chesapeake General Hospital** (736 Battlefield Blvd. N, tel. 804/482–6128). Norfolk: **Sentara Norfolk General Hospital** (600 Gresham Dr., tel. 804/628–3551). Virginia Beach: **Sentara Bayside Hospital** (800 Independence Blvd., tel. 804/363–6137).

Arriving and Departing

By Plane **Newport News/Williamsburg International Airport** (tel. 804/877–0221), formerly Patrick Henry International, in Newport News, served primarily by USAir, opened a new terminal in 1992. **Norfolk International Airport** (tel. 804/857–3351), located between Norfolk and Virginia Beach, is served by American, Continental, Delta, Northwest, Southeast, TWA, United, and USAir. Limousine service is available.

By Car The I–664 road creates a circular beltway through the Hampton Roads area. I–664 connects Newport News and Norfolk, via Suffolk. I–64 runs northwest through Norfolk to intersect with I–664 in Hampton and I–95 at Richmond. U.S. 58 and Route 44 (toll road) connect I–64 to Virginia Beach.

By Train **Amtrak** (tel. 800/872–7245) provides service between Boston (and intervening points) and Newport News (9304 Warwick Blvd., tel. 804/245–3589), with one train daily in each direction. At Newport News, a shuttle bus connects to Norfolk.

By Bus **Greyhound Lines** (22 S. Armistead Ave., Hampton, tel. 804/722–9861; 9702 Jefferson Ave., Newport News, tel. 804/599–3900; 701 Monticello Ave., Norfolk, tel. 804/627–5641; 1017 Laskin Rd., Virginia Beach, tel. 804/422–2998; 609 Washington St., Portsmouth, tel. 804/397–7839) typically has half a dozen departures daily, both north and south, from each city.

Getting Around Hampton, Newport News, Norfolk, Virginia Beach, and the Eastern Shore

By Car The area is well served with expressways and interstate highways, but you'll have to share these routes with a lot of local drivers as well. Because the ragged coastline is constantly interrupted by water, driving from one town to another usually means going through a tunnel or over a bridge, either one of which may create a traffic bottleneck. The entrance to the tunnel between Hampton and Norfolk can get very congested, especially on weekends, so listen to your car radio for updated traffic reports. In congested periods, use the less-traveled I–664. The 17½-mile Chesapeake Bay Bridge-Tunnel is the only connection between Virginia Beach and the Eastern Shore; U.S. 13 is the main route up the spine of the Eastern Shore peninsula into Maryland.

By Boat The **Elizabeth River Ferry** conveys pedestrians from Waterside, in Norfolk, to Portsmouth, whose Olde Towne is dense with 18th- and 19th-century houses. The ferry—it's a five-minute trip, more fun than driving through the tunnel—departs Norfolk every 30 minutes, on the quarter hour. *Tel. 804/640–6300. Fare: 75¢ adults, 50¢ children, senior citizens, and travelers with disabilities. Operates daily 7 AM–9:45 PM.*

Guided Tours

Orientation **Historic Trolley Tours** operates in Virginia Beach June–September, Wednesday and Thursday 9–11:30 AM. *24th St. and Atlantic Ave., tel. 804/498–0215. Fare: $6.*

The **Hampton Circle Tour** (tel. 804/727–1102) is a self-guided driving trip that passes all of Hampton's attractions. Maps are available from the Tourist Information Center, or just follow blue-and-white tour signs.

The **Norfolk Tour** (tel. 804/441–5266 or 804/441–5266) is a free self-guided walking or driving tour of the city's most popular attractions; at each stop you can pick up a leaflet with directions to the others, all designated with blue-and-gold signs. A cassette guide for use in cars is available for $6.95.

The **Norfolk Trolley**'s guided tour of the historic downtown area allows you to get on and off as you please. Tickets are available at the Tidewater Regional Transit (TRT) kiosk at the Waterside. *Tel. 804/627–2896. Fare: $2.50 adults, $1.25 children, senior citizens, and travelers with disabilities. Operates May–Sept.*

Portsmouth's **Olde Towne Trolley Tour** capsules the inside story of major historical events since 1752. It departs from the Portside Information Center. *Portside, tel. 804/393–5111. Admission: $2.50 adults, $1.25 senior citizens and children. Open late May–early Sept., daily noon–4.*

The **Virginia Beach Tour** (tel. 800/822–3224 or 804/473–4888) is a self-guided driving trip past both beach and historic points. Maps are available at the visitors center, but signs mark the route.

Boat Tours **American Rover Sailing Tours** (tel. 804/627–7245), which operates a striking 135-foot topsail schooner, cruises Hampton Roads's nautical historical landmarks and the Norfolk naval base.

The ***Spirit of Norfolk*** (tel. 804/627–7771) explores Norfolk harbor on luncheon and dinner cruises with live entertainment and dancing.

The *Carrie B* (tel. 804/393–4735), a scaled-down reproduction of a Mississippi riverboat, cruises Hampton Roads to give visitors a look at the naval shipyard and the site of the encounter of the *Monitor* and the *Merrimack* during the Civil War.

Discovery Cruise (tel. 804/422–2900) features a handsome luxury yacht that explores Virginia Beach's Broad Bay.

Wharton's Tours (Newport News, tel. 804/245–1533) offers a comprehensive cruise of the harbor and special voyages on the James River, and a short segment of the Intracoastal Waterway, a series of canals that extends from Boston, Massachusetts, to Brownsville, Texas.

The *Miss Hampton II* (tel. 804/727–1102) sails down Hampton River, passing the site where Blackbeard's head hung on a stake, and Hampton University's handsome campus, and across Hampton Roads and along the line of aircraft carriers, cruisers, and other warships at the Norfolk naval base. The trip includes a stop at Fort Wool, situated on an artificial island off Hampton, where remnants of fortifications dating from the early 19th century to World War II may be explored.

Tangier Island Cruises (tel. 410/968–2338) makes seasonal trips to Tangier Island (*see* Chapter 10, Maryland's Eastern Shore), a small, remote island in the Chesapeake Bay that was settled in 1686.

Exploring

Hampton, Newport News, Norfolk, Virginia Beach, the Eastern Shore

Numbers in the margin correspond to points of interest on the Southeast Virginia map.

The Virginia Peninsula, extending southeast from the area of Williamsburg into the Chesapeake Bay, defines the port of Hampton Roads on the north and contains the cities of Newport News and ❶ Hampton. **Newport News,** on the James River, is said to take its name from a Captain Newport, whose return with supplies was "good news" to the early colonists. The world's largest privately owned shipyard is here.

A world history of seagoing vessels and the people who sailed them occupies **The Mariners' Museum** in Newport News. Many of the authentic scale models hand-carved by August Crabtree are so tiny that you must view them through magnifying glasses; they portray mankind's shipbuilding accomplishments from ancient Egypt to 19th-century Britain. Among the more than 50 full-size craft on display are a Native American bark canoe, a sailing yacht, a speedboat, a gondola, a Coast Guard cutter, and a World War II Japanese submarine. In one gallery visitors can often watch the progress of a boat under construction; in another are ornate and sometimes huge figureheads from the bows of sailing ships; in another, the watermen's culture of the Chesapeake Bay is explored. Examples of nautical gear—for example, trailboards, rudder heads, and paddle boxes—are on display, along with a selection of the intricate whale-tusk carvings called scrimshaw. Photographs and paintings recount naval history and the story of private-sector seafaring. A permanent "Age of Exploration" gallery opened in 1992. *100 Museum Dr. (I–64 Exit 258A), tel. 804/595–0368. Admission: $6.50 adults (two*

American Express offers Travelers Cheques built for two.

Cheques *for Two*℠ from American Express are the Travelers Cheques that allow either of you to use them because both of you have signed them. And only one of you needs to be present to purchase them.

Cheques *for Two* are accepted anywhere regular American Express Travelers Cheques are, which is just about everywhere. So stop by your bank, AAA* or any American Express Travel Service Office and ask for Cheques *for Two*.

Pack light.

Take the one number you need for any kind of call, anywhere you travel.

Checking in with your family back home? Calling for a tow truck? When you're on the road, the phone you use might not accept your calling card. Or you might get overcharged by an unknown telephone company. Here's the solution: dial 1 800 CALL ATT.℠ You'll get flawless AT&T service, competitive calling card prices, and the lowest prices for collect calls from any phone, anywhere. Travel light. Just bring along this one simple number: 1 800 CALL ATT.

Southeast Virginia

for $9), $5.50 senior citizens and active military, $3.25 students and children 6–12. Open Mon.–Sat. 10–5. Closed Christmas Day.

The **War Memorial Museum,** housing more than 60,000 of Virginia's artifacts from all over the world, including weapons, uniforms, wartime posters, photographs, and other memorabilia, traces military history from 1775 to Desert Storm and includes a history of African-Americans and women. The **Vietnam War Memorial** is on the grounds of Huntington Park. Held annually is a "Christmas in the Field" Civil War reenactment, which is performed the second weekend of December. *9285 Warwick Blvd. (Rte. 60), tel. 804/247–8523. Admission: $2 adults, $1 children, senior citizens, and active military. Open Mon.–Sat. 9–5, Sun. 1–5; closed Thanksgiving, Christmas, and New Year's.*

The **U.S. Army Transportation Museum,** at Fort Eustis, traces the history of army transportation by land, sea, and air, beginning with the Revolutionary War era. More than 90 vehicles, including experimental craft, are on display. *Besson Hall, Bldg. 300, I–64 (Exit 250A), tel. 804/878–1109. Admission free. Open daily 9–4:30. Closed Federal holidays, except Memorial Day, Independence Day, and Labor Day.*

At the tip of the Virginia Peninsula, east of Newport News, is ❷ **Hampton.** Founded in 1610, it's the oldest continuously existing English-speaking settlement in the United States, and the city is also home to the country's first aviation research facility, NASA Langley Research Center, established in 1917. The center was headquarters for the first manned space program in the United States: Astronauts for the *Mercury* and *Apollo* missions trained at this historic facility.

The **Virginia Air and Space Center,** on Hampton's downtown waterfront, traces the history of flight and space exploration. The nine-story, futuristic, $30 million center is the official repository of the NASA Langley Research Center and houses dramatic space artifacts, such as a 3-billion-year-old moon rock, the *Apollo 12* command capsule, and a lunar lander. The center also holds—among its imaginative novelties—a dozen full-size aircraft, Southeast Virginia's only IMAX theater, and hands-on exhibits that allow visitors to see themselves as "astronaut-for-a-minute." *600 Settlers Landing Rd., I–64 (Exit 267), tel. 804/727–0800. Admission to Space Center only: $3 adults, $2.50 senior citizens, $1.50 students and children. Admission to Space Center and 1 IMAX movie: $8 adults, $7.50 senior citizens, $5.25 students and children 4–12. Open Mon.–Sat. 10–5, Sun. noon–5. Closed Christmas.*

Hampton was one of Virginia's principal Colonial cities. In 1718, Blackbeard, the pirate, was killed by Virginia sailors in battle off North Carolina, and they brought his head back and mounted it on a pole at the entrance to the Hampton River. In subsequent years the city was partially destroyed three times: by the British during the Revolution and again during the War of 1812, then by Confederates preempting the Union invaders during the Civil War. The **Hampton Roads History Center,** located in the Virginia Air and Space Center, depicts this colorful history through archaeological and audiovisual exhibitions that include partial reproductions of Colonial buildings, and what looks like a pirate's skeleton. Full-scale reproductions of the gun turret of the U.S.S. *Monitor* and a portion of the C.S.S. *Virginia* casemate show how the two ironclads changed the course of naval history in a famous Civil War battle in Hampton Roads. (*See* Virginia Air and Space Center, *above,* for hours and admission.)

Little of early Hampton has survived the shellings and conflagrations of the past. Yet the brick walls of **St. John's Church,** put up in 1728, have withstood the assaults of the British and the Confederates, and the interior was rebuilt each time. Today, a stained-glass window honors Pocahontas, the Native American princess who is said to have saved the life of Captain John Smith in 1608. The communion silver on display, made in London in 1618, is the oldest such service in continuous use in this country. The parish, founded in the same year as the city, also claims to be the oldest in continuous service in America. Visitors may listen to a taped interpretation or take a guided tour (by arrangement) and visit a small museum in the parish house. *100 W. Queens Way, tel. 804/722–2567. Admission free. Open weekdays 9–2, Sat. 9–noon.*

Hampton University was founded in 1868 as a freedmen's school. The alma mater of Booker T. Washington, it has had a distinguished history as an institution of higher education for African–Americans. The **Hampton University Museum** on the waterfront campus is most notable for its extensive and diverse collection of African art, which includes 2,000 pieces from 87 ethnic groups and cultures. Other valuable holdings include Harlem Renaissance paintings, Native American art and craft work, and art from Oceania. Another small exhibition tells the history of the university. *I–64 (Exit 267), tel. 804/727–5308. Admission free. Open Sept.–May, weekdays 8:30–5, weekends noon–4; June–Aug., weekdays 8:30–5. Closed major and university holidays.*

Time Out The two-level **Buckroe's Island Grill** (1 Ivory Gull Crescent, tel. 804/850–5757) has a double identity, making it a good place to stop for a drink or a bite any time of day. Both places are open for lunch, dinner, and drinks, but the top level of this lighthouse-style building is more suited for the evening, when the bar loudly reverberates with voices of young adults and those who would like to be. There are a few tables, but there is also some seating outside on the porches. The more sedate ground-level dining room is a nice place for lunch, when a moderately priced—but limited—menu is offered.

The channel between Chesapeake Bay and Hampton Roads is the "mouth" of Hampton Roads. On the north side of this passage, Hampton's **Fort Monroe,** built in stages between 1819 and 1834, is the largest stone fort in the country and the only one on active duty that is enclosed by a moat. Robert E. Lee and Edgar Allan Poe served here in the antebellum years, and it remained a Union stronghold in Confederate territory throughout the Civil War. Afterward, Confederate president Jefferson Davis was imprisoned for a time in one of the fort's casemates (a chamber in the wall); his cell and adjacent casemates now house the **Casemate Museum.** Exhibits of weapons, uniforms, models, drawings, and extensive Civil War relics retell the fort's history, depict coastal artillery activities, and describe military lifestyle through the Civil War years. *Rte. 258 (Mercury Blvd.) in Ft. Monroe, tel. 804/727–3391. Admission free. Open daily 10:30–4:30. Closed Christmas, Thanksgiving, and New Year's Day.*

❸ South of Hampton Roads, **Norfolk** is reached from the peninsula by the Hampton Roads Bridge-Tunnel. There's plenty to see in this old navy town, but the sites are rather spread out so you'll probably want to drive or take bus tours. Helpful blue-and-gold Norfolk Tour signs point the way from one major attraction to the next.

The springtime Azalea Festival is held at the 175-acre **Norfolk Botanical Gardens,** located near the airport, on the eastern edge of the city. Here is an abundance of azaleas, rhododendrons, and camellias, and a special feature: a fragrance garden for the blind, which also has identification labels in braille. A delicately landscaped Japanese garden has trees native to that country, including unusual strains of cherry and maple. From April to October, boats and trackless trains carry visitors along routes to view seasonal plants and flowers, including 4,000 varieties of roses on 3½ acres. Year-round, visitors can stroll 12 miles of paths. Eleven marble statues of famous artists, carved in the late-19th century by Moses Ezekiel, enhance the natural beauty of the gardens. Lakeside is ideal for picnics. *Azalea Garden Rd., tel. 804/441–5831. Admission: $2.50 adults, $1.50 senior citizens; $3 per person for admission and tour. No tours Thanksgiving, Christmas, or New Year's. Gardens open year-round. Boat and train tours: $2.50. Open daily 8:30–dusk.*

The **Hermitage Foundation Museum** occupies a 16th-century English Tudor–style house that was reproduced by a textile tycoon at the turn of the century. It contains the largest privately owned collection of Oriental art in the United States, including ivory and jade carvings, ancient bronzes, and a 1,400-year-old marble Buddha from China. The decorative-art collections include Tiffany glass, Persian rugs, and furniture from the Middle East, India, Europe, and America. Visitors may picnic on the 12 acres of grounds along the Lafayette River. *7637 North Shore Rd., tel. 804/423–2052. Admission: $4 adults, $1 children under 18, free to military. Open Mon.–Sat. 10–5, Sun. 1–5.*

By any standard the **Chrysler Museum** downtown qualifies as one of America's major art museums, and the *Wall Street Journal* calls it one of the 20 best. The permanent collection includes works by Rubens, Gainsborough, Renoir, Picasso, and Pollock—a list that suggests the breadth you'll find here. The classical and pre-Columbian civilizations are also represented; the decorative-arts collection includes exquisite English porcelain, and the Institute of Glass shows artifacts from ancient Rome as well as Tiffany pieces. Comfortably arranged exhibition spaces make a visit a particularly agreeable experience. *245 W. Olney Rd., tel. 804/664–6200. Admission free; $3 donation suggested. Open Tues.–Sat. 10–4, Sun. 1–5.*

The Federal-style redbrick **Moses Myers House,** built by its namesake in 1792, is exceptional, and not just for its elegance. In the long Adam-style dining room, a wood secretary displays under glass a collection of fine china—and a set of silver Kaddish cups, for Moses Myers was Norfolk's first permanent Jewish resident. A transplanted New Yorker, Myers made his fortune in Norfolk in shipping, then served as a diplomat and a customshouse officer. His grandson married James Madison's grandniece, his great-grandson served as mayor, and the family kept the house for five generations. The furnishings, 70% of them original, include family portraits by Gilbert Stuart and Thomas Sully. *331 Bank St., tel. 804/622–2787. Admission: $2 adults, $1 students, free to military. Combination ticket with Willoughby-Baylor House and/or Adam Thoroughgood House in Virginia Beach: $4 for all three sites. Open Jan.–Mar., Tues.–Sat. noon–5; Apr.–Dec., Tues.–Sat. 10–5, Sun. noon–5.*

The **Douglas MacArthur Memorial** is the burial place of the controversial war hero. An "army brat" with no hometown, the general designated this navy town as the site for a monument to himself because it was his mother's birthplace—and perhaps because no one as well known as he had a monument nearby (MacArthur had a formidable ego). In the rotunda of the old City Hall, converted according to MacArthur's design, is the mausoleum; 11 adjoining galleries house mementos of MacArthur's career, such as his signature corncob pipe and the Japanese instruments of surrender that concluded World War II. Next door the general's staff car is on display and a 24-minute biography is screened continuously. *Bank St. and City Hall Ave., tel. 804/441-2965. Admission free. Open Mon.–Sat. 10–5, Sun. 11–5.*

St. Paul's Church, constructed in 1739, was the only building to survive the bombardment and conflagration inflicted by Lord Dunmore, the last royal governor, on New Year's Day, 1776; a cannonball remains embedded in the southeastern wall. An earlier church on this site had been built in 1641, and today the churchyard contains graves dating to the 17th century. The interior was restored to the Colonial style in 1912, following Victorian alterations in the last century. *St. Paul's Blvd. and City Hall Ave., tel. 804/627-4353. Admission by contribution. Open Tues.–Fri. 10–4.*

Built in 1794, the **Willoughby-Baylor House** downtown is a red-brick town house that combines the Federal and Georgian styles. The authentic period antiques are not original to the house, but they follow an inventory made in 1800 on the death of Captain William Willoughby, who built the house. The herb-and-flower garden is also in keeping with the era. *601 E. Freemason St., tel. 804/622-1211. Admission: $2 adults, $1 children. Combination ticket with Moses Myers House and/or Adam Thoroughgood House in Virginia Beach: $4 for all three sites. Open by appointment only, within these hrs.: Jan.–Mar., Tues.–Sat. noon–5; Apr.–Dec., Tues.–Sat. 10–5, Sun. noon–5.*

The Waterside, at 333 Waterside Drive, bills itself as Tidewater's festival marketplace. This shopping center on the harbor has a nautical motif, and like other developments of the Rouse Company (Harborplace in Baltimore, the 6th Street Marketplace in Richmond) it has spurred the economic revival of the downtown area. Musical performances and temporary art exhibitions take place in the public spaces. The Waterside is a comfortable place to eat and shop, and its TRT kiosk (tel. 804/623-3222) is a source of visitor information and the launching point for all sorts of tours. *Tours depart hourly late May–Labor Day, Mon.–Sat. 10–10, Sun. noon–8; Labor Day–late May, Mon.–Sat. 10–9, Sun. noon–6.*

Time Out **Doumar's** (20th St. and Monticello Ave., tel. 804/627-4163) is a Norfolk institution. This drive-in restaurant, founded in 1934 by Abe Doumar—inventor of the ice-cream cone—is still operated by his family. Here, veteran waitresses carry to your car the specialties of the house: barbecue, natural limeade, and ice cream in fresh waffle cones made according to an original recipe.

The **Norfolk Naval Base,** on the northern edge of the city, is an impressive sight and home to more than 130 ships of the Second Fleet. Among the boarders is the USS *Theodore Roosevelt*, a nuclear-powered carrier with a crew of 6,300, said to be one of the largest warships in the world. The submarine piers and the heliport are also memorable sights. Visitors pass by but may not enter the windowless, top-secret Fleet Anti-Submarine Warfare Training Center building. Tour buses operate year-round, departing from the TRT kiosk at the Waterside and from the naval-base tour office. *Hampton Blvd., tel. 804/623-3222 (TRT), 804/444-7955, or 804/444-1577 (naval base visitors office). Tour: $5 adults, $2.50 children, senior* *citizens, and the disabled. Tour hrs. vary seasonally. Naval base open daily 9:30–4:30.*

The newest addition to Norfolk's much–redeveloped waterfront is **Nauticus,** the National Maritime Center, which opened mid–1994 and has already become one of the area's busiest attractions. With 70+ high-tech exhibits on three "decks," the site displays concepts as ancient as shipbuilding right next to interactive displays that encompass the modern naval world. Weather satelites, underwater archaeology, and the Loch Ness Monster all come together here in a stimulating and informative enironment. There are additional fees for the AEGIS Theater and Virtual Adventures. *One Waterside Drive, tel. 804/664-1000, Admission: $10 adults, $7.50 children 4–17, $8.50 seniors and military. Call for hours.*

Southwest of Norfolk, across the Elizabeth River, is the town of **❹ Portsmouth** with its well-maintained Olde Towne buildings. The **Portsmouth Naval Shipyard Museum** on the waterfront can be reached conveniently by the pedestrian ferry—a diverting experience in itself—from the Waterside in Norfolk. The museum's exhibits of naval history include models of 18th-century warships, and visitors can board the retired coast guard lightship (a floating lighthouse) whose quarters below deck have been furnished authentically. *2 High St., Portsmouth, tel. 804/393–8591. Admission: $1. Open Tues.–Sat. 10–5, Sun. 1–5.*

The 18th- and 19th-century houses of **Olde Towne Portsmouth,** which are not open to the public, can be seen comfortably on a tour organized by Norfolk Trolley, whose trolleys run between the historic neighborhood and the waterfront portside center. (*See* Guided Tours, *above.*)

Immediately south of Portsmouth (follow signs) is the much younger **❺** town of **Chesapeake** (established 1963), whose principal attraction for visitors is the entrance to the **Great Dismal Swamp.** That forbidding name was assigned to the area by William Byrd on one of his early 18th-century surveying expeditions. Today the swamp is a 106,000-acre National Wildlife Refuge that harbors bobcat, black bear, and more than 150 varieties of birds. A remarkably shallow lake—3,000 acres, 6 feet deep—is surrounded by skinny cypress trees that lend the scene a primeval quality. Several cleared and marked nature trails make this a spectacular contrast to downtown Norfolk, less than 20 miles away. *Great Dismal Swamp National Wildlife Refuge, Rte. 32 and follow signs, Box 349, Suffolk 23434, tel. 804/986–3705. Open daily sunrise–sunset.*

East of Norfolk, on the cape where the mouth of the bay meets the ocean, the historic **Old Cape Henry Lighthouse** marks the site where the English landed on their way to Jamestown in 1607. You can still climb to the top of the old lighthouse in summer; a new, working lighthouse is closed to visitors. *Tel. 804/422–9421. Admission: $2 adults, $1 children 7–18. Open mid-Mar.–Oct., daily 10–5.*

Inland from the Cape Henry lighthouses and the army installation at Fort Story, and south of U.S. 60, botanists will have a field day at **Seashore State Park.** Spanish moss grows no farther north than here, and blue spruce appears no farther south. The park is also a haven for red and gray fox, raccoon, opossum, water snake, and other denizens of swamp and dune. Boardwalks built just above the water level let you get close to flora and fauna while keeping your feet dry, and there are campgrounds, picnic areas, and guided tours. *Tel. 804/481–4836. Admission: Memorial Day–Labor Day, $2.50* *car; Sept.–May, $1 car (weekends only). Open daily 8 AM–sundown. Visitor center open daily 9–6.*

❻ The heart of **Virginia Beach,** a stretch of the ocean shore from Cape Henry south to Rudee Inlet, 6 miles of crowded public beach and a busy 40-block boardwalk, has been a popular summertime gathering place for many years. Recently renovated, the Boardwalk and Atlantic Avenue have unique lighting, teak benches, oceanfront park, and a 2-mile resort bike trail. Yet never in living memory has this been a place for peaceful communion with nature. In the surf and at the amusements on land, the crowds generate a certain excitement that should appeal most strongly to young people. One advantage of the commercial concentration here is the easy access to sailing, surfing, and scuba equipment rentals. The farther north visitors go on Virginia Beach, the more beach they will find in proportion to bars, T-shirt parlors, and video arcades. There's free entertainment from April through Labor Day weekend, nightly, at the 24th Street stage or 24th Street Park on the Boardwalk.

Along the oceanfront, the **Lifesaving Museum of Virginia,** set in a 1903 Seatack Lifesaving Station, contains ship models, shipwreck mementos, and a large collection of lifesaving equipment; one exhibit dramatically illustrates the Battle of the Atlantic, which took place just off the Virginia coast during World War II. *24th St. and Atlantic Ave., tel. 804/422–1587. Admission: $2.50 adults, $2 senior citizens and military, $1 children 6–18. Open Mon.–Sat. 10–5, Sun. 12–5; closed Mon. Oct.–Memorial Day.*

Inland from the bay shore is an attraction of earlier vintage, the **Adam Thoroughgood House** of about 1680, named for the prosperous plantation owner who held a land grant of 5,350 acres and who died in 1640. This little (45- by 22-foot) brick house, probably constructed by a Thoroughgood grandson, recalls the English cottage architecture of the period, with a protruding chimney and a steeply pitched roof. The four-room early plantation home has a typical 17th-century garden with characteristic hedges. *1636 Parish Rd., tel. 804/622–2787. Admission: $2 adults, $1 children. Combination ticket with Moses Myers House and/or Willoughby-Baylor House: $4 for all three sites. Open Jan.–Mar., Tues.–Sat. noon–5; Apr.–Dec., Tues.–Sat. 10–5, Sun. noon–5.*

The sea is the subject at the **Virginia Marine Science Museum** on General Booth Boulevard, almost 2 miles inland from Rudee Inlet at the southern end of Virginia Beach. A massive facility with more than 200 exhibits, and a very popular state attraction, this is no place for passive museum goers; many exhibits require participation. Visitors use computers to predict the weather and solve the pollution crisis, watch the birds in the salt marsh through telescopes on a deck, handle horseshoe crabs, take a simulated journey to the bottom of the sea in a submarine, and study fish up close in tanks that re-create various underwater environments. *717 General Booth Blvd., tel. 804/425–3474. Admission: $4.75 adults, $4.25 senior citizens, $3.75 children 4–12. Open daily 9–5 (until 9 Mon.–Sat., mid-June–Labor Day).*

U.S. 13 runs north from Virginia Beach via an engineering marvel: the 17½-mile Chesapeake Bay Bridge-Tunnel (toll, $10), which gives travelers the rare experience of being surrounded by the sea while never leaving their cars. An observation pier and a restaurant are located 4 miles from the southern end. The northern end is Virginia's Eastern Shore, where the wildlife, the sea, and the sun are abundant and human beings—except on popular Chincoteague—are not.

Driving north on U.S. 13, travelers encounter historic towns that preserve period structures in especially secluded environs. You will have to leave the main highway to experience the quaint towns and fishing villages that still carry an aura of simpler times. Nineteenth-century **Cape Charles,** once the southern terminus of the new railroad and the largest and busiest city on the Eastern Shore in Virginia, today is less energetic, but its residential areas still maintain their charm. Eighteenth-century **Eastville,** 15 miles above the bridge-tunnel and bisected by Route 13, has been the county seat since 1677; here you can see historic structures such as the old courthouse, erected in 1732, and a debtor's prison, raised in 1814. **Onancock,** a 300-year-old port, began as a settlement of four or five Indian families. Today it is one of the loveliest towns on the Eastern Shore of Virginia. Here you can visit a general store that dates to 1842 or walk down to the wharf and imagine yourself waiting for a steamer to Baltimore. At day's end look west across Chesapeake Bay and you can see the sun set over water—a rare sight for East Coast residents.

❼ Route 175, which meets U.S. 13 just 63 miles north of the bridge-tunnel, leads to unpopulated **Assateague Island,** a 37-mile-long national wildlife refuge and national seashore that extends north into Maryland. The ocean beaches and the hiking and biking trails here are extensive and unsullied. In addition to the pristine scenery, as many as 300 species of birds can be seen here, including migrant geese and swans. The island's best-known residents are the wild ponies, supposedly descended from Spanish workhorses that survived a shipwreck off these shores. Remember that these are wild animals, so you shouldn't get too close. Visitors should bring their own food and drink; island facilities are limited to bathhouses and water fountains. *Admission: $3 car, $1 cyclist or pedestrian. Wildlife drive closed to cars before 3 PM. Visitor center (tel. 804/336–6577) open daily 9–4; sometimes later, depending on season.*

❽ Many know the name of **Chincoteague Island** from Marguerite Henry's book for children, *Misty of Chincoteague,* first published in the 1940s. Chincoteague, smaller and closer to shore than Assateague, makes a sobering contrast to its neighbor. The dozens of billboards along Route 175, on the drive from the mainland, suggest the overdevelopment that is spoiling the place as substandard accommodations proliferate in the scramble for tourist dollars. An annual custom recalls a simpler time: On the last Thursday in July the ponies from Assateague are driven across the channel to Chincoteague, where they are placed at auction; those that remain unsold swim back home. During the rest of the year, the proximity to fine beaches and natural beauty justifies a sojourn here.

Chincoteague's Oyster Festival on Columbus Day weekend celebrates a major local industry with a food fair at which oysters are served in every conceivable form, from stew to fritters. Tickets to the festival, limited to 2,000, must be purchased well in advance from the Chamber of Commerce (tel. 804/336–6161). The **Oyster and Maritime Museum** on Chincoteague tells the history of the area. *Maddox Blvd., tel. 804/336–6117. Admission: $2 adults, 50¢ children. Open June–Oct., daily 10–5; call ahead for winter hrs.*

Chincoteague's other seasonal fairs, the **Seafood Festival** and **Harvest Festival** (held the first Wednesdays of May and October, respectively) also attract local gourmands. Tickets, which are usually sold out months in advance, can be purchased from the chamber of commerce (tel. 804/787–2460).

❾ Southwest of Chincoteague, on **Wallops Island,** NASA's Wallops Flight Facility was the site of early rocket launchings. Today, although satellites are sent up occasionally, atmospheric research is the main activity. Visitors can see a collection of spacecraft and exhibits and videos on the space program. *Tel. 804/824–2298 or 804/ 824–1344. Admission free. Open July–Aug., daily 10–4; Sept.– June, Thurs.–Mon. 10–4.*

What to See and Do with Children

Hampton Carousel is an operating antique: Its prancing steeds and bright-colored chariots carry visitors round and round to the tunes of carnival music. The 1920 carousel, a fixture at the former Buckroe Beach Amusement Park in the city for 60 years, has been meticulously restored by expert artisans. *Located off Settlers Landing Rd., in a downtown waterfront park near the Virginia Air and Space Center, tel. 804/727–6381. Admission: 50¢. Open Apr.–Sept. 15, daily noon–8; Sept. 16–Dec., Mon.–Sat. 10–6, Sun. noon–6; times may vary, depending on weather.*

Nauticus, the National Maritime Center, Norfolk *(see above).*

Peninsula SPCA, across the street from the Virginia Living Museum *(see below),* has a petting zoo with deer, donkeys, sheep, goats, turkeys, and wild animals, such as a caged jaguar, tiger, and leopard. *523 J. Clyde Morris Blvd., Newport News, tel. 804/595–1399. Admission: $1 donation. Open weekdays 10:30–5, Sat. 10:30–4:30, Sun. noon–5.*

Portsmouth Children's Museum has rooms where children can learn engineering and scientific principles by playing with bubbles and blocks. *Cnr. Court and High Sts., tel. 804/393–8393. Admission: $1.50, good also for Art Center Gallery, Lightship, and Portsmouth Naval Shipyard Museum. Open Tues.–Sat. 10–5, Sun. 1–5.*

Virginia Air and Space Center, Hampton *(see above).*

Virginia Living Museum in Newport News is a two-part facility. Outdoors, animals indigenous to the region live in wild or simulated wild lakefront habitats that allow visitors to observe their natural behavior. A trail leads to the water's edge, where otter and blue heron can be spotted, then upland past de-scented skunks, lame bald eagles (wounded by hunters), and cute but unpettable bobcats. A 40-foot-tall outdoor aviary puts visitors into a wetlands habitat. Indoors, the Planetarium offers more celestial sights; call for show times. *524 J. Clyde Morris Blvd., Newport News, tel. 804/595–1900. Admission: $5 adults, $3.25 children 3–12. Planetarium admission: $2.50 adults, $2 children 4–12 (children under 4 not permitted in planetarium). Combination admission: $5.50 adults, $3.75 children. Open mid-June–Labor Day, Mon.–Sat. 9–6, Thurs. 9–9, Sun. 10–6; Sept.–mid-June, Mon.–Sat. 9–5, Thurs. 9–5 and 7–9, Sun. 1–5.*

The **Virginia Marine Science Museum** *(see above)* in Virginia Beach sponsors an annual free Easter candy hunt and games for children.

Virginia Zoological Park in Norfolk is the largest in the state, with 110 species living on 55 acres—including rhinos and ostriches as well as such domesticated animals as sheep. With the assistance of docents, children may handle some animals. Elephant demonstrations are regularly scheduled during summer months. Next door, Lafayette Park has picnic shelters and facilities for tennis, basketball, football, and softball. *3500 Granby St., Norfolk, tel. 804/441–2706. Admission: $2 adults, $1 senior citizens and children 2–11; free after 4 on Sun. and Mon. Open daily 10–5.*

Off the Beaten Track

Matters of the spirit and the flesh are on the agenda at the **Association for Research and Enlightenment,** founded by the psychic Edgar Cayce, in Virginia Beach. Cayce was known for his ability to diagnose the causes of illness by "reading" a case history; his writings on history, philosophy, and other topics have been collected in the library here. Following a brief slide show on Cayce, visitors may have their ESP quotient determined by an electronic apparatus. A meditation garden features a pond stocked with goldfish, and a meditation room overlooks the ocean. Lectures and movies are scheduled in the afternoon. *67th St. and Atlantic Ave., Virginia Beach, tel. 804/428–3588. Admission free. Open Mon.–Sat. 9–8, Sun. 11–8.*

Shopping

Ghent (Colley Ave. and 21st St., Norfolk) is a picturesque neighborhood with an eclectic mix of chic shops.

Gifts **The d'Art Center** (125 College Pl., Norfolk, tel. 804/625–4211) allows you to watch painters, sculptors, glass workers, quilters, and other artists at work in their studios; the creations are for sale in two galleries on the premises.

Rowena's Jam and Jelly Factory (758 W. 22nd St., Norfolk, tel. 804/627–8699) offers tours of the factory Monday through Wednesday, but you must make arrangements in advance. For sale in the shop are homemade jams, cooking sauces, fruit curds, and cookies. This tour is accessible to the disabled.

Outlet Stores **The Great American Outlet Mall** (3750 Virginia Beach Blvd., Virginia Beach, tel. 804/463–8665) contains more than 40 off-price and manufacturers' outlets, including Fieldcrest, Cannon, and Van Heusen.

Sports and Outdoor Activities

Participant Sports

Boating and For canoe and fishing-boat rentals, try **Northwest River Park** (tel.
Canoeing 804/421–3145) in the Chesapeake; **Munden Point Park** (tel. 804/426–5296) in Virginia Beach; **Newport News Park** (tel. 804/886–7911; rentals available). The **Mariners' Museum** (*see above*), in Newport News, rents boats for use on Lake Maury on museum grounds.

Fishing North of Hampton, charters are offered from April to October by **Al Hartz Poquoson Charter Boats** (E. River Rd., Poquoson, tel. 804/868–6821); in Hampton, there's **Chesapeake Charter Service** (519 Bridge St., tel. 804/723–0998). **James River Fishing Pier** (tel. 804/247–0364), in Newport News, is open April through mid-November. Freshwater anglers will want to try Airfield Lake, 6 miles east of Wakefield on Route 628 or Sleepy Hole Park in Portsmouth.

In Norfolk, charters and pier fishing are offered in season at **Harrison Boat House** (414 W. Ocean View Ave., tel. 804/588–9968) and **Willoughby Bay Marina** (1651 Bayville St., tel. 804/588–2663).

On Chincoteague Island, bait and tackle are available from **Barnacle Bill's** (tel. 804/336–5188), and boat rentals from **Captain Bob's** (tel. 804/336–6654) and **R&R Boats** (tel. 804/336–5465).

In Wachapreague, charters and boat rentals, tackle and bait are available at **Wachapreague Marina** (tel. 804/787–4110).

Golf **Hampton Golf and Tennis** (tel. 804/727–1195) has an 18-hole course. **Dell Run Golf Course Newport News Park** (tel. 804/886–7925) offers two 18-hole courses. **Kiln Creek Golf and Country Club's** (tel. 804/988–3222) 6,888-yard course with numerous bunkers and water hazards is one of the most challenging. **Lake Wright** (tel. 804/461–2246) in Norfolk and **Cypress Point** (tel. 804/490–8822), **Owl's Creek** (tel. 804/428–2800), **Hell's Point** (tel. 804/721–3400), and **Honey Bee** (tel. 804/471–2768) in Virginia Beach have 18-hole courses. **Sleepy Hole** (tel. 804/393–5050) in Suffolk has an 18-hole course.

Water Sports **Chick's Beach Sailing Center** (tel. 804/481–3067), in Virginia Beach, offers Hobie Cat and Windsurfer rentals and lessons. **Lynnhaven Dive Center** (Virginia Beach, tel. 804/481–7949) and **Scuba Ventures** (Virginia Beach, tel. 804/473–0847) offer scuba lessons, gear, and trips.

Spectator Sports

Auto Racing **Langley Speedway** (tel. 804/865–1992) in Newport News features late-model stock cars, grand stock, all-American stock, and ministock. Races are run from March to October.

Baseball The **Tidewater Tides** of the International League, an affiliate of the New York Mets, play at Metropolitan Park (tel. 804/461–5600) in Norfolk, April–September.

Football **Peninsula Poseidons** (semi-pro) of Class AAA Mason-Dixon League play at Todd Stadium (tel. 804/873–1113) in Newport News on Saturdays, August through October.

Hockey The **Hampton Roads Admirals** of the East Coast Hockey League play at Norfolk's Scope (tel. 804/640–1212).

Beaches

Ocean View Beaches, 14 miles of beach along the Chesapeake Bay in Norfolk, have waters that are much calmer than those of the ocean—and safer for children. Sea trout and flounder make good fishing here.

Virginia Beach's oceanfront becomes crowded during the summer, and the lively boardwalk scene may be a greater attraction than the sand or the water.

Buckroe Beach, in Hampton, has adequate parking and a nearby park.

The **Eastern Shore** of Virginia has 5 miles of well-maintained beach, with bathhouses and picnic areas, on the southern end of Assateague Island at Tom's Cove Hook. Nearby, ponies roam the 10 miles of unsupervised Wild Beach, but do not approach the ponies, as they're wild and will bite.

A small but beautiful beach with a turn-of-the-century gazebo fronts on Chesapeake Bay in the town of **Cape Charles.**

Dining and Lodging

Chincoteague oysters, a delicacy on seafood menus across the country, come no fresher than on or near Chincoteague itself, a few miles from where they were tonged or dredged. The more urban restaurants of Virginia Beach, Norfolk, Portsmouth, Newport News, and Hampton offer a wide range of cuisine, and they are likely to serve dinner much later than the restaurants of the Eastern Shore.

Accommodations on the Eastern Shore are typically destinations in themselves, with clean, quiet beaches within easy reach. The many hotels of Virginia Beach maintain higher prices and may require a minimum stay of two or three days; some visitors will want to consider hotels and motels in Norfolk and farther north as bases of operation.

Highly recommended establishments are indicated by a star ★.

Eastern Shore **Channel Bass Inn.** The small dining room of the inn (*see* Eastern
Dining Shore Lodging, *below*) is a lightly formal ensemble of Colonial and Continental French elements: antique Queen Anne chairs at the seven well-spaced tables, and seashell-shaped, gilded-glass sconces on the walls, on which are also hung Oriental and Impressionist art. The chef (and owner) has studied in both Spain and the south of France, and his oils and seasonings are frequently redolent of that region. The soufflé of crabmeat (prepared for two) is distinguished by a judicious use of curry. Because reservations are made for the entire evening, there's a $50 no-show penalty; guarantee space by credit card. With an average check of $120–$180 per couple, the Channel Bass Inn is the most expensive restaurant in this book. *6228 Church St., Chincoteague, tel. 804/336–6148. Reservations required. Dress: casual but neat. AE, DC, MC, V. Closed a week before Christmas until after New Year's; open on weekends Jan.–mid-Feb.; nightly rest of yr. No lunch. $$$$*

The Garden and the Sea Inn. The restaurant part of this five-room bed-and-breakfast specializes in fresh local seafood and vegetables prepared French-style. The menu is not extensive, but it is select, and it changes frequently. Specialties include delicious scallops with sautéed cabbage and parsley; Chesapeake Bay fish grilled with herbs and lemon butter; bouillabaisse; duck breast with cassis berries; and veal scaloppine with capers and wine sauce. The building was built in 1802 as Bloxom's Tavern and enlarged before the end of the century. *Turn west off Rte. 13 at Rte. 710 (First Virginia Bank) and go ¼ mi (Box 275), New Church 23415, tel. 804/824–0672. Open Apr.–Oct. Reservations recommended. Dress: casual. AE, D, DC, MC, V. $$–$$$*

Landmark Crab House. Ask for a table by the window at this beachside restaurant, for although the cavernous dining hall is not much to look at in itself, there are wide views of the water from three sides. The servings are as generous as the vista. Whole loaves of fresh white bread precede the meal, and every entrée allows a visit with a large plate to the conventional crab salad bar. A creamy crab imperial, baked in a terrine, is touted as the specialty; the crab cakes are a slightly drier alternative. Beef dishes, well represented on the regular menu, often appear as specials. A children's menu that includes hamburgers makes this a spot for family dining rather than for couples in search of a romantic evening out. *N. Main St.,*

Chincoteague, tel. 804/336–5552. Reservations advised. Dress: casual. AE, D, DC, MC, V. $$–$$$

Trawler Restaurant and Lounge. Situated on Route 13 in Exmore, this inland restaurant maintains a nautical attitude in both decor and menu. "Rick and Steve" is a delicious combination of scallops, shrimp, and crabmeat sautéed in butter with fresh garlic and mushrooms. The menu also includes she-crab soup, crab cakes, and seafood quiche. Meals are accompanied by sweet-potato biscuits, which have achieved a widespread reputation (and whose recipe is a guarded secret, despite requests from national magazines) and salad bar. Three dining areas are decorated with wildlife drawings and hand-carved duck decoys, mostly by local artists. (The Eastern Shore is widely known for its decoy carvers.) *Rte. 13, tel. 804/442–2092. Reservations accepted. Dress: casual. MC, V. $$*

Lodging **Channel Bass Inn.** This three-story, beige clapboard house, built in
★ the 1870s and expanded 50 years later, was renovated in 1978; today it's an inn of impeccable luxury. The soundproof rooms are individually decorated with appointments such as four-poster beds and Erté prints; the excellent restaurant (*see* Eastern Shore Dining, *above*) draws diners from hours away. *6228 Church St., Chincoteague 23336, tel. 804/336–6148. 10 rooms. Facilities: restaurant (see Eastern Shore Dining, above). AE, D, DC, MC, V. Open weekends Jan.– mid-Feb.; nightly rest of yr. $$$$*

Miss Molly's. This gray wood house, built in 1886 by a prosperous clammer, is a Victorian turn on Queen Anne architecture, with "gingerbread" accents. The surrounding picket fence offers a cozy touch consistent with the ambience within. Breakfast is served in a gazebo attached to a corner of the back porch. The American Empire antiques correspond to the period in which the house was constructed. The sunny master bedroom, where Marguerite Henry wrote the novel *Misty of Chincoteague*, is the only room with a private bath. The building was gutted and renovated in 1982. *4141 N. Main St., Chincoteague 23336, tel. 804/336–6686. 7 rooms, 2 share bath. No credit cards. Closed Jan.–mid-Feb. Rates include breakfast and afternoon tea; no smoking. $$$*

Colonial Manor Inn. At press time, the family that has owned the Colonial Manor since 1936 had it up for sale; call ahead to find out if there's been a change of ownership. If not, you can definitely rely on the homespun attitude and decor of this charming inn, located in an 1882 three-story wood-frame house. None of the rooms has a telephone, yet all have running water and TV; the harbor is five blocks away, and several restaurants are nearby. Continental breakfast is complimentary. *84 Market St., Onancock 23417, tel. 804/787–3521. 14 rooms. No credit cards. $$*

Pickett's Harbor. At the southern tip of the Eastern Shore sits this putty-colored clapboard house with redbrick ends and siding. Built in 1976 according to a Colonial design, the home features 200-year-old floors, doors, and cupboards from several James River farms that were installed to ensure authenticity. Suitable antiques and reproductions furnish the rooms, two of which have private bath. All the guest quarters overlook small sand dunes and the bay beyond, and the backyard has 17 acres of private beach; this is very much a retreat. *Rte. 600, Box 96, Townsend 23443, tel. 804/331–2212. 6 rooms, 2 with bath. No credit cards. Rates include full breakfast. $$*

Island Motor Inn. Located on the Intracoastal Waterway, this two-story motel offers ocean and bay views from every room. Guests can relax on their private balconies and watch the passersby on the boardwalk or simply gaze at the beautiful sunset. Despite a popular location, this laid-back motel has managed to maintain its homey-ness. *4391 N. Main St., Chincoteague 23336, tel. 804/336–3141. 48 rooms. Facilities: restaurant, outdoor fireplace grill, pool, health and fitness room. AE, D, DC, MC, V. $*

Hampton
Dining
★

Victor's. The Radisson Hotel Hampton, in which this establishment is housed, offers restaurants with a variety of settings and fares, but Victor's is its top-of-the-line eatery. Its mauve-and-green decor gives the dining room a contemporary look, and high windows overlook an adjacent marina and river. The menu has a good selection of seafood, but it also has a creditable list of chicken, veal, and pasta dishes. A typical three-course meal might include oysters or clams on the half-shell, shrimp *LaRaine* (shrimp and sea scallops sautéed in lime and ginger sauce), and chocolate fettuccine. Possible entrée substitutes include Virginia crab cakes, filet Mignon, and sautéed medallions of veal. During the summer, the outdoor under-the-awning Oyster Alley serves a shorter and lighter menu that includes salads, sandwiches, and desserts from noon to 9. Its marina-side setting keeps the restaurant from all traffic except that which passes on the river or boardwalk. *Radisson Hotel Hampton, 700 Settlers Landing Rd., tel. 804/727–9700. Reservations advised. Dress: casual. AE, D, DC, MC, V. $$–$$$*

Captain George's. One in a chain of six, this smorgasbord restaurant has a nautical motif. A Chesapeake Bay mural dominates the largest of four dining rooms, with polyurethane tabletops embedded with seashells, sections of rope, and small brass boat fixtures. Although there is an ample à la carte menu, the main attraction is the all-you-can-eat buffet of fried, steamed, and broiled seafood. Highlights of the 70-item buffet are steamed Alaskan crab legs, steamed shrimp with Old Bay seasoning (a locally made favorite), broiled flounder, steamed mussels, and she-crab soup. Among the 15 desserts are baklava and five fruit cobblers. *2710 W. Mercury Blvd., tel. 804/826–1435. Reservations only for 10 or more. Dress: casual. AE, MC, V. No lunch. $$*

Fisherman's Wharf. This restaurant, decorated with ship figureheads and other seagoing paraphernalia, occupies the top floor of a waterfront building constructed several decades ago when the lobsters inexplicably moved southward along the Atlantic coast. They later moved back north, again inexplicably. A seafood-dominated buffet of up to 75 items, including king crab legs, mussels, cherrystone clams, and fish, is set up nightly and is popular locally. Prime rib is added several nights a week. The regular menu also emphasizes seafood—the tasty Hampton-style crab cake features backfin crabmeat flecked with bits of peas and carrots—but has a few other specialties, such as fried chicken strips in honey sauce. *14 Ivy Home Rd., tel. 804/723–3113. Reservations suggested. AE, D, DC, MC, V. $$*

Garden of the Heart Restaurant. This restaurant in the heart of the Old Hampton area, near the Air and Space Center, is divided into several rooms but is still on the small side. The evening menu includes, among other items, steak Diane prepared tableside, quail, and poached swordfish. But the chef is flexible; if you request a specific meal in advance, the chef will go to the market and then prepare the meal to your liking. During both lunch and dinner, this restaurant attracts a business and tourist crowd. *49 W. Queens Way, tel. 804/722–5022. Dress: casual. Reservations suggested. AE, D, MC, V. Closed Sun. $$*

The Grate Steak. Farm implements and unfinished pine walls decorate the four windowless dining rooms where tables are draped with vinyl cloths printed in a blue floral calico pattern. Consistent with this rusticity, diners step up to a common barbecue pit and grill for themselves the steak, shrimp, or chicken of their choosing. The shrimp has already been treated with wine butter and Old Bay seasoning, the chicken breast marinated in teriyaki sauce. Make-it-yourself salad bars feature baked potatoes, among other selections. Prime rib, served on the bone (as often it is not in this region), is slowly roasted by a professional chef. *1934 Coliseum Dr., tel. 804/827–1886. Reservations only for 6 or more. Dress: casual. AE, D, DC, MC, V. No lunch. $$*

Lodging **Radisson Hotel Hampton.** The nine-story Radisson has the premier location in town, right at a marina and a block away from the Virginia Air and Space Center. Guests cross the lobby's white-marble floors to Victor's Restaurant (*see* Hampton Dining, *above*) or Signals bar, where a DJ spins discs Wednesday through Sunday nights and where a light lunch is served. Upstairs, most rooms look over the harbor or the handsome plaza in front of the Virginia Air and Space Center. Rooms not facing the waterfront are less popular, but also less expensive. *700 Settlers Landing Rd., 23669, tel. 804/727–9700 or 800/333–3333, fax 804/722–4557. 172 rooms. Facilities: restaurant, outdoor café in summer, bar, outdoor pool, whirlpool, Nautilus; racquetball courts across the street. AE, D, DC, MC, V. $$$*

Holiday Inn Hampton. Halfway between Colonial Williamsburg and Virginia Beach, this complex of buildings stands on 13 beautifully landscaped acres. A four-story atrium with plants and fountains and conference facilities are recent additions. About half the rooms have a pink-and-green decor, with pink sofas, green carpets, and a floral pattern on curtains and bedspreads; even the wood furniture is pink. Other rooms have a darker look, with cherrywood dressers and tables, green bedspreads and curtains, and rust-colored carpets. Sofas convert into extra beds in many rooms. Some rooms overlook the indoor pool in the atrium; others have doors that open, motel-style, directly onto the parking lot. *1815 W. Mercury Blvd., 23666, tel. 804/838–0200 or 800/842–9370, fax 804/838–0200. 320 rooms. Facilities: restaurant, bar, indoor pool, outdoor pool, whirlpool, sauna, fitness course, exercise and games rooms. AE, D, DC, MC, V. $$*

Newport News **Herman's Harbor House.** As you drive through the residential neigh-
Dining borhood, you may think you've gone off-course, but keep on driving.
★ Herman's, located at the end of Deep Creek Road, serves the area's best crab cakes, accompanied by ample portions of vegetables. The diverse menu also includes other Tidewater-style seafood dishes, steak, veal, and pasta, as well as homemade desserts. On Friday and Saturday nights there's an all-you-can-eat seafood buffet. *Take I–64 (Exit 258-A) to Warwick Blvd. to 663 Deep Creek Rd., tel. 804/930–1000. Reservations accepted. Dress: casual. AE, MC, V. $$*

Peninsula Room. A recent addition to the Kiln Creek Golf and Country Club, this restaurant is modern and chic and has some tables situated along windows that overlook the golf course. A British Isles menu (roast leg of lamb, stoved chicken casserole, and Irish stew) delicately balances meat with equally hearty seafood such as seared salmon and crabmeat au gratin. The Peninsula Room also boasts a large, sophisticated wine cellar and a Sunday brunch. *1003 Brick Kiln Blvd., tel. 804/874–2600. Reservations accepted. Dress: casual. AE, DC, MC, V. Closed Sun. and Mon. dinner, Sat. lunch (Manchester Grill open daily). $$*

Norfolk **La Galleria.** In just a few years this restaurant has earned a reputa-
Dining tion as one of the best in Norfolk. The decor, which is not done in the
★ usual homey southern style, may appear cold to some, but it is im-

pressively Roman. Decorations include large urns imported from Italy, Corinthian columns, and a long, sculpted wall adorned with frames and half frames: The interior design may explain the restaurant's name. A pianist entertains with soft music. Menu choices include *vongole al casino* (baked clams sprinkled with herbs, garlic, and bread crumbs) as one of the appetizers, and a variety of excellent pastas and main courses, such as *salmone La Galleria* (salmon sautéed in herbs, garlic, and white wine). A predinner visit can be made to d'Art Center (*see* Exploring, *above*) across the street, a working community for the visual arts. *120 College Pl., tel. 804/623–3939. Dress: casual but neat. Reservations suggested. AE, DC, MC, V. $$$*

The Riverwalk. Through picture windows, and in good weather from the veranda, guests can watch passersby on the boardwalk and along the Elizabeth River while they dine. A distinctive appetizer is the blackened jumbo sea scallops; follow it with lemon-pepper fettuccine with shiitake mushrooms and fresh sun-dried tomatoes in a basil sauce. Other pastas, some served with meat, make light but satisfying meals. A seafood platter with portions of fresh catch, scallops, and broiled large shrimp stuffed with backfin crabmeat is a specialty, as is the filet Oscar—filet mignon and backfin crabmeat in a béarnaise sauce. *Omni International Hotel, 777 Waterside Dr., tel. 804/622–6664. Reservations advised. Dress: casual. AE, D, DC, MC, V. $$$*

★ **The Ship's Cabin.** This often-mentioned restaurant is best known for its seafood but has good steaks as well. For an appetizer try the Oysters Bingo—Eastern Shore salt oysters lightly rolled in batter, sautéed in butter, and served hot in the shell with bits of scallions and parsley in white wine. If you're really hungry and can handle a hearty portion, order the filet mignon with backfin crab and asparagus as your entrée. Bread is served with the meal and is baked fresh daily on site; the blueberry bread is almost a dessert in itself. Window-side booths in one room look across tufted sand dunes to the Chesapeake Bay and the lights of the Chesapeake Bay Bridge-Tunnel; the other dining rooms, lighted by fireplace and candles, provide even cozier settings. *4110 E. Ocean View Ave., tel. 804/362–4659. Reservations advised. Dress: casual. AE, D, DC, MC, V. $$$*

★ **Freemason Abbey Restaurant and Tavern.** A Victorian atmosphere prevails in this former church building that's more than 118 years old and features 40-foot-high cathedral ceilings and large windows that look onto the old-style business district. The upstairs, the reconstructed-steel mezzanine of the former church, offers more intimate dining, while downstairs you can get lighter fare or sit at the bar and lounge. On Wednesday Freemason Abbey features a lobster special, and on Thursday prime rib heads the menu. For an appetizer try the artichoke dip. *209 W. Freemason St., tel. 804/622–3966. Reservations accepted. Dress: casual. AE, MC, V. $$*

Il Porto. Plenteous portions of pasta, seafood, and veal are served in a dining room with a river view, and on the terrace during warm weather. The bar is bright and spacious, and a piano player entertains most nights. *The Waterside, 333 Waterside Dr., tel. 804/627–4400. Reservations advised. Dress: casual. AE, D, DC, MC, V. $$*

Kelley's. The TV set in the small dining room lends Kelley's an Irish-tavern ambience, and the cuisine follows suit. The large cheeseburger is the most popular item, but the rich soups (she-crab, clam, broccoli, and a daily special) are highlights of the menu, too. Food is served on the patio when weather permits, even on warm winter days. *1408 Colley Ave., tel. 804/623–3216. Dress: casual. Reservations not necessary. AE, MC, V. $*

Lodging **Hilton Airport.** Don't let the gray cement exterior scare you away; the interior of this six-story highway-side Hilton is neither drab nor harsh. The hotel has an atrium, a concierge floor, some king-size beds, and a free shuttle to the airport. *1500 N. Military Hwy., 23502, tel. 804/466–8000 or 800/422–7474, fax 804/466–8000. 246 rooms, 4 suites. Facilities: 3 restaurants, 2 bars, coffee shop, outdoor pool, tennis court, health club. AE, D, DC, MC, V. $$$*

Norfolk Waterside Marriott. This 1991 addition to the redeveloped downtown area of Norfolk is connected to Waterside shopping area by a ramp and is close to Towne Point Park, site of many festivals. The handsome lobby, with wood paneling, a central staircase, silk tapestries, and Federal-style furniture, sets a high standard that continues throughout the hotel. The ambience is European. Rooms are somewhat small, but each has everything the business traveler could ask for—including two telephones, voice mail, and a modem hook-up. *235 E. Main St., 23510, tel. 804/627–4200 or 800/228–9290, fax 804/628–6466. 397 rooms, 8 suites. Facilities: 2 restaurants, lounge, indoor pool and sun deck, Jacuzzis, valet parking. AE, D, DC, MC, V. $$$*

Omni International Hotel. Modern is the word for the decor, from the bright, spacious lobby to the ample rooms and large suites. A few Oriental artifacts moderate the sleek lines of the lobby. Services follow more traditional lines. A ground-floor bar with dramatic 30-foot windows overlooks the river. Many rooms have a beautiful view over the Elizabeth River and the city's working harbor. This property is convenient to the Waterside shopping area. *777 Waterside Dr., tel. 804/622–6664 or 800/843–6664, fax 804/625–4930. 419 rooms, 24 suites. Facilities: restaurant, lounge, outdoor pool, valet parking. AE, D, DC, MC, V. $$$*

Old Dominion Inn. This motel, family owned and operated, has touches suggestive of a country inn. Guest rooms are entered not from the parking area but from interior hallways. The three-story building, completed in 1989, with Colonial Williamsburg decor, has late-18th-century antiques in the lobby and reproductions in guest rooms. Ceilings have crown moldings along the perimeter and an anachronistic fan in the center. The inn is across from Old Dominion University on busy Hampton Boulevard, but the guest rooms are set back from the road, out of range of most traffic noise. *4111 Hampton Blvd., 23508, tel. 804/440–5100. 60 rooms. AE, D, DC, MC, V. Rates include Continental breakfast. $$*

★ **YMCA of Tidewater.** The rooms at this Y have daily maid service, private bath, and no curfew for guests—who are of all ages, both genders, and all faiths. Even though rooms have no phone or (with a few exceptions) TV, this is one of the all-time American hotel bargains. The six-story building is located in a historic, largely residential neighborhood, 2½ blocks from the Chrysler Museum. Yet the Y's biggest asset is the extraordinary sports facility on the premises, freely accessible to all guests. *312 W. Bute St., 23510, tel. 804/622–6328 or 804/622–9622. 76 rooms. Facilities: indoor pool, indoor track, racquetball court, whirlpool, Nautilus. MC, V. $*

Portsmouth **Holiday Inn Waterfront.** With the Portsmouth waterfront just out
Lodging the door, and Olde Town's attractions so nearby, this hotel is very well situated. The undistinguished appearance of the building hides a pleasant atmosphere: Public and guest rooms vary in size, but all feature modern decor, and some private guest-rooms share water views. The restaurant overlooks the Elizabeth River, and Norfolk's downtown skyline on the opposite shore. *8 Crawford Pkwy., 23704, tel. 804/393–2573 or 800/465–4329, fax 804/399–1248. 264 rooms, 6*

suites. Facilities: outdoor pool, restaurant, lounge, convention services. AE, D, DC, MC, V. $$

Virginia
Beach
Dining

The Lighthouse. All tables in the six dining rooms overlook the ocean or the inlet (most overlook both) through picture windows. The bare lacquered wood tables are set with candles, fresh flowers, and linen napkins; the floors are red clay tile; the walls have dark wood paneling. Nevertheless, the main attraction here is the seafood. Enormous 2½-pound Maine lobsters come plain or stuffed with fresh crabmeat. Seafood Nadia is a mix of crabmeat, shrimp, and scallops, entwined in fettuccine. The Sunday brunch menu includes a mimosa and side dishes of apples, cheese, and sautéed mushrooms. *1st St. and Atlantic Ave., tel. 804/428-7974. Reservations advised. Dress: casual. AE, D, DC, MC, V. $$$*

Duck Inn. Just east of the Lynnhaven Bridge and just off of Shore Drive, this family seafood restaurant is near the water and within sight of the bridge-tunnel. Pine paneling sets the scene for indoor dining; the warm months allow dining on an outdoor deck, or appetizers and drinks in the gazebo. The specialty of the house, a milk-based fisherman's chowder, contains shrimp, crabmeat, and mushrooms. Crab cakes are popular here, as is the nightly buffet. *3324 Shore Dr., tel. 804/481-0201. No reservations. Dress: casual. AE, D, MC, V. $$*

Charlie's Seafood Restaurant. A funky family restaurant on the south side of Shore Drive near Lynnhaven Inlet, Charlie's is usually full of people sitting at vinyl-top tables eating some of the best seafood on the Eastern Shore. Enjoy the relaxed ambience while biting into light, crispy, tasty crabs that are beyond comparison. Or, if you are in a hurry, you can buy a quart of she-crab soup to go (packed in ice). *3139 Shore Dr., tel. 804/481-9863. No reservations. Dress: casual. AE, MC, V. $*

Lodging

Cavalier Hotels. Located in the quieter north end of town, this 18-acre resort complex combines the original Cavalier Hotel of 1927, a seven-story redbrick building on a hill, with an oceanfront high rise that was built across the street in 1973. The clientele is about evenly divided between conventioneers and families. F. Scott and Zelda Fitzgerald were regular visitors to the older section, which has been lavishly refurbished. Guests in the hilltop facility can see the water—and get to it easily by shuttle van or with the help of push-button crossing lights. The newer building overlooks 600 feet of private beach. There is a fee for tennis, but the other extensive athletic facilities are free. *Atlantic Ave. and 42nd St., 23451, tel. 804/425-8555 or 800/446-8199, fax 804/428-7957. 400 rooms in summer, 282 rooms and 10 suites in winter. Facilities: 3 restaurants, private beach, indoor pool, outdoor pool, children's wading pool, 4 tennis courts, aerobic exercise course, croquet court, volleyball court, putting green, games room, playground, children's activities, baby-sitting service. AE, D, DC, MC, V. $$$$*

Ramada Oceanfront Tower. In 1985 this five-story hotel added a 17-story tower, becoming the tallest hotel in the city. In 1986 the rooms in the older section were all renovated. Rooms that do not face the ocean directly have either a sideways view or overlook the swimming pool. Typically, as many as half the guests are conventioneers. *57th St. and Oceanfront, 23451, tel. 804/428-7025 or 800/365-3032, fax 804/428-2921. 215 rooms. Facilities: restaurant, bar, indoor-outdoor pool, outdoor pool with swim-up bar, sauna, whirlpool, Nautilus. AE, D, DC, MC, V. $$$$*

Idlewhyle Motel. This 40-year-old motel on the beach and boardwalk usually caters to families, who choose between rooms and efficiencies. The walls are a drab beige vinyl, and the furniture, of recent vintage, is serviceable. Rooms that do not face the ocean look onto the pool. *2705 Atlantic Ave., 23451, tel. 804/428–9341, fax 804/425–5355. 23 rooms, 23 efficiencies. Facilities: coffee shop, indoor pool, sun deck. AE, D, MC, V. $$*

The Arts and Nightlife

The Arts

Music The Virginia Opera (tel. 804/623–1223), performing in and around Virginia, has a widely acclaimed company joined by major guest artists; the season (October to March) often sees American and world premieres.

Scope Center (1 Scope Plaza, Norfolk, tel. 804/441–2161) and **Hampton Coliseum** (1000 Coliseum Dr., Hampton, tel. 804/838–4203) are venues for country, rap, rhythm-and-blues, and rock concerts.

Ogden Hall, at Hampton University (tel. 804/727–5308), hosts performances by recognized artists on a regular schedule.

Theater In Norfolk, the **Virginia Stage Company** (Box 3770, Norfolk 23514, tel. 804/627–1234 or 804/627–6988) performs at the Wells Theatre (118 Tazewell St., tel. 804/441–2764); Broadway shows on tour appear at **Chrysler Hall** (1 Scope Plaza, tel. 804/441–2161). The **Gallery Dinner Theatre** (6270 Northampton Blvd., Hampton, tel. 804/461–5570) hosts performances Wednesday through Sunday.

Portsmouth applauds the restoration of the art deco atmosphere in the **Commodore Theatre** (421 High St., tel. 804/393–6962), built in 1945. Crystal chandeliers and wall murals provide a handsome setting for light dinner fare with first-run movies. There are tables on the main floor and traditional theater seating in the balcony.

On the Eastern Shore, the **Trawler Dinner Theater** (Rte. 13, Lankford Hwy., Exmore, tel. 804/442–2092) offers four productions a year.

Nightlife

Rock **Adams** (Ramada Inn, 6360 Newtown Rd., Norfolk, tel. 804/461–1081) has a DJ spinning Top-40 music.

Josette's (249 W. York St., Norfolk, tel. 804/623–2000) attracts a contemporary adult crowd that comes for dancing and Top-40 sounds on Friday and Saturday nights.

The Inn Place (Ramada Inn, 950 J. Clyde Morris Blvd., Newport News, tel. 804/599–4460) is the most popular spot for rock and country.

Country **Fifth National Banque** (1849 E. Little Creek Rd., Norfolk, tel. 804/480–3600) features authentic country-western entertainment and dancing, and free dance lessons.

Dancing At the **Orient Express,** in the Norfolk Airport Hilton (1500 N. Military Hwy., tel. 804/466–8000), the latest dance tunes are performed live.

After Dark (2000 W. Mercury Blvd., tel. 804/838–7078) in Hampton hosts many kinds of live music.

David's (430 High St., tel. 804/393–6071) in Portsmouth features dancing to Top-40 with alternative music on weekends.

Spirit of Norfolk (333 Waterside Dr., Norfolk, tel. 804/627–7771) offers the area's only dinner-dance cruises with live music and entertainment. Lunch and brunch cruises are featured, too.

8 Baltimore

In 1980 the christening of two shopping pavilions called Harborplace symbolized the revival of Baltimore's formerly decaying Inner Harbor and surrounding neighborhoods; this union was the payoff of at least two decades of urban-renewal efforts by a coalition of the public and private sectors. Today the Inner Harbor is surrounded by hotels, office buildings, and attractions such as the Maryland Science Center and the huge National Aquarium. Restaurants and shops nearby are proliferating, and the city's historic structures and neighborhoods are receiving unprecedented numbers of visitors. Local sports fans took a blow when the Colts football team skipped to Indianapolis in 1983, but the city is confident that the Orioles baseball team is here to stay: Their new stadium, Oriole Park at Camden Yards near the Inner Harbor, opened with much fanfare in 1992. Because the Orioles regularly play to sellout crowds who are as attracted to the surroundings as they are to the game itself, the stadium's design has been copied by other cities.

Before the 1970s it was a joke to speak of Baltimore as a tourist destination. Middle-class residents had been steadily fleeing for the suburbs since World War II, and there had been a corresponding decline in the quality of entertainment and accommodations, not to mention the level of public safety, in the downtown areas. The city's only glory lay in its past.

Here, at the end of the broad Patapsco River that empties into the Chesapeake Bay, a town was established by the Colonial government in 1729; it was named for George Calvert, First Lord Baltimore, the founder of Maryland. The town grew as a port and shipbuilding center and enjoyed booming business during the War of Independence. A quantum leap came at the turn of the 19th century: From 6,700 in 1776, the population reached 45,000 by 1810. During the War of 1812, because it was the home port for a significant portion of U.S. navy vessels and for privateers (many of them the compact and swift Baltimore Clippers) that preyed on British shipping, the city was a natural target for the enemy. After capturing and torching Washington, D.C., the British fleet sailed up the Patapsco River and bombarded Baltimore's Fort McHenry, but in vain. The 30-foot by 42-foot, 15-star, 15-stripe flag was still flying "by the dawn's early light," a spectacle that inspired Francis Scott Key to write the "Star-Spangled Banner."

After the War of 1812, Baltimore prospered as a slave market, and during the Civil War the population's sympathies were divided between North and South, provoking riots. The first bloodshed of the Civil War occurred in Baltimore when the Sixth Massachusetts Regiment was stoned by an angry group of Baltimoreans. (This is a town whose regional identity has always been, and remains, ambiguous.) President Lincoln, mistrusting the loyalty of certain city officials, ordered them summarily detained—an act that was no doubt strategically effective but was probably unconstitutional.

In the postbellum period, Baltimore became a manufacturing center, notably of iron, steel, chemical fertilizer, and textiles. It also became the oyster capital of the world, packing more of those tasty mollusks than any other place in 1880. After a 1904 fire destroyed 1,500 structures, Baltimore rebuilt valiantly and rode the economic roller coaster over two world wars and the Great Depression. The city's manufacturing base became a liability in the 1950s and '60s as U.S. competitiveness in that sector faltered.

Today, Baltimore's Inner Harbor serves as the pulse of not only a vibrant, growing metropolis but of the city's environs as well. The downtown renaissance at Charles Center and the Inner Harbor spurred a growth in tourism, making it a $1-billion-a-year industry by the mid-1980s. Historic neighborhoods such as Bolton Hill, Federal Hill, Fells Point, Otterbein, and Roland Park (developed by Frederick L. Olmsted, designer of New York City's Central Park) are home to businesspeople and families who only a few years ago might have lived in the suburbs. Baltimore has starred in several movies recently, including *Sleepless in Seattle, Her Alibi, The Accidental Tourist,* and *Diner.*

In addition to offering its own attractions, Baltimore is a great city from which to plan day trips. Within 1½ hours by car are historic Annapolis; Washington, D.C.; Pennsylvania Dutch Country; Hershey; Gettysburg; Civil War battlefields; Michener's Chesapeake Country; the Brandywine Valley; and the colony's original settlement at St. Mary's City.

Essential Information

Important Addresses and Numbers

Visitor Information Baltimore Area Convention and Visitors Association (100 Light St., 21202, tel. 410/659–7300).
Baltimore County Promotion and Tourism (400 Washington Ave., Towson, 21204, tel. 410/887–8040).
Baltimore Office of Promotion (200 W. Lombard St., 21201, tel. 410/752–8632).
Harford County Office of Tourism (220 S. Main St., Bel Air 21014, tel. 410/638–3339).
International Visitors Center of Maryland (World Trade Center, Pier Two, Inner Harbor, tel. 410/837–7150).
Visitor Information Center (300 W. Pratt St., 21201, tel. 410/837–4636 or 800/282–6632).

Emergencies For police, ambulance, fire, dial 911.

Hospitals Johns Hopkins Hospital (600 N. Wolfe St., tel. 410/955–2280).
Maryland General Hospital (827 Linden Ave., tel. 410/225–8100).

Arriving and Departing by Plane

Airport and Airlines Baltimore-Washington International Airport (tel. 410/859–7111 for information and paging), located 10 miles south of Baltimore off Route 295 (Baltimore-Washington Pkwy.), has scheduled daily flights by most major airlines, including Air Aruba (tel. 800/882–7822), Air Jamaica (tel. 800/523–5585), Air Ontario (tel. 800/776–3000), American (tel. 800/433–7300), America West (tel. 800/235–9292), British Airways (tel. 800/247–9297), Business Express (tel. 800/345–3400), Cayman Airways (tel. 800/422–9626), Colgan (tel. 800/272–5488), Continental (tel. 800/525–0280), Delta (tel. 800/638–7333), El Al (tel. 800/223–6700), Icelandair (tel. 800/223–5500), Ladeco Chilean Airlines (tel. 800/825–2332), Laker Airways (tel. 800/545–1300), Northwest (tel. 800/225–2525), Southwest (tel. 800/435–9792), TWA (tel. 800/221–2000), United (tel. 800/241–6522), and USAir (tel. 800/428–4322).

Between the Airport and Downtown
By Train Amtrak (tel. 800/872–7245) service between the BWI Airport rail station (tel. 410/672–6167) and Penn Station (Charles St. and Mt. Royal Ave.) is available daily at irregular intervals, so call ahead; the ride takes 10 to 15 minutes. Maryland Area Rail Commuter (MARC, tel. 800/325–7245) trains make the same trip in about 20

minutes, weekdays only, 7 AM–10 PM, at a fare of $2.75. Between Amtrak and MARC there are approximately 25 trains a day between the airport and Baltimore's downtown Penn Station. Continuous free shuttle-bus service links the rail station with the airport terminal less than 10 minutes away.

By Bus **Shuttle Express** (tel. 410/859–0800) provides van service between the airport and downtown hotels, every half hour, 6 AM–11 PM. Travel time is about 30 minutes; the fare, $8. Hotel vans, which are operated independently of the hotels, take 30 minutes on average. Some hotels may provide complimentary limousine service.

By Limousine **Carey Limousines** (tel. 410/837–1234 or 800/336–4646) should be reserved 24 hours in advance.

By Taxi **Airport Taxis** (tel. 410/859–1100) stand by to meet arriving flights. The ride into town on I–295 takes 15–20 minutes; the fare between the airport and downtown is about $17.

Arriving and Departing by Train and Bus

By Train **Amtrak's** (tel. 800/872–7245) trains on the northeast corridor service between Boston and Washington all stop at Baltimore's **Penn Station** (tel. 410/672–6167).

By Bus **Greyhound Lines** (210 W. Fayette St., tel. 800/231–2222) has scheduled daily service to and from major cities in the United States and Canada.

Getting Around Baltimore

The majority of Baltimore's attractions are within walking distance or a short cab ride from Inner Harbor. Beyond that area a car would be useful, for the clean and speedy metro line is somewhat limited and riding public buses can involve a number of transfers. Parking rates downtown are about $12 a day. Inner Harbor sites and other downtown attractions are best reached on foot, by water taxi, or by trolley.

By Bus **Mass Transit Administration** (MTA, tel. 410/539–5000) has more than 70 bus routes. Fare is $1.25, a transfer is 10¢, and there are additional charges for travel into zones beyond the central city area. There is also MTA bus service between Baltimore and Annapolis. Some routes have service 24 hours daily.

By Subway **MTA** (tel. 410/539–5000) operates a single metro line from downtown Charles Center north to suburban Owings Mills. Initial fare is $1.25; for the entire length one way, $1.85. Trains run weekdays 5 AM–midnight, Saturday 8 AM–midnight.

By Light Rail **MTA** (tel. 410/539–5000) began operating the new light rail service between Timonium, north of Baltimore City, and Camden Yards, offering service to the new Orioles baseball stadium and Camden Rail Station. When completed in 1996, the light rail service will connect Glen Burnie, Hunt Valley, downtown Baltimore, BWI Airport, and downtown Washington. Initial fare is $1.25.

By Taxi **Yellow Cab** (tel. 410/685–1212) provides computer-dispatched cars.

Guided Tours

Orientation **Baltimore Trolley Tours** (tel. 410/752–2015) are lively driver-guided tours through Baltimore's major attractions. The route is an endless loop (20 stops, including downtown hotels), so passengers can get on and off as they choose, with unlimited reboarding. The continuous tour operates daily, 10 AM–4 PM, every 30 minutes and costs $12 for adults, $4.50 for children 5–12 (children under 5 ride free). This is a good orientation tour because you can see as much or as little as you choose, in detail or in overview. Maps and brochures are available at major hotels and most tourist offices.

Personal Guides Group and custom tours are provided by **About Town Tours** (tel. 410/592–7770), **Baltimore Rent-A-Tour** (tel. 410/653–2998), **Diversions** (tel. 410/486–3604), and **Guidepool** (tel. 410/528–8687).

Special-interest **Bill Rohrbaugh's Charter Service** (2531 E. Monument St., tel. 410/882–7501) is a charter and receptive service offering customized itineraries—inside and outside of Baltimore—for professional groups, parties, and individuals.

Diversions, Inc. (tel. 410/486–3604) customizes an itinerary to the client's interests, inside or outside of Baltimore.

Walking **Zippy Larson's Shoe Leather Safaris** (tel. 410/764–8067) conducts neighborhood and ethnic expeditions that are popular with local residents as well as visitors because of their witty and well-researched narration. Zippy is a local woman who thoroughly researches her material.

Water Tours There are numerous opportunities to explore the harbor and the nearby Chesapeake Bay by water. Most cruise and tour boats depart from docks located in the Inner Harbor. **Clipper City** (tel. 410/575–7930) offers excursions around the harbor aboard a 158-foot replica of an 1850s topsail schooner. **Harbor Cruises, Ltd.** (tel. 800/THE–LADY or 410/727–3113) presents lunch, dinner, and evening cruises around the harbor aboard *The Bay Lady* or *Lady Baltimore* and feature live entertainment. **Maryland Tours, Inc.** (tel. 410/685–4288) offers a variety of sightseeing tours of the harbor and excursions to Ft. McHenry. **Schooner Nighthawk Cruises** (Thames St., Fells Point, tel. 410/327–7245) offers public cruises aboard a 19th-century two-masted schooner. *The Spirit of Baltimore* (tel. 410/752–SHIP), carrying 410 passengers, is the newest entertainment vessel in Baltimore and features live entertainment on its luncheon, dinner, moonlight, and Sunday brunch cruises.

Exploring

The city of Baltimore fans out northward from the Inner Harbor, with newer attractions such as the National Aquarium and Orioles Park concentrated at the center and more historic neighborhoods and sites out toward the edges. Downtown streets are laid out in a grid, although it is by no means regular. From Pratt Street, which runs east along the Inner Harbor, the major northbound artery is Charles Street. Cross streets' addresses are marked "East" or "West" according to which side of Charles Street they occur; similarly, Baltimore Street marks the dividing line between north and south.

Tour 1: Charles Street

Numbers in the margin correspond to points of interest on the Baltimore map.

Many of the city's attractions lie at the Inner Harbor or along Charles Street or within a few blocks of it. This tour begins at the intersection of Charles and Baltimore streets and heads north, involving an uphill walk. Along this route are a number of historically significant churches (*see* Baltimore for Free, *below*). Two blocks north of Baltimore Street you'll enter a neighborhood of 19th-century brownstones interspersed with modern office buildings and stores. This is also a neighborhood of distinguished art galleries, which exhibit (and hope to sell) the work of a diverse group of artists and craftspeople, including some locals. Gallery admission is usually free, and most venues are open Monday to Saturday 10–5. Galleries generally have a new show every month.

The blocks of North Charles between Saratoga and Chase streets—a stretch of more than ½ mile—are known as Restaurant Row, where the eating places offer a wide selection in price and cuisine.

❶ On Cathedral Street, one block west of Charles Street, is the **Basilica of the Assumption** (completed in 1821), the oldest Catholic cathedral in the United States. Designed by Benjamin Latrobe, the architect of the U.S. Capitol, it stands as a paragon of neoclassicism, with a grand portico fronted by six Corinthian columns suggesting an ancient Greek temple. Two towers are surmounted by cupolas. Inside, the sanctuary fills with light through nine stained-glass windows. Bells ring the Angelus daily at 6 AM, noon, and 6 PM. *Mulberry St. at Cathedral St., tel. 410/727–3564. Open daily. Tours can be scheduled by appointment.*

❷ West of the basilica is the block-long **Enoch Pratt Free Library** (400 Cathedral St., tel. 410/396–5500), the main branch of the city's public library system. The library has rooms devoted to the works and the lives of two prominent writers associated with Baltimore, Edgar Allan Poe and H.L. Mencken. It was here that Mencken's seven typescript volumes of autobiographical writings were locked up in a vault for 35 years until early 1991.

Time Out | **Louie's Bookstore Café** (518 Charles St.) is a good spot to stop for a salad or a sandwich, some evening entertainment, and to browse through a wide selection of magazines and contemporary books. There's constant socializing among the shelves and at the tables. An artsy crowd frequents Louie's, so there's almost always good people-watching.

---

❸ Return to Charles Street, where you'll find the **Walters Art Gallery** (more than 30,000 artworks spanning 5,000 years), which is housed in two wings. The older wing (built in 1904), containing Renaissance and Baroque paintings, has a sculpture court that befits this Italianate palace. The newer structure (1974) has displays of ancient, medieval, Oriental, Islamic, and Byzantine art and many 19th-century paintings. Other features of the Walters include jewelry and decorative works; Egyptology exhibits, which children fall in love with; and a wonderful gift shop filled with moderately priced souvenirs and keepsakes. *N. Charles and Centre Sts., tel. 410/547–9000. Admission: $4 adults, $3 senior citizens; children and full-time students with ID admitted free. Open Tues.–Sun. 11–5. Free entry Sat. 11–noon.*

Continuing north on Charles Street, you can't miss the marble Doric column that looms ahead at the crest of the hill, in the center of the street. (Charles Street is split by a median and renamed Washington Place for two blocks here.) The 178-foot **Washington Monument,** surmounted by a 16-foot white marble statue of the nation's first chief executive, was designed by Robert Mills, who was also responsible for the more famous Washington Monument in the nation's capital. Baltimore's version, erected in 1829, is the oldest formal monument to the Father of His Country. Built on land donated to the city by John Eager Howard, the monument—representing Washington resigning his commission—was built far from the center of the city so that if it fell it would not harm any buildings. For a $1 donation, visitors can climb the 228 steps to the top of the monument to get a bird's-eye view of the city.

Surrounding the monument, **Mount Vernon Square** is flanked by four parks, each a block in length, arranged east and west along the median of Mount Vernon Place and north and south along Washington Place. The sculptures in the parks deserve a close look; of special note is a bronze lion by Barye in the middle of West Mount Vernon Place. Take a moment to admire the brownstones along the north side of East Mount Vernon Place, inviolate in their 19th-century elegance. This neighborhood was a setting for the 1986 movie *The Bedroom Window.*

❺ On the southeast corner of East Mount Vernon Place, the **Peabody Library** has a handsome reading room: Sunshine streams through a skylight to brighten five tiers of cast-iron balconies and a black-and-white marble floor below. A quarter of a million books line the shelves. This scene may be familiar to some visitors, for it was prominent in the movie *Men Don't Leave* (1990). *17 E. Mt. Vernon Pl., tel. 410/659–8179. Admission free. Open weekdays 9–3; call for Sat. schedule.*

Head west on Mount Vernon Place, which turns into Monument Street, to visit the **Maryland Historical Society.** Maryland's heri-
❻ tage of fine living and of the Chesapeake Bay are depicted in displays of period furnishings and the Radcliffe Maritime Collection. Featured are portraits by the Peale family and Joshua Johnson, America's first black portrait artist. Two major attractions are the original manuscript of the "Star-Spangled Banner" and the world's largest collection of 19th-century American silver. *201 W. Monument St., tel. 410/685–3750. Admission: $3.50 adults, $2.50 senior citizens, $1.50 children. Open year-round Tues.–Fri. 10–5, Sat. 9–5; Oct.–Apr. also open Sun. 1–5.*

❼ Continue north on Charles Street 1½ miles to the **Baltimore Museum of Art.** The museum building was designed by John Russell Pope, who was also the architect of the National Gallery in Washington. Displayed here are Rodin's *The Thinker,* as well as works by Matisse, Picasso, Cézanne, Renoir, Degas, Gauguin, and others, with an encyclopedic collection of post-Impressionist paintings that was the bequest of the Cone sisters, who really knew their way around Paris during the early 20th century. Other strengths of the museum collections are in 18th- and 19th-century American painting and decorative arts. From the museum restaurant you can look out at 20th-century sculpture displayed in two landscaped gardens. A modern wing is the site of visiting exhibitions and other temporary shows. *N. Charles and 31st Sts., tel. 410/396–7101. Admission: $5.50 adults, $3.50 senior citizens and full-time students, $1.50 children 4–18; admission free Thurs. Open Wed.–Fri. 10–4, weekends 11–6.*

❽ The Museum of Art is contiguous to the 140-acre Homewood campus, the main campus of **Johns Hopkins University.** All of this land was once the estate of Charles Carroll, Jr., son of Charles Carroll of Carrollton, a signer of the Declaration of Independence (you can visit his residence at Museum Row; *see below*). **Homewood,** the house of

Baltimore

Broadway

Chase St.

Madison Square

Eager St.

Harford Ave.

Biddle St.

Johnston Square

Greenmount Ave.

State Penitentiary

45

Chase St.

Johns Hopkins Hospital

Church Home Hospital

Fairmount Ave.

Central Ave.

Madison St.

Monument St.

Old Town Mall

Mc Elderry St.

Aisquith St.

Fayette St.

Baltimore St.

Main Post Office

26

147

40

Ensor St.

Orleans St.

Front St.

Hillen St.

Gay St.

Fallsway

Gay St.

Police

83

TO AMTRAK PENN STATION

Guilford St.

Calvert St.

Read St.

Saint Paul St.

Eager St.

Charles St.

Cathedral St.

Read St.

Madison St.

Monument St.

Centre St.

Washington Pl.

Mt. Vernon Place

Sun Papers Building

Pleasant St.

Mercy Hospital

Saint Paul Pl.

Saint Paul St.

Davis St.

Holliday St.

30

29

Charles St.

Franklin St.

Park Ave.

Mulberry St.

Saratoga St.

Liberty St.

Greyhound Bus Terminal

Howard St.

Eutaw St.

Fayette St.

7 8 9 10

4

5

3

1

2

6

11

13

12

Maryland General Hospital

Martin Luther King, Jr. Blvd.

Biddle St.

Hoffman St.

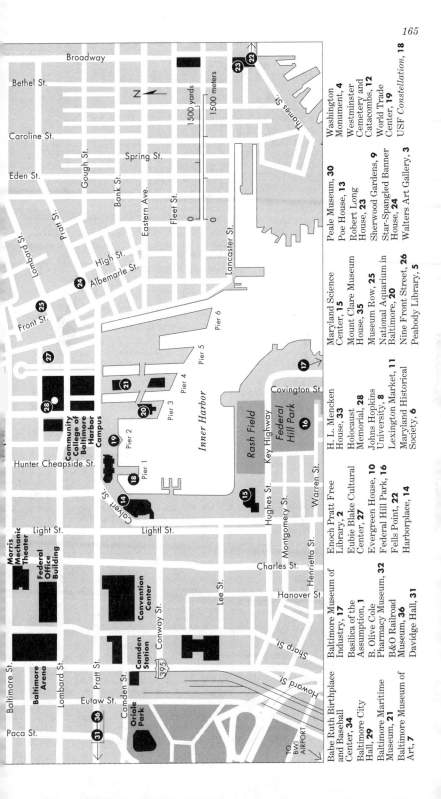

Washington Monument, **4**

Westminster Cemetery and Catacombs, **12**

World Trade Center, **19**

USF Constellation, **18**

Peale Museum, **30**

Poe House, **13**

Robert Long House, **23**

Sherwood Gardens, **9**

Star-Spangled Banner House, **24**

Walters Art Gallery, **3**

Maryland Science Center, **15**

Mount Clare Museum House, **35**

Museum Row, **25**

National Aquarium in Baltimore, **20**

Nine Front Street, **26**

Peabody Library, **5**

H. L. Mencken House, **33**

Holocaust Memorial, **28**

Johns Hopkins University, **8**

Lexington Market, **11**

Maryland Historical Society, **6**

Enoch Pratt Free Library, **2**

Eubie Blake Cultural Center, **27**

Evergreen House, **10**

Federal Hill Park, **16**

Fells Point, **22**

Harborplace, **14**

Baltimore Museum of Industry, **17**

Basilica of the Assumption, **1**

B. Olive Cole Pharmacy Museum, **32**

B&O Railroad Museum, **36**

Davidge Hall, **31**

Babe Ruth Birthplace and Baseball Center, **34**

Baltimore City Hall, **29**

Baltimore Maritime Museum, **21**

Baltimore Museum of Art, **7**

the younger Carroll, has been restored to its appearance of 1800. *Charles and 34th Sts., tel. 410/516–5589. Admission: $5 adults, $4 senior citizens, $2.50 students and children. Open Tues.–Sat. 11–4, Sun. 12–4.*

One block east of Charles Street is St. Paul Street, another major north–south artery leading out of the city. Drive north on Charles Street and St. Paul for less than 1 mile to reach the seven-acre **⑨ Sherwood Gardens,** with hundreds of thousands of tulips planted annually, and azaleas that peak in the second half of April and the first half of May. The gardens are usually at their best around Mother's Day. *Stratford Rd. and Greenway, east of St. Paul St., no tel. Admission free. Open dawn to dusk.*

St. Paul Street curves northwest to meet Charles Street, and two blocks north of that intersection, at Charles Street and Cold Spring **⑩ Lane,** stands the 48-room mansion known as **Evergreen House,** which reopened in 1990 after a three-year restoration. Built in the 1850s, Evergreen House was the home of the 19th-century diplomat and collector John Work Garrett, whose father was president of the Baltimore and Ohio Railroad (the Garrett family continued to live here until the 1950s). Today the yellow-brick building with its Corinthian columns and large collections of books, prints, paintings, and porcelain is the property of Johns Hopkins University; a tour of the mansion allows a fascinating look at the luxury that surrounded a rich American family at the turn of the century. *N. Charles St. and Cold Spring La., tel. 410/516–0895. Admission: $5 adults, $4 senior citizens, $2.50 students and children. Open weekdays 10–3, weekends 1–3.*

Return to downtown via Maryland Avenue and Cathedral Street. **⑪** On Lexington Street one block west of Howard is the **Lexington Market,** founded in 1782, the oldest, largest, and most famous of six city-owned markets. More than 130 vendors operate out of stalls, selling fresh meat, produce, seafood, baked goods, delicatessen items, poultry, and food products from around the world. *Lexington and Eutaw Sts., tel. 410/685–6169. Open Mon.–Sat. 8:30–6.*

Two blocks south and one block west of the Lexington Market is the **⑫ Westminster Cemetery and Catacombs** of the (former) First Presbyterian Church, with the grave sites of Edgar Allan Poe and other famous people. Originally dating from 1786, the cemetery was known as the Old Western Burying Grounds. In the early 1850s a city ordinance demanded that burying grounds be part of a church. So, the building was constructed on arches above the cemetery creating catacombs beneath the church. Poe's monument was donated from pennies collected by Baltimore schoolchildren in the 1930s. *W. Fayette and Greene Sts., tel. 410/706–2072. Open daily dawn to dusk.*

To visit the house where Poe lived from 1832 to 1835, drive west on Fayette Street and follow the blue-green signs for the Poe House. You'll go about seven blocks on Fayette to Schroeder Street, where you turn right, drive another two blocks to Saratoga Street, and turn right again. Amity Street is the first street on your right; turn **⑬** right and drive to the **Poe House** at the far left end. Displayed inside are changing exhibits and a video presentation about Poe's short, tempestuous life; the cold, tiny garret where he wrote his first horror story, "Berenice," has been furnished in early 19th-century period style. Occasional performances take place here. *203 N. Amity*

St., tel. 410/396–7932. Admission: $3 adults, $1 children under 12. Open Apr.–Dec., Wed.–Sat. noon–3:45.

Tour 2: Inner Harbor and Environs

At the southern edge of downtown Baltimore, the basin of the northwest branch of the Patapsco River is an almost landlocked body of water with six piers jutting into it from the north side. This is Baltimore's **Inner Harbor,** one of the city's liveliest neighborhoods, with shops, restaurants, and major cultural attractions. It's also a working port, with rental craft, water taxis, and battery-operated paddle boats (available at the foot of the World Trade Center) for those who want to enjoy a river perspective of the waterside architecture.

⓮ At the northwest corner of Inner Harbor stand the Light Street and Pratt Street pavilions of **Harborplace.** Like Boston's Quincy Market, New York's South Street Seaport, and similar complexes in dozens of other American cities, this was a development of the Rouse Company. Here two glass-enclosed shopping malls house more than 100 specialty shops and gourmet markets. Street entertainers frequently perform at an outdoor amphitheater between the two buildings. The Light Street pavilion has a food court; a skywalk across Pratt Street leads to the Gallery, another 70 shops, and about a dozen restaurants. *Pratt and Light Sts., tel. 410/332–4191. Open Mon.– Sat. 10–9, Sun. 10–6 (Light Street Pavilion has extended summer hours; some restaurants open earlier for breakfast, and most close very late.)*

Time Out Inside the Light Street Pavilion you'll find food ranging from fast and frigid to fried or fruity for you to eat by the water. **Phillips Seafood Restaurant** (tel. 410/685–6600) offers popular, moderately priced dining inside, under cover, or alongside the promenade. The piano bar is a favorite hangout for the sing-along and sailing crowd.

At the corner of the Inner Harbor between the two pavilions is the **Ceremonial Landing** used for the skipjack *Minnie V*, a turn-of-the-century oyster boat that has been restored and is now used for short informational cruises.

⓯ At the southwest corner of Inner Harbor, the **Maryland Science Center**'s most popular attraction is an IMAX movie theater: Across a screen five stories high are thrilling scenes shot from hang gliders and roller coasters. The museum also has a planetarium, and many of the museum's exhibits on the Chesapeake Bay, energy resources, and computer applications are interactive, hands-on displays that fascinate children. *601 Light St., tel. 410/685–5225. Admission: $8.50 adults, $6.50 senior citizens and students 4–17. Open July– Labor Day, Mon.–Thurs. 10–6, Fri.–Sun. 10–8; Sept.–June, weekdays 10–5, weekends 10–6.*

⓰ On the south side of Inner Harbor, **Federal Hill Park** (Battery St. and Key Hwy.) was named in 1788 to commemorate Maryland's ratification of the U.S. Constitution. Later it was the site of Civil War fortifications, built by less-than-welcome Union troops under the command of Major General Benjamin "Spoonie" Butler. Until the early 1900s, a signal tower atop Federal Hill displayed the "house" flags of local shipping companies, notifying them of the arrival of their vessels. The summit provides an excellent view of Rash Field, of Inner Harbor beyond, and of the downtown skyline. The best vantage point for photographing Baltimore, it is also a favorite spot for watching holiday fireworks.

⓱ The **Baltimore Museum of Industry,** housed in an 1865 oyster cannery, is about a half-mile walk south of Inner Harbor along Key Highway and provides more entertainment than its name might suggest. Visitors watch and help operate the functional re-creations of a machine shop circa 1900, a print shop, and a garment workroom. A restored steam-driven tugboat that plied the waterfront for the first half of this century is docked outside. *1415 Key Hwy., tel. 410/ 727–4808. Admission: $3.50 adults, $2.50 senior citizens and children. Open Memorial Day–Labor Day, Tues.–Fri. noon–5, Sat. 10–5, Sun. noon–5; Sept.–May, Wed. 7–9 PM, Thurs.–Fri. noon–5, Sat. 10–5, Sun. noon–5.*

⓲ Walking east from Harborplace along the northern edge of Inner Harbor, you'll find the **USF *Constellation*** docked at Pier One. Visitors may climb aboard this, the first commissioned ship of the United States navy and the oldest U.S. warship continuously afloat. Built at David Stoddard's shipyard in nearby Fells Point, the "Connie" was christened in 1797. It sailed to Tripoli to battle pirates during Thomas Jefferson's administration, served in the War of 1812, and was still in commission at the time of the Civil War. Nearly 80 years later, during World War II, it was the auxiliary flagship of the Atlantic fleet. A massive restoration program was begun on the *Constellation* in spring 1994; as a result, the ship may be dry-docked in another location for several months. *Pratt and Light Sts., tel. 410/ 539–1797. Admission: $3 adults, $2 senior citizens, $1.50 children 6–15. Open mid-June–Labor Day, daily 10–8; Sept.–mid-Oct., mid-May–mid-June, daily 10–6; mid-Oct.–mid-May, daily 10–4.*

⓳ The attraction at Pier Two is the **World Trade Center**: With 32 stories, this is the world's tallest pentagonal building. The 27th-floor observation deck (Top of the World) allows an unobstructed view of Baltimore and environs—a good place for orienting oneself to the city. Indoor exhibits focus on local economic growth and on Baltimore's sister cities in other nations. *Pier Two, tel. 410/837–4515. Admission: $2 adults, $1 senior citizens and children. Open Labor Day–Memorial Day, Mon.–Sat. 10–4:30, Sun. noon–4:30; Memorial Day–Labor Day, weekdays 10–4:30, Sat. 10–6:30, Sun. 11–5:30.*

⓴ At Piers Three and Four is the **National Aquarium in Baltimore,** home to 5,000 fish, marine mammals, birds, reptiles, amphibians, invertebrates, and plants that dwell in, or around, its 2 million gallons of water. In the main building, spectators watch from seven levels joined by escalators. Such docile sea creatures as horseshoe crabs and starfish may be handled by children with the supervision of volunteer guides. A rooftop glass pyramid 64 feet high encloses a rain forest: a climate controlled re-creation of an entire neotropical ecosystem that harbors two-toed sloths in the calabash trees, parrots in the palms, iguanas on the ground, and red-bellied piranhas in a pool. The stars of the Aquarium's new addition, the Marine Mammal Pavilion, are seven Atlantic bottlenose dolphins that live in a 1.2-million-gallon pool surrounded by a 1,300-seat amphitheater. Educational presentations highlighting the natural agility and intelligence of these mammals take place several times a day. The aquarium's famed large-tank exhibit, which gives visitors a multilevel view of ocean life (complete with sharks), is closed for repairs until spring 1995. A laser-light exhibit has been substituted for the interim. *Pier Three, tel. 410/576–3810. Admission: $11.50 adults; $9.50 students, senior citizens, active-duty military; $7.50 children 3–11. Open*

Nov.–Feb., Sat.–Thurs. 10–5, Fri. 10–8; Mar.–June and Sept.–Oct., Sat.–Thurs. 9–5, Fri. 9–8; July and Aug., Sun.–Thurs. 9–6, Fri.–Sat. 9–8.

㉑ The three vessels docked at Pier Four compose the **Baltimore Maritime Museum.** On the west side, the submarine **USS** *Torsk,* the "Galloping Ghost of the Japanese Coast," is credited with sinking the last two Japanese warships in World War II. The lightship *Chesapeake,* built as a floating Chesapeake Bay lighthouse in 1930 and now out of commission, remains fully operational. The *Taney* is a Coast Guard cutter that saw action at Pearl Harbor. *Pier Four, tel. 410/396–3453. Admission: $5 adults, $4 senior citizens, $2.50 children. Open summer, daily 10–5; winter, Fri.–Sun. 10–5.*

㉒ For more maritime atmosphere, take the water taxi to **Fells Point,** the center of Baltimore's thriving shipbuilding industry in the late 18th and early 19th centuries. (The USF *Constellation* was one of many distinguished craft built here.) The neighborhood today is one of cobblestone streets and more than 350 historic houses, many of them brick structures dating to the early 1700s that now serve as shops, galleries, and restaurants. Seafood dining rooms and lively
㉓ taverns make this a popular social area at night. The **Robert Long House,** built by a merchant in 1765, is the city's oldest dwelling. *S. Ann and Thames Sts., tel. 410/675–6750. Admission: $1. Open for tours daily 10 AM, 1 PM, and 3 PM and by appointment.*

Time Out While in Fells Point, wander into any one of the many pubs that line the cobblestone streets for a cold beer or soda. **Piccolo's** and **Lista's,** two new restaurants at the foot of Broadway, offer pleasant waterfront dining, inside or outside. The water-taxi stop is just a few steps away from either of them.

From Pier Six at the northeast corner of Inner Harbor, head east on
㉔ Pratt Street to Albemarle Street. The **Star-Spangled Banner House,** built in 1793, is where Mary Pickersgill hand-sewed the 15-star, 15-stripe flag that survived the British bombardment of Ft. McHenry in 1814 and inspired Francis Scott Key. The house contains Federal furniture and American art of the period. Outdoors, a map of the United States has been made of stones from the various states. A museum connected to the house tells the history of the War of 1812. *844 E. Pratt St., tel. 410/837–1793. Admission: $2 adults, $1.50 senior citizens, $1 children 13–18, 50¢ children under 13. Open Mon.–Sat. 10–4.*

㉕ Two blocks to the north, **Museum Row** comprises four institutions around a courtyard on Lombard Street between Front and Albemarle streets, all with the same admission policy and hours. The **Center for Urban Archaeology** (Lombard and Albemarle Sts., tel. 410/396–3156) displays 18th- and 19th-century ceramics and glassware discovered around Baltimore. Visitors can observe archaeologists examining the artifacts. The **Courtyard Exhibition Center** (800 E. Lombard St., tel. 410/396–9910) offers a multimedia presentation of the city's economic and social advancements since the Great Depression. The **1840 House** (50 Albemarle St., tel. 410/396–3279) is the reconstructed 19th-century row house of a wheelwright and his family, portrayed today by costumed interpreters who perform short thematic plays (about race relations, for example) set in the year 1840. An aristocratic complement to the 1840 House, **Carroll Mansion** (800 E. Lombard St., tel. 410/396–3524) was the home of Charles Carroll of Carrollton, who was the last surviving signer of the Declaration of Independence. The elegant town house is fully restored and furnished in the Empire style, as it was at the time of Carroll's death in 1832. *Single admission: $1.75 adults, $1.25 senior citizens and students, 75¢ children. Admission to all sites: $4 adults, $3 senior citizens and students, $2 children, $12 family; admission free on Sat. Open Apr.–Sept., Tues.–Sat. 10–5, Sun. noon–5; Oct.–Mar., Tues.–Sat. 10–4, Sun. noon–4.*

㉖ Two blocks north, at Baltimore Street, **Nine Front Street** is a cute two-story brick town house built in 1790 that was once the home of Mayor Thorowgood Smith. The Women's Civic League restored it and maintains it as a visitor information center. *9 Front St., tel. 410/ 837–5424. Open Tues.–Fri. 9:30–2:30.*

Since you're nearby, take note that the structure standing next door is a Baltimore curiosity—the **Shot Tower,** one of the few remaining buildings of its kind. The landmark, built in 1829 from one million bricks, stands 234 feet high, tapering toward the top and capped with pseudomedieval battlements. The tower was used in the manufacture of shot: Molten lead dropped from the top through sieves formed natural spheres by the time it landed in water at the bottom. An audiovisual presentation demonstrates the process by which high-quality ammunition was produced prior to the Civil War era when bullets replaced shot. On one nearly forgotten day in late March many years ago, an ad appeared in a Baltimore newspaper announcing that a Baltimorean would "fly" from the top of the Shot Tower . . . a hoax perpetuated by Baltimore's Edgar Allan Poe. *E. Fayette and Front Sts.*

㉗ The **Eubie Blake Cultural Center** is a tribute to the native Baltimorean and renowned composer of jazz and show tunes, best known for "I'm Just Wild About Harry." Musicians, dancers, and actors study and perform here. Exhibits depict Blake's life and career, and a gallery showcases the work of local artists. *34 Market Pl., tel. 410/396–8128. Admission free. Open weekdays noon–5.*

Across Gay Street, between Water and Lombard streets, the **㉘** **Holocaust Memorial** honors Jewish victims of the Nazi regime. Two granite-and-concrete monoliths stand beside six rows of pear trees, each row representing 1 million deaths. A startling sculpture depicts skeletal figures climbing toward a flame of hope. The sculptor is Baltimore native Joseph Sheppard, a Maryland Institute of Art graduate who now lives in Baltimore and Florence, Italy.

㉙ Walk two blocks north and one block west to reach **Baltimore City Hall** on Holliday Street, above Fayette Street. Built in 1875, it boasts mansard roofs and a gilt dome over a 110-foot rotunda, the whole supported by ironwork. In addition to its architecture, City Hall offers visitors exhibits on Baltimore's history and tours of the chambers. *100 N. Holliday St., tel. 410/396–4900. Open weekdays 8–4:30.*

Directly across the street from City Hall is **City Hall Plaza.** Originally, it was the site of the Holliday Street Theatre, which was owned and operated by the Ford Brothers, who also operated Ford's Theatre in Washington, D.C., where President Lincoln was assassinated. The "Star-Spangled Banner" was first publicly sung here.

㉚ In the next block north on Holliday Street, the **Peale Museum,** the oldest museum in the United States, built in 1814 by Rembrandt Peale to honor his father, Charles Willson Peale, has also served as City Hall. Today its attractions are temporary shows from the museum collection and a permanent exhibition on Baltimore cultural and architectural history. The museum's prize possessions, 29 paintings by members of the Peale family, are shown on the third floor. *225 Holliday St., tel. 410/396–1149. Admission: $1.75 adults, $1.25 senior citizens, 75¢ children; admission free on Sat. Open Tues.–Sat. 10–4, Sun. noon–4 (until 5 in summer).*

West Baltimore

Proceed west into the University of Maryland Hospital complex, where there are two buildings of interest. Green-domed **Davidge Hall,** built in 1812 for the sum total of $35,000, is the oldest building in the Western Hemisphere in continuous use for teaching medicine. It's located on the outskirts of town, amidst rolling fields, and it's said that from the porch, one could watch the British bombardment of Ft. McHenry. Visitors interested in the practice of medicine should add this to their list of "must sees." *522 W. Lombard St., tel. 410/706–7454. Admission free. Open weekdays 8:30–4:45.*

The **B. Olive Cole Pharmacy Museum,** a block away, contains a replica of an early 19th-century pharmacy and paintings that recount the history of pharmacies. *650 W. Lombard St., tel. 410/727–0746. Admission free. Open weekdays by appointment.*

About a mile west of the Inner Harbor on Lombard Street, turn right (north) onto Stricker Street, go one block and turn left (west) onto Hollins Street, and go to the middle of the block to the **H.L. Mencken House.** Known as the Sage of Baltimore, H. L. Mencken ruled American letters from the 1920s to the 1940s as author, editor, and columnist; at the height of his career he stood at the pinnacle of American culture. One of Baltimore's leading cultural institutions, the Mencken house on Union Square in west Baltimore is a modest row house still full of Victorian flavor. The house is furnished with Mencken family possessions (no reproductions), including one of four remaining life masks of Beethoven. Also of particular interest is Mencken's beloved garden—an English row-house garden restored to the pundit's own taste. *1524 Hollins St., tel. 410/396–7997. Admission: $1.75 adults, $1.25 children under 18; admission free on Sat. Open Tues.–Sat. 10–4, Sun. noon–4 (until 5 in summer).*

Just south of Pratt Street, on Emory Street, is the **Babe Ruth Birthplace and Baseball Center,** where the baseball legend was born in 1895. The row house has been furnished in a turn-of-the-century style, and the adjoining buildings are a museum devoted to Ruth's life and to the local Orioles baseball club. Film clips, rare photos of "The Bambino," and many other artifacts can be found here. The museum is located within three blocks of Oriole Park at Camden Yards. *216 Emory St., tel. 410/727–1539. Admission: $4.50 adults, $3 senior citizens, $2 children 5–16. Open Apr.–Oct., daily 10–5; Nov.–Mar., daily 10–4; until 7 on the days of Orioles home games.*

From Babe Ruth's house proceed west on Pratt Street to Martin Luther King Jr. Boulevard, turn left and go two blocks, then turn right onto Washington Boulevard. Go to the eighth traffic light and turn into Carroll Park on the right. At the top of the hill is a mansion owned by Charles Carroll–The Barrister, formerly one of the major landowners in the state, author of the Maryland Declaration of Independence, and member of the Continental Congress. **Mount Clare Museum House,** begun in 1754, has been carefully restored to its Georgian elegance; there are many original 18th-century furnishings, including rare pieces of Chippendale and Hepplewhite silver, crystal, and Chinese export porcelain. This is Baltimore's only remaining pre-Revolutionary mansion: Washington, LaFayette, and John Adams were numbered among the guests who visited here.

The greenhouses here provided rare trees and plants for Washington's Mount Vernon. *21230 Carroll Park, tel. 410/837-3262. Admission: $4 adults, $2 senior citizens and students, 50¢ children under 12. Open Tues.-Fri. 10-3, Sat.-Sun. noon-3.*

❸❻ Drive east along Pratt Street to the **B&O Railroad Museum,** the "birthplace of railroading in America." The 1884 roundhouse (240 feet in diameter and 120 feet high) adjoins the world's first railroad station, where one of the great collections of railroading engines and memorabilia can be found. From this station, the legendary race between the *Tom Thumb* (a working replica is inside) and the "gray" horse took place: Reportedly, the horse won when the *Tom Thumb* lost a fan belt. Samuel Morse's first transmission of Morse code, WHAT HATH GOD WROUGHT?, in 1844, passed through wires here, en route from Washington to the B&O Pratt Street Station. *Pratt and Poppleton Sts., tel. 410/752-2490. Admission: $5 adults, $4 senior citizens, $3 children. Open daily 10-5.*

Excursion to Havre de Grace

Less than 40 miles northeast of Baltimore, at the mouth of the Susquehanna River on the upper Chesapeake Bay, is the attractive town of Havre de Grace. An easy day trip from the city, the town has several small regional museums, a few historical houses, and opportunities for outdoor recreation. Along the way, there are some worthwhile sites to visit.

A little more than 30 miles northeast of Baltimore's Inner Harbor, at Exit 85 from I-95, the 75,000-acre **Aberdeen Proving Ground,** a U.S. army installation on Chesapeake Bay, has been a site for artillery testing since 1917. Tank parades and firing demonstrations take place every year on Armed Forces Day (the third Saturday in May).

The **U.S. Army Ordnance Museum** maintains the largest collection of armored fighting vehicles in the country—225 at last count. Some are one-of-a-kind inventions: "The Elephant" is a self-propelled gun built by the Germans during World War II; "The Christie" was designed in the United States in 1934 to run at a speed of 60 mph when its competition could go no faster than 8 mph. The 3-ton Ford tank of 1919, from the first line of American tanks, is the only one extant with the original Model T twin engines. General John Pershing's World War I staff car is here, and so is a 1916 Dodge used by Lieutenant George Patton in the first mechanized raid across the Mexican border. A huge 16-inch American gun from World War I is on display, as well as the first surface-to-air missile, devised by the Germans in 1945. The collection of small arms features a 15th-century matchlock, a musket whose powder ignites from a slow-burning wick. *Tel. 410/278-3602. Admission free. Open Tues.-Fri. noon-4:45, weekends 10-4:45.*

Five miles north of the proving ground, on the site of one of Maryland's oldest settlements, is the neatly laid-out town **Havre de Grace,** reputedly named by the Marquis de Lafayette. Because this "harbor of mercy" on the bay at the mouth of the Susquehanna River was shelled and torched by the British in the War of 1812, almost none of its structures dates from before the 19th century. One of the few 18th-century structures—and the town's most historically significant building—is the **Rodgers House** (226 N. Washington St.), a two-story redbrick Georgian town house topped by a dormered attic. This was the home of Admiral John Rodgers, who fired the first shot in the War of 1812; like most of the historic houses of Havre de Grace, it is closed to the public at present, but it's worth a drive past.

Housed in a converted power plant, the **Decoy Museum** has 1,500 facsimiles of duck, goose, and swan made from wood, iron, cork, papier-mâché, or plastic. Three classes of decoy—decorative, decorative floater, and working decoys—are represented, the working decoy most of all. Exhibits change periodically; a recent one featured the mannequin of a hunter in a rubber "body boot" squatting in a pool, surrounded by replica of various waterfowl species. A permanent exhibit of six human figures portrays 20th-century carvers, including the prolific R. Madison Mitchell, and a recorded narration covers the lore of the craft. In the basement—a modern workshop with electric lathes and other state-of-the-art tools—visitors can watch all stages of decoy production. A festival during the first full weekend in May features carving contests and demonstrations by retrievers. *Giles and Market Sts., tel. 410/939–3739. Admission: $2 adults, $1 senior citizens and children. Open daily 11–4, closed major holidays.*

At the southernmost lock of the defunct Susquehanna and Tidewater Canal is the **Susquehanna Museum.** From 1839 until 1890 the canal ran 45 miles north to Wrightsville, Pennsylvania, a thoroughfare for mule-drawn barges loaded with iron ore, coal, and crops. The museum, in the lock tender's cottage built in 1840, is partially furnished with modest midcentury antiques that recall its period of service. The rest of the house is devoted to town history, with old photographs of the buildings and residents, and artifacts of the local fishing industry. Outdoors, a pivot bridge across the lock has been restored and the original wooden gates have been dragged up onto land. There are demonstrations of a reconstructed lock, with vessels passing up this small segment of the canal. *Erie and Conesto Sts., tel. 410/939–5780. Admission free. Open Apr.–Dec., Sun. 1–5; candlelight tour 2nd Sun. in Dec.*

Unlike the screw-pile lighthouses at Solomons and St. Michaels (*see* Chapters 9 and 10), the **Concord Point Lighthouse** has the classic conical design. Also unlike the other two, it is too small for anyone to live in (the nearby keeper's quarters have been restored and are now open. Built in 1827, and restored in 1980, it is the oldest continuously operated Chesapeake Bay lighthouse remaining on its original site. Visitors climb 30 feet for views of the bay, the river, and the town. *Lafayette St. at the Susquehanna River, tel. 410/939–1498. Admission free. Open May–Oct., Sun. 1–5.*

Susquehanna State Park, 6 miles upriver, sits on 2,500 acres where visitors can fish, bird-watch, hike, bike, and camp. A covered stone pavilion by the river is ideal for picnics. *Rte. 155, tel. 410/939–0643. Admission: $4 per car with Maryland tags, $5 per car for out-of-state cars. Open daily 10–sunset.*

Within the park, the **Steppingstone Museum** is a 10-acre complex of seven restored turn-of-the-century farm buildings plus a replica of a canning house. Among the 12,000-plus artifacts in the collection are a horse-drawn tractor and an early gas-powered version, manual seeders and planters, and horse-drawn plows. A blacksmith, a weaver, a wood-carver, a cooper, a dairymaid, and a decoy artisan regularly demonstrate their respective crafts in the workshops. *461 Quaker Bottom Rd., tel. 410/939–2299. Admission: $2 adults. Open May–Oct., weekends 1–5.*

Ladew Topiary Gardens, 15 flower gardens planned and designed by the late Harvey Smith Ladew, include a formal rose garden, cottage garden, water garden, berry garden, and America's finest sculpted topiary trees and shrubs, which together cover 22 acres. In summer, there are special events such as concerts and polo matches. The house is filled with English antiques, paintings, photographs, and fox-hunting memorabilia and boasts the Oval Library, considered one of the most beautiful rooms in America. *3535 Jarrettsville Pike, Monkton, tel. 410/557–9570. Open mid-Apr.–late Oct., Tues.–Fri. 10–4, weekends noon–5. Admission to house and gardens: $6 adults, $4 senior citizens and students, $1 children.*

Baltimore for Free

B. Olive Cole Pharmacy Museum, *see* Other Places of Interest
Davidge Hall, *see* Other Places of Interest
Eubie Blake Cultural Center, *see* Tour 2
Nine Front Street, *see* Tour 2
Shot Tower, *see* Tour 2
Sherwood Gardens, *see* Tour 1

Houses of Worship Maryland was the first state to guarantee religious freedom, hence Baltimore has a number of significant and historic houses of worship. The **Basilica of the Assumption** (Cathedral and Mulberry Sts.), designed by famed architect Benjamin Latrobe and completed in 1821, was the first Catholic cathedral built in this country (*see* Tour 1, *above*). Nearby, **The First Unitarian Church** (Franklin and Charles Sts.), designed by Maximilian Godefroy in 1819, is famous because its founder, Dr. Channing, gave the definitive sermon for the church here. At the base of the Washington Monument is **Mount Vernon Methodist Church** (Mt. Vernon and Washington Place), built in the mid-1850s on the site of Francis Scott Key's home and place of death. **Lovely Lane Methodist Church** (2200 St. Paul St.), built in 1882, is honored with the title "The Mother Church of American Methodism." Stanford White designed the interior with wood—almost entirely black birch—and the stained-glass windows are excellent examples of Italian mosaics. Tours of the church and the Methodist Historical Society (Lovely Lane Church, tel. 410/889–1512 or 800/368–2520) are available. The buildings to the north that resemble the church are the original campus of Goucher College. Dr. Goucher, the college's founder, was a pastor at Lovely Lane Church. Baltimore's original house of worship, **St. Paul's Episcopal Church** (Charles St. at Saratoga St.), begun in 1854, is the fourth building on this site and was dedicated for St. Paul's Parish in 1732. The **Lloyd Street Synagogue** (Lloyd St., a block above Lombard St., tel. 410/732–6400), built in 1845, was the first synagogue in Maryland and the third in the United States. It has been restored and now serves as a museum and is open for touring Tuesday through Thursday and Sunday, noon–4. **Old Otterbein United Methodist Church** (124 W. Conway St., near Sharp St.), in the shadow of the Baltimore Convention Center, is the oldest ecclesiastical building in Baltimore (1785). It is open after Sunday services. **Zion Lutheran Church** (Holliday and Lexington Sts.) is the site of the first Lutheran congregation in Baltimore (1755) and offers some services in German. The **Mother Seton House** (600 N. Paca St., tel. 410/523–3443) was the Baltimore home of Elizabeth Ann Seton, first American-born saint. The home is open Sunday 1–4 and by appointment.

What to See and Do with Children

Baltimore's Child (tel. 410/367–5883), a free monthly newspaper published during the school year and available at public libraries, is a good source of information on special and ongoing events in the city.

The Baltimore Children's Museum at the Cloisters, an outstanding children's museum housed in a fanciful mock-Tudor–Gothic Revival "castle" about 7 miles north of downtown, has many interactive exhibits. Events, crafts projects, and seasonal activities are offered for kids and parents. Outdoors, deer and wild turkey share 50 leafy acres with rabbits and squirrels. Concerts take place in spring and summer in an open-air theater, and year-round indoors. There are no food facilities on the premises. *10440 Falls Rd., tel. 410/823–2550. Admission: $4 adults and children, $3 senior citizens. Open Wed.–Sat. 10–4, Sun. noon–4.*

The **Baltimore Streetcar Museum** lets visitors travel back to an era when streetcars rather than gas-powered cars dominated city roads. A free film traces the vehicles' evolution. *1901 Falls Rd., tel. 410/547–0264. Admission free. Streetcar rides: $2 adults, $1 senior citizens and children 4–11. Open weekends noon–5.*

The 150 acres of the **Baltimore Zoo**—the third-oldest zoo in the country—make a natural stomping ground for little ones who enjoy the spectacle of elephants, lions, giraffes, hippos, and penguins—among more than 1,200 animals that make this their home. At the petting zoo, children can befriend small farm animals. A ride on the "zoo-choo" or the merry-go-round provides further diversion. *Druid Hill Park, Druid Hill Lake Dr., tel. 410/366–5466. Admission: $6.50 adults, $3.50 senior citizens and children. Open daily 10–4 (till 5:30 in summer).*

At the end of the peninsula that bounds the northwest branch of the Patapsco is **Ft. McHenry,** a star-shaped brick and earthen structure built in 1803 that has also been used as a prison and a hospital. It is most famous for its role in the War of 1812, which is immortalized in the national anthem. In September 1814 a Maryland lawyer named Francis Scott Key was detained aboard a ship of truce after having obtained the release of a friend, Dr. William Beanes. The British bombardment of Ft. McHenry was about to begin, and Key knew too much about the attack plan to be released. During the 25-hour battle that ensued, Key often witnessed his country's flag drift in and out of view through the smoke and haze. "By the dawn's early light" of September 14, 1814, he saw the 30-foot by 42-foot "Star-Spangled Banner" still waving and was inspired to pen the words to a poem. The poem was set, ironically, to the tune of an old English drinking song, "To Anacreon in Heaven." The flag that Key saw had 15 stars, 15 stripes, and was hand-sewn for the fort by Mary Pickersgill, a Baltimore resident whose house in the city is also open to visitors (*see* Tour 2, *above*). A visit to the fort includes a 16-minute history film. *From Light St. take Key Hwy. for 1½ mi and follow signs. Fort Ave., tel. 410/962–4299. Admission: $2. Open Sept.–May, daily 8–4:45; June–Labor Day, daily 8–8.*

Maryland Science Center (*see* Exploring Baltimore, *above*)

National Aquarium in Baltimore (*see* Exploring Baltimore, *above*)

Off the Beaten Track

On the east side of the Inner Harbor, the **Baltimore Public Works Museum** is the oldest museum of its kind in the country. Here an unusual collection of artifacts is displayed in an unusual location: the 80-year-old Eastern Avenue Sewage Pumping Station. On show are several generations of water pipe, including wood piping nearly 200 years old; other exhibits tell the history of such city services as trash removal. Outdoors, a life-size model shows what lies underneath

Baltimore streets. *E. Falls and Eastern Aves., tel. 410/396–5565.*
Admission: $2.50 adults, $2 senior citizens, $1.50 children. Open
mid-Oct.–mid-Apr., Wed.–Sun. 10–4; mid-Apr.–mid-Oct., Wed.–
Sun. 10–5.

Shopping

Shopping Districts

The Pratt Street and Light Street pavilions of **Harborplace** (tel. 410/
332–4191), together with **The Gallery,** just across Pratt Street, contain almost 200 specialty shops that sell everything from business
attire to children's toys; markets for gourmet food, wine, and flowers; and 60 eating places ranging from fast-food stalls to expensive
restaurants.

Antique Row (700 and 800 blocks, N. Howard St.; Boutique Row: 200
block, W. Read St.) comprises more than three dozen first-rate
shops for furniture, art, books, used clothing, nostalgia, and
junque.

Art galleries are concentrated in a neighborhood of 19th-century
brownstones and modern office buildings that begins two blocks
north of Baltimore Street.

Owings Mills Town Center (tel. 410/363–1234), at the Owings Mills
exit from I–795, includes Macy's, Saks, and Hecht's; smaller specialty clothing stores; and shoe, toy, and book stores. Both fast-food and
formal restaurants are among the mall's numerous eating places.
The mall is near the northern end of the metro.

Towson Town Center (Dulaney Valley Rd. and Fairmount Ave., in
Towson, ½ mile south of I–695 at Exit 27A, tel. 410/494–8800) celebrated a grand reopening in 1991 and now features nearly 200 specialty shops. The attractive and imaginatively decorated indoor
center is anchored by Hecht's and Nordstrom department stores.
One of the mid-Atlantic region's largest malls, it has nearly a million
square feet of shopping space.

The Village of Cross Keys (5100 Falls Rd., tel. 410/323–1000), located
about 6 miles from downtown off I–83, hosts an eclectic collection of
26 boutiques and stores ranging from women's, men's, and
children's clothing shops to a print gallery, flower store, and restaurants. The open-air court offers an alternative to fluorescent-
lighted, enclosed shopping malls and is often visited by families on
weekends and—during the week—by businesspeople staying at the
Cross Keys Inn (tel. 410/532–6900). There are occasional outdoor
spring and summer concerts and promotional events held in the
courtyard.

Department Stores

Hecht's: Golden Ring Mall (tel. 410/574–1600), Marley Station (tel.
410/766–2055), Owings Mills Town Center (tel. 410/363–7700), Towson Town Center (tel. 410/337–3600), White Marsh Mall (tel. 410/
931–2000).

Macy's: Marley Station (tel. 410/760–2100), Owings Mills Town Center (tel. 410/363–7400), White Marsh Mall (tel. 410/931–7000).

Saks Fifth Avenue: Owings Mills Town Center (tel. 410/363–7200).

Food Markets

All year long the following indoor food markets, which are all at least 100 years old, accommodate vendors of fresh fish, fowl, meat, and produce: **Belair Market** (Gay and Fayette Sts.), **Broadway Market** (Broadway and Fleet Sts.), **Cross Street Market** (Light and Cross Sts.), **Hollins Market** (Hollins and Arlington Sts.), **Lexington Market** (Lexington and Eutaw Sts.), **Northeast Market** (Monument and Chester Sts.). Lexington Market is the largest and most famous, but all feature fresh, taste-tempting foods for on-premise consumption.

Specialty Stores

Antiques **Gaines McHale Antiques Ltd.** (836 Leadenhall St., tel. 410/625–1900) brings new meaning to the word "recycling." Owners Jean and Mike McHale build new pieces with old wood. Among their specialties is turning antique armoires into entertainment centers, wet bars, computer desks, and other furniture that fits the needs of the '90s.

Books **Kelmscott Bookshop** (32–34 W. 25th St., tel. 410/235–6810) is known internationally for its enormous, well-preserved stock of old and rare volumes in every major category, especially art, architecture, American and English literature, and travel. The books are clearly organized in 12 rooms on two floors of two converted town houses. This cozy place to browse is made more relaxing by recorded classical music. The shop also provides a diligent search service for out-of-print titles.

Gifts **Crafts Concepts** (Greenspring Station, Falls and Joppa Rds., tel. 410/823–2533) is a good stop-off if you're shopping for a reasonably priced but unique birthday, wedding, or house-warming gift. Of particular note are the handmade ceramic vases and plates; and the unique, hand-woven and hand-painted women's clothing and handmade jewelry.

The Store Ltd. (Village of Cross Keys, tel. 410/323–2350) is actually a retail museum of top-quality (and pricey) collections including handcrafted jewelry designs by local artist Betty Cook, reproduction calendars, stationery, and women's sportswear. Other items you can find here are state-of-the-art kitchen gadgets, coffee-table books, hats, whimsical lawn items, and lifelike stuffed animals.

Jewelry **Marley Gallery of Contemporary Jewelry, Inc.** (Festival at Woodholme Gallery, 1809 Reisterstown Rd., Pikesville, tel. 410/486–6686) offers a unique selection of fine designer jewelry from leading contemporary artists and original designs by Marley Simon. All work is done in-house. Fine timepieces by Ebel and Phillippe Cahrriol are featured, as is a complete selection of fashion jewelry.

Men's **A. J. Borenstein's Eclectic** (The Gallery, tel. 410/539–2411) supplies
Clothing the confident and colorful dresser with accessories: Italian silk and leather, Japanese neckties, bold British shirting, snappy suspenders, fine hosiery, and links both antique and new.

Women's **Bare Necessities** (Greenspring Station, Falls and Joppa Rds., tel.
Clothing 410/583–1383) has in the past received the "Baltimore's Best" award for its tasteful selection of women's lingerie and accessories. Shopping in this Victorian-accented shop is an experience not unlike a pampered spa vacation.

Ruth Shaw (tel. 410/532–7886), **Octavia** (tel. 410/323–1652), and **Jones and Jones** (tel. 410/532–9645), all located in the Village of

Cross Keys, carry women's clothing on par—in both style and price—with New York's Fifth Avenue boutiques. Among the three you'll find such genres as cruise wear, formal evening attire, and casual dress sold by stylish sales people.

The White House, Inc. began in 1985 at Harborplace and now has about 25 stores. The boutique carries white—and only white—clothing, lingerie, and accessories for women. In addition, the stores feature pearl and crystal jewelry and other gift items. Maryland stores currently include the original boutique at Harborplace's Pratt Street Pavilion (tel. 410/659–0283) and Owings Mills Town Center (tel. 410/363–0036).

Sports and Outdoor Activities

Participant Sports

Bicycling   *Best Bike Routes in Maryland* is a series of 10 well-documented maps of on-road and off-road touring routes throughout Maryland. The color-coded, waterproof, and tearproof maps are available at area bookstores, bicycle shops, and by mail order (Box 16388, Baltimore, MD 21210, tel. 410/685–3626) for $9.95 each or $29.95 for the set.

Baltimore and Annapolis Trail Park (Rte. 50 in Arnold to Dorsey Rd., tel. 410/222–6244) includes 13.3 miles of paved trails, open space, bridges, and woodlands.

Northern Central Railroad Hike and Bike Trail is a 21-mile trail that extends along the old railroad to the Maryland–Pennsylvania line, beginning at Ashland Road, just east of York Road, and heading north 20 miles to the Pennsylvania border. Parking is available at seven points along the way. It was on this line that President Lincoln rode to deliver the Gettysburg Address and on which—after his assassination—his body was carried to Gettysburg and on to Illinois, his home state. For more information and a map, write or call Gunpowder Falls State Park (Box 5032, Glen Arm, MD 21057, tel. 410/592–2897).

Canoeing   **Springriver Corp.** (6434 Baltimore National Pike, tel. 410/788–3377) offers daily canoe and kayak rentals for use on bay tributaries and lakes in the region.

Fishing   Annual licenses ($7–$12) are available at many sporting-goods stores or from the **Maryland Department of Natural Resources** (580 Taylor Ave., Annapolis 21404, tel. 410/974–3211).

The Fishin' Shop (7672 Belair Rd., tel. 410/882–4334) and **Tochterman's** (1925 Eastern Ave., tel. 410/327–6942) are bait-and-tackle shops that can also provide personal guides. **Clyde's Sport Shop** (2307 Hammonds Ferry Rd., tel. 410/242–6108), another bait-and-tackle shop, can provide a guide only for bass fishing.

Golf   **Carroll Park** (Monroe St. and Washington Blvd., tel. 410/685–8344) has nine holes. The following courses all have 18 holes: **Clifton Park** (Harford Rd. and St. Lo Dr., tel. 410/243–3500); **Forest Park** (2900 Hillsdale Rd., tel. 410/448–4653); **Mount Pleasant** (6101 Hillen Rd., tel. 410/821–5835); **Pine Ridge** (Dulaney Valley Rd., tel. 410/252–1408).

Health and Fitness Clubs The **Harbor Court Hotel** has by far the best athletic facilities. The two clubs below offer temporary membership to transients. Your hotel may provide this as a courtesy, so ask the concierge.

Baltimore Racquet and Fitness Club (218 N. Charles St., tel. 410/625–6400) offers its facilities, which include an indoor pool, squash courts, and Nautilus equipment, to nonmembers for a daily fee of $10.

At the **Downtown Athletic Club** (210 E. Centre St., tel. 410/332–0906), guests of area hotels pay a $15 daily fee to play squash and racquetball and to use the indoor pool and exercise equipment.

Jogging One conveniently located, scenic area is **Rash Field,** on the south side of Inner Harbor, adjacent to the Science Center and Federal Hill Park. Many conventioneers jog around the promenade at Baltimore's Inner Harbor, or on the path at the water's edge at Ft. McHenry.

Rafting **Springriver Corp.** (6434 Baltimore National Pike, tel. 410/788–3377) has inflatable rafts for hire on the rivers north of Baltimore.

Tennis **Carroll Park** (Monroe St. and Washington Blvd., tel. 410/396–5828) has six courts. **Clifton Park** (Harford Rd. and St. Lo Dr., tel. 410/396–6101) has nine courts. **Druid Hill Park** (Druid Hill Lake Dr., tel. 410/396–6106) has 24 courts. **Patterson Park** (Eastern Ave., tel. 410/396–3774) has six courts. These are all city maintained courts, so don't expect too much. If you're a serious tennis player, your best bets are at the various hotel courts (*see* Lodging, *below*).

Water Sports **Springriver Corp.** (6434 Baltimore National Pike, tel. 410/788–3377) has sea kayaks and white-water kayaks, in addition to rafts and canoes for hire.

Trident Electric Boat (Aquarium Dock, Harborplace, tel. 410/539–1837) rents eight-foot, two-passenger electric-powered craft for cruising the Inner Harbor waters.

Spectator Sports

The **USAir Arena** (tel. 410/792–7490), less than an hour away from Baltimore, in Landover, is the home of the Washington Bullets (basketball) and the Washington Capitals (hockey).

Baseball The **Orioles** (tel. 410/685–9800), a sometime contender in the American League East division, play their home games at Oriole Park at Camden Yards, from early April until early October.

Lacrosse The **Thunder** (tel. 410/347–2020) are members of the Major Indoor Lacrosse League, competing from January to March in the Baltimore Arena (201 W. Baltimore St., tel. 410/347–2000).

Outdoor high school and college lacrosse are very popular and fiercely played in spring. The **Johns Hopkins University team** is a perennial favorite, and games are played at the Homewood Field (Charles St. and University Pkwy.). Another hometown favorite is the Loyola Greyhounds, whose games are played at the Loyola campus (Charles St. and Cold Spring La.).

Soccer The **Spirit** (tel. 410/625–2320), a team in the Eastern Division of the Major Soccer League, plays from October to April at the Baltimore Arena.

Dining

In 1859 Oliver Wendell Holmes, Sr., called Baltimore "the gastronomic metropolis of the Union." Although other cities' culinary reputations have eclipsed Baltimore's since then, this is certainly a city where it's not difficult to eat quite well. Baltimore's restaurants offer the cosmopolitan dining advantages that one commonly finds in major cities: dining rooms that stay open later (many kitchens operate until 10 PM, especially on weekends), a large number of restaurants to choose from within a compact central area, and a variety of the cuisines of local ethnic communities, in some cases at very moderate prices.

Drive or take a taxi east from the Inner Harbor along Pratt Street to reach the Little Italy neighborhood, where there's a tempting concentration of authentic Italian restaurants near the intersection of Pratt and High streets.

Highly recommended restaurants are indicated by a star ★.

Baltimore **McCafferty's.** Named for former Baltimore Colts coach Don
American McCafferty, this is a haven for fans of both pigskin and beef. The house specialty is aged prime beef from the owner's Western ranch, and locals and visitors alike rave about its preparation. Other popular selections include lamb and salmon dishes, but what really draws attention is the restaurant's decor: Football helmets, signed baseballs, and jerseys are among the sports memorabilia on display. *1501 Sulgrave Ave., tel. 410/664–2200. Reservations recommended. Jacket and tie advised. AE, D, DC, MC, V. No weekend lunch. $$$$*

★ **The Prime Rib.** Bustling and crowded, this dark dining room just north of Mount Vernon Square features tables set close together under a low ceiling. Bankers and lawyers are much in evidence here, as are couples on expensive dates. The traditional menu is headed by the sterling prime rib and an even better filet mignon. Oysters Rockefeller and smoked trout are recommended appetizers. The wine list is surprisingly short and predominantly Californian. *1101 N. Calvert St., tel. 410/539–1804. Reservations required. Jacket and tie required. AE, D, DC, MC, V. $$$$*

Burke's. This Baltimore institution, situated at Light and Lombard streets, is famous for large frosty mugs of beer and soda. Burke's gigantic burgers, homemade soups, oyster stew, sandwiches, salads, and the city's best onion rings make the restaurant a popular eatery for lunch and after the theater and baseball games, 1 AM or later. *36 Light St., at Lombard St., tel. 410/752–4189. Reservations not needed. Dress: casual. AE, MC, V. $*

The Buttery. On Mount Vernon Square, cater-corner to the Walters Art Gallery and looking out at the Washington Monument, is this 24-hour diner, a beloved institution in this neighborhood of artists and young professionals. At the counter, or in one of two rooms of booths, diners can order from the full menu at any time. Pancakes are the most dependable breakfast item, made from a rich unclotted batter and served with eggs, bacon, sausage, or ham. The triple-decker roast beef, turkey, and ham sandwiches are generously endowed. Coffee is always fresh, as is (notably in such a place) the seasonal fruit. Ice-cream sundaes, particularly banana splits, are the most popular choices for dessert. *1 E. Centre St., tel. 410/837–2494. No reservations. Dress: casual. No credit cards. $*

Cajun **Midtown Yacht Club.** Peanut shells litter the floor of this one-room saloon on Mount Vernon Square, which resounds every night until 2 AM with juke box music and the voices of young-adult and middle-aged patrons. Dartboards and video games offer entertaining alternatives to conversation. The menu, available until midnight, stands out from typical bar fare with its strong Cajun influence. Jambalaya, a rice dish with clams and mussels; and seafood gumbo, a crab-and-shrimp stew, are among the spicy New Orleans–style selections. Clams, oysters, steamed shrimp and mussels, and crab cakes are more typical of the region and they meet the prevailing high standards. The ample hamburgers come with blue cheese, bacon, and other familiar toppings. Among the shifting selection of desserts, mud pie (made from chocolate ice cream) is a constant. Fifty brands of premium beer are available in bottles, and five are on tap. *15 E. Centre St., tel. 410/837–1300. No reservations. Dress: casual. AE, MC, V. $*

Continental **Citronelle.** Michel Richard, famed chef of Los Angeles's Citrus, has
★ brought his signature "California French cuisine" to the East Coast. Seafood dominates the menu, from a salmon terrine appetizer to a grilled swordfish entree. Such desserts as chocolate hazelnut bars are the high points of the meal, and the wine list is heavy on Chardonnays, Cabernets, and Bordeaux. Perhaps as impressive as the food are the environs: From its perch atop the Latham Hotel, Citronelle offers an unparralled view of the Washington Monument and Baltimore skyline. *Latham Hotel, 612 Cathedral St., tel. 410/837–3150. Reservations recommended. Dress: casual but neat. AE, D, DC, MC, V. $$$$*

★ **Hamptons.** A view of Inner Harbor and the distinctive National Aquarium building competes with the restaurant's interior decor: Sheraton-style tables, set with bowls of dahlias, are spaced generously in a dining room styled after an English country house. A highlight of the nouvelle menu is red snapper poached in white wine and topped with crabmeat and a leek-and-butter sauce. Bouillabaisse is loaded with crab, scallops, mussels, clams, whitefish, vegetables, and herbs. The wine list is about equally French and American, with token Australian, Italian, Spanish, and German selections. The major attraction on Sunday is the champagne brunch. Hamptons has been named among the top 40 restaurants in the United States by *Condé Nast Traveler* magazine. *Harbor Court Hotel, 550 Light St., tel. 410/234–0550. Reservations required. Jacket and tie required. AE, D, DC, MC, V. Closed Mon. $$$$*

8 East. Local celebrities as well as those from elsewhere are so common a sight at this demurely elegant retreat that they don't draw stares—which is one reason they come. Another is the menu. Scallops sautéed with sun-dried tomatoes and double-blanched garlic accompany linguine. Yellowtail flounder is broiled with lemon butter and white wine and stuffed with crab imperial. The chicken marsala's medallions of breast meat are sautéed with shallots and mushrooms and glazed with a white wine sauce. *Tremont Hotel, 8 E. Pleasant St., tel. 410/576–1199. Reservations advised. Jacket and tie advised. AE, DC, MC, V. $$$*

★ **Polo Grill.** This relatively new restaurant, located near the Johns Hopkins University campus, has a masculine, dark decor with lots of wood and brass fittings but is still a warm and comfortable place for dinner. Hosts Leonard and Gail Kaplan have a strong reputation in Baltimore and they don't disappoint. Some menu favorites include penne pasta and blackened chicken with a scattering of tomato, green peas, and pine nuts in a light Parmesan herb butter; a grilled veal chop with mixed wild mushrooms in Madeira sauce and creamy polenta; and the Oriental-style barbecued salmon with soya buerre blanc on warm spinach leaves and shiitake mushrooms. *Inn at the Colonnade, 4 W. University Pkwy., tel. 410/235–8200. Reservations advised. Jacket and tie advised. AE, D, DC, MC, V. $$$*

Baltimore Dining and Lodging

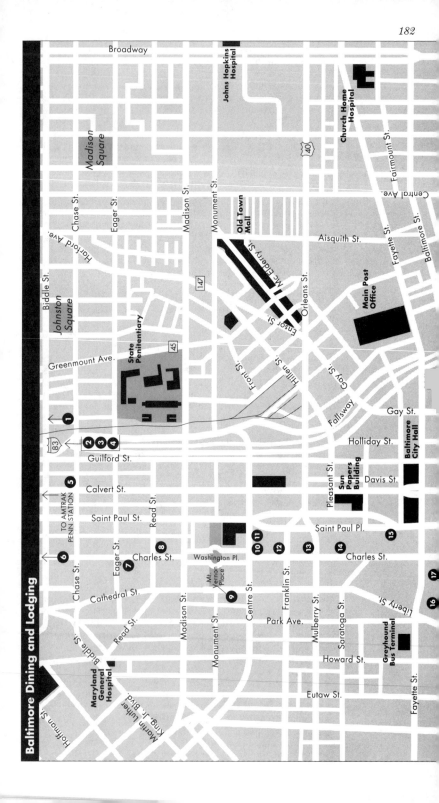

Broadway

Johns Hopkins Hospital

Church Home Hospital

Fairmount St.

Madison Square

Central Ave.

Chase St.

Eager St.

Madison St.

Monument St.

Old Town Mall

Baltimore St.

Harford Ave.

Johnston Square

Biddle St.

Aisquith St.

Fayette St.

40

147

McElderry St.

Orleans St.

Main Post Office

Ensor St.

State Penitentiary

45

Greenmount Ave.

Front St.

Hillen St.

Gay St.

Fallsway

Gay St.

1

83

2 3 4

Holliday St.

Baltimore City Hall

Guilford St.

Sun Papers Building

5

Pleasant St.

Davis St.

TO AMTRAK PENN STATION

Calvert St.

Saint Paul Place

Saint Paul St.

Read St.

10 11

15

6

12

13

14

Eager St.

8

Charles St.

Washington Pl.

Charles St.

Chase St.

7

Mt. Vernon Place

Franklin St.

17

Cathedral St.

9

Centre St.

16

Madison St.

Park Ave.

Liberty St.

Biddle St.

Read St.

Monument St.

Mulberry St.

Maryland General Hospital

Saratoga St.

Greyhound Bus Terminal

Martin Luther King Jr. Blvd.

Howard St.

Hoffman St.

Eutaw St.

Fayette St.

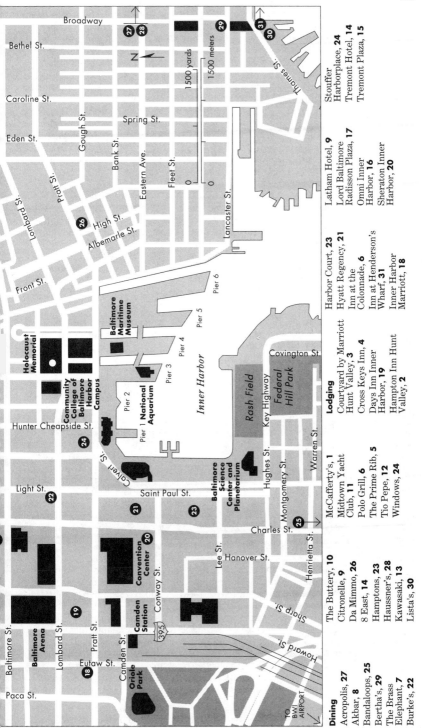

Broadway

Bethel St.

Caroline St.

Eden St.

Spring St.

Gough St.

Bank St.

Eastern Ave.

Fleet St.

Lombard St.

Pratt St.

Front St.

High St.

Albemarle St.

Lancaster St.

Holocaust Memorial

Baltimore Maritime Museum

Pier 6

Pier 5

Community College of Baltimore Harbor Campus

Pier 4

Pier 3

Pier 2

Inner Harbor

Covington St.

Hunter Cheapside St.

Pier 1 **National Aquarium**

Rash Field

Key Highway

Federal Hill Park

Light St.

Baltimore Science Center and Planetarium

Saint Paul St.

Hughes St.

Montgomery St.

Warren St.

Charles St.

Hanover St.

Lee St.

Henrietta St.

Convention Center

Camden Station

Baltimore Arena

Lombard St.

Pratt St.

Conway St.

Sharp St.

Oriole Park

Camden St.

Eutaw St.

Howard St.

Paca St.

TO BWI AIRPORT

N

1 500 yards

1 500 meters

0

0

Thames St.

Dining

Acropolis, **27**
Akbar, **8**
Bandaloops, **25**
Bertha's, **29**
The Brass Elephant, **7**
Burke's, **22**
The Buttery, **10**
Citronelle, **9**
Da Mimmo, **26**
8 East, **14**
Hamptons, **23**
Haussner's, **28**
Kawasaki, **13**
Lista's, **30**
McCafferty's, **1**
Midtown Yacht Club, **11**
Polo Grill, **6**
The Prime Rib, **5**
Tio Pepe, **12**
Windows, **24**

Lodging
Courtyard by Marriott Hunt Valley, **3**
Cross Keys Inn, **4**
Days Inn Inner Harbor, **19**
Hampton Inn Hunt Valley, **2**
Harbor Court, **23**
Hyatt Regency, **21**
Inn at the Colonnade, **6**
Inn at Henderson's Wharf, **31**
Inner Harbor Marriott, **18**
Latham Hotel, **9**
Lord Baltimore Radisson Plaza, **17**
Omni Inner Harbor, **16**
Sheraton Inner Harbor, **20**
Stouffer Harborplace, **24**
Tremont Hotel, **14**
Tremont Plaza, **15**

Windows. Picture windows allow diners to watch, from five floors up, the comings and goings in and around Inner Harbor. Less spectacular than the view, the dining room is tasteful and understated, and its tables are set far enough apart to ensure privacy at every meal. Patrons of the hotel set the tone with their relaxed demeanor and attire. The seafood grill typically includes two fish selections (for example, tuna and swordfish or salmon) and one shellfish (jumbo shrimp or soft-shell crab) in a cool tarragon vinaigrette. The kitchen is proud of its shrimp stuffed with crabmeat, prepared in a flaky phyllo dough in a caviar sauce. The wine list is heavily American—mostly Californian, with even a Maryland vintage—but France, Italy, and Germany are represented. *Stouffer Harborplace Hotel, 202 E. Pratt St., tel. 410/547–1200. Reservations advised. Jacket and tie advised. AE, D, DC, MC, V. $$$*

Bandaloops. This unusual restaurant, remarkable for its narrow structure that suggests a boxcar, has a decidedly informal and lively tone. The front room is a bar that attracts a youthful clientele. A "casual gourmet" menu means rich salads and sandwiches. The kitchen takes particular care with oysters and prepares them Cajun-style (served with spinach pasta covered with tomato-pepper butter) or in combination with steak. The wine list is heavily Californian, with Chilean and Spanish selections. Bandaloops is a five-minute ride south from Inner Harbor. *1024 S. Charles St., tel. 410/727–1355. Reservations required. Dress: casual but neat. AE, D, DC, MC, V. Closed Sun. $$*

German **Haussner's.** Since its opening in 1926 this restaurant has been one of
★ Baltimore's favorite places to come for special occasions: If you have but one meal in this city, it should be here. The restaurant, which doubles as a gallery, has walls adorned with works of art by Van Dyck, Whistler, Bierstadt, Rembrandt, Elsley, and Gainsborough to name but a few. Sculpture, statuary, ceramics, silver, and crystal fill the cabinets that border the rooms. Make no mistake, however; Haussner's fine food at reasonable prices is the major drawing card. More than 100 freshly prepared items appear on the menu, and there are dozens of vegetables to choose from. While German specialties and wild game are featured, there is something to satisfy anyone's taste, especially at dessert time. Haussner's strawberry pie is an all-time favorite. The pastries you'll see as you enter will tempt you before you've even ordered your meal. Many of the waitresses, clad in their fresh white attire, are as much an institution as the restaurant—some have worked here for 40 years or more. *3244 Eastern Ave., tel. 410/327–8365. No reservations at dinner. Dress: casual but neat. AE, D, DC, MC, V. Closed Sun. and Mon. $$*

Greek **Acropolis.** Greektown, 15 minutes by cab from the major hotels, has
★ ethnic restaurants that cost less than those in Little Italy to the west. Murals and music of Greece, and a clientele composed largely of families, give the dining room an informal but not noisy character. Portions are generous, with rockfish and red snapper leading the fresh seafood menu. Shrimp oregano are jumbo shrimp sautéed in white wine and butter and served (with a marinara sauce that contains feta cheese) over a rice pilaf baked in a lemon chicken base. Lamb Giouvetsi is baby lamb braised in olive oil and baked with orzo in a sauce of fresh tomatoes, green peppers, and onions. The good selection of Greek wines includes retsinas. *4718 Eastern Ave., tel. 410/675–3384. Reservations required. Dress: casual. AE, D, DC, MC, V. $$*

Indian **Akbar.** This small restaurant a few steps below street level on the business-and-retail Charles Street corridor is usually crowded and always filled with pungent aromas and the sounds of Indian music. Among the vegetarian dishes, *alu gobi masala* (a potato-and-cauliflower creation) is prepared with onions, tomatoes, and spices. Tandoori chicken is marinated in yogurt, herbs, and strong spices, then barbecued in a charcoal clay oven. The wine list is short and unremarkable. *823 N. Charles St., tel. 410/539-0944. Reservations advised. Dress: casual but neat. AE, D, DC, MC, V. $$*

Italian **Da Mimmo.** From Inner Harbor, it's a five-minute cab ride east to Little Italy, whose neighborhood restaurants are more expensive than the quaint location might suggest. Da Mimmo is the most worthwhile, even though the dining room can be noisy and the tables are too close together. Diners keep the reservations book filled for the cuisine alone, although there is nightly piano music. The seafood entrées are led by shrimp and red snapper; in one version, shrimp is baked with cognac and garlic and topped with breading in individual dishes. Veal is prepared with rosemary and sage, and portions are large. *Straciatelle,* an egg-drop soup, is made from an Old World recipe; and clams casino, diced with bacon, is a satisfying appetizer. Pastas are reliably fresh and properly cooked. Like the menu, the list of Italian wines is the best in the neighborhood. *217 S. High St., tel. 410/727-6876. Reservations required. Jacket and tie advised. AE, DC, MC, V. $$$$*

★ **The Brass Elephant.** The rooms of this grand pre-Civil War house on Charles Street are filled with classical music and the chatter of diners (the Teak Room is the quietest, the Oak Room the noisiest). An atrium meant to suggest a Venetian café has moss painted on pink walls, and the rest of the decor, including the elephant sconces, is just as remarkable. So is the northern Italian menu. Veal Valdostano, a favorite of the owner and chef, is a cutlet sautéed with butter, shallots, mushrooms, cream, white wine, and Fontina cheese. Hot antipasto is an unusual treat and the long wine list is extensive. *924 N. Charles St., tel. 410/547-8480. Reservations required. Jacket and tie advised. AE, DC, MC, V. $$$*

Japanese **Kawasaki.** Located amid art galleries and shops, this lively, brightly lighted dining room is a good setting for a convivial dinner. The menu offers the familiar teriyaki and tempura dishes, but the standouts here are the sushi and the sashimi; they are the best in town, and their preparation can be seen at the sushi bar in the front dining room. An illustrated menu is a great help for first-timers and those who can never remember the names of their favorite sushi. *413 N. Charles St., tel. 410/659-7600. Reservations advised. Dress: casual but neat. AE, DC, MC, V. Closed Sun. $$*

Mexican **Lista's.** Owners Kathy and Ruben Evangelista have struck the right chord with their "new Mexican" restaurant, whose popularity has certainly been helped along by its dockside location. The water taxi that runs between the Inner Harbor and nearby Fells Point keeps busy shuttling patrons to the door of this restaurant, which offers both indoor and outdoor dining. Once you've settled in with a margarita and chosen from the variety of fish, chicken, and more traditional Mexican dishes (all rated with one to four chili peppers, depending on how spicy they are), you can scan the displays of southwestern arts and crafts (which are available for sale). *1637 Thames St., tel. 410/327-0040. Reservations recommended. Dress: casual but neat. AE, D, DC, MC, V. $$*

Seafood **Bertha's.** All over the region, visitors who see the bumper sticker "Eat Bertha's Mussels"—come here to find out why that curious slogan is so enthusiastically displayed. This family-run establishment on Fell's Point, first opened as a bar in 1972, has gradually expanded into two cozy but uncramped dining rooms. The unusual menu partially reflects the Caledonian heritage of one of the married proprietors. The Scottish afternoon tea, offered every day except Sunday, is a rich array: Scotch eggs (hard-boiled eggs deep-fried with a sausage coating); sausages baked in dough blankets; cheese-tomato pasties; fresh-baked scones with lemon, jam, and butter; and various dessert pastries. On the main menu, the ballyhooed mussels are the outstanding item. They come steamed, with a choice of eight butter-based sauces (such as a garlic sauce with capers or—in late summer through the fall—a basil-pesto sauce made with home-grown basil); or as a Turkish appetizer, stuffed with sweet-and-spicy rice. Stuffed shrimp, crab cakes, and paella Valenciana (mussels, chorizo sausage, chicken, scallops, and shrimp on a bed of rice) fill out the menu. *734 S. Broadway, tel. 410/327–5795. Reservations required for tea, accepted at other times only for parties of 6 or more. Dress: casual. DC, MC, V. $$*

Spanish **Tio Pepe.** Candles illuminate the whitewashed walls of these cellar
★ dining rooms, which are usually hopping (the Shawl Room is quietest), and the menu represents all regions of Spain. The staple is paella à la Valenciana (chicken, sausage, shrimp, clams, and mussels with saffron rice); a less well known Basque recipe for red snapper includes clams, mussels, asparagus, and boiled egg. For appetizers, be certain to sample the mushrooms from the caves of Segovia and the shrimp scampi. The short but diverse wine list has many Spanish vintages, and there is a more expensive reserve list. The staff have a rich tradition of training and service behind them, and it's obviously successful. Make reservations well in advance. *10 E. Franklin St., tel. 410/539–4675. Reservations required. Jacket and tie required at dinner. AE, DC, MC, V. $$$*

Havre de *Restaurants in Havre de Grace do not appear on the Baltimore Din-*
Grace *ing and Lodging map.*

Continental **Crazy Swede.** A nautical theme prevails in this restaurant on the
★ first floor of a former hotel on a tree-lined avenue. Windows and mirrors on all sides keep the dining room well lighted whether or not the sailboat lanterns at the tables are burning. In winter the tables are covered with cloths in the blue-and-white scheme; in summer the wooden tables are bare except for straw mats. Anything on the diverse surf-and-turf menu can be ordered Cajun-style, prepared with the moderately spicy house seasoning. One popular choice for this treatment is shrimp scampi with garlic on a bed of rice. Broiled flounder is stuffed with a rich crab imperial. Veal Christopher is sautéed with shallots and served with a sauce of backfin crabmeat. *400 N. Union Ave., tel. 410/939–5440. Reservations advised. Dress: casual but neat. AE, D, MC, V. $$$*

German **Josef's Country Inn.** This unique restaurant is small and cozy—much like what you'd expect to find in the Bavarian countryside—and is very unassuming from the outside. Complete luncheon and dinner menus are highlighted by German specialties, which are served in a tidy European setting with 75 seats. *2410 Pleasantville Rd., tel. 410/877–7800. Reservations advised. Dress: casual. AE, DC, MC, V. $$$*

Seafood **MacGregor's.** Behind the original redbrick facade of a bank built in 1928, the dining rooms on two levels, with glass walls on three sides, look onto Chesapeake Bay. The decor includes carved duck decoys, mounted guns, and antique prints of the town. An outdoor deck with a gazebo is in use from May to October. Among the entrées on a recent menu, orange roughy (a whitefish from New Zealand) is served with a dill remoulade, and seafood Alfredo combines shrimp, scallops, lobster, and crab with linguine. Rare at a seafood house, here is a memorable dessert menu: Chocolate Sin is a fallen soufflé made without flour and with four kinds of imported chocolate; butter almond torte is only slightly less rich. *331 St. John's St., tel. 410/939–3003. Reservations advised. Dress: casual but neat. AE, DC, MC, V. $$$*

Vandiver Inn. One of the three dining rooms is a glassed-in sun porch; the other two have stained-glass windows and photographs of the town in 1866, the year the building was constructed. The chairs and tables—the latter draped with white linen cloths—are solid mahogany antiques. Candles at tables and a crystal chandelier in one room illuminate dinner. The prix fixe menu changes with the chef's fancy, but light seasonings are the rule. A recent menu featured fresh grilled marlin with a lime hollandaise sauce, and rack of lamb accompanied by the inn's meaty crab cakes. A Chambord cheesecake with a black-chocolate crust is made with fresh raspberries and raspberry liqueur. The Vandiver also has four warm, Victorian-style guest rooms with antiques and comfortable furnishings (*see* Lodging, *below*). *410 S. Union Ave., tel. 410/939–5200. Reservations required. Dress: casual but neat. AE, MC, V. No lunch. Closed Mon.–Thurs. $$$*

Fortunato Brothers. On the first floor of a two-story redbrick building in Havre de Grace's historic district is this bustling Italian eatery, which opened in 1990. The floors are covered in maroon-and-white tiles, and the walls, except where wood-paneled, are papered to match; the wood tables are bare. The menu features homemade spaghetti, ziti, ravioli, and shells (stuffed with ricotta cheese) in a mild and thick homemade meat sauce. All the pastas come with a small dinner salad and garlic bread, making this an exceptional bargain. Homemade meat lasagna, served in large portions, is the biggest hit. Fortunato Salad is an alternative meal-in-itself, featuring ham, turkey, and mozzarella. Pizza and submarine sandwiches are well represented on the menu. A conspicuous omission at a restaurant in this waterside town is seafood. An alarming omission is alcohol, but a beer-and-wine license is expected in 1991. *103 N. Washington St., tel. 410/939–1401. Reservations accepted. Dress: casual. No credit cards. $*

Lodging

Accommodations in the vicinity of Inner Harbor will give visitors ready access to all major attractions of the city. The redevelopment of this neighborhood and the subsequent revival of downtown have intensified competition among hotels and kept the level of service high while restraining prices. Away from the water and as far north as the more gracious Mount Vernon, travelers can find reminders of an older Baltimore and some relative bargains. All hotels listed are within a short drive or a half-hour's walk of Inner Harbor. Lodging reservations must be made well in advance for Preakness weekend, the third weekend in May.

Highly recommended lodgings in each price category are indicated by a star ★.

Category	Cost*
$$$$	over $175
$$$	$140–$175

$$	$115–$140
$	under $115

All prices are for a standard double room, excluding service charge.

Baltimore **Harbor Court.** In spite of its less central location on the west side of
$$$$ Inner Harbor, this well-managed, eight-story, red-brick tower built
★ in 1986 has become the most prestigious transient address in Baltimore. The decor is ersatz English country house à la Ralph Lauren. A ground-floor "library" stocked with collectors' editions and dominated by a Chinese lacquer screen is the domain of a concierge who personifies an obliging staff. Guest rooms reflect the expensive, meticulous look of the public areas: 18th-century English landscapes and portraits, a marble floor in the bath. The staterooms (business-class accommodations) are distinguished by canopied four-posters. Suites feature wood parquet floors. The most desirable—and most expensive—rooms have a harbor view. Courtyard rooms have the advantage of quiet, except for the occasional screech of a peacock. *550 Light St., 21202, tel. 410/234–0550 or 800/824–0076, fax 410/659–5925. 195 rooms, 8 suites. Facilities: 2 restaurants, bar, indoor pool, sauna, whirlpool, workout room, tennis court, racquetball court. AE, D, DC, MC, V.*

Inner Harbor Marriott. This 10-story hotel, one of the city's largest, boasts surprisingly quiet, brightly lighted public areas that are decorated in a nondescript contemporary style. The best views are from those rooms that face the Inner Harbor and Camden Yards, which is just a few blocks away. Some rooms have black-and-white nature photographs and make prominent use of the color jade. Guests on the 10th floor enjoy concierge-level privileges such as bathrobe and shoeshine. *Pratt and Eutaw Sts., 21201, tel. 410/962–0202 or 800/228–9290, fax 410/962–8585. 525 rooms, 14 suites. Facilities: restaurant, bar, indoor pool, sauna, whirlpool, workout room. AE, D, DC, MC, V.*

★ **Latham Hotel.** When this 13-story building, built as an apartment house in 1924, was converted to a hotel in 1985, it filled the luxury hotel vacuum. It's a favorite of upscale business travelers, rivaled only by the Harbor Court (*see above*). The hotel faces the Washington Monument in Mount Vernon Square, with churches, museums, restaurants, and the Peabody Conservatory of Music in the immediate neighborhood. The lobby is distinguished by a library with dark wood paneling that suggests a men's club. Guest rooms are decorated largely in pastels, with horticultural prints. Rooms with park views are the best choice. *612 Cathedral St., 21201, tel. 410/727–7101 or 800/528–4261, fax 410/789–3312. 104 rooms, 10 suites. Facilities: 2 restaurants. AE, D, DC, MC, V.*

Stouffer Harborplace. The most conveniently located of Baltimore hotels—across the street from the shopping pavilions, where the Inner Harbor area renaissance began—the Stouffer meets the needs of tourists, business travelers, and conventioneers alike. While the guest-room decor is light and cheerful, the furnishings—oversize pieces of stained mahogany veneer accented with brass—take up an inordinate amount of space. Rooms with harbor view are the most popular. Guests on the 12th-floor concierge level, accessible only by card-key, may have free breakfast and snacks (and cocktails at a charge) in a staffed club room. *202 E. Pratt St., 21202, tel. 410/547–1200 or 800/468–3571, fax 410/539–5780. 622 rooms, 60 suites. Facilities: restaurant, bar, indoor pool, sauna, whirlpool, workout room. AE, D, DC, MC, V.*

$$$ Hyatt Regency. This stretch of Light Street is practically a highway, but the unenclosed skyways allow ready pedestrian access to the Harborplace mall and the convention center. While the Harbor Court next door strives for the ambience of a country inn in the big city, the Hyatt achieves the charm of an airport hotel in a downtown location. The reserved, though polite, staff does little to dispel the somewhat desolate atmosphere. Guest rooms have basic furnishings, with small tables instead of proper desks; the views are of the harbor or the city. The 12th floor is the club level, with free Continental breakfast and hors d'oeuvres available. Frequent stay (Gold Passport) participants get hair dryer and newspaper and may use the health club free of charge. Over the past few years the public areas have lost some of their original shine and glitz, but still the lobby features glass elevators and the chain's trademark atrium. *300 Light St., 21202, tel. 410/528–1234 or 800/233–1234, fax 410/685–3362. 487 rooms, 9 suites. Facilities: 2 restaurants, bar, outdoor pool, 3 tennis courts, sauna, whirlpool, workout room, running track. AE, D, DC, MC, V.*

Inn at the Colonnade. Directly across the street from Johns Hopkins University, within walking distance of the Baltimore Museum of Art, and just 10 minutes north of downtown, this suburban inn offers luxuriously appointed European-style accommodations in a central location. Business travelers and conventioneers will appreciate the comfortable setting and state-of-the-art facilities for board meetings, conferences, and workshops. But the inn also offers amenities necessary for personal comfort, such as rich and warm furnishings, an attractive indoor swimming pool, whirlpools, complimentary transportation to your center-city destination, VCR and classic video library, and excellent dining and cocktail facilities. The inn is dedicated to European elegance and service. *4 W. University Pkwy., tel. 410/235–5400 or 800/222–8733, fax 410/235–5572. 125 rooms and suites. Facilities: restaurant, lounge, indoor pool, shuttle service, 3,100 sq ft of meeting space, reception room. AE, D, DC, MC, V.*

Inn at Henderson's Wharf. This inn was actually built in the mid-1800s as a B&O Railroad tobacco warehouse. Situated at the water's edge in historic Fells Point, the inn is less than a mile from Baltimore's Inner Harbor and is linked by water taxi. The richly decorated, warmly inviting bed-and-breakfast–style accommodation offers waterfront or garden views from all of its 38 rooms. A complimentary European breakfast is offered, and the inn is equipped with meeting and banquet facilities, a modest excercise facility, and is pleasantly "smoke free." Adjacent to the inn is the **Fells Point Marina**, with slips to 150 feet. All possible amenities are available to visiting yachtsmen. Just a two-minute walk from the heart of Fells Point, there is bountiful nightlife nearby. *1000 Fell St., Fells Point 21231, tel. 410/522–7777 or 800/522–2088, fax 410/522–7087. 38 rooms. Facilities: gym, valet and concierge services, shuttle service. AE, DC, MC, V.*

Lord Baltimore Radisson Plaza. The highlight of this 23-story hotel built in 1928 is its cavernous art deco lobby, whose dark green walls, set off by elaborately carved brown-and-gold moldings, are dimly lit by frosted-glass sconces. The Jazz Age elegance does not extend to the guest rooms, renovated in 1986, which are somewhat cramped. Rooms on the south side have the best view, and from the top three floors you can see the water. Rooms on the east side, with views of a wall and an alley, are the least desirable. The hotel is quiet, clean, and comfortable, and its location is central. Staff are polite but harried, apparently overworked. A restaurant serves three meals a day; the lobby bar hosts ethnic happy hours (Mexican on Wednesday, Italian on Thursday, etc.). *20 W. Baltimore St., 21202, tel. 410/ 539–8400 or 800/333–3333, fax 410/625–1060. 440 rooms, 4 suites. Facilities: 2 restaurants, bar, whirlpool, sauna, workout room. AE, D, DC, MC, V.*

Omni Inner Harbor. Baltimore's largest accommodation, with more than 700 rooms in twin towers, also houses the largest ballroom in the city, making the hotel especially popular with guests and conventioneers alike. Rooms are standard, but what is most outstanding about the Omni are its fine restaurants. A $15 million renovation in 1991 brought wining and dining to the fore with the Corner Bar, which features light dining and a Library of Liquors (replete with ladder for the top shelf). At Jackie's you can get light fare all day, including eggs and designer pizza. The Baltimore Grille, where the Sunday-brunch buffet begins, is a classic steak house featuring grilled seafood, steak, poultry, and wild game, all served with 22 condiments from a tableside cart. In 1991 the restaurant received the *Wine Spectator* magazine award for its extensive collection of wines—more than 220 vintages are available here, many by the glass. *101 W. Fayette St., 21201, tel. 410/752–1100 or 800/843–6664, fax 410/752–0832. 703 rooms, 6 suites. Facilities: 2 restaurants, bar, outdoor pool, workout room. AE, D, DC, MC, V.*

★ **Sheraton Inner Harbor.** A relaxed atmosphere prevails here in spite of heavy traffic from the adjacent convention center. The chrome-and-glass construction of the lobby resembles that of many others, yet it does admit abundant sunlight on bright days. While the standard rooms are among the smallest of the major hotels in town, all were renovated in 1990 and all contain coffeemakers. The Sheraton has the only certified kosher hotel kitchen in Baltimore, available for functions and room service by arrangement. The Sheraton is the official hotel of the Baltimore Orioles. *300 S. Charles St., 21201, tel. 410/962–8300 or 800/325–3535, fax 410/962–8211. 339 rooms, 20 suites. Facilities: restaurant, bar, indoor pool, sauna, workout room. AE, D, DC, MC, V.*

★ **Tremont Hotel.** Built in the 1960s as an apartment house on a quiet downtown block, the 13-story Tremont was renovated in 1983 to become a small European-style hostelry with an elegant home-away-from-home ambience. The lobby and the hotel's 8 East restaurant are intimate and private—qualities that attract guests who might be easily recognized. Like the Tremont Plaza (*see below*), which is owned by the same company, the hotel has only suites; they come in two sizes, all with kitchen, microwave, toaster oven, and coffeemaker. A view to the north, which includes the Washington Monument, is more impressive than the view of shady Pleasant Street. The level of service is unsurpassed by that of any other hotel in town: The concierge will arrange local transportation, in most cases free of charge. Staff will also do guests' personal shopping (groceries, clothing). Room phones have conference and speaker functions. *8 E. Pleasant St., 21202, tel. 410/576–1200 or 800/638–6266, fax 410/244–1154. 60 suites. Facilities: restaurant, bar. AE, D, DC, MC, V.*

$$ **Cross Keys Inn.** Located in a quiet wooded setting about 10 minutes north of downtown, the Village of Cross Keys, the inn is a nice respite from the bustle of the city but still offers meeting rooms, ballrooms, and conveniences for the businessperson. Accommodations are steps away from the clusters of wonderful and whimsical shops and boutiques and a fair selection of dining options. A legendary feature of this property is the Sunday Champagne Brunch offered at the Crossroads Restaurant: Get there early, as folks start lining up well in advance. Dinners are good here, too, but if you have a breakfast meeting, make it at the Roost, where Baltimore's most powerful

start their day. The Inn offers complimentary van service within a 15-minute radius, which hits most of Baltimore's main attractions. There's free parking and a secluded pool. *5100 Falls Rd., 21210, tel. 410/532-6900 or 800/532-5397, fax 410/532-2403. 148 rooms. Facilities: 2 restaurants, lounge, meeting rooms, outdoor pool, AE, DC, MC, V.*

★ **Tremont Plaza.** In 1984 this 37-story apartment building in the densest part of the business district was converted into a hotel. The building's plain gray facade and the minuscule brass-and-marble lobby belie the tasteful guest rooms decorated in earthtones. Like its sister property, the Tremont Hotel one block north, this is a suite hotel; all units—there are six sizes to choose from—have kitchen with microwave, toaster oven, and coffeemaker. The best views, of the city and the small park in the center of St. Paul Place, are from rooms numbered 06. The concierge floors (30 and above) have larger rooms, and their guests receive free breakfast and cocktails. The restaurant Tugs has a nautical decor and a menu rich in seafood, but the hotel's major culinary distinction is its gourmet delicatessen, judged the best in town by readers of *Baltimore* magazine. *222 St. Paul Pl., 21202, tel. 410/727-2222 or 800/638-6266, fax 410/685-4215. 250 suites. Facilities: restaurant, bar, outdoor pool, sauna, workout room. AE, D, DC, MC, V.*

$ **Courtyard by Marriott Hunt Valley.** About 15 minutes from downtown, in an affluent suburb that is a growing corporate center, this motel provides comfortable and affordable chain lodging. The simple guest rooms are as standardized as Courtyard's signature white-stucco exterior; a coffee service, including cups and hot water, is the only unusual touch in the rooms. The neighbors are office buildings, which means that all the rooms enjoy quiet nights, and uninteresting views during the day. *221 International Circle, Hunt Valley 21030, tel. 410/584-7070 or 800/321-2211, fax 410/584-8151. 146 rooms, 12 suites. Facilities: restaurant, bar, indoor pool, whirlpool, weight room. AE, D, DC, MC, V.*

Days Inn Inner Harbor. Less than three blocks from the Inner Harbor and the baseball stadium, this nine-story redbrick building, built in 1984, provides reliable and relatively economical accommodations in the center of town. Guest rooms, featuring heavy use of lavender, are not drab but are sparsely furnished; each has a small desk, a television (some with remote control), and a refrigerator. Rooms on the west side have views of the stadium. *100 Hopkins Pl., 21201, tel. 410/576-1000 or 800/325-2525, fax 410/576-9437. 250 rooms, 8 suites. Facilities: restaurant, bar, outdoor pool. AE, D, DC, MC, V.*

Hampton Inn Hunt Valley. Built in 1986, this seven-story building stands across the road from a farmer's market and is next door to a restaurant; downtown is about a 15-minute drive. The guest rooms are simply and brightly decorated: the carpets are mauve, and so are the bedspreads, which have squiggly sea-green stripes. Furniture is basic: The only extra is a small refrigerator. Free coffee is served, and on Tuesday and Thursday from 5:30 to 7 there are free cocktails. *11200 York Rd., Hunt Valley 21031, tel. 410/527-1500 or 800/426-7866, fax 410/771-0819. 126 rooms. AE, D, DC, MC, V. Rates include Continental breakfast.*

Havre de Grace *Hotels in Havre de Grace do not appear on the Baltimore Dining and Lodging map.*

$ **Spencer-Silver Mansion.** This house was built in 1886 of gray granite
★ quarried at Port Deposit, 5 miles up the Susquehanna—the same kind of granite that was used in the Brooklyn Bridge and the United

Nations building. Characteristic Victorian features include stained-glass windows, a wraparound porch, and a turret. One guest room is a round turret room; another has a queen-size brass bed and a view of the diverse garden. All rooms are furnished with period antiques supplemented by select reproductions. The formal parlor is graced by a brass chandelier with ornate glass globes. *200 S. Union Ave., 21078, tel. 410/939–1097. 4 rooms, 1 with bath. No credit cards. Rates include breakfast.*

Vandiver Inn. This three-story wood house, built in 1886 and listed on the National Register of Historic Places, sits on a 1-acre property 1½ blocks from the bay. Green with a dark green trim on the outside, the inn evokes a Victorian ambience indoors, with antique beds and other period pieces. The O'Neil and the Rodgers suites have their own porches. Another porch extends the width of the house front, and the gazebo in the backyard is as old as the house itself. The Vandiver's true claim to fame, however, is the cuisine in its restaurant (*see* Dining, *above*), which makes good use of local seafood complemented by the chef's sauces. *410 S. Union St., 21078, tel. 410/939–5200 or 410/939–5202. 4 rooms, 2 with bath; 4 suites. Facilities: restaurant. AE, MC, V. Rates include full breakfast.*

The Arts and Nightlife

Events listings appear in the "Maryland Live" Friday supplement to the *Baltimore Sun*; the Thursday "Accent Plus" supplement to the *Evening Sun*; the monthly *Baltimore* magazine; and the *City Paper*, a free weekly distributed in shops and street-corner machines.

The Arts

Film **Baltimore Museum of Art** (Art Museum Dr., tel. 410/396–7100) and the **Enoch Pratt Free Library** (400 Cathedral St., tel. 410/396–5430) screen themed repertory programs.

Music **Meyerhoff Symphony Hall** (1212 Cathedral St., tel. 410/783–8000), the home of the Baltimore Symphony Orchestra, led by maestro David Zinman, is the city's principal concert hall.

Friedberg Hall (E. Mt. Vernon Pl. and Charles Sts., tel. 410/659–8124) of the Peabody Conservatory of Music is the scene of recitals, concerts, and opera performances by students, faculty, and distinguished guests.

Pier Six Concert Pavilion (Pier 6 at Pratt St., tel. 410/625–4230) began more than 10 years ago as a temporary summer-entertainment venue but was rebuilt in 1991. It is now open May–September.

Theater **Center Stage** (700 N. Calvert St., tel. 410/685–3200), a repertory theater that has performed works by Shakespeare and Samuel Beckett, is the state theater of Maryland.

Fells Point Corner Theater (251 S. Ann St., tel. 410/276–7837), a center for acting and directing workshops, stages eight off-Broadway productions a year, with performances on weekends.

Lyric Theater (140 W. Mt. Royal Ave., tel. 410/685–5086) hosts plays and musicals in addition to opera productions.

Morris A. Mechanic Theatre (Baltimore and Charles Sts., tel. 410/625–4230) houses road shows of Broadway hits and serves as a testing ground for Broadway-bound productions.

Spotlighters Theater (817 St. Paul St., tel. 410/752–1225) stages a variety of works ranging from Shakespeare to musicals; there is one production a month, with performances on weekends.

Vagabond Players (806 S. Broadway, tel. 410/563–9135) perform recent Broadway hits throughout the year, on Friday, Saturday, and Sunday.

Nightlife

Bars and Lounges   In recent years, "pub-crawling" has become a popular pastime in Fells Point, where the young professionals who call the neighborhood home mingle with visitors from throughout the city and surrounding areas. Many of the bars offer outdoor or rooftop tables and serve domestic and local brews. Most also have notable bar food, often a seafood specialty. Entertainment runs the musical gamut from rock and reggae to jazz and blues.

At the harborside **Explorer's Club** in the Harbor Court Hotel (550 Light St., tel. 410/234–0550), the most remarkable sights are the elephants and monkeys in the murals, and the eclectic furnishings include elephant tusks and leopard-skin chairs that might have been collected by a 19th-century great white hunter. A pianist performs every night, a full jazz band on Friday and Saturday nights.

Blues   **8x10** (8 E. Cross St., tel. 410/625–2000) is a venue where rhythm and blues often shares the bill with so-called progressive rock (*see below*).

Comedy   **Comedy Factory Outlet** (Lombard and Light Sts., tel. 410/244–5233), **Slapstix Comedy Club** (34 Market Pl., tel. 410/659–7527), and **Winchester's Comedy Club** (102 Water St., tel. 410/576–8558) are filled with chuckles, giggles, titters, snickers, snorts, guffaws, jeers—and sometimes dead silence.

Rock   **Max's on Broadway** (735 S. Broadway, tel. 410/675–6297) has showcased a Bruce Springsteen colleague, Nils Lofgren, who hails from nearby Bethesda.

Singles   **Hammerjack's Inner Harbor Concert Hall** (1101 S. Howard St., tel. 410/659–7625) is a place where hard rock and heavy metal predominate and young people congregate.

8x10 (8 E. Cross St., tel. 410/625–2000) emphasizes the blues, yet rock and occasional jazz can be heard here as well.

Sports Bars   **Balls** (200 W. Pratt St., tel. 410/659–5844) and the **Baltimore Original Sports Bar** (34 Market Pl., tel. 410/244–0135) are places where fans banter about trivia, dispute scores, and commiserate over cheating scandals while watching sports programming on the telescreen.

9 Annapolis and Southern Maryland

Annapolis, capital of Maryland, contains one of the highest concentrations of 18th-century architecture in the United States, including more than 50 pre-Revolutionary buildings. This considerable Colonial and early republican heritage is largely intact and, because it's all within walking distance, highly accessible; a visitor can do Annapolis justice in a single well-planned day.

Puritan settlers relocating from Virginia in 1649 established the town of Providence at the mouth of the Severn River, a tributary of Chesapeake Bay. Lord Baltimore, who held the Maryland Royal charter, named the area around the town Anne Arundel County, after his wife. Anne Arundel Town was established in 1684 on the south side of the Severn, across from Providence, and in 1694 this town became Annapolis, the colonial capital city. From 1783 to 1784 Annapolis served as the nation's capital as well—the first peacetime capital of the United States.

Throughout the 18th century Annapolis was a major port, important in the tobacco trade. Today Baltimore is the principal Chesapeake port, but Annapolis remains a favored destination of oystermen and yachtsmen, and on warm days City Dock is thronged with sails billowing against a background of red-brick waterfront shops and restaurants. The sailboat and powerboat shows in October are events of national importance, and the nautical atmosphere of the town is accentuated by the regular presence on city streets of the strikingly uniformed midshipmen of the United States Naval Academy.

South of Annapolis and Washington, D.C., the Western Shore peninsula of Maryland is prominently cleft by the Patuxent River, a 110-mile tributary of Chesapeake Bay, which separates Calvert County in the north from St. Mary's County in the south. The river's name, in the language of the original natives, meant "where tobacco grows," and it was this stinking "sotweed"—along with the seafood industry—that supported the local economy for centuries. Tobacco and cornfields commonly border the highways across the flat terrain of this coastal plain region, an area for touring and fishing. Calvert County also has a couple of rare bay beaches.

Essential Information

Important Addresses and Numbers

Visitor Information **Annapolis and Anne Arundel County Conference and Visitor's Bureau** (26 West St., Annapolis 21401, tel. 410/280–0445).
Charles County Tourism (Star Route 1, Box 1144, Port Tobacco 20677, tel. 410/932–6004).
City of Annapolis Office of Public Information and Tourism (City Hall, 160 Duke of Gloucester St., Annapolis 21401, tel. 410/269–6125).
St. Mary's County Tourism (Box 653, Leonardtown 20650, tel. 410/475–4626).
Tourism Council of Calvert County (Dept. of Economic Development, County Courthouse, Prince Frederick 20678, tel. 410/535–4583).
Tri-County Council For Southern Maryland (Box 1634, Charlotte Hall 20622, tel. 410/884–2144).
Visitor Information Center (City Dock, Annapolis 21401, tel. 410/268–8687).

Emergencies Throughout the region, dial **911** for emergency assistance.

Hospitals **Anne Arundel Medical Center** (Cathedral and Franklin Sts., Annapolis, tel. 410/267–1260).
Calvert Memorial Hospital (Rte. 4, Prince Frederick, tel. 410/535–4000).
St. Mary's Hospital (234 Jefferson St., Leonardtown, tel. 410/475–8981).

Late-night **Leader Drugs** (609 Taylor Ave., Annapolis, tel. 410/268–5007) is
Pharmacy open until 10 PM.

Arriving and Departing

By Car Annapolis is normally 35–45 minutes by car from Washington, D.C., on U.S. 50 (Rowe Blvd. exit), but during the evening rush hour, after 3:30 PM, the trip can take two hours. From Baltimore, following Route 3/97 (heavily patrolled by unmarked cars with radar) to U.S. 50, travel time is the same. To tour Southern Maryland, follow Route 2 south from Annapolis, and Route 4, which continues through Calvert County.

By Bus Maryland's Mass Transit Administration (MTA) offers regularly scheduled bus service from Baltimore to Annapolis (about 1 hour and 20 minutes one way from downtown—exact fare is required). Bus No. 210 departs from the Baltimore State Office Building Complex at Preston and Eutaw streets several times daily. One-way fare is $2.85. For schedules, tel. 410/539–5000.

Getting Around Annapolis

On-street parking is scarce in the historic downtown areas of the city. The lot at the Navy-Marine Corps Stadium is on the right of Rowe Boulevard as you come into town from Route 50. Annapolis Department of Public Transportation (tel. 410/263–7964) has shuttle bus service (30¢) every hour between the lot and downtown from 6:30 AM until 8 PM.

Guided Tours

Orientation **Historic Annapolis Foundation Tours** (Old Treasury Building, State House Circle, tel. 410/267–8149) and **Three Centuries Tours** (48 Maryland Ave., tel. 410/263–5357 or 410/263–5401) offer two-hour walking tours with similar itineraries that may include the State House, St. John's College, the Naval Academy, the Hammond-Harwood House, and the Chase-Lloyd House. Three Centuries' guides wear Colonial dress.

Maryland State House Tours (State House Circle, Information Desk, tel. 410/974–3400) are offered free of charge daily at 11 AM and 3 PM, except Thanksgiving, Christmas, and New Year's Day.

Boat Tours **Chesapeake Marine Tours** (tel. 410/268–7600) has departures from City Dock; tours last from 45 minutes to 7½ hours and range as far as St. Michaels, a preserved 18th-century fishing village on the Eastern Shore of the Bay.

Wm. B. Tennison, the oldest Coast Guard–licensed passenger vessel on Chesapeake Bay, is a bugeye sailboat "chunk built" from logs in 1899 and long used as an oyster boat. Now a power boat operating from May to October, the craft carries passengers on one-hour cruises of Solomons Harbor and the Patuxent, departing Wednesday to Sunday at 2 PM from the dock at the **Calvert Marine Museum** (Box 97, Solomons 20688, tel. 410/326–2042).

Exploring

Annapolis

Numbers in the margin correspond to points of interest on the Southern Maryland and Annapolis maps.

① A good place to begin a tour of **Annapolis** is at the **visitor center** at the
② **City Dock,** on the waterfront. Boats dozens of feet long, under motor and sail power, moor right at the edges of Dock Street and **Market Square** (also called Market Space), an open dockside area roughly the size of four city blocks, ringed with restaurants with outdoor seating. On the east side of the dock is another visitor information booth; the Markethouse pavilion at the center of the square offers gourmet refreshments; the **Kunta Kinte Plaque,** on the sidewalk at the head of the dock, commemorates the 1767 arrival of the African slave immortalized in Alex Haley's *Roots*. On some summer evenings Market Square is the site of a band concert.

③ The **Victualling Warehouse Maritime Museum,** on Main Street just off Market Square, occupies the site of a Continental army storehouse during the War of Independence, when Annapolis was a vital link in the chain of supply. Exhibits on the history of maritime commerce include a diorama of the city's waterfront in the 18th century and artifacts of Colonial-era trade. *77 Main St., tel. 410/268–5576. Admission free. Open Mar.–Dec., daily 9–5; Jan.–Feb., daily 10–4.*

④ Head northeast on Randall Street to visit the **United States Naval Academy;** the visitor center is in Ricketts Hall, by the gate at Randall and King George streets. Here visitors can join a one-hour guided tour or set out on an independent expedition. The academy, founded in 1845 on the site of a U.S. army fort, occupies 329 riverside acres. The most prominent structure on campus is the bronze
⑤ dome of the interdenominational **U.S. Naval Chapel;** the building contains the crypt of the Revolutionary War hero John Paul Jones ("I
⑥ have not yet begun to fight!"). A museum in **Preble Hall** tells the story of the U.S. Navy with displays of miniature ships and flags from the original vessels. There are periodic full-dress parades of midshipmen and, in the warmer months, noontime musters. Yet the most remarkable sight may be the representative student quarters—considerably neater than the typical college dorm room. *Tel. 410/267–3363 or 410/263–6933. Admission free. Open daily 9–5. Tours: $3 adults, $1 children. Tours depart Mar.–Dec., Mon.–Sat. 11 AM and 1 PM; Sun. 12:30 PM and 2:30 PM.*

⑦ Leaving the Naval Academy via Maryland Avenue will take you past the three-story, redbrick **Hammond-Harwood House** (1774), the only verified full-scale example of the work of William Buckland, Colonial America's most prominent architect at his death in 1774. Buckland was famous for his woodwork, including that of the Chase-Lloyd House across the street and George Mason's Gunston Hall (near Mount Vernon). The Hammond-Harwood is distinguished by exquisite moldings, cornices, and other carvings, including garlands of roses above the front doorway. These refinements were garnishes on a manorial wedding present from Matthias Hammond, a lawyer and revolutionary, to a fiancée who jilted him before it was finished. After this disappointment, Hammond never married. The Harwood family inhabited the house in the second half of the 19th century and during the first quarter of this century, and since then the house has been on show under various auspices. Today the interior is fur-

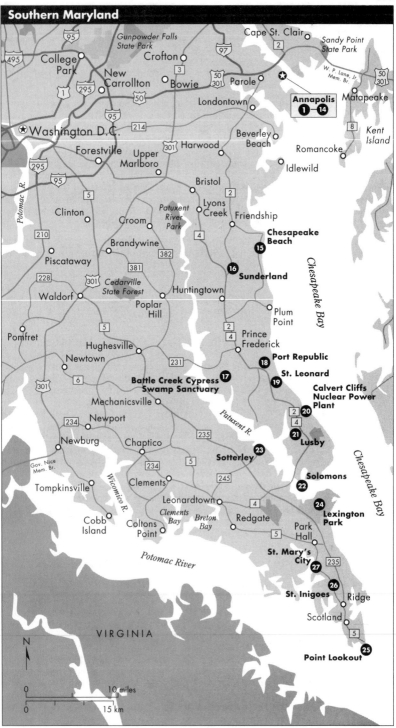

Southern Maryland

Gunpowder Falls State Park

Cape St. Clair

Sandy Point State Park

College Park

Crofton

New Carrollton

Bowie

Parole

Annapolis **1** **14**

W. P. Lane, Jr. Mem. Br.

Matapeake

Kent Island

Washington D.C.

Forestville

Upper Marlboro

Harwood

Londontown

Beverley Beach

Romancoke

Idlewild

Piscataway

Clinton

Croom

Patuxent River Park

Bristol

Lyons Creek

Friendship

Chesapeake Beach **15**

Brandywine

16 **Sunderland**

Waldorf

Cedarville State Forest

Huntingtown

Poplar Hill

Plum Point

Chesapeake Bay

Pomfret

Hughesville

Newtown

Prince Frederick

18 **Port Republic**

Battle Creek Cypress Swamp Sanctuary **17**

19 **St. Leonard**

Calvert Cliffs Nuclear Power Plant

Mechanicsville

Newport

Newburg

Chaptico

Patuxent R.

20

21 **Lusby**

23 **Sotterley**

Gov. Nice Mem. Br.

Clements

Tompkinsville

Clements Bay

Breton Bay

Leonardtown

Redgate

Solomons **22**

Chesapeake Bay

24 **Lexington Park**

Cobb Island

Coltons Point

Park Hall

Potomac River

St. Mary's City **27**

26

St. Inigoes

Ridge

Scotland

VIRGINIA

N

0   10 miles

0   15 km

Point Lookout **25**

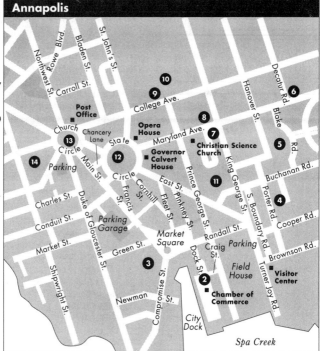

Annapolis

nished with period pieces, the garden tended with a regard for period authenticity. *19 Maryland Ave., tel. 410/269–1714. Admission: $4 adults, $3 students. Open Mon.–Sat. 10–4, Sun. noon–4.*

To appease the planter Edward Lloyd IV, Matthias Hammond extended octagonal wings from his house rather than build to a height that would block Lloyd's view of the harbor from the **Chase-Lloyd House** across the street. The Lloyd house was the completion in 1774 of work begun in 1769 by Samuel Chase, a future Supreme Court justice. The redbrick house has a massive but graceful facade with a central section that juts out dramatically from beneath a pediment. The interior is William Buckland's handiwork, including a parlor mantelpiece decorated with tobacco leaves (the source of the wealth that made the house possible, and a carved motif that can often be found throughout many early Maryland homes) carved in marble. The staircase parts dramatically around a Palladian window (a triple window whose center segment is taller than its flanks and arched). For most of this century the house served as a home for elderly Episcopalian women. *22 Maryland Ave., tel. 410/263–2723. Admission: $2. Open Mar.–Dec., Tues.–Sat. 2–4; Jan.–Feb., Tues., Fri., and Sat. 2–4.*

It's one block north on King George Street and a left on College Avenue to **St. John's College.** The most famous alumnus of St. John's is Francis Scott Key, who wrote the verses of the "Star-Spangled Banner," but since 1937 the college has been best known for a Great Books curriculum that is structured on reading the works of more than 100 classic authors, from Homer to Freud, in seminars.

McDowell Hall, approached from College Avenue by a long brick path up a gradual slope, is a grand sight under its golden cupola. Begun in 1742 to serve as the governor's residence, it was never used for that purpose and took half a century to complete. This is the third-oldest academic building in the country, just as St. John's— founded as King William's School in 1696—is the third-oldest college in the country after Harvard and William and Mary. The huge tulip poplar called the Liberty Tree, on the lawn fronted by College Avenue, is perhaps 600 years old. Here colonists and Native Americans concluded treaties in the 17th century, revolutionaries rallied in the 18th, and Union troops encamped in the 19th. The Liberty Tree, still standing on campus, is a 400-year-old tulip tree that served as a rallying point for meetings of the Sons of Liberty prior to the Revolutionary War. College commencement takes place here in spring. The **Carroll-Barrister House** (tel. 410/263–2371), now the college admissions office, was built in 1722 at Main and Conduits streets and moved to the campus in 1957; it was the birthplace of the Charles Carroll who helped draft Maryland's Declaration of Rights.

A two-block walk south from St. John's on Prince George Street will
⑪ take you to the **William Paca House and Gardens,** whose raised portico and dormer windows (windows that emerge from the roof) give it a strikingly steep aspect when viewed from the front. Since the entrance is only a few feet from the sidewalk, the 37-room redbrick mansion looms over Prince George Street. The house, built in 1765, and the gardens, originally finished in 1772 and restored in the present century, are what remain of the estate of William Paca, a signer of the Declaration of Independence and a governor of Maryland. The adjacent 2-acre garden permits a longer perspective on the house from the rear plus attractions of its own: a Chinese Chippendale bridge, a pond, a wilderness area, and formal arrangements. *186 Prince George St., tel. 410/263–5553. Admission: $4 house, $3 gardens, $6 both. Open Jan.–Feb., Fri.–Sat. 10–4, Sun. noon–4; Mar.–Dec., Mon.–Sat. 10–4, Sun. noon–4.*

⑫ East Street leads to State Circle, where the domed **Maryland State House** of 1780 is the oldest state capitol in continuous legislative use and the only one that has housed the U.S. Congress. When Congress convened here in 1783–1784, it accepted the resignation of George Washington as commander-in-chief of the Continental army and ratified the Treaty of Paris, which concluded the War of Independence. Both proceedings took place in the Old Senate Chamber, whose intricate woodwork—featuring the ubiquitous tobacco motif—is attributed to William Buckland. Here, too, is the Charles Willson Peale painting, *Washington at the Battle of Yorktown.* The Maryland House and Senate meet in other chambers in the building. On the grounds is the oldest public edifice in Maryland, the minuscule redbrick **Treasury** of 1735. *State Circle, tel. 410/974–3400. Open daily 9–5.*

Chancery Lane, an alleyway that runs alongside the State House Inn, leads from State Circle to Main Street, where the boutiques, bookstores, and gift shops are pleasant for browsing.

Time Out Deli sandwiches, milkshakes, and other ice-cream concoctions are the bill of fare at **Chick and Ruth's** (165 Main St.), a longtime local counter-and-table institution with friendly waitresses, where the person on the next stool eating the Reuben sandwich may be a state legislator.

---

⑬ Main Street leads uphill to Church Circle, where the Episcopal **St. Anne's Church** (1858), the third church of that name on this site, incorporates some of the structure of an earlier church. The parish was founded in 1692, with the Protestant king of England William III donating the communion silver, which is still in service. The churchyard has the grave of the last Colonial governor, Sir Robert Eden. *Church Circle, tel. 410/267–9333. Open daily 8–5.*

On Franklin Street, a block west of Church Circle, an ivy-covered
⑭ redbrick former church houses the **Banneker-Douglass Museum of Afro-American Life.** Changing exhibits, lectures, and films present a picture of African-American life in Maryland. *84 Franklin St., tel. 410/974–2893. Admission free. Open Tues.–Fri. 10–3, Sat. noon–4.*

Southern Maryland

Calvert County, on the Western Shore, is less than an hour's drive south of Annapolis via Route 2, and offers compelling bayside scenery that includes the imposing Calvert Cliffs and several miles of
⑮ southern Maryland's bay beaches. The town of **Chesapeake Beach** in northern Calvert County (follow the signs from Route 2) was founded in 1900 as a business venture, a seaside resort linked by rail to Washington, D.C., and Baltimore. In time, the decline of train travel and of the traditional middle-class Chesapeake Bay vacation led to the town's demise as a business. Grand hotel, racetrack, casino, and boardwalk attractions are gone, but the 1898 railroad station survives to house the **Chesapeake Beach Railway Museum** and its poignant collection of relics from a brief heyday. *Rte. 261, Chesapeake Beach, tel. 410/257–3892. Admission free. Open May–Sept., daily 1–4; Apr. and Oct., weekends 1–4.*

To the west, **All Saints Episcopal Church** (1775), a mile south of
⑯ **Sunderland,** is the redbrick replacement for a log building that served as the sanctuary of an Episcopal parish founded in 1692. Traffic noise from the highway junction mars the calm of the hilltop site, yet the trees and the 18th-century tombstones are handsome; family plots, fenced with wrought iron, hold the graves of generations. Indoors, the clay-tile floor, classic white box pews, and plain windows set off the subtle blue-and-rose stained-glass window over the altar. *Jct. Rtes. 2 and 4, Sunderland, tel. 410/257–6306. Open daily 10–5.*

Just past Sunderland, Route 2 merges with Route 4 and continues south to **Prince Frederick.** This is the county seat, a town of only 1,800. Prince Frederick has been destroyed by fire three times in its history; each time, the county courthouse went up in flames. The current courthouse, on Main Street, is a white-columned, redbrick building with a green tin roof and dates to 1916.

Six miles southwest of Prince Frederick (take Route 2/4 and follow the signs to Gray's Road, off Route 506), glimpses of the forest pri-
⑰ meval can be found in the **Battle Creek Cypress Swamp Sanctuary,** which boasts the northernmost stand of bald cypress trees in the United States. The 10-acre swamp, thick with the 100-foot members of an ancient species, can be comfortably inspected from a ¼-mile elevated boardwalk at the bottom of a steep but sturdy column of steps. Attendants at the nature center alert visitors to the seasonal permutations of the vegetation and the activities of squirrels, owls, and other wildlife. Indoor exhibits include a working beehive under glass. *Rte. 506, tel. 410/535–5327. Admission free. Open Apr.–Sept., Tues.–Sat. 10–5, Sun. 1–5; Oct.–Mar., Tues.–Sat. 10–4:30, Sun. 1–4:30.*

⑱ In **Port Republic, Christ Episcopal Church** (1772) is notable for its Biblical garden planted with species mentioned in the scriptures.

Nearby, in a small grove of trees, is a classic one-room schoolhouse, **Port Republic School No. 7,** built in the 1880s. Until 1932 a single teacher taught children in seven grades here. The schoolhouse has been restored and furnished with archetypal desks, inkwells, and a school bell. Since 1868 the grounds have been the venue the last Saturday in August for the oldest state tournament of the official state sport, jousting. *3100 Broomes Island Rd. (Rte. 264), Port Republic, tel. 410/586–0232 (school) or 410/586–0565 (church). Admission free. Church open dawn–dusk. School open June–Aug., Sun. 2–4.*

Behind 2½ miles of scenic Patuxent riverfront stretch 512 acres of woods and farmland on which more than 70 archaeological sites have yielded evidence of 9,000 years of human habitation. At the **Jefferson Patterson Park and Museum** in **St. Leonard,** visitors follow an archaeology trail to inspect artifacts of the successive hunter-gatherer, early agricultural, and plantation societies that exploited the resources of this area. Primitive knives and axes, fragments of Native American pottery, and Colonial glassware are among the items that have been recovered and are on display here. Stroll along the nature trails to take a look at wildlife, antique agricultural equipment, and fields of crops. *Mackall Rd., Rte. 265, St. Leonard, tel. 410/586–0050 or 410/586–0055. Admission free. Open Apr. 15–Oct. 15, Wed.–Sun. 10–5.*

Still in St. Leonard but on the eastern side of the peninsula, **Flag Ponds Nature Park** is one of the few Chesapeake Bay beaches in Calvert County open to the public. In addition to the shoreline and its fishing pier, the attractions include 3 miles of gently graded hiking trails, observation decks at two ponds, a boardwalk through wetlands, and indoor wildlife exhibits. Indigenous wildflowers, notably the blue flag iris, are abundant on the 327 acres, the location of a busy fishery during the first half of this century. As the boundaries contain both marshland and cliffs, they hold a diversity of plant and animal life. *Rte. 2/4, St. Leonard, tel. 410/586–1477 or 410/535–5327. Admission: $6 car. Open Memorial Day–Labor Day, weekdays 9–6, weekends 9–8; Sept.–May, weekends 9–6.*

The waterside **Calvert Cliffs Nuclear Power Plant,** the first such plant in the state, is ¼ mile south of Flag Ponds. The generator towers, rising before the cliffs, make an incongruous sight. Atop the cliffs, overlooking the reactor and Chesapeake Bay, a restored barn from 1818 has bundles of strong-smelling tobacco hanging from the ceiling and stuffed into hogshead barrels; it also houses sophisticated exhibits on atomic energy. A computer quiz linked to a scale-model reactor allows visitors to manipulate the fuel rods (it buzzes to signify human error). Youngsters can burn off excess energy at stationary bicycle-generators. On the grounds are the foundations of a 19th-century farmhouse and a heavily populated wildlife sanctuary that boasts spectacular snowy egrets, wild turkey, and white-tailed deer. Some 80 acres of this land are still under cultivation, producing wheat and corn. From the observation deck on a clear day observers can spot the Eastern Shore. *Rte. 2/4, Lusby, tel. 410/260–4676. Admission free. Open daily 10–4.*

The Calvert Cliffs run along most of Calvert County's western shore, and range in height from 40 to 100 feet. In their clay are embedded fossils of the Miocene era, which began 15–20 million years ago. More than 600 species have been recovered, and specimens are on view at the nuclear plant visitor center. Visitors can scavenge for, and keep, shark's teeth and other fossils along the beach, which is reached on foot by a 2-mile trail from the parking lot of the 1,600-acre **Calvert Cliffs State Park.** Access to the cliffs themselves is prohibited because of the danger of landslides. A children's playground has swings, slide, and jungle gym. Fishing and picnicking are permitted. *Rte. 2/4, Lusby, tel. 410/888–1410. Open Fri.–Sun. 10–6. Schedule for rest of week varies, so call for additional hours.*

㉑ In **Lusby,** along Route 765, **Middleham Chapel,** erected in 1748 on the foundations of a "chapel of ease," which was originally built in 1684, is a small redbrick cruciform structure, the oldest of that design in the state. Visitors must park carefully on the highway and climb a dozen steps to approach the sanctuary, whose acute roofline and lack of ornament lend it a storybook cuteness from the front. Indoors the atmosphere is cozy though solemn. Among the exposed beams in the ceiling hang anachronistic fans, which get a lot of use on summer Sundays in this swampy climate. The chapel is surrounded by tall hickory trees and tombstones as old as the 18th century. A bell given to the congregation in 1699 still calls the faithful to worship. *Rte. 765, Lusby, tel. 410/326–9507. Admission free. Open by request.*

㉒ On the tip of the peninsula, in **Solomons,** where the Patuxent empties into the Chesapeake, you'll find a tranquil, relaxed town that attracts many boaters, who rate its charms on a par with St. Michaels and Annapolis. The aptly situated **Calvert Marine Museum** recounts the histories of both the river and the bay. The bright and spacious exhibition hall contains models and life-size examples of business and pleasure boats that represent phases in local maritime history. Blacksmith and ship's carpenter shops have been re-created. In the supervised Discovery Room, children may sift through a tray that has shark's teeth and other fossils among the sand and gravel. A videotape explains the historical context for all the sights. Outside, small craft of different periods are on display in a waterside shed.There are also cruises on a converted 1899 bugeye sailboat. The greatest spectacle, however, is the restored Drum Point Lighthouse, built in 1883 and transported here in 1975: It is of the squat yet graceful screw-pile design, a sexagonal house poised like an insect on six slender legs. Tours of the cramped quarters are somewhat strenuous; senior citizens, preschoolers, and persons with heart problems are discouraged from taking them. *Rte. 2/4 at Solomons Island Rd., Solomons, tel. 410/326–2042. Admission: $3 adults, $2 senior citizens and children. Open daily 10–5; lighthouse open Apr., weekends 10–5; Memorial Day–Labor Day, daily 10–5.*

Affiliated with the museum is the **J.C. Lore & Sons Oysterhouse,** a processing plant built in 1934 and converted to a museum of the local seafood industries, displaying the tools of the trades and illustrating the work of oystermen, crabbers, and fishermen. The oyster house, a short walk south of the museum, is on the harbor-front strip of Solomons Island Road, where visitors find restaurants, antiques shops, and plentiful parking. *Open Memorial Day–Labor Day, daily 10–5.*

Travelers new to the area often fail to notice that they have crossed over to an island on entering Solomons on Route 2/4. But they cannot miss the Patuxent River when they cross the 1⅓-mile Thomas Johnson Bridge that arches into St. Mary's County, a peninsula that protrudes into the Chesapeake, with the Patuxent and the Potomac rivers on either side of it. Here Route 2/4 becomes simply Route 4.

㉓ Head north on Route 5/235 to Hollywood and turn east on Route 245 to reach **Sotterley.** This is a distinguished plantation house that, while not ranking with Shirley and its James River neighbors in Virginia, tends to be overlooked by visitors and guides. Not only is it surrounded by the only working 18th-century plantation in Maryland open to the public, it is the earliest known (1727) posted-beam structure in the United States: In place of a foundation, cedar timbers driven straight into the ground support the house. Sotterley is a sampler of architectural styles and interior design from the last two centuries, and the walls are hung with portraits of the successive owners. Like the secret closet built to conceal children from pirates, each feature of the house presents its own little history lesson. On the grounds, one of the original slave cabins has been restored. Sotterley overlooks the Patuxent; if you're sailing past on a boat you may dock, telephone, and be picked up and brought to the house by station wagon. *Rte. 245, near Hollywood, tel. 301/373–2280. Admission: $5 adults, $4 senior citizens, $2 children. Open Apr.–May and Nov.–Dec. by appointment; June–Oct., Tues.–Sun. 11–4.*

In rural St. Mary's County the lone magnet for commercial development—strips of fast-food restaurants and shopping malls—is the
24 Patuxent Naval Air Station in **Lexington Park,** which lies south of Route 4, between Route 235 and the bay. Located at the north gate of the station is the **Naval Air Test and Evaluation Museum,** the only facility in the country for testing naval aircraft. Vintage aircraft are parked alongside automobiles in the front lot, among them an imposing 25-ton twin-turboprop Hawkeye. Indoors, visitors are welcome to climb into an F-4 cockpit procedures trainer. An exhibit on contraptions that failed their tests includes the improbable Goodyear Inflatoplane: One of the portable rubber aircraft, fully inflated, is on display. The museum shop stocks a wide assortment of airplane models and accessories. *Rte. 235, Three Notch Rd., Lexington Park, tel. 301/863–7418. Admission free. Open Fri.–Sat. 11–4, Sun. noon–5.*

25 **Point Lookout,** at the farthest tip of the peninsula, about 20 miles south of Lexington Park, was the site of a Union prison during the Civil War. The prison was so placed because of the point's convenient location, just across the Potomac River from the Confederate state of Virginia. Conditions in the penitentiary evidently fell short of the standards of the much later Geneva Convention, for nearly 3,500 Confederate soldiers died here in the last two years of the conflict. All that remain of the prison are some earthen fortifications, partially rebuilt, known as Fort Lincoln. Park attendants and psychics report sightings of Confederate soldiers who, they believe, were imprisoned here. On the approach on Route 5, two memorial obelisks remind vacationers of the bloody background of this place, and a small museum within the park supplies some of the details. Today the place has resumed its antebellum function as a recreational area; the 500-acre state park offers camping and boating facilities, nature trails, and a beach for swimming. The RV campground, with hook-ups, is open year-round; tent camping facilities close in winter months. *Rte. 5, Point Lookout, tel. 301/872–5688. Admission free. Park open 8 AM–11 PM. Museum open Apr.–Memorial Day and Labor Day–Oct., weekends 10–6; Memorial Day–Labor Day, daily 10–6.*

26 The pre-Revolutionary plantation of **St. Inigoes** has been displaced by a naval installation, but nearby (watch for the signs on Route 5) survives **St. Ignatius Church,** built in 1758 by Roman Catholics (Maryland's first settlers were Catholics, and the 1649 Toleration Act guaranteed religious freedom in the colony). A church dating to the 1630s had stood on the same spot; the graveyard is one of the oldest in the United States. Several veterans of the Revolution are buried here, alongside Jesuit priests who served at this church named for the founder of their society. To see inside the church, ask for the key at the sentry box of the naval installation next door. *Villa Rd., off Rte. 5, St. Inigoes, tel. 410/863–2149. Admission by contribution. Open daily 9–4.*

㉗ Historic **St. Mary's City** is Maryland's birthplace: It was here in 1634, on St. Clement's Island, that its first colonists stepped ashore and celebrated a thanksgiving mass under Father Andrew White. Here, too, the first act of religious tolerance in the New World was enacted, guaranteeing the freedom to practice whatever religion one chose. The settlement served as Maryland's capital city until 1695, when the legislature moved to Annapolis. The county seat was then moved to Leonardtown, and St. Mary's City practically disappeared from the maps. Fortunately, in the early 1970s, a vast archaeological/reconstruction program began. A project that was in its early days carried out in earnest has to date revealed nearly 200 individual sites that have been explored or are in the process of rediscovery. The entire 800-plus acres have become a living-history museum, and although the city is less well known than Virginia's Williamsburg, its project is no less ambitious. *Rte. 5, tel. 301/862–0990. Admission: $5 adults, $2 children. Open late Mar.–late Nov., Wed.–Sun. 10–5.*

The historic complex includes several notable restored buildings. The **State House of 1676,** like its larger and grander counterpart in Williamsburg, has an upper and a lower chamber for the corresponding houses of parliament. This is a 1934 reproduction, based on contemporary documents; the original was dismantled in 1829 to provide bricks for Trinity Church nearby. The small square-rigged ship docked behind the State House is a reproduction of the *Maryland Dove,* one of two vessels (the other being the *Ark*) that conveyed the original settlers from England. The nearby **Farthing's Ordinary** is a reconstructed inn.

The lives of the colonists' predecessors are being re-created at the **Chancellor's Point** area of the complex, where an authentic woodland Indian longhouse has been constructed. A nature trail winds through the marshes, woods, and beaches of 66 acres.

The **Godiah Spray Tobacco Plantation** is named for a fictional planter. The Spray family and its indentured servants are portrayed by interpreters who enlist visitors in such daily household chores as cooking and gardening or in working the tobacco field. The buildings, including the main dwelling house and outbuildings, were constructed with period tools and techniques.

Also part of the city is **St. Mary's College,** an intimate state-run, liberal arts school that, among other roles, functions as the cultural center for the surrounding community. The institution boasts a peaceful campus that overlooks the St. Mary's River (which feeds into the Chesapeake Bay) and makes a delightful place for a picnic, especially in fall or spring when the humidity level is low and the breeze blows off the water. In summer you can sunbathe along the beach and watch sailboarders catching crosswinds from the Bay. Although the river is warm and safe for swimming, beware of sea nettles that lurk below the water's surface. Their sting can be quite painful.

What to See and Do with Children

Battle Creek Cypress Swamp Sanctuary, Calvert County
Calvert Cliffs Nuclear Power Plant, Lusby

Calvert Cliffs State Park, Lusby
Calvert Marine Museum, Solomons
Flag Ponds Nature Park, St. Leonard
Jefferson Patterson Park and Museum, St. Leonard
St. Mary's City, St. Mary's County
Naval Air Test and Evaluation Museum, Lexington Park
United States Naval Academy, Annapolis

Off the Beaten Track

About 8 miles south of Annapolis (via Rte. 2, on Mayo Rd.), at Edge-water on the South River, is the **Londontowne Publick House,** an 18th-century inn and terminus to a ferry route to Annapolis. It's the only remaining building of a once thriving community and is fur-nished as it might have looked during that period. There are more than 10 acres of landscaped and wooded gardens, in addition to themed walks, including a Spring Flower Walk and an American Wildflower Walk. A few picnic tables are on the premises, and cater-ing is available for special functions, but otherwise visitors must bring their own provisions. *839 Londontown Rd., Edgewater, tel. 410/222–1919. Admission: $5 adults, $3.50 senior citizens and stu-dents, $2.50 children 6–18 years. Open Mar.–Dec., Tues.–Sat. 10–4. Sun. noon–4.*

Shopping

Shopping Districts and Malls

Annapolis Mall (109 Annapolis Mall, Annapolis 21401, tel. 410/841–6111) presents more than 125 clothing and shoe stores, home design and appliance centers, audio and video outlets, boutiques, general merchandise department stores, and restaurants.

Downtown Annapolis offers fun shopping, including arts and crafts, funky and foolish fashion, home decor, whimsical junk, outdoor ap-parel, clothing and necessities for salts and would-be sailors, and, of course, souvenirs.

Antiques

Annapolis Antique Gallery (2009 West St., Annapolis, tel. 410/266–0635) is a consortium of 20 dealers with an inventory that ranges from Victorian to art deco.

Ron Snyder Antiques specializes in 18th- and 19th-century American furniture displayed in seven tastefully decorated rooms. *2011 West St., Annapolis, tel. 410/266–5452. Open Tues.–Sun.*

Furniture Barn (Rte. 2/4, Solomons, tel. 301/326–4575) shows and sells the handiwork of the Amish community, reproductions of their own distinctive furniture.

Grandmother's (Dowell Rd., Dowell, tel. 301/326–3366) showcases restored trunks and country oak furniture; its branch store, **Grand-mothers II** (Solomons Island Rd., Solomons, tel. 301/326–6848), is in a complex of similar shops at Harmon House.

Sports and Outdoor Activities

Participant Sports

Bicycling   Ten different waterproof and tear-proof maps of the "Best Bike Routes in Maryland" are available for $9.95 each, or $29.95 for the set from Box 16388, Baltimore 21210, tel. 800/394–3626, or from most bike shops.

The Baltimore & Annapolis Trail (Earleigh Heights Rd., Severna Park, tel. 410/222–6244) runs through 13 miles of farmland, forests, urban, and suburban neighborhoods from Annapolis to Glen Burnie. It follows the old Baltimore & Annapolis Railroad and is open sunrise to sunset to hikers, bikers, runners, and rollerbladers. **Pedal Pushers Bike Shop** (546 Baltimore and Annapolis Blvd., Severna Park, tel. 410/544–2323) rents bikes for the B&A Trail.

Cycle 90 (Solomons Island Rd., Solomons, tel. 301/326–2864) and **Mike's Bikes** (447 Great Mills Rd., Lexington Park, tel. 301/863–7887) rent bicycles.

Point Lookout State Park and **St. Mary's City** are both perfect for biking; in northern St. Mary's County, around Mechanicsville, the roads have wide shoulders to accommodate the horse-drawn vehicles of the Amish and Mennonite communities.

Fishing   **Anglers** (435 Revel Hwy., Annapolis, tel. 301/757–3442) sells and rents fishing equipment.

Chesapeake Bay Sportfishing and Charters (Box 304, Deale 20751, tel. 410/867–4101 or 800/675–4103) offers sportfishing trips, customized yacht charters (power or sail), and Chesapeake Bay excursions. Charters can be designed for any size group.

"Samuel Middleton" Fishing Charters (2 Market Space, Annapolis 21401, tel. 410/263–3323) charters a vintage Chesapeake Bay fishing boat for a day (or half-day) jaunt on the bay. Later, you can have your catch prepared at the Middleton Tavern, which overlooks the harbor.

There is a pier at **Flag Ponds Nature Park** (*see* Southern Maryland in Exploring, *above*); anglers under 16 years of age do not need a license here.

Fishing is no longer permitted from the bulkhead in **Solomons**; anglers must charter sailboats or rent smaller vessels with outboard motors. **Bunky's Charter Boats** (Solomons Island Rd., Solomons, tel. 301/326–3241) can provide them.

Scheibels (Wynne Rd., Ridge, south of Lexington Park, tel. 301/872–5185) sends out groups on "head boats" for fishing in the bay.

Golf   **Eisenhower Golf Course** (Generals Hwy., Crownsville, tel. 410/222–7922), northwest of Annapolis; **Twin Shields Golf Club** (Rte. 260, Dunkirk, tel. 301/257–7800), northwest of Chesapeake Beach; and **Breton Bay Country Club** (Rte. 243, tel. 301/475–2300), southwest of Leonardtown, have 18-hole golf courses.

Health and Fitness Clubs   **Merritt Health and Fitness Center** (1981 Moreland Pkwy., Annapolis, tel. 410/263–5400) offers a three-visit membership for $5 to guests at any Annapolis hotel. Facilities include Nautilus and

Stairmaster equipment, stationary bicycles, racquetball and squash courts, and whirlpools.

Swimming **Arundel Olympic Swim Center** features an outstanding facility that includes an indoor 50-meter by 23-meter swimming pool, large spa, wading pool, and two 1-meter diving boards. Disabled accessible. *Riva Rd., Annapolis, tel. 410/222–7933. Open daily. Call for hours.*

Tennis The Annapolis Department of Parks and Recreation (tel. 410/263–7958) maintains six lighted courts at **Truxton Park** (Forest Dr. and Hilltop La.) and 10 lighted courts at **Annapolis High School** (Riva Rd.).

The Calvert County Department of Parks and Recreation (tel. 301/535–1600) supervises four courts at **Hollowing Point Park** (Rte. 231, Prince Frederick), four courts at **Dunkirk Park** (Rte. 4, Dunkirk), and four lighted courts at **Cove Point Park** (Rte. 765, Lusby).

Water Sports In Annapolis, **N.E.W. Highspire Yacht Services** (306 2nd St., Annapolis, tel. 410/263–2838) and **Paradise Bay Yacht Charters** (410 Severn Ave., Annapolis, tel. 410/268–9330 or 800/877–9330) offer well-maintained sail and power yachts. Captained and bareboat charters are available for a day, weekend, week, or longer.

Zanhiser's Sailing Center, in Solomons (C St. at Back Creek, tel. 410/326–2166), and **Scheibel's,** in Ridge (Wynne Rd., tel. 301/872–5185), south of Lexington Park, will arrange yacht charters.

Sailing Instruction **Annapolis Sailing School** (601 Sixth St., Annapolis, tel. 410/267–7205) is "America's oldest and largest sailing school," where the inexperienced can take a two-hour basic lesson. In addition, live-aboard, cruising, and advanced-sailing programs are available, as are boat rentals. **Womanship** (Boathouse, 410 Severn Ave., Annapolis, tel. 410/267–6661 or 800/342–9295) is the sailing program *by* women, *for* women, at all levels of experience.

Spectator Sports

The **United States Naval Academy Athletic Association (NAAA)** (ticket office, tel. 410/268–6060) offers 33 varsity sports, most notably football. The team plays home games in the fall at the Navy-Marine Corps Stadium on Rowe Boulevard in Annapolis. You can enjoy the excitement and tradition of Navy sports from fall through spring.

Boat Races **Annapolis Yacht Club** (tel. 410/263–9279) sponsors sailboat races at 6:30 PM each Wednesday in July and August in Annapolis Harbor, starting at the Eastport bridge.

Zanhiser's Sailing Center (tel. 410/326–2166) has details of the annual powerboat and sailing-yacht races that are held at Solomons in August.

Jousting The **Amateur Jousting Club of Maryland** (Box 367, Glen Arm 21057, tel. 410/592–5952) can provide details on about 48 jousting tournaments and events that take place from April through November. The longest-running tournament of the state sport is held the last Saturday in August at Christ Episcopal Church in Port Republic.

Beaches

Anne Arundel County has **Sandy Point State Park** (Rte. 50, 12 mi east of Annapolis, tel. 410/974–2149), with a mile of beach for fishing and swimming, 22 launching ramps for boats, rock jetties extending into the bay, and a fishing pier.

Dining and Lodging

Dinner reservations in Annapolis are recommended throughout the summer and at times of Naval Academy events. Hotel reservations are necessary, even a year in advance, during the sailboat and powerboat shows in October and Naval Academy commencement in May. The restaurants of Calvert and St. Mary's counties in southern Maryland offer excellent opportunities to experience local seafood dishes. Be certain to sample the famous St. Mary's County stuffed ham.

Highly recommended establishments are indicated by a star ★.

Annapolis
Dining

The Corinthian. This is one of the most formal dining rooms in Annapolis, yet the ambience is in keeping with the town's prevailing resort air. Candlelight and piped-in classical music accompany a cheerful waiter's recitation of the day's specials. The distinctive crab cakes are made with angel-hair pasta as binder. All beef is dry-aged three weeks, including the New York strip steak and the filet mignon. This is also the place for an elegant breakfast any morning of the week. *Loews Annapolis Hotel, 126 West St., tel. 410/263–1299. Reservations advised. Jacket and tie advised. AE, DC, MC, V. $$$*

Harry Browne's. This elegant dining room sits quietly across from Maryland's statehouse and is a popular place for entertaining special guests and friends. Featuring attentive service and Continental cuisine, Harry Browne's is especially busy during the legislative session (mid-January–late March) and during June Week at the Naval Academy. In the lounge, there's entertainment ('70s and '80s music) Thursday–Sunday, and jazz on Monday nights. *66 State Circle, tel. 410/263–4332. Reservations advised. Dress: casual. MC, V. $$$*

Middleton's Tavern. This waterfront building has served as a tavern since it was built in 1750. The present chef, a 40-year veteran, long ago perfected his own rich version of crab imperial, called crab Middleton, and his heavy Cuban black-bean soup is a rare treat in this neighborhood. Decor and furnishings are vaguely Colonial; at night the wood tables bear blue-and-white-check tablecloths. In winter the fireplaces are alight in all four dining rooms. In the warmer months, three dozen tables are set up under an awning out front, yards from the City Dock, where diners can watch the lively stream of pedestrian traffic. Acoustic pop music is performed nightly in the Oyster Bar lounge. Upstairs on Friday and Saturday a piano player takes requests for standard favorites (*see* Nightlife, *below*). *2 Market Space, tel. 410/263–3323. Reservations advised. Dress: casual. MC, D, V. $$$*

The Treaty of Paris. Named for the agreement that concluded the American War of Independence, this restaurant is situated on the ground floor of the 200-year-old Maryland Inn. Brick-hearth fireplaces and vintage prints create a historical ambience in the three dining rooms, yet the cuisine is quite contemporary. Recent entrées were sautéed duck breast, dressed with raspberry and shallots; and chicken breast Normandy (prepared in applejack brandy with Brie, scallions, and white mushroom sauce). A house gazpacho is heavy with seafood and suitably spicy. Mussels, shrimp, scallops, oysters, and clams atop fettuccine are in turn covered with a rich chardonnay sauce. Adjoining the smallest dining room is the **King of France Tavern,** a small bistro where jazz and folk music are performed Thursday through Monday nights. Jazz guitarist Charlie Byrd is often featured here. Breakfast is served, as well. *Maryland Inn, 16*

Church Circle, tel. 410/263–2641. Reservations advised. Jacket and tie advised. AE, DC, MC, V. $$$

Buddy's Crabs and Ribs. In Annapolis, this has become the place to relax and "crack crabs." Featuring Chesapeake Bay steamed hard crabs, this family restaurant and raw bar is a casual spot for enjoying the local lifestyle. Buddy's serves dinner, a daily luncheon buffet, and a popular Sunday brunch. *100 Main St., tel. 410/626–1100. Reservations not necessary. Dress: casual. AE, MC, DC, V. $$*

Marmaduke's Pub. Across the drawbridge in the Eastport section of Annapolis, this watering hole is a favorite among sailors and hamburger-lovers. This is a pub in every sense of the word: You might find yourself next to a mariner on an around-the-world trip, or a government official. Tuesday night is Darts Night. If you enjoy Broadway musical hits, pay a visit on Friday or Saturday night for the sing-along (*see* Nightlife, *below*). Local Wednesday-evening sailing races are videotaped and shown here afterwards—allowing some claims to be upheld, while briefly bruising some windy egos. *301 Severn Ave., tel. 410/269–5420. Reservations not necessary. Dress: casual. AE, DC, MC, V. $$*

McGarvey's Saloon and Oyster Bar. This casual, fun spot, situated just a block from the Annapolis dock, offers excellent East Coast seafood, steaks, burgers, interesting specials, and finger food. The full menu is available daily until 1 AM. *8 Market Space, tel. 410/263–5700. Reservations accepted. Dress: casual. AE, MC, V. $$*

Lodging **Annapolis Marriott Waterfront.** The most comfortable vantage points for enjoying the bustle of City Dock are the 20 private balconies in this waterfront luxury hotel. The other, less expensive rooms also look out on the water or over the Annapolis historic district. Most guests are business travelers and conventioneers, and hotel services are oriented to them, with exercise equipment reserved for occupants of concierge-level (top-floor) rooms. The lively outdoor bar at the water's edge is especially popular on summer nights. *80 Compromise St., 21401, tel. 410/268–7555, 800/336–0072, or 800/228–9290. 150 rooms. Facilities: restaurant, 2 bars. AE, D, DC, MC, V. $$$$*

★ **Governor Calvert House.** The original brick structure, built in 1727 on property owned by Charles Calvert, second governor of Maryland, was expanded in the 19th century to become the mayor's residence, then more extensively in 1986 to serve as a full-service, intermediate-size hotel—large for an inn, small for the well-equipped conference center it is. The Colonial and Victorian era rooms are furnished in period antiques, the modern additions with quality reproductions. Governor Calvert House is also the registration desk for three other neighboring properties of Historic Inns of Annapolis: Robert Johnson House, with 30 rooms; State House Inn, with nine rooms, three of them "Jacuzzi suites"; and Maryland Inn, with 44 rooms, a restaurant, a tavern, a wine bar (and breakfast not included). *58 State Circle, 21401, tel. 410/263–2641 or 800/847–8882. 51 rooms. AE, DC, MC, V. Rates include Continental breakfast. $$$$*

Loews Annapolis Hotel. Because of the hotel's distance, six blocks from City Dock, it offers a panorama of downtown and the water from rooms (with balconies) on the top two floors. All rooms have been completely refurnished and redecorated with wallpapers in bright, flowery patterns; guest quarters come in more than a dozen sizes and shapes, at various prices, but each has a desk and a bathroom phone. Business travelers are a large proportion of the guests here, and the hotel's conference center—in a converted railroad powerhouse next door—and fitness facilities are provided with the business traveler in mind. *126 West St., 21401, tel. 410/263-7777 or 800/223-0888. 220 rooms. Facilities: 2 restaurants, bar, Nautilus, aerobics workout room, whirlpool. AE, DC, MC, V. $$$$*

Gibson's Lodgings. Three detached houses stand together on the other side of a fence from the United States Naval Academy. Although one formal dining room here is equipped for gatherings of up to 50, the inn's character is predominantly that of bed-and-breakfast intimacy. Furnishings of the guest rooms and common rooms reflect a harmoniously eclectic taste, with brass and wood beds suited to their respective rooms. A hallway lined with mirrors is a striking feature. The most unusual room is the first-floor room designed for disabled access, with a specially equipped bathroom and a small private porch. Six other rooms have private bath, TV, and phone. Free parking in the courtyard is a big advantage in the heart of a small city with heavy traffic. *110–114 Prince George St., 21401, tel. 410/ 268-5555. 20 rooms, 7 with bath; 2 suites. Facilities: conference space, parking. AE, MC, V. Rates include Continental breakfast. $$*

★ **Prince George Inn.** This three-story brick Italianate Victorian town house was built in 1884. The rooms, all of which share baths, are similarly decorated in antiques of the period, and one room is distinguished by a bay window. All rooms face the street, with views of either Prince George Street or, beyond neighboring yards, Maryland Avenue, but traffic noise is inconsiderable at night. An unusually large breakfast buffet, with home-baked pies or tarts, is served on either of two glassed-in porches or in the gazebo in the garden. *232 Prince George St., 21401, tel. 410/263-6418. 4 rooms. MC, V. Closed Jan.–mid-Feb. Rates include breakfast. $$*

William Page Inn. Built in 1908, the dark brown, cedar-shingle, wood-frame structure was the local Democratic party clubhouse for 50 years. Today its wraparound porch is furnished with Adirondack chairs, and among the period antiques indoors are appropriate Victorian reproductions. All rooms have a queen-size bed and no phone; only the sloped-ceiling third-floor suite with dormer windows and an Italian-marble bathroom with Jacuzzi has TV. Guests in two rooms walk out into the hall to reach a bathroom. Breakfast is served in the common room. *8 Martin St., 21401, tel. 410/626-1506. 4 rooms, 2 with bath; 1 suite. AE, MC, V. Rates include Continental breakfast. $$*

Calvert County Dining

Lighthouse Inn. The first-floor dining room has a view of Solomons Harbor on Back Creek; from the nearly floor-to-ceiling windows of the second floor, diners look onto the creek toward the Patuxent River. Indoors, the polished wood tables are illuminated by gas lanterns, and the ceiling beams have been exposed and the floors carpeted. The chef seasons his crab cakes following a recipe that is closely guarded in the competitive crab market. The catch of the day, which can take inventive form, is frequently sautéed. In the warm months, the harbor can be watched from the partially covered "quarterdeck," where lighter fare is served. *Solomons Island Rd., Solomons, tel. 410/326-2444. Reservations advised. Dress: casual. AE, D, DC, MC, V. No lunch Mon.–Fri. Lunch outdoors on weekends, weather permitting. $$$*

Old Field Inn. This wood-frame house was built in 1885 by a branch of the Briscoe family that once owned Sotterley Plantation in St. Mary's County. In two of the three dining rooms, Oriental rugs lie on wood floors; the tables in all three rooms have linen cloths and candlelight in the evening. Veal Oscar puts a local resource to effective use: Sautéed crabmeat enhances the veal, along with asparagus and béarnaise sauce. Standouts in the seafood sampler—an appetizer prepared for two—are clams casino (with bacon, cheese, and vegetables), stuffed mushroom caps, fried crab balls, and fried shrimp. *485 Main St., Prince Frederick, tel. 410/535–1054. Reservations advised. Dress: casual but neat. AE, D, MC, V. No lunch weekends. $$$*

Solomons Crabhouse. The long, narrow dining room of this converted firehouse is typically packed with boaters, anglers, local residents, and vacationers, many of them smashing hard-shell crabs with knockers (wood mallets) and pouring from pitchers of cold beer as country-and-western music booms from the stereo. Crab legs, another specialty, are served with shrimp; a captain's serving is two pounds of crab and one of shrimp, and a mate's serving is half that. *Rte. 2/4, Solomons, tel. 410/326–2800. Reservations advised. Dress: casual. AE, MC, V. No lunch Mon.–Thurs. $$$*

Solomons Pier. Because this restaurant sits on a pier in the Patuxent River, a place at any one of the bare wood tables enjoys a good view of the water. The ample steamed platter combines lobster, mussels, oysters, clams, and shrimp. Lobster may also be ordered stuffed with crab imperial. For lunch, sample the cheesy crab quiche; at dinnertime ask for Miss Elva's well-known almond shrimp. The dance floor is in the dining room, and on weekends a DJ spins light rock-and-roll oldies and light contemporaries (*see* Nightlife, *below*). *Solomons Island Rd., Solomons, tel. 410/326–2424. Reservations advised. Dress: casual but neat. AE, D, DC, MC, V. $$$*

Penwick House. You'll get the feeling that you've entered another time zone when you visit Audrey Davenport's Penwick House. Glowing candlelight, fresh flowers, Oriental rugs, waiters in historic costumes, a garden and an enclosed patio, and a fireplace offer an atmosphere that almost equals the food. Enjoy the heritage that embodies Maryland cuisine, which includes hearty soups, fresh seafood, beef, pork, and chicken cooked in southern-Maryland style. Along with your entrée, try the pumpkin muffins, and after your meal at least share one of the homemade desserts. The Sunday brunch (10:30–2) has become a local tradition. *Rte. 4, Pennsylvania Ave. extended at Ferry Landing Rd., Dunkirk, tel. 301/855–5388 or 410/257–7077. Reservations advised. Dress: casual. AE, D, MC, V. Closed Mon. $$*

Lodging
★ **Back Creek Inn.** Behind this wood-frame house built by a waterman in 1890 are an outdoor deck and a Jacuzzi; beyond that the lawn leads to the very edge of Back Creek. A cottage on the grounds holds a one-bedroom apartment, and an extension to the main house completed in 1986 contains two suites. In the guest rooms colorful quilts cover the beds, three of which are brass. Three rooms enjoy views of either the Patuxent or Back Creek; the others face the garden or a quiet street. The suites and the cottage have TV. *Calvert and A/Alexander Sts., Solomons 20688, tel. 410/326–2022. 4 rooms, 1 with bath; 2 suites; 1 cottage. Facilities: Jacuzzi. No credit cards. Closed Dec.–Feb. $$*

Davis House. On the Back Creek side of narrow Solomons Island stands this three-story, white wood-frame house built by a local seafood magnate in 1906 and operated as a bed-and-breakfast since 1985. Two rooms look onto the creek, and four face the yard. All are furnished with period antiques and reproductions in comparable proportions, and each room features an ornate armoire; none has phone or TV. On weekends, a very large breakfast—almost a brunch—is served in the formal dining room, on the screened porch, or in the garden, as guests prefer and weather permits. *Charles and Maltby Sts., Box 759, Solomons 20688, tel. 410/326–4811. 7 rooms, 5 with bath. MC, V. Closed Dec.–Jan. Rates include breakfast. $$*

Holiday Inn Conference Center and Marina. The five-story waterfront hotel, built in 1987, was enlarged in 1990 and all its rooms remodeled. Each guest has a water view (if you count the swimming pool); rooms look onto the cove, the open creek, or the courtyard. The facility was designed to accommodate plenty of convention and meeting business, and it provides the snazziest amenities, including whirlpools in some suites. Rooms here are heavily booked, so early reservations are advised. *155 Holiday Rd., Box 1099, Solomons 20688, tel. 410/326–6311 or 800/356–2009. 326 rooms. Facilities: restaurant, 2 bars, outdoor pool, 2 tennis courts, Nautilus equipment, sauna. AE, D, DC, MC, V. $$*

St. Mary's County Dining

★ **Evans Seafood.** Diners select live lobsters, which may then be stuffed with crab imperial, lightly breaded crabmeat with a white-wine-and-cream sauce. Seafood imperial combines crab, scallops, and shrimp in a similar manner. Hard-shell crabs and crab soup are made with spicy recipes that are jealously guarded. This waterside restaurant is a major regional attraction where an hour-long wait for dinner is not unusual (reservations are not accepted for groups of fewer than 10). Waiting diners have a beer and stroll along the seawall or the 300-foot pier. Inside seating includes some water views—but two of the four dining rooms face the parking lot. *Rte. 249, Piney Point, tel. 301/994–2299. Reservations required for 10 or more. Dress: casual. MC, V. No lunch weekdays. Closed Mon. $$*

The Reluctant Navigator. It's no surprise to the visitor to find that this restaurant, with its casually dressed diners seated before linen tablecloths in a wood-paneled dining room with a fireplace, has the atmosphere of a yacht club. After all, there may be as many as 200 sailboats docked outside. Crab cakes fare well here against a formidable regional competition, and Sunday brunch is a lively occasion. When the restaurant is closed in the winter, the bar remains open and serves an abbreviated menu. *Potomac View Farm, Rte. 249, Tall Timbers, tel. 301/994–1508. Reservations advised. Dress: casual. AE, MC, V. Closed Dec.–Feb. $$*

★ **Spinnakers Restaurant at Point Lookout Marina.** Established by former students from St. Mary's College, this burgeoning restaurant has brought all the best of southern Maryland to the shores of Smith Creek. When partners John Spinnichia (a.k.a. "Spinach") and Michael Gould aren't in the kitchen baking bread or cooking what *Nightline* commentator Ted Koppel has called "the world's best gold-medal crab cakes," they're probably behind the bar mixing drink specials such as Outriggers (peach schnapps and orange juice) and Russian Quaaludes (coffee liqueur, cream, and Irish whiskey). Contributing to Spinnakers's friendly atmosphere are the subdued lighting, fresh flowers, and linen-covered tables, but really it's the genuinely enthusiastic staff that makes dining here such a comfortable experience. When in season, the soft-shell crabs caught fresh from the creek outside are a sure bet, especially when complemented by a glass of wine from Catoctin Vineyards, in the mountains in Maryland. Leave enough room for a homemade dessert—rum raisin should be one of your choices. Sunday brunch here has fast become a tradition. *Point Lookout Marina, 32 Millers Wharf Rd., Ridge, tel. 310/872–4340. Reservations recommended. Dress: casual. D, DC, MC, V. Closed Tues. No lunch. $$*

Lodging

Patuxent Inn. This three-story hotel, built in 1982 on an overdeveloped strip of Route 235 near the Patuxent Naval Air Test Center, is charming compared with its surroundings—and the best equipped of its impersonal type in St. Mary's County. Guest rooms are furnished with mock-Colonial furniture, and their windows face either the highway or the woods in back. Many guests are those with business at the air base, and that tends to keep rates to the government's per diem level. Since the mood here is hardly that of a resort, it's a surprise to find a pair of lighted tennis courts, a jogging trail, and a pool. *Rte. 235, Box 778, Lexington Park 20653, tel. 301/862–4100. 120 rooms. Facilities: restaurant, bar, outdoor pool, 2 tennis courts, jogging trail. AE, DC, MC, V. $$*

★ **Potomac View Farm.** Construction of this white wood-frame "telescope" house (built in progressively smaller sections) began in 1830. This is emphatically a farmhouse, not a manor, and it is furnished accordingly with handsome but simple oak furniture and decorative quilts. Yet there are elegant touches in some rooms, such as the 10-foot ceilings with crown moldings. Whimsical folk touches include a life-size wooden cow in the living room. One of the restored outbuildings, originally the gardener's cottage, is now a room with its own bath. A one-bedroom kitchenette apartment attached to the main house but entered through a separate door also has its own bath. The remaining rooms share five baths, so there is rarely a wait. As its name suggests, the inn sits by the water on working farmland: 120 acres planted with corn and soybeans. The proprietors also operate the marina, where terrestrial arrivals may arrange excursion charters. *Rte. 249, Tall Timbers 20690, tel. 301/994–0419. 6 rooms, 1 cottage. Facilities: restaurant, bar, outdoor pool, beach, 200 boat slips, gas dock, boat-launching ramp. AE, MC, V. Rates include full breakfast. $$*

The Arts and Nightlife

The Arts

Music **Annapolis City Dock** is the scene of free summertime concerts; the **U.S. Naval Academy Band** (tel. 410/267–2291) performs on Tuesday evening, and the **Starlight Series** (tel. 410/280–1247) takes place on Sunday evening.

Theater **Maryland Shakespeare Festival** is part of the Chesapeake Summer Arts Festival at **St. Mary's College** (tel. 301/862–0243) in St. Mary's City.

When the **Colonial Players** (108 East St., Annapolis, tel. 410/268–7373) go on vacation, **Annapolis Summer Garden Theater** (Compromise and Main Sts., tel. 410/268–0809) takes over, staging the same mix of musicals and plays, including occasional works by local authors.

Nightlife

Dancing At **Solomons Pier** (Solomons Island Rd., Solomons, tel. 410/326–2424) a DJ spins pop tunes of the 1960s and 1970s and lighter recent hits.

Jazz **King of France Tavern** (16 Church Circle, Annapolis, tel. 410/263–2641) sees bands jam from 9 PM on Monday.

Middleton's Tavern (At The City Dock, Annapolis, tel. 410/263–3323) features live acoustical music nightly at the upstairs bar; on Sunday nights from 7 to 10 join the Sunday Blues.

Folk **King of France Tavern** (16 Church Circle, Annapolis, tel. 410/263–2641) hosts folk performances from 9 PM on Thursday.

Piano Bar **Vera's White Sands** (Rte. 4, Lusby, tel. 410/586–1182) has a comfortable lounge overlooking the St. Leonard's Creek marina.

Sing-along **Marmaduke's Pub** (3rd and Severn Sts., Eastport, Annapolis, tel. 410/269–5420) has a sing-along in its upstairs pub on Friday and Saturday nights.

10 Maryland's Eastern Shore

THERE IS NO LIFE WEST OF THE CHESAPEAKE BAY reads the bumper sticker on a pickup truck crossing the Chesapeake Bay Bridge to Maryland's Eastern Shore. You need to spend only a little time in this region to understand that it is a unique area whose natives truly are cut from a different cloth: They're committed to their land and their bay, and are fiercely independent people (yet dependent on the bay). Most, in fact, would probably not be too disappointed if the counties east of the bay were to secede from the state, and many have never ventured off this peninsula.

Captain John Smith, who explored the Chesapeake Bay region in 1607–8, may have expressed it best when he noted in his diary that "Heaven and earth never agreed better to frame a place for man's habitation . . . truly a delightsome land." Of the bay's resources he recorded, "That abundance of fish, lying so thicke with their heads above the water as for want of nets . . . we attempted to catch them with a frying pan . . ."

The Chesapeake Bay—in actuality, the drowned valley of the Susquehanna River, which before the last ice age flowed directly into the Atlantic Ocean—is unquestionably Maryland's major natural resource, the focal point of an immense seafood, shipping, and recreational industry. It's the largest estuary in the United States and one of the most productive bodies of water in the world. Comprising 3,237 square miles, the bay is 195 miles long—if straightened, the shoreline would reach from Baltimore to Honolulu, with a few hundred miles to spare—and 37.5 miles across at its widest point, near the mouth of the Potomac River. At the William Preston Lane Jr. Memorial Bridges, its narrowest point, it is but 4 miles across.

In addition to the Chesapeake Bay, the Eastern Shore offers beautiful historic towns and fishing villages that have little changed over the years, and a distinctive shore hospitality unequaled in most other East Coast regions. The long, flat roads with nicely paved shoulders provide a good surface for long bike rides and exploring, and there are numerous cozy bed-and-breakfasts posted between towns. Also, there's Ocean City, an ever-growing, flamboyant Atlantic resort town, as well as more modest hamlets with good quiet beaches.

Essential Information

Important Addresses and Numbers

Visitor Information
Caroline County Commissioner's Office (Box 207, Denton 21629, tel. 410/479–0660).

Dorchester County Tourism (501 Court La., Room 103, Cambridge 21613, tel. 410/228–1000 or 800/522–TOUR, fax 410/228–1563).

Kent County Chamber of Commerce (118 N. Cross St., Box 146, Chestertown 21620, tel. 410/778–0416).

Ocean City Tourism Office (4001 Coastal Hwy., Ocean City 21842, tel. 410/289–8311 or 800/OC–OCEAN).

Somerset County Tourism (Box 243, Princess Anne 21853, tel. 410/651–2968 or 800/521–9189).

Talbot County Chamber of Commerce (805 Goldsborough St., Box 1366, Easton 21601, tel. 410/822–4606).

Wicomico County Convention & Visitors Bureau (Civic Center, 500 Glen Ave., Salisbury 21801, tel. 410/548–4914).

Worcester County Tourism (105 Pearl St., Box 208, Snow Hill 21863, tel. 410/632–3617).

Emergencies Throughout the region, dial 911 for emergency assistance.

Hospitals **Dorchester General Hospital** (300 Byrn St., Cambridge, tel. 410/228–5511).
Easton Memorial Hospital (219 S. Washington St., Easton, tel. 410/822–1000).
Peninsula General Hospital (100 E. Carroll St., Salisbury, tel. 410/543–7101).

Late-night **CVS Pharmacy** (11905 Coastal Hwy., Ocean City, tel. 410/524–5101)
Pharmacies is open daily until 9 in winter and daily until 10 in summer.
Rite-Aid Drugs (94th St. and Ocean Hwy., Ocean City, tel. 410/723–2425) is open until 9 PM, 10 PM Memorial Day–Labor Day.

Arriving and Departing

By Plane **Cambridge/Dorchester Airport** (tel. 410/228–4571) is 3 miles east of Cambridge on Bucktown Road. **Easton Municipal Airport** (tel. 410/822–8560), 2 miles north of Easton on Route 50, is served by **Maryland Airlines** (tel. 410/822–0400) from Baltimore-Washington International Airport. Other services are offered by **Easton Jet** (tel. 410/820–8770) and **East Coast Flight Services** (tel. 410/820–6633).

Ocean City Airport (tel. 410/289–0927) is 6 miles southwest of Ocean City on Route 611.

Salisbury-Wicomico Regional Airport (tel. 410/548–4827), 5 miles north of Salisbury off Route 50, is served by **USAir** (tel. 800/428–4322).

By Car To reach the Eastern Shore from Baltimore or Washington, D.C., cross the Chesapeake Bay by the toll bridge (toll collected eastbound only, $2.50) northeast of Annapolis; continue on U.S. 50, a divided four-lane highway in good repair with a 55 mph speed limit. A car is indispensable for touring the Eastern Shore, except within Ocean City—and even there it's your most effective means of transportation.

By Bus **Greyhound Lines** (tel. 800/231–2222) makes several runs daily in both directions between Baltimore or Washington and Easton (FastStop Convenience Store, Rte. 50, 2 miles north of town, opposite airport, tel. 410/822–3333), Cambridge (501 Maryland Ave., tel. 410/228–4626), Salisbury (350 Cypress St., tel. 410/749–4121), and Ocean City (2nd St. and Coastal Hwy. at the Rte. 50 bridge, tel. 410/289–9307).

Getting Around Ocean City

By Bus **"The Bus"** (tel. 410/723–1607) travels the 10 miles of Coastal Highway 24 hours a day with service about every 10 minutes. Bus-stop signs are posted every other block, and there are shelters at most locations. A $1 ticket is good for 24 hours.

Guided Tours

Orientation The **Historical Society of Talbot County** (Box 964, 25 S. Washington St., Easton 21601, tel. 410/822–0773) offers walking tours of the town's historic district.

Boat Tours The **Ocean City Public Relations Office** (tel. 410/289–2800 or 800/626–2326) has information on boats that make scenic cruises of ½–2 hours from Ocean City, taking 25 to 150 passengers.

The paddle wheeler *Maryland Lady* (Box 316, Salisbury 21803, tel. 410/543–2466) takes sightseeing, lunch, brunch, and dinner cruises on the Wicomico River.

The Patriot (Box 1206, St. Michaels 21663, tel. 410/745–3100), a 65-foot motor yacht, departs three times daily (at 11, 1, and 3 PM) for 90-minute cruises on the Miles River, from May to October. It passes many magnificent estates that front the river, including Bel Aire, Perry Hall, Wheatlands, The Anchorage, and The Willows.

Exploring

Numbers in the margin correspond to points of interest on the Maryland's Eastern Shore map.

A central approach to the Eastern Shore, the William Preston Lane Jr. Memorial Bridges reach into Chesapeake Bay from Sandy Point State Park, about 10 miles northeast of Annapolis, to **Kent Island,** the largest island in the bay and a thriving trading post since 1631, when it became the first permanent settlement in Maryland. The bridge toll of $2.50 for cars is collected at Sandy Point.

❶ In **Stevensville,** the largest town on Kent Island, the oldest surviving building is the **Cray House,** a two-story, mansard-roof cottage of post-and-plank construction that was completed in 1815. Set in a little yard surrounded by a picket fence, and furnished with period pieces, the restored house allows a glimpse into the middle-class life of the early 19th century. *Cockey's La., Stevensville, tel. 410/758–2300. Admission free. Open May–Oct., Sat. 1–4, and by appointment.*

Christ Episcopal Church is the sanctuary for what could be the state's oldest continuous religious congregation, one that dates to the settlement of the island. The curious Carpenter's Gothic structure, built in 1880, is mostly of wood, but the lancet chimney (a gap in the center has the shape of a lancet window in a medieval church) is made with bricks from a church of 1652 that stood nearby. *Rte. 18, Stevensville, tel. 410/643–5921. Open by appointment.*

❷ About 10 miles inland are the remains of the village of **Wye Mills,** named for a gristmill built in 1671. The mill has been reconstructed twice, in 1720 and 1840. During the War of Independence, Washington's troops at Valley Forge ordered flour and other supplies from here. The present structure is powered by a waterwheel, and visitors can watch the mill's gears turn and apparatus grind: Cornmeal, whole wheat, and buckwheat flour produced here are on sale. *Rte. 662, Wye Mills, tel. 410/827–6909 or 410/685–2886. Admission free. Open Apr.–Dec., weekends 11–4.*

The mill sits on the line between Queen Anne's and Talbot counties, both of which claim it as a landmark. Some yards south, on the other side of the junction of Routes 662 and 404, and indisputably in Talbot County, is the Maryland State Tree: The 450-year-old **Wye Oak** is an imposing 95 feet tall and 37 feet around at its thickest; its branches spread out 145 feet, casting plenty of shade on sunny days. Although this mammoth tree is in its declining years, it's nonetheless still very impressive. A 29-acre park with a picnic area and tables is open to the public.

❸ The affluent town of **Easton,** 13 miles south of Wye Mills, has a well-preserved downtown full of buildings dating from Colonial through Victorian times. The **Talbot County Courthouse** of 1794, still in use, is one of two courthouses in the state built in the 18th century (the

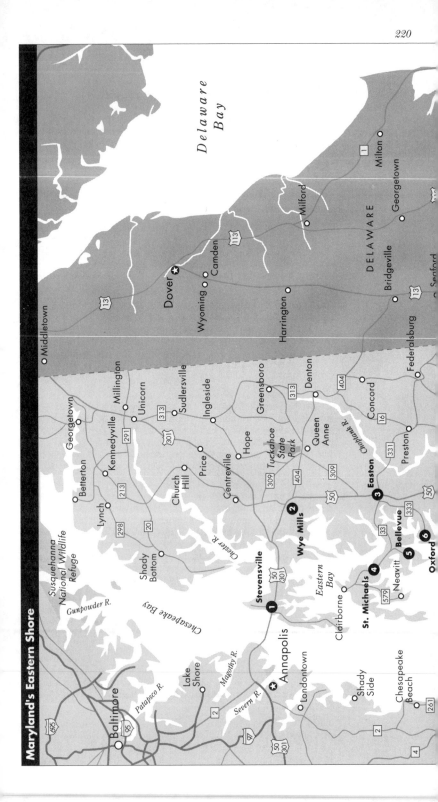

Maryland's Eastern Shore

Delaware Bay

Milton

Georgetown

11

DELAWARE

Milford

113

Bridgeville

Camden

Dover ✪

Wyoming

Seaford

13

Harrington

13

Middletown

Federalsburg

Georgetown

Millington

Denton

Concord

Sudlersville

404

16

Kennedyville

Unicorn

313

291

Ingleside

313

Preston

331

Betterton

US 301

Hope

Greensboro

Queen
Anne

Choptank R.

Lynch

213

Price

Church
Hill

*Tuckahoe
State
Park*

309

Easton

50

Shady
Bottom

298

20

Centreville

309

404

3

Bellevue

333

50

Chester R.

Wye Mills

2

33

6

Oxford

Stevensville

50
301

Eastern
Bay

4

St. Michaels

Neavitt

5

*Susquehanna
National Wildlife
Refuge*

Gunpowder R.

Clairborne

579

Chesapeake Bay

1

Baltimore

695

95

Patapsco R.

Lake
Shore

Magothy R.

Annapolis ✪

Londontown

Shady
Side

Chesapeake
Beach

261

2

Severn R.

2

97

50
301

4

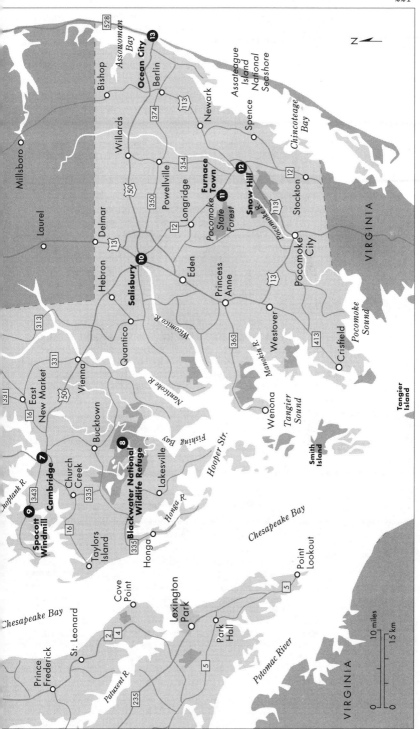

two wings were added in 1958). It is an elegant little brick structure with a two-tier cupola that recalls Colonial Williamsburg and is topped by a weather vane. Rebellious citizens gathered here to protest the Stamp Act in 1765 and to adopt the Talbot Resolves, a forerunner of the Declaration of Independence. *Washington St., Easton, tel. 410/822–2401. Open weekdays 9–5.*

A federal town house is now the home of the **Historical Society of Talbot County,** a source of information on the Eastern Shore and a starting point for guided tours of the area. The restored three-story brick structure, with a fourth dormered story under the roof, was built by a Quaker cabinet maker in 1810. An adjacent museum shows changing exhibits of local history. The small wood-frame house in the garden behind was built in 1795. *25 S. Washington St., Easton, tel. 410/822–0773. Admission: $2 adults, 50¢ children. Open daily 10–4.*

The **Third Haven Friends Meeting House,** built by Quakers in 1682, is believed to be the oldest wood-frame house of worship in the country. No doubt it is the oldest still in use; meeting takes place Sunday at 10 AM. The Quaker William Penn and the Catholic Lord Baltimore are among those who have attended over the centuries. The white building is strikingly plain inside and out, with the simplicity that the sect reveres. The building remains unheated; a stove was deemed a frippery. *405 S. Washington St., Easton, tel. 410/822–0293. Open daily 9–5.*

On the second full weekend in November the town of Easton erupts in the **Waterfowl Festival,** a convention of decoy carvers and painters. Their work, which draws on the wildlife of this area, is offered for sale in galleries and at auction. Related events include goose- and duck-call competitions and demonstrations by retrievers. Seafood stalls are plentiful. *40 S. Harrison St. (Box 929), Easton 21601, tel. 410/822–4567.*

❹ Route 33 follows the contours of the Miles River to reach **St. Michaels,** 9 miles west of Easton. The harborside village, historically a shipbuilding center because of the abundant timber nearby, was a focus of attack in the War of 1812. During one attack, citizens diverted British fire from strategic targets by adroitly placing lanterns in the fog.

Just one house in "the town that fooled the British" was struck during the shelling. That structure, known as the **Cannonball House,** built in 1805, is privately owned and not open to the public, but you can see it on Mulberry Street at the northwest edge of St. Mary's Square.

This square, dedicated to public use in perpetuity, is the core of a neighborhood whose architecture has remained largely unchanged since the 19th century. A 17th-century cabin of axe-hewn half-timber houses is part of the **St. Mary's Square Museum,** which preserves local artifacts. Most prominent in the collection is a shipyard bell that still rings at the start of the workday, at lunch, and at quitting time. The museum also occupies the adjoining Teetotum Building, a yellow clapboard house of the Civil War era named for a children's toy it was thought to resemble. *St. Mary's Sq., St. Michaels, tel. 410/745–9561. Admission by contribution. Open May–Oct., weekends 10–4.*

Talbot Street, the town's main drag, is lined with seafood restaurants and boutiques that sell summer fashions, crafts, bowls of potpourri, and the like. Even the hardware store is also a "gift shop."

Time Out **Justine's,** at Talbot and Cherry streets, is an old-fashioned ice-cream parlor whose menu is up-to-date enough to feature frozen yogurt. A full range of candy toppings is available, and there's a small selection of sandwiches to serve as appetizers for dessert.

Cherry Street leads across a footbridge to the **Chesapeake Bay Maritime Museum** at Navy Point (automobiles use Mill Street one block west). The museum is a complex of six exhibition halls on 17 acres. Exhibits trace the history of the Bay and its traditions in boat building, commercial fishing, navigation, and waterfowling. Major features include a restored log-bottom "bugeye" (a two-masted skipjack native to the Chesapeake Bay and used for oyster dredging), a skipjack, and a racing log canoe. In the Bay Building, artifacts and illustrations, including a dugout canoe hewn by Native Americans and a later crabbing skiff, recount the history of the great estuary. The Waterfowl Building contains carved decoys and stuffed birds, including wood ducks, mallards, and swans; another collection assembles the outlawed firearms that put many species in danger of extinction. Several outlawed hunting boats are shown outdoors in a small shelter called a corncrib. The Small Boat Shed (1888) is a cavernous hall first erected as a steamboat ferry depot and railroad terminal in Claiborne, 6 miles away. Here the shed contains racing and fishing boats and the tools of the fishing trade, among them a wire-mesh crab pot and wood oyster-tongs. The lighthouse on the pier, built in 1879 at Hooper Strait (in the southern bay) and moved here in 1966, is of screw-pile design (a sexagonal house poised on six slender legs and used for marking shoals) and virtually identical to the one at Solomons Island in southern Maryland (*see* Chapter 9); the interior is a surprisingly spacious apartment with wood floors and quaint stoves—built for a single tenant but ideal for a young couple. Two or three construction projects are under way in the Boat Shop, where visitors can observe from a raised deck and examine augers, awls, and planes in a glass display case. The second-story porch allows a breezy respite from the sightseeing march. *Navy Pt., St. Michaels, tel. 410/745-2916. Admission: $5 adults, $4.50 senior citizens, $2.50 children. Open Jan.–Mar., weekends 10–4; Apr.–Oct., daily 10–5; Nov.–Dec., daily 10–4.*

❺ **Bellevue,** 7 miles south of St. Michaels via Routes 33 and 329, is the departure point for the **Oxford-Bellevue Ferry,** believed to be the oldest privately owned ferry in continuous operation in the United States. In 1683 the Talbot County Court "pitcht up on Mr. Richard Royston to keepe a Ferry," and it has been running across the Tred Avon River ever since. *N. Morris St. at The Strand, Oxford, tel. 410/745-9023. Ferry rates: $4 car and driver one way, $5.75 same-day round-trip; 25¢ car passenger, 50¢ pedestrian, $1.50 bicycle, $2 motorcycle. Operates weekdays 7–sunset, weekends 9–sunset. Closed Dec. 25–Feb.*

❻ **Oxford,** founded in 1683, is one of the oldest towns in Maryland, but few of the buildings put up before the middle of the 19th century still stand. The prevailing style is Victorian Carpenter's Gothic. One exception is the Robert Morris Inn, at Morris Street and the Strand, on the rise overlooking the ferry terminal. The inn, expanded gradually from a four-room core from 1710, was once the house of the Liverpool merchant Robert Morris and his son. The junior Morris signed the Declaration of Independence, enlarged the family fortune, helped to finance the Revolution, and ended up in debtor's prison after failing at land speculation.

On the riverbank, the **Customs House** is a Bicentennial replica of the shed from which Jeremiah Banning, the first federal collector of customs, kept track of the traffic in and out of this crucial 18th-century port. Often immobilized by gout, Banning watched the ships through a spyglass. The replica version is simply but comfortably furnished with antiques of the period and attended by a docent who will tell the story of the port and direct visitors to points of interest in the town. The original structure, built in 1777, stands on private property across the harbor. *N. Morris St., Oxford, tel. 410/226-5122. Admission free. Open Apr.–Oct., Fri.–Sun. 3–5.*

The **Oxford Museum,** an unusually well maintained local museum, is three blocks down Morris Street, adjacent to the town offices at Market Street. On display are models and pictures of sailboats, some constructed at the Cutts and Case shipyard, which is still in business. Oxford was the site of one of the first Chesapeake regattas (1860), hence the full-scale racing boat that sits by the door. Other artifacts include the lamp from a lighthouse on nearby Benoni Point, a sail-maker's bench, and an oyster-shucking stall. Docents elaborate on the exhibits, which set the context for a walking tour of the blocks nearby (tour booklet $1 here and at most local merchants). *Morris and Market Sts., Oxford, tel. 410/226-5122. Admission free. Open May–Oct., Fri.–Sun. 2–5.*

Opposite the museum is the **Town Park,** a leafy area with benches and an unobstructed view of the Tred Avon River, and a serene spot at which to take a breather.

❼ Situated on the south shore of the Choptank River, 15 miles southeast of Oxford and about a dozen times as big, is the deep-harbor port of **Cambridge,** best reached by taking Route 50 south. This is the second-largest port in Maryland, used heavily by the seafood-processing plants nearby. At press time, work on the revitalization of the port area, now called Sailwinds Park, was scheduled to begin in December 1994. The complex will eventually comprise a visitor center and museum complex, a hotel, a marina, a shopping area, a playground, and a park. The new Festival Hall is already hosting public events and concerts (tel. 410/228–SAIL).

The most important of the Cambridge buildings is the **Meredith House** (1760), a three-story, redbrick Georgian structure that houses the collections of the Dorchester County Historical Society. This regional museum features artifacts of Native Americans and colonists; a child's bedroom has antique toys and dolls; and the Governor's Room holds personal effects of the six Maryland chief executives who sprang from the county. A smokehouse, a blacksmith's shop, formal gardens, and a medicinal herb garden have been restored. *Greenway Dr. and La Grange St., tel. 410/228-7953. Admission free. Open Thurs.–Sat. 10–4.*

Near the town of Church Creek on Route 16, 7 miles southwest of Cambridge, is the tiny **Old Trinity Church** of 1675, extensively altered in the 19th century but now restored to its 17th-century appearance. It is possibly the oldest Episcopal church in the country in continuous use. On display is a Table of Marriages, a chart that details proscribed relationships. The silver chalice given by Queen Anne and the cushion she knelt upon when she was crowned are sometimes exhibited. In the churchyard are the graves of four governors of Maryland and several members of the distinguished political and clerical Carroll family. *Rte. 16, near Church Creek, tel. 410/228-2940. Open Wed.–Mon., 9–5.*

The **Wild Goose Brewery** is the Eastern Shore's only microbrewery. Take the tour and see every step of the operation—then sample some of its highly regarded ale, amber or lager. *20 Washington St., Cambridge, tel. 410/221–1121. Tours daily 10–3.*

❽ **Blackwater National Wildlife Refuge,** 5 miles farther south on inland Route 335, is 11,000 acres of marshland protected by the Department of the Interior. Canada geese are prominent among the waterfowl that winter here; the hawkish, fish-eating osprey hatches its offspring in June; the bald eagle, as seen on the national coat of arms, makes frequent appearances. Another (less majestic) endangered species on the premises is the fox squirrel. Drivers and cyclists follow a 5-mile road through several habitats; pedestrians follow a network of trails. Exhibits and films in the visitor center provide background. *Rte. 335 at Key Wallace Dr., tel. 410/228–2677. Admission: $3 car, $1 pedestrian or cyclist. Drive open daily sunrise–sunset. Visitor center open June–Labor Day, weekdays 8–4; Sept.–May, weekdays 8–4, weekends 9–5. Closed federal holidays.*

❾ **Spocott Windmill,** located 6 miles west of Cambridge on Route 343, is the only existing post windmill for grinding grain in Maryland. Although the post type windmills were common in England as early as the 1100s, it wasn't until the early 17th century that they became common in Virginia and Maryland—particularly in the eastern counties where the terrain is generally flat. This is an authentic replica of one destroyed in a great blizzard in 1888. Also on the property and open to the public is the miller's tenant house and a one-room schoolhouse dated 1868. The windmill is operated from time to time in fair winds. *Rte. 343, tel. 410/228–7090. Admission free; donations accepted. Open Mon.–Sat. 10–5.*

❿ **Salisbury,** about halfway across the peninsula on Route 50, is the largest city and, with the barge traffic along the Wicomico River, the second-largest port on the Eastern Shore. This is an industrial town of more than 20,000 people, one in eight of whom packages chickens for a living. Around the intersection of Elizabeth Street and Poplar Hill Avenue is a six-block historic district; a brochure with a walking tour is available from the Chamber of Commerce (300 E. Main St., Box 510, 21803, tel. 410/749–0144). These are Victorian houses: Few buildings survived the fire of 1886. One structure that did remain after the fire was the wood **Poplar Hill Mansion,** built in 1805 by a Revolutionary officer. The Federalist house is notable for a large Palladian window and a 12-foot-wide arched front hallway. *117 Elizabeth St., Salisbury, tel. 410/749–1776. Admission: $1.50. Open Sun. 1–4.*

At Schumaker Pond, the newly opened and enlarged **Ward Museum of Wildfowl Art** illustrates and reviews the history of decoy carving. Replicas of simple 1,000-year-old figures made from reeds by Native Americans share space with lifelike works of the 19th and 20th centuries. More than 2,000 works of art and related artifacts are displayed: The 30,000-square-foot structure includes exhibition and gallery spaces, a gift shop, a library, and research areas. Artists from all parts of the world participate in the World Championship Carving Competition held here in April. This is a craft whose premium pieces have commanded hundreds of thousands of dollars at auctions. *Schumaker Pond at Beaglin Park Drive (3416), Salisbury 21802, tel. 410/742–4988. Admission: $4 adults, $3 senior citizens and college students, $2 children.*

Highway 12 provides the direct route southeast from Salisbury to Snow Hill, a distance of 19 miles. When you've gone 14 miles, you'll

⓫ find **Furnace Town,** where the huge outdoor Nassawango Iron Furnace (1828–1850) is now inactive. Visitors learn about its past by
strolling around the extensive re-creation of a 19th-century industrial village complete with broom house, blacksmith shop, smokehouse, printshop, church, and company store. A visitor center has
background information and exhibits. In addition, there are nature
trails, bird watching, living history programs, and an elevated
boardwalk that traverses the cypress swamp. *Old Furnace Rd.,
Rte. 12, tel. 410/632–2032. Admission: $1.50 adults, 75¢ children.
Open Apr.–Oct., daily 11–5.*

⓬ The Pocomoke River port of **Snow Hill** is no longer the shipping center it was in the 18th and 19th centuries, but the summertime
cruise-tours that depart from Sturgis Park (tel. 410/632–0680 or
800/345–6754) recall the river's importance. The story of the town is
told in the **Julia A. Purnell Museum,** where spinning wheels, mouse-
traps, and other miscellany illustrate the 100-year life of the woman
for whom it is named, an ordinary citizen who died in 1943. *208 W.
Market St., Snow Hill, tel. 410/632–0515. Admission free. Open
weekends 1–5.*

The redbrick **All Hallows Episcopal Church** at Church and Market
streets, completed in 1756 on the site of an earlier sanctuary and
containing a Bible from Queen Anne, is one of the Snow Hill historic
structures that appear in a walking-tour brochure available at the
Purnell Museum or, on weekdays, at Town Hall (Green and Bank
streets).

On the Atlantic side of the peninsula, 29 miles east of Salisbury on
⓭ Route 50, **Ocean City** lies on a ¼-mile-wide strip of barrier island
that extends north into Delaware. To the west are the Isle of Wight
and Big Assawoman bays. Coastal Highway (Hwy. 1) is the main artery through town; "Olde Towne" Ocean City is situated on the south
end of the island, and "Condo Row" runs from 90th to 110th Street.
The large residential areas of Little Salisbury and Caine Woods are
home to approximately 7,500 year-round residents. This population
often swells to more than 250,000 in summer, however, when vacationers flock to the 10 miles of white-sand beach and 3-mile boardwalk with shops, pubs, restaurants, hotels with big decks and
rocking chairs, a restored 19th-century carousel, water parks, a
fishing pier, and stomach-churning amusement rides. Along the
lower Boardwalk—below 1st Street—are the stores selling Dolles
and Candy Kitchen saltwater taffy, Thrasher's french fries, and
Fisher's caramel popcorn—traditional souvenirs to take home from
Ocean City. To the south of Ocean City lies the continuing narrow
strip island, the Assateague Island National Seashore (*see* Beaches,
below).

What to See and Do with Children

Trimper's Amusement Park, at the south end of the Boardwalk, has a
number of rides, including a double-loop roller coaster. Of special interest is the Hirschell Spellman Carousel, dating to 1902. The outdoor portion of the amusement complex is open when there are
crowds and features a double ferris wheel; the indoor portion is open
year-round, but weekends only November–March. *Boardwalk and
S. 1st St., Ocean City, tel. 410/289–8617. Pay per ride.*

The **Jolly Roger Amusement Park** boasts two miniature golf courses,
a water park, a roller coaster, kiddie rides, and a petting zoo. *30th
St. and Coastal Hwy., Ocean City, tel. 410/289–3477. Admission to*

park free; rides priced individually. Open Easter–May 1, weekends noon–midnight; May–Sept., daily noon–midnight.

Salisbury Zoological Park, said to be one of the finest small zoos in North America, offers spectacled bears of a small (5- to 6-foot) South American species distinguished by light fur around the eyes. Also dwelling on the 12 acres are monkeys, prairie dogs, lions, panthers, alligators, llamas, bison, bald eagles, and plenty of waterfowl. *750 S. Park Dr., Salisbury, tel. 410/548–3188. Admission free; donations accepted. Open daily 8–7:30.*

Off the Beaten Track

Although commercialism has begun to creep into the Eastern Shore communities of Easton, Oxford, and St. Michaels, there is still a place—**Tilghman Island,** situated on Route 33—that remains mostly untainted. This is an authentic waterman's village where in the spring and summer you'll see skipjacks (oyster boats) tied, awaiting the beginning of the oystering season (September–April). These indigenous boats are the only working fleet of sailboats in North America. In the 1800s there were about 1,500 of them sailing the bay; today there are fewer than 30.

Just a short drive beyond the Knapps Narrows Bridge, on the one small road on the island, is **Harrison's Chesapeake House–Country Inn and Sportfishing Center,** on the left (tel. 410/886–2123), where "Captain" Buddy and his wife Bobbie Harrison oversee every detail of the 100-year-old restaurant-provisions center, geared mostly to hunters and outdoorspeople. The Harrisons exude friendliness and work hard to accommodate their guests: For example, they have devised the "Buddy Plan," which includes all the elements needed for goose- and sea-duck-hunting packages, and fishing packages for parties from one to 100. The moderately priced restaurant offers an equally hospitable atmosphere, and on the menu is a variety of seafood specialties—only a handful of dishes are non-seafood. You'll be hard-pressed to find fresher fish anywhere in these parts. Dress is casual, and sometimes bluegrass and country music are featured; the tone is always relaxed here.

On the water, across the busiest drawbridge in the country, is the **Tilghman Island Inn** (tel. 410/886–2141), at the confluence of the Chesapeake Bay and Choptank River, about 200 yards from Harrisons. The intimate resort has a fine restaurant and private tennis court, swimming pool, croquet court, biking, fishing, and boating facilities, and a dock. The modestly priced menu at the restaurant specializes in seafood, but there's a good variety of other items that you'd probably expect to find in a big-city bistro, not a small-town place like Tilghman. To top it off, everything is well prepared.

Smith Island, Maryland (tel. 410/651–2968 for self-guided tour brochure), and **Tangier Island, Virginia,** are two fishing communities in the Chesapeake Bay, each with fewer than 1,000 residents. One of the most remarkable characteristics associated with these islands is that the natives have not lost the accents of their 17th-century English ancestors, and they are very difficult to understand. A midday visit by passenger ferry will allow plenty of time for a leisurely meal and a stroll around the island; large areas of wildlife refuge are not open to visitors. While you're here, take advantage of whatever seafood is in season: Some of the local specialties served at the islands' inns include soft-shell crabs, crab cakes, crab soup, oysters, and clam fritters. *Ferries to Smith and Tangier islands depart from*

Crisfield on Rte. 413 at southeastern point of Maryland's Eastern Shore (see below).

The *Captain Tyler 2* departs from Somers Cove Marina in Crisfield for the 1-hour, 10-minute cruise to Smith Island. Visitors receive a seafood luncheon and island tour as well. To reach Crisfield follow Route 13 south from Salisbury. Turn at Westover and take Route 413 south to Crisfield. *Tyler Cruises: Box 41, Rhodes Point, tel. 410/ 425-2771. For a tour to Tangier contact Tangier Island Cruises, 10th and Main Sts., Crisfield, tel. 410/968-2338.*

Shopping

Of the towns of the Eastern Shore, St. Michaels has the largest variety of boutiques and specialty stores.

Christmas Decor **The Blue Swan** (200 Talbot St., St. Michaels, tel. 410/745-9346) sells seashell ornaments, wood Santas and elves, crystal, glass, and other furnishings for the holiday season—all year long. The store is just one in a neighborhood of curiosity shops.

Outlet Stores **Carvel Hall Cutlery** (Rte. 50, Queenstown, tel. 410/827-6904) is a unique outlet for the famous Crisfield manufacturer and offers heirloom-quality utensils and seafood tools at factory prices. The store is open daily 9:30-6; closed Thanksgiving Day, Christmas, and New Year's Day.

Chesapeake Village Outlet Center (Rte. 50, near Grasonville, tel. 410/827-8699), 10 miles east of the Bay Bridge, is composed of 19 "factory direct" labels, among them Liz Claiborne, Capezio, Nike, and Evan Picone.

Eastern Shore Factory Stores (Piney Narrows Rd., Chester, tel. 410/ 643-5231), on Kent Island, is a complex of 29 merchants, including American Tourister, Anne Klein, and Corning Glass.

At **Salisbury Pewter** (Rte. 13, Salisbury, between the town of Salisbury and the Delaware border, tel. 410/546-1188), visitors can watch craftspeople turning pewter by hand at the factory showroom and select from a variety of Early American designs for sale at very reasonable prices.

Sports and Outdoor Activities

Participant Sports

Bicycling **Oxford Mews** (Morris St., Oxford, tel. 410/820-8222) and **Town Dock Marina** (305 Mulberry St., St. Michaels, tel. 410/745-2400) rent bicycles. On the **boardwalk** in Ocean City, try Caroline, 1st, 2nd, 6th, 9th, 14th, 15th, 16th, 17th, 21st, 23rd, 26th, 28th, and 72nd streets for rentals. Boardwalk riding is permitted in summer 6 AM–10 AM only.

Viewtrail 100, a specially marked 100-mile biking circuit in Worcester County, uses secondary state and county roads between Berlin and Pocomoke City, supervised by the University of Maryland Extension Service (Box 219, Snow Hill 21863, tel. 410/632-1972).

Ocean City has designated a portion of the bus lanes on Coastal Highway for the use of bus and bicycle traffic. Traffic does get heavy, however, so exercise caution. Bicycle riding is allowed on the Ocean City boardwalk from 5 AM to 10 AM during summer months and 5 AM to 4 PM the rest of the year. A bike trail connects Ocean City with Assateague Island, and the island itself is criss-crossed by a number of clearly marked paved trails.

Fishing   For fishing on Chesapeake Bay, contact **Eastern Bay Charters** (Box 452, St. Michaels 21663, tel. 410/745–2329) or **Eastern Shore Yacht Charters** (Box 589, Oxford 21654, tel. 410/226–5000).

The Fishing Center (Shantytown Rd., West Ocean City 21842, tel. 410/213–1121) sends out groups of 20 to 100 day-trippers on the *Ocean City Princess* and *Miss Ocean City*, both head boats. They also run *The Bay Queen* for quieter (and closer) bay fishing. Private charters can also be arranged here. **Bahia Marina** (21st St. and the Bay, Ocean City 21842, tel. 410/289–7438) will arrange deep-sea charters to fish for marlin, shark, and tuna. This is the home of the head boat *Judith M*. Other charters leave the Talbot Street pier and Dorchester Street pier in South Ocean City daily.

Free public fishing piers on the **Assawoman Bay** and **Isle of Wight Bay** are at 3rd, 9th, 40th, and 125th streets and at the inlet in Ocean City. Other fishing and crabbing areas include the Route 50 bridge, Oceanic Pier, Ocean City Pier at Wicomico Street and the boardwalk, and Shantytown Village.

Golf   There are 10 excellent golf courses in the Ocean City area. For a complete listing of courses and details, contact **Worcester County Tourism** (105 Pearl St., Box 208, Snow Hill 21863, tel. 410/632–3110 or 800/854–0335) or the **Ocean City Public Relations Office** (tel. 410/289–2800 or 800/OC–OCEAN). **The Bay Club** (9122 Libertytown Rd., Berlin, west of Ocean City, tel. 410/641–4081) has 18 holes. **Nassawango Country Club** (3940 Nassawango Rd., Snow Hill, tel. 410/632–3114 or 410/957–2262) has 18 holes. **Ocean City Yacht Club** (11401 Country Club Dr., Berlin, tel. 410/641–1779) has 36 holes.

Tennis   Ocean City's public tennis courts (tel. 410/250–0125) are located on 41st and 61st streets and require reservations. Courts on 14th, 94th, and 136th streets are first come, first served.

Water Sports   **Ocean City Public Relations Office** (Dept. of Tourism, City Hall, 4001 Coastal Hwy., Box 158, Ocean City 21842, tel. 800/OC–OCEAN) publishes a guidebook called *Sea for Yourself* and a small brochure entitled "Get Hooked On Ocean City," which lists information on charter fishing and headboats, marinas and boat rentals, scenic cruises, diving charters, speedboat cruises, sailing yachts, and public boat ramps. The office has also published a brochure entitled "Camping In and Around Ocean City," which lists campgrounds, RV parks, camping stores, and bike and canoe rentals.

Sailing, Etc. (5305 Coastal Hwy., Ocean City, tel. 410/723–1144) rents sailboats, catamarans, and Windsurfers and teaches sailing and windsurfing.

Town Dock Marina (305 Mulberry St., St. Michaels, tel. 410/745–2400) rents sailboats, runabouts, and pedal boats.

Spectator Sports

Air Show   The **Antique Fly-In,** a convention of vintage aircraft including World War I biplanes, takes place in mid-May on the grass landing strip of the former Francis du Pont estate at Horn Point, 4 miles northwest of Cambridge. The Dorchester Heritage Museum (tel. 410/228–1899) has up-to-date information.

Volleyball The **Eastern Volleyball Association** (tel. 410/250–2577) coordinates a series of professional and pro/am tournaments on the beach at Ocean City each summer.

Beaches

There are no Chesapeake Bay beaches of any consequence on Maryland's Eastern Shore.

On the Atlantic, south of the 10 miles of white sand at Ocean City, the northern portion of **Assateague Island National Seashore,** an immaculate and untamed 37-mile-long barrier island, extends south into Virginia. Swimming, biking, hiking, fishing, picnicking, and camping are permitted in this national park, and there is a boat ramp. A visitor center with informative exhibits on the birds and wild ponies that inhabit Assateague is located at the entrance, 6 miles south of Ocean City. Legend has it that the first horses to come to the island swam ashore from a Spanish galleon in the 1600s. It's important to note that the ponies that roam the dunes really are wild and should not be ridden, fed, approached, or played with. Each year there are reported cases of these seemingly harmless ponies biting and kicking visitors who try to make contact with them. *Rte. 611, tel. 410/641–1441 or 410/641–3030. 1-wk park admission: $3 cars, $1 bicycles and pedestrians. Open 24 hours. Visitor center open daily 8:30–5:30.*

Dining and Lodging

Innovative kitchens and classic crab houses—representing both ends of the price scale—offer the most promising dining opportunities. Yet even the less expensive restaurants here are expensive by the standards of, say, the Western Shore in southern Maryland. Hotels throughout the region fill up months, even a year, in advance of Easton's Waterfowl Festival in November and the Annapolis power and sailboat shows on two October weekends. At those times hotels typically require two- or three-day minimum stays; many smaller inns have minimum stays all year long.

Highly recommended establishments are indicated by a star ★.

Cambridge **Glasgow Inn.** In a 6-acre park across the street from the Choptank
Lodging River sits this plantation house, white brick with a clapboard wing, built in 1760 and restored in 1987. The generally Colonial decor includes prints of the period and four-posters carved with rice designs or turned to resemble spools. Some rooms have quilted hangings; one room contains French provincial furniture, white with hand-painted detailing. The ample common space includes a screened porch that faces the river, with a daybed on which guests have been known to choose to spend the night. The grounds are practically a refuge for birds, and eight public tennis courts are a block away. *1500 Hambrooks Blvd., Cambridge 21613, tel. 410/228–0575. 7 rooms, 3 with bath. MC, V. Rates include full breakfast. $$$*

Church Creek **Loblolly Landings.** Essentially a retreat for lovers of the great out-
Dining doors, this unique B&B is situated very near the Blackwater Wildlife Refuge. At present, there are only two rooms available in the main lodge, though the owners plan to have a total of 10 rooms ready by the middle of 1995. The 10-room bunkhouse is for travelers willing to rough it; guests are asked to bring along bedrolls or sleeping bags. Bicycles and canoes are available for rental, and there is an archery course on the property (bring your own bow and arrows).

An adjacent 3,500-foot grass runway is available for guests who want to fly in. Well-behaved cats and dogs are allowed. *2142 Liners Rd., Church Creek 21622, tel. 410/397–3033. Reservations advised, especially in fall. AE, D, MC, V. $$*

Easton
Lodging

John S. McDaniel House. This three-story white clapboard house with green roof and shutters, built in 1890, is dominated by an octagonal tower. A circular turret room on each floor is distinctively Victorian. All rooms were renovated in 1988 and furnished with period reproductions; the beds have quilts; pictures of waterfowl hang on the white-with-gray-trim walls; and two rooms have brass beds. Ceiling fans augment the central air-conditioning. When weather permits, the large buffet breakfast with freshly baked bread can be taken on the wraparound porch amid rocking chairs and other wicker furniture. *14 N. Aurora St., Easton 21601, tel. 410/822–3704. 7 rooms, 5 with bath. AE, MC, V. Rates include full breakfast. $$*

Kent
Dining

Kent Manor Inn. The pinks on walls and tablecloths complement the porcelain on display in glass cases and above the marble fireplaces. Reproductions of Impressionist paintings hang on the walls. This is a large facility; a solarium serves as a second dining room, and the staff can attend to more than 100 people at a time. Among the specialties, salmon Chesapeake is Norwegian salmon and blue crab topped with a tangy sauce. Veal saltimbocca is prepared with mushrooms, spinach, and prosciutto. Kent Manor–baked chicken breast is a boneless chicken breast stuffed with artichoke hearts and cheese. *500 Kent Manor Dr., Stevensville, tel. 410/643–5757. Reservations advised. Dress: casual but neat. AE, MC, V. Closed Dec. 25. $$$*

The Narrows. The atrium dining room, with a mix of uncovered wood and Formica tables, is decorated with potted ficus trees and stuffed waterfowl. Large windows on three sides (and, in spring and fall, a glass-enclosed "greenhouse") allow diners to watch the activity of the fishing and pleasure craft on the waterway that separates Kent Island, opposite, from the mainland. In warm weather, meals are also served on the dock, where sailors can tie up their vessels before dinner. Cream of crab soup contains one pound of crabmeat per gallon, along with chicken stock and heavy cream. Strip steak Quimby, named for a prominent local family, is prepared with a sauce made of brandy, onions, freshly ground black pepper, and cream. *Rte. 50 at Kent Narrows, Grasonville, tel. 410/827–8113. Reservations advised. Dress: casual but neat. DC, MC, V. Closed Dec. 24–25 and Jan. 1. $$$*

★ **Harris Crab House.** The restaurant's location, on the mainland side of Kent Narrows, enables boaters to sail up and dock their boats at slips provided by Harris's; roof-deck dining offers expansive water views. Harris Crab House supplies clams for the chowders of many New England restaurants, and the dining room here resembles a processing plant, with concrete walls painted white and exposed rafters in the ceiling. A light, eggless batter is used on the clams, which are then breaded and deep-fried. Little breading is used in the crab cakes. The crabs are spicy enough to promote plenty of beer drinking. *Sewards Marina Rd. (Rte. 50), Grasonville, tel. 410/827–8104. No reservations. Dress: casual. No credit cards. Closed Jan.–Feb. $$*

Lodging
★

Kent Manor Inn. In 1987 the innkeeper added the west wing of this three-story wood house on a 226-acre working farm on Kent Island. The addition was designed to match the old two-story east wing built in 1820. An overall restoration brought four-posters and other Victorian reproductions and Impressionist paintings to hang above marble fireplaces. Half of the rooms face Thompson Creek. Rooms on the first and second floors open onto verandas; those on the third floor have sloped ceilings, dormer windows, and window seats. Dogs are welcome. *500 Kent Manor Dr., Stevensville 21666, tel. 410/643–5757. 24 rooms, some accessible for guests with disabilities. Facilities: restaurant, bar, outdoor pool, volleyball court, horseshoes, croquet. AE, MC, V. Rates include Continental breakfast. $$$*

Ocean City
Dining

Fager's Island. The fun begins at the end of the day when Tchaikovsky's *1812 Overture* accompanies every sunset over the Assawoman Bay. The restaurant and bar create a unique American café–style atmosphere, with a beautiful bayside setting. There are more than 100 beers on the menu, inlcuding one brewed especially for Denise and John Fager, the hospitable owners. Major wine publications agree that the wine list is, unexpectedly, one of the best in Maryland. In the dining room, which has plenty of windows that overlook the water, sun, and waterfowl, you'll enjoy some of the finest seafood the area has to offer, as well as prime rib with fresh-shaved horseradish. Also recommended is the fresh tilapia fish baked in parchment, or the swordfish steak—charbroiled and topped with a compound lime butter. As the night progresses, the adjoining bar comes to life and the crowd gets younger, but old-timers won't ever feel out of place here. *60th St. at The Bay, Ocean City, tel. 410/723–6100. Reservations suggested. Dress: casual. AE, DC, MC, V. $$$*

★ **The Hobbit.** Dedicated to Bilbo Baggins and other literary creations of J.R.R. Tolkien, the dining room has murals depicting scenes from the classic novel, and wood table lamps are carved in the shapes of individual hobbits. The burgundy carpeting and table linen complement the redwood trim on the walls. The room's wedge shape allows a view of Assawoman Bay from two angles, and new-age or classical music plays in the background. Veal with pistachios is sautéed in a sauce of Madeira wine, veal stock, prosciutto, mushrooms, shallots, and heavy cream. Hobbit Catch is the fish of the day (typically swordfish, tuna, or salmon) sautéed in butter with white wine, artichoke hearts, capers, and mushrooms. The full menu and a selection of snacks are offered in the adjoining bar. *101 81st St., tel. 410/524–8100. Reservations advised. Dress: casual but neat. MC, V. $$*

Seasons. The dining room decor is muted: sea-foam green carpeting, white walls trimmed in peach, beige linen tablecloths. Freshly cut flowers grace each table, but the sea-level view of the surf brooks no competition. In one preparation, shrimp is sautéed with garlic and finished with brandy. Tournedos Dijon are small cuts of beef tenderloin in a mustard cream sauce with cognac. The wine list, more Californian than French, includes a selection of wines by the glass. *Carousel Hotel and Resort, 118th St. and Coastal Hwy., tel. 410/524–1000. Reservations advised. Dress: casual but neat. AE, D, DC, MC, V. $$*

Lombardi's. With a local reputation for being the best pizza kitchen in Ocean City, Lombardi's produces a consistent thin-crust pie baked with the traditional toppings. The one unusual option is the white pizza: Mozzarella, olive oil, garlic, and onions are not accompanied by tomato sauce. Cheese steaks and cold-cut sandwiches are the alternatives to pizza. The dining room furnishings, cozy wood booths and tables, are augmented by photographs of Ocean City and the house specialty; the adjacent solarium provides additional seating. Full bar service includes a fairly priced selection of beers. *9203 Coastal Hwy., tel. 410/524–1961. No reservations. Dress: casual. MC, V. $*

Lodging **Dunes Manor Hotel.** You can't overlook this 11-story pink stucco building with the peaked roof that looks like a Victorian seaside inn—even though it was built in 1987. Guest quarters have a pink-and-green decor, botanical prints, and light oak furniture that includes an armoire to hide the TV. Each room offers a refrigerator, an ocean view, and a private balcony accessible through French doors. Every day at 3:30 the owner presides over afternoon tea in a lobby notable for a large double staircase and a brass chandelier. *28th St. and oceanfront, Ocean City 21842, tel. 410/289–1100 or 800/523–2888. 160 rooms, 10 suites. Facilities: restaurant, bar, indoor-outdoor pool, whirlpool, exercise room. AE, DC, MC, V. $$$$*

Hotels at Fager's Island: Coconut Malorie Hotel and **Lighthouse Club Hotel.** Although the two hotels at Fager's Island are relative newcomers to the beach scene, the restaurant and bar are well known and established fixtures. The Coconut Malorie Hotel is an 85-suite Caribbean-style hotel with full amenities and stylish decor, including marble bathrooms and Haitian art; offering a different ambience is the Lighthouse Club Hotel, a 23-suite maritime inn that is designed to represent a typical Chesapeake Bay lighthouse. No creature comfort has been overlooked at either accommodation. The Coconut Malorie features a Grecian white-marble lobby, palm trees, and a waterfall. The Lighthouse "Lightkeeper" suites are ultraspacious with fireplaces and double marble Jacuzzis, four-poster beds, and other luxurious amenities. The Lighthouse Club Hotel is connected to the restaurant by an arched, lighted footbridge. Fager's Island is Ocean City's magical place. *56–60th Sts. at the Bay, Ocean City, 21842, tel. 410/723–6100 or 800/767–6060, fax 410/723–2055. 85 suites at Coconut Malorie, 23 at Lighthouse Club. Facilities: restaurant, bar, health club, pool, sun deck, Jacuzzis. AE, MC, V. $$$$*

Carousel Hotel and Resort. The older and smaller section of this complex was built in 1965 by Bobby Baker, an aide to Lyndon Johnson, who operated it as a weekend playground for Washington politicians, lobbyists, and their friends. In those days the core of Ocean City was at least 80 blocks away; today this is a busy neighborhood and the Carousel is a family establishment. All rooms, whether in the original four stories or in the 22-story addition of 1974, have a fully equipped kitchenette. The predominant color is turquoise; shell paintings decorate the walls. Views are of the ocean or of Assawoman Bay. This is a well-equipped recreational facility, and its indoor ice rink is an unusual beachfront attraction. *118th St. and Coastal Hwy., Ocean City 21842, tel. 410/524–1000 or 800/641–0011. 265 rooms. Facilities: restaurant, delicatessen, 3 bars, indoor pool, saunas, whirlpool, exercise room, 3 lighted tennis courts, ice-skating rink. AE, D, DC, MC, V. $$$*

Dunes Motel. Half the rooms are oceanfront efficiencies in a five-story building of 1978, with windows that slide open for access to the beach or (on the upper story) to admit the sea breeze. Rooms in the older three-story building have a small refrigerator and no view of the water. This dependably clean place to stay is located conveniently at the north end of the boardwalk. *27th St. and Baltimore Ave., Ocean City 21842, tel. 410/289–4414. 103 rooms. Facilities: restaurant, outdoor pool, wading pool. AE, MC, V. $$$*

Oxford
Dining

Pope's Tavern. A pressed-tin ceiling and large display windows remain from when this restaurant was a grocery store. Ship models decorate both dining rooms, where the hardwood floors are uncarpeted and fireplaces provide warmth in cold weather. Blue-and-gray linen cloths on the tables are covered with glass, candles, and fresh flowers. Shrimp and crab Norfolk, sautéed in white wine and butter, is heavily seasoned. Chicken Patricia is a boneless chicken breast sautéed in white wine with a sauce of green peppers, mushrooms, scallions, and butter. Sunday brunch is known for meaty crab cakes and freshly baked muffins. A mostly Californian wine list includes a selection of Australian vintage. *Oxford Inn, 1 S. Morris St., tel. 410/226–5220. Reservations advised. Dress: casual but neat. MC, V. Closed Tues. $$*

Dining and Lodging **Robert Morris Inn.** Situated near the Bellevue-Oxford Ferry terminal, on the Strand, this friendly inn offers a convenient location and a variety of accommodations, including efficiencies, river cottages, and simple bedrooms, some with bay windows, others with porches. Some rooms are modestly furnished and none have telephones or TVs; there's no room service or porter service. The hallmark of this famous inn is that it provides simple comfort, quiet hospitality, and excellent food. The main dining room has crystal chandeliers, red-and-silver wallpaper, murals depicting 18th-century river scenes, and pink table linen. Nautical prints adorn the walls of the Tap Room, which is made more elegant by the pine flooring and paneling. In the more informal Tavern are oak panels and slate floors, and tables have lacquered tops. Among the house specials is the seafood cakes au gratin—a mix of crab and shrimp, baked with Monterey Jack and cheddar cheeses. The crab and shrimp Norfolk is meticulously prepared with just the right amount of sherry. Author James Michener, who often dined here while working on his epic novel *Chesapeake*, was especially fond of the inn's crabcakes. For an after-dinner drink, consider the Irish tea, fortified with coffee liqueur and whiskey. *Box 70, Oxford 21654, tel. 410/226–5111. Facilities: restaurant. MC, V. $$*

Lodging **Oxford Inn.** This inn was built as a private home in 1872, served as a watermen's bar during the seafood industry boom in the early part of this century, and later as a grocery store. The innkeepers have raised the roof and added a third floor; guests can spy Town Creek from the dormer windows. Rooms were renovated in 1990. The furniture is a collection of antiques, mostly early 20th-century American; rocking chairs and quilts are standard. Public tennis courts and a children's playground are across the street. *1 S. Morris St., Box 627, Oxford 21654. 13 rooms, 7 with bath. Facilities: restaurant. MC, V. Rates include Continental breakfast. $$$*

Pasadena Inn and Conference Center. The newly restored 240-year-old mansion and guest cottages, owned and operated by Schwaben International, are comfortably situated on Oak Creek in Royal Oak. The accommodation offers a tranquil setting for families, receptions, bicycle touring, conferences, and weekend getaways. Guests can borrow a rowboat, canoe, paddleboat, or bicycles. There are horseback-riding facilities about 7 miles away. The Pasadena is situated about 3 miles from St. Michaels. Amenities include a full country breakfast, and à la carte American dinners are available nightly to guests and to the public. Smoking is not permitted in the guest rooms but is allowed in a lower-level public room and on the porches. *Box 187, 25876 Royal Oak Rd., Royal Oak, 21662, tel. 410/745–5053. Facilities: restaurant, outdoor pool, bicycles, boats. MC, V. $$*

St. Michaels Dining **Lighthouse.** Paneling and captain's chairs are of traditional design, but the blond wood lends a light, contemporary appearance to this restaurant's interior. Tables are set with mauve tablecloths and candles. Large windows—and an outdoor deck—allow diners to watch the comings and goings in the marina below. Following an appetizer (perhaps shrimp with Dijon mustard sauce) or a soup (lobster bisque with brandy), a sorbet is served. Among the entrées, stuffed soft-shell choron is a pair of soft-shell crabs stuffed with crab imperial and shrimp, then lightly breaded and fried. *Saumon en papillote* is salmon cooked with celery, white wine, and lemon. The dessert cart carries a large selection. *101 N. Harbor Rd., tel. 410/756–9001. Reservations advised. Dress: casual but neat. AE, DC, MC, V. $$$*

Town Dock. The long L-shaped bar—a magnet for merriment in the evening—dominates the lounge. Formerly an oyster-shucking shed built in the 1830s, the room seems to be made entirely of polished dark wood, including the exposed beams in the low ceilings. The two more spacious main dining rooms behind provide wide views of St. Michaels Harbor. Of the menu selections, Parma is a mix of shrimp, scallops, and lobster in a sherry cream sauce, atop a mound of fettuccine. Veal Simone is sautéed and served with a cream sauce and shrimp. Desserts include bananas Foster, a combination of bananas, brown sugar, rum, cinnamon, nutmeg, butter, and ice cream flambéed at tableside. *305 Mulberry St., tel. 410/745–5577. Reservations advised. Dress: casual. AE, MC, V. Closed Mon., Tues., Sept.–May. $$$*

Lodging **Inn at Perry Cabin.** An early 19th-century Colonial Revival farmhouse was expanded, renovated, and opened as an inn in 1990. The proprietor is the widower of the designer Laura Ashley, and the decor is characterized by the rich yet restrained fabric designs she popularized. The ambience suggests an English country house with its handsome yet cozy library and spectacular gardens. Afternoon tea and fresh flowers in guest rooms and common areas are distinctive touches; many rooms have heated towel racks and private balconies. The inn sits on 25 acres of property along the Miles River. Call ahead about special policies. *308 Watkins La., 21663, tel. 410/745–2200 or 800/722–2949. 11 rooms, 8 suites. Facilities: restaurant, bar, swimming cove. AE, DC, MC, V. $$$$*

St. Michaels Harbor Inn and Marina. A favorite with bay boaters, this multigable clapboard structure, built in the mid-'70s, is a postmodernist takeoff on the town's Victorian architecture. Part of the waterfront complex is the 60-slip marina that sits just across the harbor from the Maritime Museum. The rooms in this all-suite facility have dockside patios or verandas and—on the third floor—large dormer windows. Interiors are soothingly spare: white walls, a mirror here, a botanical print there; fabrics have muted floral or simple geometric patterns; a brass ceiling fan is the most colorful element. Rooms have wet bar and refrigerator. The odd angles and slopes in many ceilings add interest, and the views of the sailboats in the harbor are diverting. *101 N. Harbor Rd., St. Michaels 21663, tel. 410/745–9001, fax 410/745–9150 or 800/955–9001. 46 suites. Facilities: restaurant, bar, outdoor pool, workout room, whirlpool, 60-slip marina. AE, DC, MC, V. $$$*

★ **Victoriana Inn.** This attractive inn was originally built as a private residence by Dr. Clay Dodson, a U.S. army officer during the Civil War. The two-story wood house, white with blue trim, is across a footbridge from the Maritime Museum. Guest rooms, which face the cove or the inn's own gardens, are furnished with 19th-century antiques; one has a canopied four-poster bed. All rooms have rocking chairs and air-conditioning, and handwoven floral rugs lie on polished wood floors. The sun room, where breakfast is served, has a VCR. At the center of tourist and maritime activity, with a view of the harbor's picturesque sailboat traffic, this inn is a haven in an increasingly popular town. Call ahead for special policies. *205 Cherry St., St. Michaels 21663, tel. 410/745–3368. 5 rooms, 1 with bath. MC, V. Rates include full breakfast. $$$*

Wades Point Inn. Amid fields of corn and gladiolus, on a 120-acre farm 5 miles south of St. Michaels, stand three adjoining brick Colonial and wood-frame Victorian buildings. The oldest structure was built in 1820 by Thomas Kemp, the Baltimore shipwright who built the famous Baltimore clipper ship, *The Chasseur* (nicknamed "The Pride of Baltimore"). The newest part of the property was added in 1989 by the present innkeepers, John and Betsy Feiler. The houses are about 100 feet from the Miles River, and some rooms enjoy views of the Chesapeake Bay. Wood floors and painted walls are the rule in some guest rooms; others have a carpet and wallpaper. Some rooms have four-poster beds, and one has a canopied bed; two rooms boast intricate moldings around the ceiling; most guest quarters have a private porch or balcony. Two brightly sunlighted corner rooms in the summer wing provide the closest look at the water. A 1-mile trail through the property accommodates joggers and bird-watchers. If you're seeking solitude and lots of fresh salt air, you'll find no better location in Maryland. *Wades Point Rd., Rte. 33, Box 7, St. Michaels 21663, tel. 410/745–2500. 24 rooms, 15 with bath. MC, V. Rates include Continental breakfast. $$$*

The Arts and Nightlife

The Arts

Chamber Music The **Historical Society of Talbot County** (25 S. Washington St., Easton, tel. 410/822–0773) sponsors occasional concerts.

Popular Music **Ocean City Convention Center** (4001 Coastal Hwy., Ocean City, tel. 410/289–2800 or 800/626–2326) presents big-band dances and star entertainers throughout the year.

Northside Park Recreation Center (125th St. and the Bay, Ocean City, tel. 410/250–0125) is frequently the site of free outdoor concerts.

Theater **Tred Avon Players** is a versatile community theatrical troupe that performs musicals, comedies, and melodrama at the Oxford Community Center (Rte. 333, Oxford, tel. 410/226–5904).

Avalon Theatre (Dover and Harrison Sts., Easton, tel. 410/822–3355), a restored venue for the performing arts, is in an especially attractive building. It is home to the Talbot Chamber Orchestra and the Eastern Shore Chamber Music Festival, and host to other performances as well.

Nightlife

Dancing **Longfellow's** (125 Mulberry St., St. Michaels, tel. 410/745–2624) has Top-40 programs on Saturday night.

Bonfire (71st St. and Ocean Hwy., Ocean City, tel. 410/524–7171) plays the slower new tunes for an over-30 crowd.

Tiffany's (24th and Philadelphia Sts., Ocean City, tel. 410/289–3322) rocks with live entertainment for the young set.

Live Rock At the **Washington Street Pub** (20 N. Washington St., Easton, tel. 410/822–9011) the Saturday-night acts are more or less countrified.

In Ocean City, the **Paddock** (17th St. and Coastal Hwy., tel. 410/289–6331), and the **Purple Moose** (108 S. Boardwalk, tel. 410/289–6953) are heavily booked all summer long with diverse programs.

Teenagers **Under 21 Club** (Boardwalk at Worcester St., tel. 410/289–6313), for dancers 16–21 only, has a DJ whose sets are occasionally interrupted by a live act. No alcohol is served.

Index

The only guide to explore a
Disney World® you've never seen before:
The one for grown-ups.

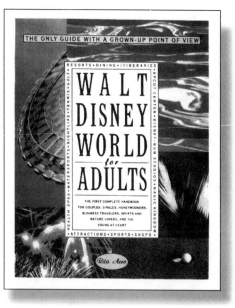

0-679-02490-5 $14.00 ($18.50 Can)

This is the only guide written specifically for the millions of adults who visit Walt Disney World® each year <u>without</u> kids. Upscale, sophisticated, packed full of facts and maps, *Walt Disney World® for Adults* provides up-to-date information on hotels, restaurants, sports facilities, and health clubs, as well as unique itineraries for adults. With *Walt Disney World® for Adults* in hand, you'll get the most out of one of the world's most fascinating, most complex playgrounds.

At bookstores everywhere, or call **1-800-533-6478**.

Fodor's

Fodor's Travel Guides

Available at bookstores everywhere, or call 1–800–533–6478, 24 hours a day.

U.S. Guides

Alaska

Arizona

Boston

California

Cape Cod, Martha's Vineyard, Nantucket

The Carolinas & the Georgia Coast

Chicago

Colorado

Florida

Hawaii

Las Vegas, Reno, Tahoe

Los Angeles

Maine, Vermont, New Hampshire

Maui

Miami & the Keys

New England

New Orleans

New York City

Pacific North Coast

Philadelphia & the Pennsylvania Dutch Country

The Rockies

San Diego

San Francisco

Santa Fe, Taos, Albuquerque

Seattle & Vancouver

The South

The U.S. & British Virgin Islands

USA

The Upper Great Lakes Region

Virginia & Maryland

Waikiki

Walt Disney World and the Orlando Area

Washington, D.C.

Foreign Guides

Acapulco, Ixtapa, Zihuatanejo

Australia & New Zealand

Austria

The Bahamas

Baja & Mexico's Pacific Coast Resorts

Barbados

Berlin

Bermuda

Brittany & Normandy

Budapest

Canada

Cancún, Cozumel, Yucatán Peninsula

Caribbean

China

Costa Rica, Belize, Guatemala

The Czech Republic & Slovakia

Eastern Europe

Egypt

Euro Disney

Europe

Florence, Tuscany & Umbria

France

Germany

Great Britain

Greece

Hong Kong

India

Ireland

Israel

Italy

Japan

Kenya & Tanzania

Korea

London

Madrid & Barcelona

Mexico

Montréal & Québec City

Morocco

Moscow & St. Petersburg

The Netherlands, Belgium & Luxembourg

New Zealand

Norway

Nova Scotia, Prince Edward Island & New Brunswick

Paris

Portugal

Provence & the Riviera

Rome

Russia & the Baltic Countries

Scandinavia

Scotland

Singapore

South America

Southeast Asia

Spain

Sweden

Switzerland

Thailand

Tokyo

Toronto

Turkey

Vienna & the Danube Valley

At last — a guide for Americans with disabilities that makes traveling a delight

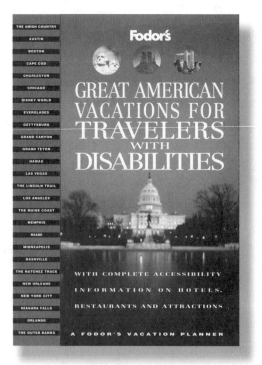

0-679-02591-X $18.00 ($24.00 Can)

This is the first and only complete guide to great American vacations for the 35 million North Americans with disabilities, as well as for those who care for them or for aging parents and relatives. Provides:

- Essential trip-planning information for travelers with mobility, vision, and hearing impairments
- Specific details on a huge array of facilities, along with solid descriptions of attractions, hotels, restaurants, and other destinations
- Up-to-date information on ISA-designated parking, level entranceways, and accessibility to pools, lounges, and bathrooms

Fodor's At bookstores everywhere, or call **1-800-533-6478**